JAPANESE TALES

J A P A

SELECTED, EDITED, AND TRANSLATED BY

PANTHEON BOOKS
NEW YORK

N E S E

ROYALL

TYLER

T A L E S

All rights reserved under International and Pan-American Copyright
Conventions. Published in the United States by Pantheon Books, a
division of Random House, Inc., New York, and simultaneously in
Canada by Random House of Canada Limited, Toronto.

Library of Congress Cataloging-in-Publication Data
Japanese Tales.
(Pantheon fairy tale and folklore library)
Bibliography: p.
Includes index.
1. Tales — Japan.   I. Tyler, Royall.   II. Series: Pantheon fairy
tale & folklore library.
GR340.J33   1987   398.2/0952   86-17017
ISBN 0-394-52190-0

Book design by Susan Mitchell
Manufactured in the United States of America
First Edition

FOR LIZ

CONTENTS

ODD PATHS TO SALVATION

WATER

CLOSED WORLDS

HAUNTS II

DREAMS

SCARES AND NIGHTMARES

FOXES II

BEYOND THE RULES

PARENT AND CHILD

ACKNOWLEDGMENTS

John Dower introduced me to Pantheon and so began the book. Susan Tyler, my wife, read and reread my drafts, continually making suggestions; discussed countless questions of form and content with me, always offering wise and well-informed advice; and kept me going with batches of cookies. Wendy Wolf, my editor, was always quick and helpful. How can I thank them enough?

A NOTE
ON
PRONUNCIATION

Japanese is easy to pronounce. The consonants work when spoken just as they are written in this book. The vowels sound roughly as in Italian. Each syllable in Japanese gets equal stress (quite unlike Italian) and in principle each vowel is a separate syllable. For example, the name Tadaie is pronounced tah-dah-ee-ay.

O's and U's with a macron or long mark over them (ō or ū) are supposed to last twice as long as plain ones — the difference between sOft and sOfa. For example, the name Sōō is pronounced, not "Sue," but more like "SO, O magnificent one, I have a humble suggestion."

A few names, like Urin'in, have an internal apostrophe which the reader can ignore since it hardly affects pronunciation.

INTRODUCTION

These tales from medieval Japan are by turns curious, touching, disturbing, funny, gross, and sublime. No doubt they will give everyone who
reads them a different impression, but I think first of how civilized they
are. There have never been better losers than the Palace Guards in no. 8,
who laugh wholeheartedly at their own awful discomfiture; and no warrior was ever wiser than the hero of no. 67. Most people in the stories
are quick to laugh or cry but slow to kill or seek revenge, and their gods
(with a few local exceptions) are kind.

Nearly all the stories come from tale collections put together between
about A.D. 1100 and 1350, though the earliest (no. 106) was written
down in the early 700s and the most recent (no. 209) in 1578. Most tell
about things that happened in the two centuries between 850 and 1050,
a classic period in Japanese civilization.

THE WORLD OF THE TALES

Nowadays we associate tales mainly with country people. No doubt
villagers told tales in Japan a thousand years ago too, but if the aristocracy had not been equally fond of stories, the ones in this book would
never have been written down. People's ideas about the world then were
rather different from ours, and from those of the modern Japanese. It is
true, for example, that fox lore still survives in Japan, and that possession
by fox spirits is still a factor in a very few people's lives; but it has been
a long time since someone like a regent could encourage such goings-on
as those in no. 47. The rumor of a modern prime minister practicing fox
magic would be too weird to make sense.

Even time was different then. Day and night were each divided into
six "hours" which expanded and contracted as the seasons turned. Since
the calendar was lunar, instead of solar like the modern world's, the
"months" followed the moon's phases. That is why in this book I use the
word "moon" instead of "month," for a "moon" and a solar month are
not the same. The New Year came sometime in our February, as it still
does in the Chinese calendar today.

There was no fixed reference point in Japanese history comparable to the birth of Christ or the Hegira. Instead, the flow of the years was divided into "year periods," which might range in length from a year or two to about twenty. Year periods did not correspond to the reign of an emperor or to anything else easy to describe, and they could start or stop at any time. Each had its own name: for example, Shōtai (898–901) and Engi (901–923). No. 171 tells how Yōrō (717–724) got its name. The people in charge of deciding year periods, and of all matters relating to the calendar, were top yin-yang diviners (see below) like the Kamo no Tadayuki of nos. 162 and 165. Of course, all dates in this book have been converted to the modern Western calendar.

People's names, then as now in Japan, were written with the surname first, but they were a little different in other ways from their modern counterparts. For example, the full name of the regent in no. 47 is Fujiwara no Tadazane. "Fujiwara" is his family or clan name; "no" is a particle like the French *de* or the German *von;* and "Tadazane" is his personal name. In other words, Fujiwara no Tadazane means "Tadazane of the Fujiwara [clan]." Similar names are Minamoto no Yorinobu (no. 67) and Tsunezumi no Yasunaga (no. 130). Names like these have about as much meaning as ours do — usually rather little.

The names of Buddhist monks and nuns are distinctive. In these stories a monk has only one name, usually the one he acquired on entering religion. Buddhist names often have some sort of fortunate meaning. In no. 101, for instance, Dōken ("Wise about the Way") receives in a vision the new name Nichizō ("Sun-store"). Monks' names sound quite different from laymen's names, although both are written with Chinese characters, because they are pronounced according to entirely different principles.

THE CAPITAL AND THE PROVINCES

The center of Japan, about the year 1000, was "the Capital": the city now known as Kyoto. It sprang up in 794 when the emperor moved to the site from Nara (see below), and for centuries was practically the only city in the land. Among its roughly 100,000 inhabitants, those who "really mattered," both men and women, probably numbered no more than a few thousand, but they gave a sort of glow to all the rest. Thanks to them the Capital, seen from the provinces, was a sort of Parnassus: the home of elegance, wit, romance, learning, the arts — in short, of all civilization. The rest of the population consisted of the lower aristocracy and officialdom, servants of many degrees, craftsmen, petty merchants, guards, priests, Buddhist monks of various kinds, etc. There seems also to have been a twilight zone, not outstandingly large, of assorted ne'er-do-wells and thieves. Government income came from dwindling crown lands; the aristocracy lived off the income from their growing private estates; and religious institutions prospered from pious donations and from their own landholdings. Nothing like a middle class developed until centuries later.

The streets of the Capital were laid out in the same regular grid pattern as the Chinese capital of the time. (Modern Kyoto is still patterned this way, although none of the buildings mentioned in these stories survive.) The major east-west avenues were numbered (First Avenue, Second Ave., etc.), while the north-south ones were named (East Omiya Avenue). Smaller, intermediate streets were also named (Horikawa Street).

The central north-south thoroughfare was Suzaku Avenue. It began at the Suzaku Gate, the central gate in the south wall of the palace compound, and ran down to the Rashō Gate, the central, southern gate into the city itself. The flute-playing demon of no. 167 lived high in the structure of the Suzaku Gate, and the Rashō Gate sheltered the equally musical demon-thief of no. 64.

Naturally the Imperial Palace occupied a commanding position in the city. Located at the north end of Suzaku Avenue, it was actually a complex of buildings inside a large, rectangular walled compound that occupied about three hundred acres. Within the compound were several hundred buildings including the emperor's personal residence (in a sub-compound of its own), the various halls of government, and many other structures either functional or ceremonial. No. 59, for example, starts with a scene of gentlemen arriving at the palace, apparently for a council to be held near the Great Hall of State. In no. 207, a warrior of the Palace Guard arranges to meet his colleagues by a gate at the northeast corner of the palace compound, while at the next gate south lurks the dastardly toad of no. 10.

Rivers flow on either side of Kyoto, east and west. To the east is the Kamo, which every visitor has seen. Riverside Palace (Kawara-no-in), where Retired Emperor Uda met the ghost (nos. 190, 191), was on the west bank of the Kamo. To the west flows the deeper Katsura River, where two holy men (nos. 116, 161) came to grief.

The city lies in a basin surrounded on three sides by mountains. This makes it miserably hot in summer, which is why the empress was wearing "a nearly transparent gown" when the hermit first glimpsed her in no. 125. Ladies often dressed that lightly in summer, at least in private. To the northwest rises Mount Atago, where another hermit had his false vision (no. 121); to the north stretches a range where a man met a mountain god in the form of a white dog (no. 129); and to the northeast towers Mount Hiei, where all sorts of curious things went on (nos. 33, 34, and others).

About thirty miles south of Kyoto is Nara, which became Japan's first "permanent" capital in 710. (Before then the imperial residence had moved every time an emperor died.) Nara appears often in these tales because the eighth century was such a crucial period in the development of Japanese civilization, and because the religious institutions founded there remained important later on. Tōdaiji, no doubt the single most famous Buddhist temple in Japan and a must for every tourist, appears in nos. 23, 24, and 25; while the great Shinto shrine of Kasuga (nos. 31, 45) still preserves the music and dance tradition honored by hell itself in no. 46.

The rest of Japan consisted of sixty-six provinces, whose names and boundaries were different from those of the modern Japanese prefectures. Those mentioned most often are the ones closest to the Capital, like Ōmi around the southern end of Lake Biwa; Yamato, where Nara is located; and Harima, which included the site of modern Kobe. For a courtier, the ends of the earth were represented by the nine provinces of Kyushu, such as Hizen, where Nagasaki eventually grew up; and Mutsu and Dewa in the far north of Honshu. Of the stories that take place in these more remote regions, many involve visitors from the Capital or persons bound for the Capital.

EMPERORS, MINISTERS, OFFICIALS, SERVANTS

The great nobles of this court-centered world, men whose birth destined them for the top ranks and posts in the government, figure prominently in the tales. Naturally the emperor had a special aura, even for the members of the nobility; but it is touching to glimpse (nos. 32, 67) how impressive even a provincial governor could look in his own province.

Provincial governors were appointed and sent out from the Capital, although sometimes (no. 8) they stayed in the Capital and had their provinces run by subordinates on location. Dazzling in the hinterland, at court they impressed no one because they came too low in the official hierarchy. A special provincial post, however, was that of viceroy of Kyushu. The viceroy was normally of considerable rank, but no one coveted his office since Kyushu was so far away. In fact, appointment as viceroy of Kyushu could amount to exile. Fujiwara no Yamakage (no. 105) seems not to have minded too much, but Sugawara no Michizane's appointment as viceroy of Kyushu meant his downfall and led to his becoming a vengeful god (nos. 101, 103).

The emperor was of course supposed to rule Japan, and these stories assume that he really did. But it is remarkable how often, in Japanese history, real power has been held not by the figure with the great title, but by someone who is officially his subordinate. The great shogun who unified Japan in 1600 after a century of war legitimized his power with the fiction that he was ruling for the emperor at the emperor's request. History provides many other such examples. No doubt it is natural that effective power should have passed from office to office, from clan to clan, and even from class to class over time. What is more surprising is that the emperor should never have been deposed, and should always have remained the ultimate source of legitimate political authority.

In the time of these stories, real power had been captured by the Fujiwara clan, headed by a regent whose position was hereditary in one Fujiwara line. The Fujiwara were wealthier than the imperial family, and their "private" house administration rivaled the "public" (imperial) government nominally headed by the emperor, especially since so many of the top posts in the "public" government were inevitably held by the top Fujiwaras. Since most of the great lords belonged to the Fujiwara clan, this book is full of Fujiwaras great and small. Tadazane has already been mentioned, but the ultimate Fujiwara potentate was the Regent Michinaga (966–1027), whose little dog saves him from hostile magic in no. 63. Of the rest, most bore the surname Minamoto. Tōru (nos. 190, 191) was an illustrious Minamoto.

The regent's standing illustrates this state of affairs perfectly, for although there was no slot at all for a regent in the government's official table of organization, he outranked every other official at court even if he held no other office. Normally his daughter was the emperor's wife (no. 125), and therefore the mother of the next emperor. (No woman was allowed to succeed to the throne between 770 and 1630.) Michinaga had three emperors as his sons-in-law and four as his grandsons.

Under these circumstances emperors were often children, or at least very young, and usually abdicated early. A retired emperor enjoyed a good deal more freedom than a reigning one. Retired Emperor Kazan (no. 39), forced to abdicate by the Fujiwara, ended up leading a life of Buddhist practice. As a reigning emperor he could never have left Kyoto on pilgrimage to see a holy man, as he does in the story. Retired emperors could even wield real influence. In the twelfth century they came to compete with the regents for power at court, leaving the reigning emperor, as usual, to play a largely ceremonial role.

The highest formal post in the government was that of chancellor, the senior minister of state. Anyone weeping with joy to see an ox eat a handful of grass would be bound to raise a smile, but he is particularly amusing when he is a chancellor (no. 197). Below the chancellor came the Minister of the Left, then the Minister of the Right. Minamoto no Makoto, visited by angels in no. 44, was a Minister of the Left; while the "Sage Minister" of the Right, Fujiwara no Sanesuke, appears in no. 53 and elsewhere.

In theory the chancellor was to be a man of outstanding character who could serve as an example for the emperor and the officials. The office was not supposed to be filled unless a suitably superior candidate was available. In fact the chancellor's appointment depended largely on his standing in the Fujiwara clan. In any case, since the office carried little real power, eligible candidates often declined the honor — one reason why the post was often vacant. The Minister of the Left had far more genuine authority since he was the legal head of the government, and responsible for the working of the Council of State (no. 11). The Minister of the Right could substitute for him as needed, and did so as a matter of course when the Minister of the Left served concurrently as regent.

Below the ministers were three grades of counselors. (Major Counselor Yasumichi and his fox-infested mansion appear in no. 80.) The two top grades belonged, like the ministers, to the Council of State. Among the many other, lower offices were those of controller (no. 11) and chamberlain. The controllers (there were between six and nine of them) supervised essential administrative activities which linked the Council of State with the central and provincial bureaucracies. Chamberlains were generally younger and of much lower rank than the officials just described, but their office was unusually glamorous because at least some of them, being private secretaries to the emperor, had frequent access to him. One chamberlain is the victim of a naughty joke in no. 7, and another has a strange dream in no. 56.

Several stories concern members of the Palace Guards and the Imperial Police. Both were needed. Security in the Capital was doubtful, especially at night, even without the parades of demons that people occasionally met in the dark, deserted streets (see below). Robberies were not uncommon, and passersby could be murdered under the very walls of the palace compound. It is probably only since the seventeenth century that Kyoto has been as safe as it and other Japanese cities are now.

The Palace Guards consisted of Gate Guards, Military Guards, and Inner Guards, each divided into Left and Right contingents. All six contingents besiege a mansion in no. 8, but only the Inner Guards come to grief. Since the Inner Guards served physically closer to the emperor and were therefore grander than the others, their undoing in no. 8 is all the funnier. The leading officers of the guards were captains of various grades, like the gallant young man of no. 78. In fact the post of senior captain of the Inner Guards (either contingent would do, but Left was preferable since it meant higher prestige) was one of the most desirable of all for a very high-born young man (no. 168).

The Imperial Police had their headquarters just outside the palace compound. Their chief (no. 102) was normally a counselor and had direct access to the emperor. They could be brave (no. 79) and they could be rough. For their dirty work they routinely used freed convicts like the ones in no. 173 who force a poor young man to carry a strangely heavy corpse.

Below all these came the humble people who made up the bulk of the Capital's population. When they appear in these stories they are nameless. The men seem usually to be *saburai,* or capable of being *saburai* if only they could find a job. The heroes of nos. 74 and 174 are that sort of person. The word meant "servant," someone who served a nobleman in any one of many capacities. It comes from the same verb as the familiar *samurai,* or "warrior," but in those days its meaning was less specialized. The assumption that a young man of humble station was or should be a *saburai* illustrates the overwhelming importance of the aristocracy in the life of the Capital.

HOUSES

Emperor or commoner, people lived in single-story houses where they sat and slept on the floor, as many Japanese still do. "Bed" in this book refers only to a sleeping-place, not to a piece of furniture or to any other structure. Covers were often just a layer of robes. *Tatami,* the thick straw flooring for which "traditional" Japanese houses are now famous, had not yet been invented. Floors were polished boards spread with straw mats. Having no permanent outside wall, rooms had no windows and generally no outside door. Interior doors were sliding panels.

The boundary between outside and inside was a sort of continuous shelf a few feet wide which ran all around the house. "Veranda" is the word for it in these stories, although it was not really a veranda at all. The outside rooms opened onto this shelf. A gentleman might sit on the veranda to talk with a lady inside, the two often being separated by a hanging blind. In one episode (no. 213), a holy monk steps straight out of the empress's room onto the veranda and does something quite disgusting.

The rooms along the veranda could be closed off by latticework shutters, which were backed by boards and divided horizontally into upper and lower panels. When both panels were in place the room was supposed to be secure from sun, wind, rain, and prying eyes. However, the upper panel could swing up and outward, horizontally, leaving the room open. In no. 44 a gentleman finds three little angels dancing on an open shutter panel.

The elaborate mansions of the great lords were composed of separate pavilions (sometimes referred to as "wings") linked by covered, open-sided galleries. There was a large garden around them, and a pond in front with an island in it. No. 139 gives an idealized description of such a garden. The mansion faced south. On its east and west sides it had an entrance, and just inside each entrance a "middle gate" which gave access to the corresponding "wing" of the mansion proper. In no. 71 a devoted monk sits by a middle gate of the chancellor's mansion to pray for the chancellor's recovery.

MEN, WOMEN, AND MANNERS

You would not guess from these stories that a court lady of Michinaga's time wrote one of the world's greatest novels, though the Jijū of no. 57 does seem capable of practically any stroke of genius. Women played a major role in cultural life, but their presence here is subdued. In fact, the book contains not a single woman's name. "Jijū" and the other seeming names are actually nicknames. Women did not use their personal names in public. Two woman writers of the age are known only as "Michitsuna's mother" and "Takasue's daughter." "Mitsutō's sister" is another example. Although no. 68 is really about her, not her brother, the story names and describes her brother before ever mentioning her, and never names her at all.

Proper women stayed hidden, physically as well as figuratively, though peasant women must have been too active to imitate them. Not that women never went outside. But among the aristocracy, a gentleman seldom saw a lady's face plainly in broad daylight. There was usually a curtain between them, and even when they were in bed together it was dark or at best dim.

This is obvious in no. 177. When the young monk, newly arrived in the lady's house, hears rustling in a room nearby, he knows right away what is going on: curtains on a portable frame are being moved in so that the lady can talk to him from behind them. He will not actually see her. This movable, curtained enclosure, forming a tiny room inside a room, plays a role in several stories (nos. 58, 73, 125).

The monk does not see the lady until he takes a walk outside and spots a hole in one of the shutters that enclose her room for the night. (The literature of the time is full of men peering through such cracks and holes.) Naturally he falls in love. Later on, when she allows him into her room knowing that he will be joining her in bed, she still has a cushion laid for him *outside* her curtains. The only light in the room is from a dim lamp behind a screen. No doubt the lamp is out and her maids all asleep when he finally lies down beside her. She never sits simply talking with him face to face.

Courting men were like bees visiting shy flowers, and courtship took place largely in the dark. Heichū (no. 57) has never seen the lady he is so desperate to make love to, and when he finally gets into her room it is naturally pitch dark. He can only assume that the woman lying there is the one he is courting; in fact, he must check whether she is a woman at all by feeling over her face and her long, cool hair.

Both men and women seem to have wept freely and often in response to emotion. Courtship always involved tears. When you wept you dried your eyes with your sleeves, and if your grief was deep enough your sleeves got pretty wet. A man with conspicuously dry sleeves might appear insincere. Heichū (no. 56) knew this so well that he took a little bottle of water with him when he went courting, to dampen himself as needed.

The transition from lover to husband was a passage from darkness and secrecy to daylight and public recognition. No. 220 summarizes this process. The bridegroom spends two nights with the bride, leaving while it is still dark. On the third night he stays in bed with her on into the morning, for her parents and household, and in fact for her, to see. Was there nothing else to getting married in those days? Of course there was, but this, together with some discreet rituals, was the gist of the "wedding." Moreover, aristocratic husbands, who might have lesser wives and concubines as well as a principal wife, did not normally live with their wives but only visited them. The wife in no. 54 lives with her parents in a great lord's mansion, and her husband just spends the night with her. The emperor did not live with his principal consort either (no. 125). In this sense, more modest people lived what seem more normal lives. The husband and wife of no. 130 obviously live together; and the husband of no. 134 is afraid of his wife in a manner recognizable the world over.

Only women used the portable curtains just described, but in formal circumstances high-ranking men too might speak from behind blinds. The governor in no. 8 does just this when he finally admits his victims to his mansion. The emperor normally spoke or watched from behind blinds. Being made of thin bamboo or rush strips, blinds were more or less transparent to someone in a dim space looking out at a bright scene. Often rooms were screened from the outside only by blinds, like the residence of the Dragon King in no. 183.

The tendency to avoid face-to-face contact also encouraged conversations conducted not directly but through servants. It was beneath a lord or lady's dignity to speak directly to a humble person, even through a curtain or blind, and a servant would carry messages back and forth instead. Approximate equals would likewise become acquainted through letters and messages carried by intermediaries. This was possible because people had so many servants.

It is difficult for us now to imagine a life so peopled by servants of all degrees. In no. 133 a man goes back to see the wife he left many years ago. It saddens him to find the house falling to ruin, but his wife's plight and the force of his own cruelty only sink in when he discovers that she has been too poor to keep a single servant. Even the starving young man of no. 172 has a servant to open the door for him. The poor woman in no. 175, abandoned by her husband, is reduced to living "a sad life in her poor, dreary house, alone but for a pair of maids." Better-off people had servants and "retainers" of all sorts.

As a result, a man's "household" was much larger than what we would call his "family," and whatever happened to him affected this larger group. The fox-girl of no. 82 takes the randy hero home to a beautiful house bustling with servants who welcome her effusively. In fact, to evoke a fine, prosperous residence, it was not enough to praise the size or luxury of the building. The place had also to be "bustling," which meant that it had lots of servants and visitors. If it was not "bustling," it looked forlorn and gave the impression that the occupant, whatever his or her means, had little real standing in the world.

With so many servants, people were seldom, if ever, alone in our sense of the word. A lady like the one in no. 177 may have slept within her curtains, but several maids slept in the same room. Someone was always within earshot, if not within sight. The writers of the time did not insist on this since it was obvious to them and their readers, and since in any case servants did not really "count" in relation to their masters; but we need to be reminded. No one of the slightest standing went anywhere entirely alone. Even the wanderer of no. 127 has a servant with him on his travels, and so does the threadbare monk of no. 155.

MAGIC, HEALING, AND RELIGION

One thing that makes these tales unlike recently collected Japanese folk-tales, despite the continuity of many motifs, is religion. Medieval Japan was as steeped in religion as medieval Europe, and people thought in religious terms far more often than nowadays. Buddhism was dominant, but other religious or magical traditions were important too. None were mutually exclusive, at least not in any sense that might sound serious to a Christian or a Moslem.

The magic and religion in these stories fall into four main categories: yin-yang lore, Chinese yoga, the cults of the native Japanese gods, and Buddhism. The first two can be dealt with fairly quickly. The native gods, however, will require fuller treatment, together with such preoc-cupations as spirit possession, dreams, healing, and the fear of pollution. I will save Buddhism till last, even though I will have to refer to it often before then, just because Buddhism looms so large. Magic, spirit powers, healing, etc. are, after all, subjects familiar to us in a general way from many cultures; and so is the quest for right conduct and salvation which finds its expression in Buddhism as in other religions. But Buddhist ideas, the names and roles of Buddhist divinities, and the other trappings of the Buddhist faith are too complex to treat consecutively until the other, lesser topics are safely out of the way.

YIN-YANG LORE

The yin-yang tradition came to Japan from China. In the West, most people know now that "yin" means the dark, moist, cold, passive, female principle of the universe, while "yang" means the bright, dry, hot, active, male principle. This is not wrong, of course, but it represents such a high level of philosophical abstraction that it has little to do with yin-yang lore as it figures in these stories. Yin-yang knowledge, intricate and practical, involved astrology, geomancy, purification, divination, and offensive or defensive magic.

I have called the yin-yang masters in this book "diviners" because they appear most commonly in that role. They were often called in to fathom the meaning of puzzling events and to prescribe appropriate action (nos. 63, 164). They could also be asked to determine auspicious or inauspi-cious days and to interpret dreams. Purification rites come up in nos. 162 and 179. Both the government and private patrons considered such func-tions essential. The government's table of organization included a Bureau of Divination, which employed the top members of the profession like Abe no Seimei (nos. 59, 60, and others) and Kamo no Tadayuki (nos. 162, 165). Although hereditary in certain families, the profession required long training. As already noted, such men also played a key role in the establishment of the official calendar.

Yin-yang diviners practiced magic at the request of their patrons. In no. 59, for example, Seimei defends a young gentleman against a hired diviner's curse. Such magic was lethal (no. 163). A common countermeasure against curses and other misfortunes, foreseen by the diviner thanks to his art, was seclusion. The potential victim had to shut himself up strictly at home, admitting no one and talking to no outsider. No. 14 describes the particularly horrid way a demon broke through a man's seclusion, sensibly ordered by a diviner.

CHINESE YOGA

The Chinese tradition of ascetic self-cultivation entered Japan early, but was then overwhelmed by Buddhism. It is represented here by a few old stories. The ascetic's goal was the eternal one of freedom from mortality and from the constraints of the body. A truly accomplished ascetic could shed his gross physicality and take on a new, spiritual body as an Immortal; and one nice thing about being an Immortal was that you could fly. One ascetic who thought he could fly made a big mistake (no. 90), but the wizard of no. 88 managed beautifully. (This wizard is known to have mastered Chinese yoga, but it is true that he mixed Buddhist esoteric practices with it.)

In time the idea of the Immortal came, under Buddhist influence, to be associated with certain ascetic monks who were devoted to the Lotus Sutra (see below).

THE NATIVE GODS

Japan has always been full of gods. There are now shrines to them even on the roofs of department stores. In medieval times people often thought of Japan as the "land of the gods," thus expressing a natural love for the beautiful Japanese islands and their human community.

In the centuries covered by these stories there were countless cults to these gods, and some were very strong. On the whole, though, the worship of the native Japanese gods did not constitute a clear-cut religion. We are often told that the two main religions of Japan are Buddhism and Shinto, and that Shinto ("the Way of the Gods") is the "native religion of Japan." But Shinto has only existed as a self-conscious religion since the late nineteenth century, when it developed in response to a movement of political and religious ideas which is foreign to the world of these tales. The earlier cults of local, regional, or even national significance celebrated a great variety of divine presences in symbiosis with Buddhism.

Philosophically and organizationally, Buddhism was far more highly developed. A handful of important shrines tried with limited success to keep Buddhism at arm's length, but most were as much dominated by their associated Buddhist temples as the emperor was by the Fujiwara regent. Not that this domination involved force. Many legends tell how the native gods accepted Buddhism gladly, listened eagerly to its teaching, and sometimes even claimed Buddhist-sounding titles.

All this helps to explain why the stories talk more about Buddhist divinities than about the native gods. Although the court honored the gods, it was so steeped in Buddhism that it did not think deeply about them. The Kasuga God, the clan god of the Fujiwara, upheld Buddhism with affecting conviction (no. 31). In fact, his shrine was thoroughly dominated by Kōfukuji (no. 45 and others), the oldest ancestral temple of the same Fujiwara clan. The God of Fire and Thunder (no. 101) is very different, but he still insists that Buddhism moves him deeply and has so far deterred him from destroying Japan completely.

The Kasuga God and the God of Fire and Thunder were major divinities. So was the divine presence at Kumano, a great pilgrimage center whose name alone appears in these stories. Others were more remote. No. 30 shows how gentlemanly a provincial god could be, but the mountain gods Kōya and Nifu, eager to help found a great Buddhist temple, are impressively rugged (no. 26). The war between the mountain god and the wizard (no. 88) is one of Japan's most famous legends. Nos. 77 and 188, with their legends of human sacrifices offered to monkey gods, conjure up a world that must have seemed almost as strange to the original readers of these stories as it does to us.

Some gods had animal forms. In addition to monkeys, these stories include a dog (no. 29) and a snake and centipede (no. 187). Animals could also be divine messengers: the deer for the Kasuga God; the monkey for the Hie God (no. 41). The fox is associated with Inari, a god of plenty, and that is probably how the fox gets into the rite that starts no. 47. Later in the same story, the fox itself is a god. (Fox spirits, who occupy a lower level than gods, are discussed below.)

Humblest of all, perhaps, were the road gods (nos. 159, 178). Their direct descendants can still be seen along the roads in some parts of

Japan. Now as then, most road gods "have a man part and a woman part," as no. 159 puts it. The road god in both stories appears as an old man, the single most likely form for a native god to take when appearing to a human.

All the gods thrived on human attention and in fact required it. Naturally they received offerings of food and drink, as well as rites and festival observances. But in these stories the gods especially enjoy music and dance. The divine applause described in no. 48 was one accepted sign of a god's pleasure. The God of Good Fortune's lust for music (no. 47) seems demented; but the Kasuga God nicely disposes of the idea that music has nothing, or nothing important, to do with genuine religion (no. 45).

COMMUNICATING WITH THE GODS

Not only did human beings address the gods, but the gods spoke to humans. Shamanistic possession is now banished from the religion that identifies itself as Shinto, but in the world of these stories it was quite normal. So was a keen interest in divinely inspired dreams.

A god might deliver an oracle through a human medium. Hitokotonushi, the name of the god who opposes the wizard in no. 88, means "Master of the Single Word" and suggests the practice of giving one-word oracles, yes or no. In the story, though, Hitokotonushi accuses the wizard at length through one of the emperor's own attendants. This sort of spontaneous possession of a household member by a god occurs in no. 31, and also in no. 163 where a man discovers, thanks to "an oracle delivered in his own home," that an enemy is plotting to kill him. However, there were plenty of professional mediums, too. Some worked in healing, as explained below under that topic. Others belonged to the staffs of major shrines like those of Kasuga or Hie. In no. 41 a Hie Shrine medium is seen delivering oracles to a crowd of pilgrims.

Shrine mediums were women, as were most other professional or spontaneous mediums. Young boys sometimes gave oracles, though none do in this book. Of shamanic men, most seem to have been monks like the one who has the great vision in no. 101, or like the monk described in no. 88 as "the vessel of the God of Hakusan." Many monks were involved with spirit possession as healers, often acting in partnership with a woman medium.

An absorbing or outstandingly apt oracle was uncommon. What people sought instead, at both shrines and Buddhist temples, was dreams. The

Buddhist divinities did not possess mediums, but they and the gods could speak or otherwise signify their will in dreams.

The common procedure was to do a seven-day retreat at a temple or shrine, in the hope of getting a sign from the divinity in the form of a dream. If none came, you could do a second seven-day period or even a third. The dream seems always to come just before the last dawn of the retreat (no. 45). In no. 174, a young man prays at a temple for relief from poverty, and by acting on his dream message he becomes rich.

A medieval Japanese story may not identify a communication from a god or a Buddhist divinity as a dream, but may describe it instead as though it were a normal, waking event. (In most such instances the circumstances still make it clear that the communication is a dream, and sometimes another version of the story may say so plainly.) This suggests that dream experience and waking experience were not always sharply distinguished from each other, and that dream experience could be accepted as perfectly authentic. Some sacred dreams, although unsought, carried great weight. In a fascinating example (no. 197), a monk dreams that a certain temple has a black ox and that this ox is actually a buddha. The dream starts a mass pilgrimage (it really happened) to worship the Buddha-Ox.

Besides sacred dreams, these tales contain other kinds of dreams which show how fascinating people found the theme. Examples are the complementary dreams dreamed simultaneously by both members of a couple (nos. 130, 134), and the extraordinary Buddhist morality dream of no. 198.

HEALING

The literature of the time rarely acknowledges that the Japanese had acquired from China (as well as undoubtedly developed also on their own) knowledge of medicine and drugs. The physician who appears briefly in no. 125 must have known about such things, but his treatment is not even mentioned. Instead, the emphasis is on spiritual rather than physical processes, and especially on exorcism.

Several stories contain a passage like this one (no. 72): "Then Emperor Daigo happened to become very ill. All sorts of prayers and rites tried on his behalf brought him no relief. Finally an official remembered the holy man of Mount Shigi . . ." The first thing to do, apparently, was to bring in one or more Buddhist monks (depending on the patient's means) to perform rites and chant sacred texts. A rite alone could work, for a healer once cleansed an entire province of an epidemic with his masterful performance of an elaborate ritual (no. 127). Usually chanting was essential too. When the chancellor was ill (no. 71), "all the best-known monks crowded into his mansion, which rang with the din of their chanting."

In most cases, spirits are involved on both sides of the struggle between the healer and the sickness. In no. 70 a Buddhist divinity, invoked by chanting monks, drives away a horde of nasty spirit-children. More often, though, the healing spirit is not a standard divinity but a protector spirit personally linked to the healer. A famous example is the Sword Guardian (no. 72), a spirit controlled by the holy man of Mount Shigi.

As for the evil spirits who cause sickness, their nature and motivation are usually shadowy. Although one story (no. 74) features a remarkable account of a healing session from the afflicting spirit's standpoint, we learn nothing about why the patient should have been singled out for torment. The afflicting spirit has only been dragooned into service by a minor god, and the minor god is apparently acting on behalf of a bigger god whose reasons are unfathomable. In these stories, the only kind of afflicting spirit with a relatively clear identity is a fox.

Fox spirits still make people ill in Japan. The reasons why they possess people may be hard to make out, especially when you doubt (as a modern reader or observer can hardly help doing) that foxes really are autonomous entities, external to the possessed person, who just move in when they feel like it. In these tales, two motives are given. The first is exceptional: a man sends a fox to deliver a message to his household, and the fox obeys by possessing the man's wife and speaking through her mouth (no. 83). The second is more common: the fox explains that it has possessed the patient only because it hopes to be given some food (nos. 124, 206).

These last two stories show clearly how a monk and a woman medium worked together. As the monk chanted sacred texts and spells, the medium went into a trance. Meanwhile the protector spirit or spirits who served the monk would force the afflicting power to move into the medium, where the monk could question it. After asking what it was and why it was there, he might go on to scold it for its mischief. Finally he would send it away and the medium would regain consciousness.

AFTER DEATH

If healing fails, the patient may die. There are several deaths and corpses in these stories, although no births. A corpse may pollute the place where it lies and the people who come into contact with it, and the spirit of the deceased may appear as a ghost.

Proper treatment of the dead has always been vital in Japanese religion. First, the body had to be properly disposed of. (No. 133 evokes horribly the fate of an untended corpse.) This could be done by cremation or by disposing in one way or another of the whole body. Toribeno, the Capital's major burning ground, appears in several stories (nos. 15, 131). In other instances the corpse was carried to a charnel ground, often a ravine near the foot of the mountains where it might be abandoned, or at best buried in a shallow grave. In two stories (nos. 27, 46) the body is hung in a tree. It could also be left in a cave (the saving spirit in no. 148 speaks from such a cave) or even on the top floor of a city gate (no. 65). For the living, these spots belonged to another, alien world of which the hellish, volcanic landscape of Tateyama (nos. 147, 216) is an extreme example.

Proper care of the spirit took more devotion than disposal of the body. Buddhist rites had to be performed daily for the first seven days after death (no. 216), then every seventh day thereafter until the forty-ninth day. The schedule of observances thinned out after that, but it ran on another year or two for the individual spirit. When it was over, the spirit joined a family's collective ancestors, who were honored jointly.

Without this care spirits were miserable, and could easily linger on as harmful or unhappy ghosts. In any case, people who died violently or in acute distress were likely to become ghosts (no. 133). In extreme cases, an unhappy ghost could become a harmful god (no. 28). The God of Fire and Thunder (nos. 101, 103), a model of this kind, was originally the statesman Sugawara no Michizane. Michizane died heartbroken, in unjust exile. When his ghost started causing disasters, he was first posthumously promoted in rank, then a major shrine to him was built in Kyoto and his worship developed into a widespread cult.

Death was a difficult issue for most native gods, who abhorred any taint of blood, sickness, or death. No doubt the people of pre-Buddhist Japan found ways to deal with this problem. Buddhism seems to have met a need, however, since so much of its teaching was concerned with the fate of the soul after death, and since in principle its divinities felt no such revulsion. In fact, the care of the dead became in time the fundamental task of Buddhism in Japanese society. Buddhist monks conducted mortuary rites, Buddhist ascetics practiced in the mountains which were the "other world" of the ancestral spirits, and Buddhist temples grew up in association with the places where the dead were disposed of. In no. 46 a woodcutter hears groans from a coffin hanging in a tree and goes to warn "the priests of the temple nearby." The temple may have had this sort of connection with the place.

The native gods' attitude toward death is beautifully illustrated in no. 41. A monk is making daily pilgrimages from Kyoto to the Hie Shrine, over a low mountain pass to the east of the city. On his way home one day he finds a young woman weeping because she cannot dispose of the corpse of her mother who has just died. The villagers will not help her because they are busy with preparations for a festival in honor of their local god; if they touch the corpse, the god will be angry and misfortune will strike the whole village. The monk generously helps carry the body away. Now, however, he is polluted himself and must either break off his pilgrimages or risk the Hie God's wrath. Though afraid, he decides the next morning to make his pilgrimage as usual. On arrival he keeps well away from the sanctuary building. When the god nonetheless orders him (through a medium) to approach, he is so terrified that he almost faints.

This fear of pollution was so deeply ingrained in the Japanese that it influenced the Buddhist establishments themselves, even though it had no canonical basis in Buddhist teaching. When thieves manage to rob a temple of its big bronze bell (no. 143), the key to their success is their certainty that the monks of the temple will not go near a dead body. Likewise, the temple monks in no. 174 are afraid that the hero of the story will die of starvation right before their altar and in so doing pollute the temple. This fear was not confined to shrines and temples, for a courtier polluted by direct contact with death could not appear at court, as no. 132 suggests.

BUDDHISM

Buddhism began in India about 500 B.C., and first came officially to the Japanese court's attention in the mid-sixth century A.D. In between it had permeated Southeast Asia, Central Asia, China, and Korea, and gone through a thousand years of evolution. In time it all but vanished from India and faded in China. During the thirteenth century, certain Japanese Buddhists even began claiming that the center of Buddhism was now Japan.

So old, complex, and sophisticated a religion is hard to summarize, even for the limited purpose of introducing these stories. Perhaps it is best to begin with some basic terms.

This book is full of Buddhist "monks," with a few "priests" scattered here and there. Some were saintly, some frivolous, some worldly and rich. The religious or quasi-religious population was large, as in medieval Europe, and many monks who appear in these stories were sons of great families. Subclasses of varying standing and outlook made up the religious population, but I have not tried to distinguish them in translation. Instead, I have called everyone a monk unless he is obviously ministering to the laity; then I have called him a priest. I have left out all ecclesiastical titles.

Monks had boys of varying ages (acolytes) to serve them, and often disciples studying under them. In their all-male society, there naturally occurred certain things that are made quite explicit in nos. 154 and 155.

Monks were attached more or less closely to religious establishments conventionally called "temples" in English, although in many cases the word "monastery" might do as well. (It is also simply a useful convention to call the native gods' holy places "shrines.") Typical temple names are Tōdaiji, Kōfukuji, and Tennōji, where the element -ji means "temple." Another pronunciation of the same -ji element is -dera, which occurs in such temple names as Shigadera, Koyadera, and Miidera. Two other endings that for our purposes also mean "temple" are -in (Urin'in) and -dō (Rokkakudō). Nos. 22 through 26 are a tiny sampling of Japan's many temple origin legends.

Important temples were large and complex communities. Kōfukuji and Tōdaiji in Nara, Mount Hiei near Kyoto, and the Mount Kōya of no. 26 each had a total population of many thousands, and consisted of countless buildings great and small. They also had vast, widely scattered estates which supported their activities. The most prominent temple complex in these stories is Mount Hiei. Mount Hiei is first of all a mountain about 3,000 feet high that rises near the northwest corner of Kyoto. The temple complex that grew up there after about A.D. 800 came to wield enormous religious, political, and even military power. Since its doings were of special interest to the nobles, almost all of whom had relatives on the mountain, there was a lot of traffic, material and intellectual, between Kyoto and Mount Hiei.

Buddhist scriptures are called sutras. The one most commonly mentioned here is the Lotus Sutra, but the Heart Sutra (nos. 74, 182), the Sutra of Golden Light (no. 149), the Diamond Wisdom Sutra (no. 151), and others also appear. "Sutra," a Sanskrit word, means a text accepted by the tradition as having been spoken by the Buddha. The Japanese used Chinese translations.

Shakyamuni, the historical Buddha, was called Shaka in Japan. Shaka was a man and taught as a man, without claiming to be a god or to share in any divine nature. His aim was simply to teach the way things are. One who understood his message would be free from bondage to the complex seductions of the physical and mental realms, characterized above all by the round of birth and death. This theme remained vital throughout Buddhist history, and the Japanese monks followed through on it as thoroughly as anyone. Although the Buddhist cosmos became filled with divine beings, Buddhist philosophy continued to hold that these divinities had no ultimate existence, but only pointed to, or acted from, a reality beyond name or description: the ways things really are.

Since "the way things really are" obviously does not exclude the round of birth and death (we are all born and we all die), medieval Japanese Buddhism taught routinely that enlightenment and the world which enslaves us are not different from each other. It would be foolish even to try explaining this paradox further, but I mention it because it underlies no. 38, the story of a saint and a prostitute. It demonstrates that to the enlightened eye (the saint's), all things, even the incarnation of base, enslaving desire (the prostitute), speak of their true nature, which is freedom and enlightenment.

The effort to realize or, better, to embody this understanding had profound consequences in Buddhist thought and practice. One approach held that the path toward freeing onself from slavery (that is, toward opening the eye of enlightenment) went through close embrace with this apparently enslaving world. Since the detailed Buddhist code of conduct for monks is designed precisely to discourage anything of the kind, those who took this approach were likely to break various rules. Traces of a line of adepts who do seem to have lived beyond the rules may be seen in nos. 182 and 211, and perhaps in no. 212. All three monks were from the same temple in Nara, and at least the first two were from the same lineage; the visionary of no. 101 may have been connected with them. Meanwhile, the monk's life told in no. 213 is a garland of triumphant affronts to respectability.

A related approach avoided rule-breaking, upholding instead orthodox conduct to achieve the same enlightened embrace of the world of birth and death. This was the tradition founded in Japan by Kōbō Daishi, who is still a powerful presence in Japanese Buddhism. Kōbō Daishi taught that all objects of sense and thought are the "preaching" of the Cosmic Buddha, and stressed for everyone the possibility of enlightenment *in this body*. His own legend naturally exemplifies this achievement, for he did not die (no. 26). Instead, he entered eternal meditation on his mountain.

Kōbō Daishi and the others all practiced one variety or another of the Esoteric Buddhism that underlies the Buddhism of these stories. One or two terms from this tradition need explaining. Nos. 26, 87, 88, and 101 mention the vajra (a Sanskrit word), which is a ritual as well as a symbolic implement. "Vajra" is variously translated "diamond" or "thunderbolt," and refers to spiritual power. The Vajra-Bearer (no. 101) is therefore a being of pure power. The Vajra-Realm Mandala is paired (nos. 101, 127)) with the Womb-Realm Mandala: both complementary diagrams of the cosmos sum up a vast and complex understanding of "the ways things are." The healing described in no. 127 works because the healer endows the mandalas with living potency and so briefly transforms the area around him into a perfect realm where sickness is impossible.

BUDDHIST DIVINITIES

Shaka must have seemed more than human to his disciples, though he preached purely as a man, for people's tendency to deify great beings and principles is very strong. In any case, as Buddhism developed and spread it was influenced in many ways by other, theistic religions. By the time it reached Japan it was rich in divinities, having even absorbed the Hindu gods Indra and Brahma, who appear in these stories respectively as Taishaku (nos. 11, 147) and Bonden (no. 36). Of course the Buddhist divinities have Sanskrit names, but I will use their Japanese names as they appear in these tales. I have retained two Sanskrit titles, though, because they are so well known in English: buddha and bodhisattva.

Buddhas. "Buddha" means a fully enlightened being. Naturally the title applies to Shaka himself, who is mentioned here once as a divinity (no. 101) and once as a mountain (no. 88). But it also applies to other divinities who represent one aspect or another of the timeless, universal character of enlightenment.

Buddhism came to teach that Shaka, the buddha of our age, was one of a line of buddhas extending out of the remote past and into the indefinite future. Two of the past buddhas, Bibashi and Kashō, appear here (nos. 101, 197). The next buddha after Shaka is Miroku, who at present is still technically a bodhisattva. He will descend into our world eons from now, as no. 88 explains. According to a Japanese legend (nos. 22, 88, 102), the earth will then be covered with gold. This no doubt means that the earth will be made new, since Miroku has at times been worshipped in Japan as a deity of world renewal. In the meantime he waits in the Inner Sanctum of the Tosotsu Heaven (nos. 73, 86), which is a kind of paradise where certain earnest practitioners longed to go. One monk (no. 73) reached the gate but unfortunately could not get in. The Tosotsu Heaven was associated with salvation achieved through the Lotus Sutra (nos. 73, 111).

Dainichi ("Great Sun"), described as "the Cosmic Buddha" in no. 101, is associated especially with Kōbō Daishi's teaching. He is philosophically interesting, but too abstruse ever to have been popular.

No buddha required sole allegiance, but many people (like the nun in no. 160) centered their devotion by choice on Amida, whom the Japanese imagined and depicted as a simple buddha in meditation. Amida is the loftiest savior figure in the Japanese Buddhist pantheon. His name means both "Infinite Light" and "Infinite Life." In the thirteenth century there emerged a trend toward exclusive faith in Amida, but this development lies outside the world of these stories.

Amida presides over a paradise that lies a vast distance away from our world, toward the west. This paradise is sometimes called the Pure Land and sometimes the Land of Bliss. Amida established it for all those who have faith in him, and he vowed that whoever calls his name sincerely shall be reborn there. That is why the key practice for the Amida devotee is simply to chant Amida's Name, "Namu Amida Butsu" ("Hail Amida Buddha!"). Many people in these stories call on Amida, but none so urgently as the robber who actually hears Amida answer him from the depths of the sea (no. 115). Calling the Name was also a common practice at funerals, for the benefit of the deceased (nos. 143, 203).

Unlike the "enlightenment in this body" approach just described, Amida faith was almost entirely concerned with the life to come. At the moment of death, Amida would come down from his paradise in a blaze of glory, preceded by the two Bodhisattvas Kannon and Seishi, and by a joyous host of musicians and saints, to welcome the soul into the Land of Bliss (nos. 118, 119). The people around the dying person would not see this vision, but they would know by certain signs that the soul had gone to glory: they would hear strains of celestial music, smell an indescribably sweet fragrance on the air, and see a purple cloud trailing away from the spot in the direction of the west (nos. 113, 160).

Voluntary renunciation of the body (rather than "suicide") is an identifiable strain in Japanese spiritual endeavor, especially in medieval times. A few people thirsted so strongly for paradise that they sought death to hasten their journey there. The way to seek Amida's paradise in this manner was by drowning. The sea off Tennōji (mentioned in no. 43) was a well-known place for this, but the two stories on the theme here (nos. 116, 161) involve the Katsura River near Kyoto. Both show in different ways how dangerous the practice was, and how complex piety could be.

Bodhisattvas. A bodhisattva is, in theory, a being who has vowed not to enter final Nirvana (enlightenment) until all beings in the world can enter it with him, and who in the meantime helps and saves all those who are caught in the round of birth and death. For example Amida, as a buddha, does not intervene directly in this world, although he welcomes to his far-off paradise the soul of anyone who calls his Name with faith. On the other hand Kannon, as a bodhisattva, works actively in the world to save those in distress.

The Bodhisattva Kannon, together with the relatively obscure Seishi, accompanied Amida to welcome the soul into the Land of Bliss. But Kannon's religious role in Japan was much broader and more autonomous than that of an attendant to Amida. It was based partly on the "Kannon Sutra," actually a chapter of the much longer Lotus Sutra, where Amida is only briefly mentioned, and partly on other scriptures and traditions.

Kannon is often identified as the "Goddess of Mercy." The "mercy" is quite right, but for Japan the "goddess" part is doubtful, if only because in terms of the Lotus Sutra a female bodhisattva is impossible. Sexually specific depictions of Kannon are all male. In any case, the variety of Kannon's forms makes the question less interesting than it might sound. The "Kannon Sutra" tells how Kannon may take any conceivable form to save beings from any conceivable peril. (In no. 137, for example, he appears as a huge snake.) Moreover, Nyoirin Kannon (no. 23), Thousand-Armed Kannon (nos. 70, 98, and others), and Eleven-Headed Kannon (nos. 27, 82, and others) are only some of the forms of Kannon that are depicted in religious art.

The main image on the altar of a temple dedicated to Kannon would be a specific form such as Eleven-Headed Kannon, and that form alone would be associated with that temple. Nyoirin Kannon usually has six arms, Eleven-Headed Kannon looks quite normal except for a sort of crown formed of faces with different expressions, and Thousand-Armed Kannon has about that number of arms. The thousand-armed form simply shows graphically the countless ways Kannon saves beings from danger (sickness in no. 70, a frightful snake in no. 98), but the reasons for the other forms are more complicated. All wield saving power.

Kannon has a paradise called Fudaraku in Japanese. Potalaka, its Sanskrit name, is visibly the same as that of the famous Potala Palace in Lhasa, until recently the home of the Dalai Lama. (For the Tibetans, the Dalai Lama is an incarnation of Kannon.) Some mountains in Japan were thought of as Fudaraku, but the Japanese knew that Buddhist texts identify it as a mountain at the southern tip of India.

To the Japanese, the location of Fudaraku meant that Kannon's paradise, unlike Amida's, was in our own world and that in principle it could be reached in this body. A few people, like the man in no. 157, tried to sail there. But although Fudaraku was a geographically real place, it was so remote from Japan that the journey there was actually impossible. In other words, to set out for Fudaraku meant to renounce one's body. (Perhaps the idea of sailing to Fudaraku was colored by legends of island paradises in the sea, as in nos. 106 and 186.) The devotees who did so can have had little doubt about this. They had themselves cast adrift from somewhere on the Pacific coast of Japan, sometimes sealed in a cabin aboard a rudderless boat. Only a story like that of the nice little road god who sailed to Fudaraku (no. 159) can make the theme bearable.

People could hardly imagine paradise without imagining hell. Medieval Japan imagined hell vividly. Whereas Kannon normally saved people from earthly dangers, the Bodhisattva Jizō specialized in saving people from hell. He was naturally very popular. The Kasuga God in no. 215 was identified with Jizō, among other Buddhist divinities. Jizō looks like a mild little monk (nos. 104, 180). The wizard of the mountains (no. 88) rejected him on the grounds that he did not look tough enough to keep the unruly Japanese people in line, and perhaps the wizard was right; but many miracle stories show what a tireless savior Jizō is.

The Bodhisattvas Monju and Fugen are closely associated with the Buddha Shaka, especially in connection with Shaka's preaching of the Lotus Sutra. One monk sees, in a vision of this preaching, "the Buddha, flanked by Monju and Fugen, [sitting] before him on his Lion Throne" (no. 120). Monju embodies the Buddha's wisdom. In no. 24 an Indian monk recognizes a Japanese saint as an incarnation of Monju.

Fugen embodies the Buddha's Teaching and rides a white elephant (nos. 38, 121). Since he plays a major role in the Lotus Sutra, he shared particularly in the Sutra's popularity. The touching idea that Fugen could manifest himself as a woman of pleasure (no. 38) got sympathetic response, for a major medieval play is based on it, and the theme lived on in later woodblock prints.

The Bodhisattva Kokūzō had no popular cult in Japan, but some scholar-monks honored him because invoking Kokūzō could dramatically improve one's power to understand and remember sacred texts (no. 177). Kokūzō's decision to manifest himself as a beautiful woman (also no. 177) is akin to Fugen's appearing as a prostitute. It illustrates perfectly the enlightened tactic of using people's own weaknesses and desires to draw them toward the true goal.

Lower Buddhist Divinities. A third class of Buddhist divinities has a less exalted standing than the buddhas and bodhisattvas, but includes divinities who are prominent in these stories. There are, first of all, the protectors. The protective attitude of the native gods toward Buddhism has already been noted, but Buddhism had a corps of official protectors before it even reached Japan. They guard the buddhas, the bodhisattvas, and the devotee as well. The only one who figures here is Bishamon. Images of such divinities show them as warriors, often trampling demons underfoot, and that is why Bishamon wields his spear so effectively (no. 146). He could also dispense wealth (no. 155).

A class of wrathful divinities, associated especially with Esoteric Buddhism, represent energy-in-action, destroying whatever impedes enlightenment. Even important, peaceful divinities can take on a wrathful appearance. Kannon, for instance, has at times a terrifying form that is visualized surrounded by flames. Fudō ("The Unmoving"), the wrathful emanation of Dainichi, appears in several stories, and is still popular. He is especially to be found on mountains, near a waterfall. Usually blue-black in color, Fudō sits or stands on a rock and is surrounded by flames (no. 95). Practices associated with him involve the energy of fire (no. 34). Sometimes this energy is turned to the purpose of healing (nos. 74, 126). The fierce ascetic of no. 73 is also a powerful healer, and it is Fudō who carries him up to the Tosotsu Heaven.

Two stories feature a gorgeous feminine divinity named Kichijōten, probably descended from the Indian goddess Lakshmi. Though well known as an object for a monk's sexual fantasies (no. 20), she was actually one of many divinities you could pray to for wealth (no. 172).

There is also the king of hell. In Buddhism there are multiple hells, just as there are multiple paradises and heavens. In these stories, though, hell is not too complicated. No. 149 evokes it nicely. Emma, the king of hell and judge of the dead, appears in nos. 46, 149, and 215. He was usually imagined in Japan as a Chinese magistrate, aided by a whole bureaucracy of assistants, officials, bailiffs, etc. Fortunately, he could be influenced by savior figures like Jizō.

RELICS AND IMAGES

Faith in the miraculous powers of relics and of specific holy images was common in Japan. "Relics" were not the bones of saints, however, as in the Christian world, but were certain hard bone fragments or mineral particles (perhaps gallstones) that survived cremation and that were believed to come from the Buddha Shaka. The relics mentioned in no. 43 are of this kind, and so are the dreamed ones in no. 209. Relics were thought to be filled with divine power.

Boons, miracles, or spiritual power did not always come from a divinity generally conceived, but were sometimes granted by specific icons (statues or paintings). No. 27, which relates the miraculous origin of a particular image of Eleven-Headed Kannon, shows how special a person's relationship with such an image could be. Appeals to the Kannon of Hasedera (nos. 76, 173, 174) were addressed not to Kannon in general but to the image of Eleven-Headed Kannon enshrined at that temple. The Fudō who takes a monk up to the Tosotsu Heaven (no. 73) is "the one [the monk] himself had made, life-size, and enshrined in his temple"; and the wizard in no. 88 receives an important dream message from the Miroku that he himself had made and enshrined.

BUDDHIST TEXTS

Sutras are of course full of philosophy, and Buddhist philosophy is fascinating. But it can be said too that not all sutras convey their philosophical message ecomomically; that the point of some sutras is not philosophical; and that some do not even make sense unless you are an advanced initiate. In any case, the Chinese versions used in Japan are difficult for the poorly educated to understand; and being Chinese rather than Japanese, they are unintelligible as language when spoken aloud or chanted. An important aspect of the sutras has always been outside their meaning, for their sound alone, when they are chanted, carries power. Examples here include the monk who has dedicated himself to chanting the Sutra of Diamond Wisdom (no. 151), and the monk who heals the chancellor by chanting the Sutra of Golden Light (no. 149). However, the issue would be a minor one without the Lotus Sutra, which figures in twenty-nine tales and is the supreme power text in the world of these stories.

The Lotus Sutra. The Lotus Sutra is probably the single most important sutra in Japanese Buddhism. Its impressive parables, its awesome vision, and its fervently put message of universal salvation give it endless appeal. The Sutra's full title is "Sutra of the Lotus of the Wonderful Teaching," and in Chinese, "Wonderful" is the title's first word. This "Wonderful," written on the only scrap of paper left from an ancient copy of the Sutra, saves a man from a demon in no. 148: such was the Lotus Sutra's power. In one branch of Japanese Buddhism, chanting the title alone became a fundamental observance that many people still do today.

The Lotus Sutra states that it was preached by the Buddha Shaka on Vulture Peak, a real mountain in India. The mountain's Chinese name was applied to a good many hills and mountains in Japan, and the image of the Buddha preaching the Lotus Sutra on Vulture Peak became in Japan an image of paradise (no. 120).

At the time of these stories, study of the Lotus Sutra was basic for a great many monks, especially those on Mount Hiei (no. 177). Temples might sponsor lectures on it for the laity (no. 138), and lay patrons often had monks lecture on it in order to gain spiritual merit for themselves or others (no. 139). In fact, the Sutra itself describes the enormous merit to be gained from honoring it. Another way to acquire this merit was to copy out the text. No one here copies the Sutra for himself, although people certainly did so; but the hero of no. 149 copies it, like a sort of scribe, for patrons who think his beautiful writing will bring them still more merit than if they copied it on their own. Often people copied the Sutra intentionally for the benefit of someone else, especially for the dead (nos. 81, 216, and others).

Chanting the Sutra worked much the same way as copying it. You could chant it as a regular practice on your own behalf. A holy man could also heal someone by chanting it (no. 128), and a saint (no. 66) gets himself thrown in jail so that he can chant the Sutra for the benefit of the prisoners. The dead particularly valued hearing the Sutra chanted for them because it helped to dissolve their lingering attachment to the earth. In no. 159 a god goes to paradise thanks to a monk's chanting of the Lotus, and in no. 216 the flames of hell dim at the sound.

The Lotus Sutra's saving power did not take the spirit to any one paradise, the way devotion to Amida always meant rebirth in the Land of Bliss. But it was often linked to rebirth in the Tosotsu Heaven, where Miroku, the Future Buddha, waits to be born into our world (no. 111). For women, though, there was a catch. Apparently the Tosotsu Heaven was too lofty for them. In these stories, all the women are reborn into the Tōri Heaven, a lower realm presided over by the deity Taishaku (nos. 81, 111, 147). Standard Buddhist teaching defined women as spritually inferior to men. In the Lotus Sutra a young girl dramatically attains enlightenment, thus giving hope to all women; but she has to pass through a male incarnation, however briefly, in order to do so.

Many monks chanted the Sutra in order to purify themselves spiritually. The most successful of them memorized it, as the monk in no. 177 finally manages to do. Singleminded chanting of the Lotus, a common ascetic practice, could endow one with miraculous powers (no. 151), the greatest of which was simply endless life (nos. 85, 86, 100). With his power of flight, the Immortal of no. 85 closely resembles the Chinese-style Immortals discussed earlier.

As with the Amida and Kannon cults, devotion to the Lotus Sutra could lead to renunciation of the body. The Sutra itself contains a clear model of such action: a bodhisattva who burns his own body as an offering to the Buddha. Self-immolation in the Lotus tradition was done by fire (no. 157). In no. 22 the emperor himself follows this example on a small scale by lighting a flame on his own finger (no doubt dipped in perfumed oil) and then cutting off the finger as an offering. The Lotus ascetic of no. 158 chooses another, but no less distressing way.

Mantras and Daranis. Besides the sutra texts there were much shorter formulas which carried concentrated power. Some were called mantras and others daranis. For "mantra" I use the Sanskrit word because it is relatively familiar in English. "Darani" is the Japanese version of the Sanskrit word properly written "dharani" in our alphabet.

Many mantras invoke specific divinities. The Name of Amida, already explained, is a kind of mantra; so is the title of the Lotus Sutra. But the Mantra of Fudō and the Mantra of Fire (no. 34) are better examples. Both illustrate a peculiarity of most mantras: they are not even in Chinese but in hopelessly distorted Sanskrit. In other words, they are unintelligible not only as spoken but also as written text. The unusual Chinese characters used to write them convey only sound, not meaning. Buddhist mantras in Japan are "mystical" indeed.

The same is true of the generally longer formulas known as daranis. Some sutras give daranis that are described as summing up the deep meaning of the whole text, however long. The Sonshō Darani, a greatly revered example of the genre, occurs three times in these stories as an extraordinarily powerful protective spell (nos. 85, 108, 168).

SACRED MOUNTAINS

For reasons connected as much with Chinese, Buddhist, and pre-Buddhist ideas as with Japan's nebulous "love of nature," landscape figured prominently in medieval Japanese religion. "Landscape" means mountains, for in Japan most landscape *is* mountains and valleys. There was a tendency in Japanese Buddhism to affirm that mountains, valleys, rivers, etc. (in other words, all of nature) did not just symbolize but *were* enlightenment (no. 38).

Buddhist ideas of paradise and hell were projected onto countless mountains. In standard Japanese Buddhist cosmology, a great mountain named Shumisen stands at the center of the universe. Above its summit, which is the Tōri Heaven, rise level after level of increasingly ethereal heavens, while on the earth beneath it are multiple levels of hells. Japanese mountains could easily support several paradises. The Kasuga Mountain (no. 31) was associated with Kannon's Fudaraku paradise,

Vulture Peak where the Buddha preached the Lotus Sutra, and others. It also had a hell. So did Mount Hiei. Mount Fuji (no. 32) was crowned with all sorts of paradises, and its hell became famous after the thirteenth century. The volcanic hells of Tateyama are vividly described in nos. 147 and 216.

Most prominent of all, in these stories, are the mountains of the Ōmine range south of Nara. They have been revered since the earliest times, and their sacred character still lingers on today. Golden Peak (now Sanjō-ga-take on Japanese maps) is the chief peak of the range. No. 101 describes both its paradise and its hell. No. 88 passes on the shamelessly tall tale that Golden Peak was originally a corner of Vulture Peak in India and flew to Japan in A.D. 552, which means that the mountain is nothing less than the Buddhist Teaching itself. Nos. 23 and 102 both involve the legend that Golden Peak is full of gold, although there actually is no gold in the Ōmine Mountains. Small gold buddhas recently discovered at the temple site on Golden Peak may have been offered there by Emperor Uda (nos. 190, 191) in 900; and Lord Michinaga (no. 63) made a grand pilgrimage there in 1007.

Apart from being Buddhist paradises or hells, sacred mountains in Japan also had local gods of their own. Zaō Gongen, the god of the Ōmine Mountains, was especially famous: the wizard En no Gyōja called him into existence as a sort of guide for the people of Japan (no. 88). Zaō Gongen is closely related to wrathful Buddhist divinities like Fudō and looks very fierce indeed. He became the patron god of the mountain ascetic tradition, founded by En no Gyōja, and images of him can now be found on many Japanese mountains.

SUPERNATURAL MONSTERS AND BEASTS

The supernatural monsters and beasts in these stories include demons, tengu, foxes, badgers, dragons, turtles, snakes, and a boar. All can be found in recently collected Japanese folktales, but not as deeply colored by Buddhism as they are here.

Demons are a motley crew. As no. 169 puts it, "some were red dressed in green, some were black with a red loincloth, some had one eye or no mouth, and most were just indescribable." They are also terrifying. In no. 14 a rider sees behind him "a red face with one amber-yellow eye as huge and round as a cushion. The thing was greenish and nine feet tall. The three fingers on each hand had five-inch, knifelike nails, and the hair was like a snarl of weeds." Since they are called *oni* in Japanese, I have consistently translated them as "demons," with two exceptions: in no. 92

they are "devils" and in no. 169 they are "monsters." (Actually, the *oni* of no. 92 seem to be exotic humans.)

Demons frequent abandoned storehouses or isolated chapels, the upper stories of city gates, mountain clearings, bridges, and other obviously twilight-zone places. A human who detects one nearby expects to be eaten, and with good reason, for some people do get eaten (nos. 11, 12, 146). Fortunately, though, demons are not always so murderous. They like parties (no. 169), and some seem to like playing music (nos. 64, 167). At times they cannot be bothered to harm a human seriously (nos. 74, 170), though the least their mere presence will do is frighten someone half to death.

A recurring motif is that of the "demons' night procession." One night each month (clearly indicated on your calendar, as long as you took the trouble to consult it) the demons would parade through the streets of Kyoto, and you risked your life if you went out of doors. Having other things on his mind, one young man runs straight into them and is lucky to get off with nothing worse than a few days of fever (no. 168). In no. 74 the demons spit on a man they find cowering under a bridge, and he discovers to his horror that they have made him invisible.

In so Buddhist a land as medieval Japan, even demons were bound sometimes to be religious. In most demon stories, demons simply exist; there is no speculation about how they got that way. No. 97, however, presents a Buddhist morality demon: he used to be a human being, but singleminded hate turned him into a demon and got him stuck in that form forever. Some demons actually serve Buddhist divinities or are Buddhist divinities in disguise (nos. 98, 172). Still others are pious devotees, hungry only for the mystic sound of the Lotus Sutra (no. 100).

Tengu, another kind of troublesome creature, play tricks on humans. They are shape-changers. Tengu live in the mountains — not in the wholly deserted mountain wilderness, but closer to where people, for instance monks, live or pass by. Many sacred mountains had their tengu, including Mount Ibuki (no. 118) and Mount Hira (no. 35). Mount Hiei (nos. 34, 120) seems to have teemed with them. Several stories even have them visiting the Capital (nos. 35, 119, 120).

In these stories tengu appear as a kite (nos. 35, 120), a kestrel (no. 119), a warrior-monk (no. 35), a decrepit old monk (nos. 34, 120), a cheerful, well-fed monk (no. 123), the Buddha Shaka (no. 120), and the Buddha Amida (no. 118). In effect, they often parody the solemn Buddhist world. Unfortunately, the form most familiar in art and illustration (that of a long-nosed, winged mountain ascetic) does not appear here, perhaps because the image developed relatively late. As birds of prey, they are natural enemies of snakes (no. 35) and may even carry off a monk (nos. 35, 118). They also are known to carry off children.

A tengu's greatest pleasure seems to be tormenting pious monks (nos. 33, 34). No doubt anyone leading a life of religious practice, in any tradition, has to distinguish at times between true inspirations and those that "come from the devil." Japanese monks had to look out not only for tengu talons but for tengu visions, since tengu could create outrageously convincing hallucinations. One unhappy ascetic is done in by a fake Amida with all his saints (no. 118), while in no. 120 a tengu's Lotus Sutra show works all too well, even though the tengu himself has warned his spectator not to believe it.

The badger and the boar too can conjure up deceptive visions, however much they may sound like "real" animals. One badger puts on a wonderful show as the Bodhisattva Fugen (no. 121) and another haunts a chapel in the form of an absurdly tall monk (no. 122). The one boar in this book stages a fake funeral for the benefit of a lonely traveler (no. 52). However, all these tricks end in the trickster's death, whereas tengu do not get killed.

A far greater trickster is the fox. In these stories foxes leave monks alone, instead pestering laymen with confusing visions and illusions (no. 208). Perhaps the foxes' lack of interest in monks has to do with their relatively more familiar presence in the everyday human world. It was a commonplace that an abandoned mansion, like the one in no. 84, soon became a foxes' lair; and even an inhabited mansion could be infested with foxes (no. 80). Apparently foxes could move into a house just the way raccoons and even skunks do in the United States, but I wonder whether a raccoon family has ever carried on the way these foxes do.

Some fox tricks are simple mischief. Whereas tengu and their colleagues like to play on religious feelings, foxes play especially on sexual desire. The fox counterpart to the tengu vision of Amida and his saints (no. 118) is the dream-marriage of the fox-enchanted hero in no. 82. Foxes are famous in Japan for masquerading as beautiful women — so much so that if a man runs across a pretty girl alone, especially at twilight or in the evening, he is a fool if he does not suspect her of being a fox. In other words, enchantresses are, literally, foxy ladies. The stunning fox-woman of no. 47 is another example. She does not exactly mislead the regent who sees her, but she certainly plays on his maleness.

Foxes do not appear to women as handsome men, but possess them instead as spirits. Not that a fox speaking through a woman's mouth talks about anything romantic. Often, all the fox wants is food (nos. 124, 206). In the end, though, something else seems to be going on — something that has as much to do with the woman as the fox-bewitched man's infatuation has to do with himself. No. 125 seems to support this impression. At the beginning of the story, the empress is possessed by a fox which the healer manages to transfer to a medium and then capture. Next, the empress is overwhelmed to the point of insanity by the healer's own lust. It is hard to believe that the original fox had nothing to do with her susceptibility.

The Dakini rite of no. 47 involves foxes in some sort of messenger role. "Dakini" refers to a triad of demonic figures who were absorbed into Esoteric Buddhism, and who became associated in Japan with the god Inari, who grants abundance and whose messenger is the fox. The story's God of Good Fortune, a by-product of the Dakini rite, is so foxy that he even smells like a fox.

The fox in no. 209 is probably a messenger too, signifying that a magic channel of communication between the dreamer and the higher divinities stands open. (The appearance of the golden relics seems to confirm this.) Although I do not know just why the white fox should have asked the dreamer to wear red, the image is fascinating.

Dragons and snakes constitute an entirely different class of creatures. Both are closely associated, in all Japanese folklore, art, and literature (including these stories), with water. Related associations are with thunder and lightning on the one hand and with lust on the other — in other words, with primordial manifestations of energy and vitality. The boundary between dragons and snakes is often vague, but on the whole dragons are nobler and are more likely to be thunder-beings than snakes, while snakes are more likely than dragons to stand plainly for lust. Neither is given to gratuitous mischief, but snakes can sometimes be destructive.

Japanese dragons have distinguished continental ancestors. In the Buddhist sutras they appear as spirits of the cosmic waters who honor and protect the Teaching, while imperial imagery in the Sino-Japanese tradition is full of dragons. For instance, the emperor's face is "the dragon visage," and an angry emperor has "ruffled scales."

Perhaps the dragon is best thought of as the energy of the water cycle: rain, river, sea, vapor, and rain again. The image of a dragon sporting among the clouds, obviously representing rain and the blessing its brings, is so common in East Asian painting that it is familiar to many in the West. The dragon of no. 36, a Lotus Sutra devotee, makes rain, and dragon gods were normally invoked in rainmaking rites (no. 183). The emperor, who blesses his people from high atop a metaphorical mountain, is dragonlike because it is from mountains that the life-giving waters flow down to the plain. Dragon (or snake) shrines are common on watershed summits and ridges for this reason.

Practically any body of water in Japan may harbor a Dragon King.

Mano Pond (no. 35) may be imposing; but Sarusawa Pond (nos. 37, 183), which practically every visitor to Nara has seen, is unimpressive; and the pool at Kōzen (no. 183), the site of rainmaking rites even into the twentieth century, is tiny. In fact the Dragon King of no. 183 lives in a cave on a mountainside, where the waters begin their journey to the fields below.

A proper Dragon King lives in a splendid palace. The dragon of no. 183 has his inside a cave, but a dragon with a pond will have his palace at the bottom of the pond. No. 184 provides a fine example. The Dragon Palace at the bottom of the sea, well known in Japanese lore, does not figure directly in these stories, but it is probably related to the Eternal Mountain of no. 106.

Snakes, the most ambiguous of all "real" creatures, can be gods or at least supernatural powers; can embody sinful, especially lustful thoughts; and can be a form of Kannon (no. 137). Their lack of dignity in comparison with dragons no doubt has to do with their familiarity in normal life.

No. 187 features a snake god who resembles a dragon in many ways, but who lacks a dragon's philosophical or poetic aura. He controls a fruitful island, and lives high up on the island for the same reason that dragons often live on mountains. (A related god still lives high on a small sacred island in Lake Biwa.) The snakes of several other stories are more plainly water-beings. In no. 98 a mass of snakes even looks like water, and in no. 136 a snake tries for no particular reason to drag a wrestler into a deep pool.

Snakes are easily recognizable even to us as an image for evil, deluded, or lustful thoughts. In these stories a snake seems sometimes to be lust itself. The woman in no. 111, frantic with frustrated sexual desire, turns into a huge snake and pursues the man she wants. In no. 109 a young man dreams a girl makes love to him, then wakes up to discover that a snake has made him ejaculate; while in no. 110 a young woman ends up mesmerized by a snake that has accidentally seen between her legs. Four stories associate the snake motif with a young girl's sexual fantasies (nos. 107, 108, 112, and 185).

An avowedly Buddhist context may give snakes a wider, moral significance. In no. 139, a young girl's only sin is to love her plum tree's blossoms so much that she cannot forget them even after death. As a result of this clinging to the pleasures of her past life, she is reborn as a little snake that wraps itself around the plum tree. The story makes a pretty Buddhist sermon againt attachment to the things of this world, but it too, of course, may allude silently to sexual fantasies.

The last animal to mention is the turtle. The immortal lady of no. 106 is a turtle. Marine turtles are magic creatures who stand for immortality and who seem related, like dragons and snakes, to ideas of spiritual transformation (nos. 103, 104, and 105).

Japanese scholars distinguish a body of writing they call *setsuwa bungaku*. The term just means "tale literature," but it refers specifically to about forty-five collections (they vary greatly in language, quality, and intent) put together between A.D. 822 and roughly 1350. Of the 220 stories in this book, 210 come from ten of the more important of these medieval collections, while the remaining 10 are from other medieval works outside "tale literature." (All the sources are listed in "The Works These Tales Come From," in the back of the book.) However, 165 of the stories, far more than a two-thirds majority, are from two collections, the masterpieces of the genre: *Uji shūi monogatari* ("A Later Collection of Uji Tales," early thirteenth century) with 54, and *Konjaku monogatari shū* ("Tales of Times Now Past," ca. 1100) with 111.

What are the subjects of "tale literature"? One category of stories deals with China and India. *Konjaku*, for instance, devotes the first 185 of its more than 1,000 tales to India, and the second 181 to China. Needless to say, I left such tales out because they are about the wrong country.

The second and by far the largest category deals with Buddhist topics. If I had kept the same proportion of Buddhist stories as in my sources, *Japanese Tales* would be a far more pious book, for the medieval collections include many more Buddhist stories than any other kind. A good many, like nos. 115 and 137, must have been used in preaching; while others evoke the miraculous origins of famous temples (no. 26) or images (no. 27), or the deeds of great monks (nos. 182, 213).

The third category of stories concerns the court and its world. Some of these tales are very good (nos. 7 and 191, for example), but I found many others unsuitable: brief items about court manners or about the doings of great lords; scenes of court life interesting only to the initiated; curious incidents in history and politics; a few accounts of battles; moments of triumph for master artists, craftsmen, horsemen, wrestlers, players of court football (*kemari*), etc.; and numerous anecdotes about particularly successful, moving, or unusual poems. Many of these items can hardly be called stories at all. They interested compilers and readers less as entertainment than as examples of conduct, judgment, or skill.

The fourth category, from which I have drawn the most heavily, consists of legends and popular tales. However, this category is the smallest of the four, and for this reason alone *Uji shūi, Konjaku,* and the other sources should not be thought of primarily as folktale collections.

What is the relationship between "tale literature" and the modern folktale? A comparison with *Ancient Tales in Modern Japan,* a recently published volume of folktales told by village storytellers in the twentieth century (see Bibliography), can serve as an illustration. Fanny Hagin Mayer's work shares five stories with *Japanese Tales:* no. 127 (my no. 3); no. 183j (my no. 17); no. 140 (my no. 169); no. 69 (my no. 174); and no. 164 (my no. 217). A few of its stories also include parts of tales present in this book — for example, no. 99 (my no. 75), no. 30 (my no. 107), and no. 311 (my no. 219). The two works also share various motifs. This is remarkable in a way, since six hundred to eight hundred years separate the sources for each. On the other hand, *Ancient Tales in Modern Japan* represents fairly the range of the modern Japanese folktale, whereas *Japanese Tales* exaggerates the folktale content of the medieval collections. Seen in this light, the resemblances are not necessarily impressive. However ancient the recently collected folktales may be, many things have changed in the last eight hundred years. For instance, nos. 3 and 169 in this book follow the symmetrical "good old man/bad old man" pattern well known in modern folktales, and well represented in Fanny Hagin Mayer's book; yet they are the only examples of this pattern in all my sources. The *kappa,* a water-goblin that has become almost the emblem of Japanese folklore, is not to be found in medieval tale literature at all. Above all, farmers and their preoccupations, so basic to the modern folktale, are rare in the older literature.

Although they do include popular elements, the medieval collections are not folk literature. The compilers and their readers were highly literate, and particularly conscious of history. Of course educated people were bound to be interested in history anyway, but the Chinese tradition of meticulous record-keeping influenced the Japanese, who also valued detailed records. In this spirit, many stories give precise information by which they can be dated. (I have indicated these dates whenever possible in the notes, usually with the help of the modern Japanese commentators.) The compilers' interest in accuracy is only emphasized by occasional gaps in the sources, especially in *Konjaku.* Here the compiler seems to have left a blank when he found he was missing a name, so that he could fill it in later. The stories were supposed to be true, and it was the transmitter's responsibility to situate them correctly in his and his reader's world.

Where did the compilers get their tales? The preface to *Uji shūi monogatari* gives a fascinating glimpse of a compiler at work on an important collection, now unfortunately lost. This was *Uji no Dainagon monogatari* ("The Uji Major Counselor's Tales"), put together by a high-ranking courtier named Minamoto no Takakuni (d. 1077) who retired to Uji, between Kyoto and Nara. There he would "enjoy the cool reclining on a mat and fanning himself with a great big fan. He would call over any passerby, high or low, and get the person to tell him a story, which he would take down in a big notebook, straight from the teller's lips." The anonymous author of the preface surmises that the equally unknown *Uji shūi* compiler meant to continue Takakuni's work.

Perhaps Takakuni used written sources as well; later compilers surely did. Anyway, written and oral sources probably did not exclude each other even for a single tale. In cases where an earlier, written version certainly existed, a compiler still might not use it, at least not directly. He might rely instead on an intermediate written version; on his own familiarity with several versions, written or oral; or on someone else's telling. In fact the distinction between "written" and "oral" may not be very useful for *Japanese Tales*. Take the example of Takakuni noting down tales from "any passerby, high or low." A "high" passerby would have been someone whose thinking had been formed largely by the written word, whether poetry (which was essential then) or prose; and Takakuni would still have edited his telling. A "low" passerby might have been illiterate or semiliterate, and Takakuni would have tidied up his words even more.

Every compiler put his mark on his work. Some seem to have reduced a lot of material to skeleton notes, while others developed stories lovingly. At the very least, there was the question of choosing the kind of language to write in.

Writing in medieval Japan could vary between classical Chinese and pure, natural Japanese. These and many transitional styles are present in "tale literature." (People then wrote in Chinese rather as the medieval Europeans wrote in Latin, though they could not speak it.) Written language was not the same as speech. Even the pure Japanese of *Uji shūi* probably does not simply transcribe speech, for Japanese was a literary language too, with many masterpeices to its credit by the time the *Uji shūi* compiler lived. His stories evoke natural speech thanks to the writer's craft, and their consistency of tone could only have been imposed on them by a fine writer.

Who were the "compilers" I keep mentioning? There is not much to say about them. Most collections, like *Uji shūi*, are anonymous. No one knows who put together *Konjaku*, although scholars make one conjecture or another. Perhaps the man was a monk; and perhaps several people worked on it. At any rate all the compilers, whether monks or laymen, must have been educated men with some knowledge of court society. Takakuni, for his part, was a former member of the Council of State.

Among my ten source collections normally classified as "tale literature," the compilers are known only for the following works, from which I got thirty tales: *Hosshinshū* ("Those Who Awoke to Faith," early thirteenth century); *Kojidan* ("Anecdotes of the Past," ca. 1215); *Kokonchomonjū* ("Things Seen and Heard, Old and New," 1254); *Shasekishū* ("A Book of Sand and Pebbles," 1287); and *Tsurezuregusa* ("Essays in Idleness," ca. 1330). Three more tales are from *Kasuga Gongen genki* ("The Miracles of the Kasuga God," 1309), which, though not counted as part of "tale literature," is a fine collection of miracle stories. Some of these compilers were monks and some laymen, and all except perhaps the *Shasekishū* compiler were of distinguished birth and knew the world of the Capital. I name and describe them in "The Works These Tales Come From."

TRANSLATION AND EDITING

All my translations are edited, more or less so depending on the character of the original. Of course studiously faithful translations are valuable, but I felt they would be out of place in this book. These are very old stories, after all, from a distant country. If their genius is to shine for us, in our time, they need a little combing and brushing to rid them of small idiosyncrasies which might turn our attention from what matters. I have taken no casual liberties, however, and have not denatured the stories in any way. It is true, though, that in a few instances I combined elements from different sources into a single tale — the outstanding example is no. 213. Throughout, I worked especially on four problems: the titles of the stories, their style, the large amount of unfamiliar information many contain, and their form.

Although nearly every tale has a title in the original, I made up all the titles in this book. The old ones sound like this: "How Retired Emperor Uda Revealed the Ghost of Minister of the Left Tōru, of Riverside Palace" (no. 190), and this: "How the Fox of Kōya River Changed into a Woman and Rode on the Croups of Horses" (no. 207). Old-fashioned titles like these are usefully descriptive, but they seem awfully poker-faced.

As for style, I have already noted the variety of languages in the sources. Classical Chinese (no. 101) produces a very different effect from pure conversational Japanese (no. 150). There are also differences of tone, since some originals sound light, others serious or stiff. The style of *Konjaku* is often rather plodding. I tried to blend all these variations into about the same sort of English. Occasionally I found I had to change the order of the statements in the narration so as to make a story sound natural in English — an interesting discovery. The medieval Japanese did not value forward movement in a story as much as we do.

The originals often supply information that for the uninitiated modern reader makes the text unnecessarily obscure. Names and titles of historical people, and the names of precise locations, are displayed prominently; while elsewhere details of architecture, costume, equipment, etc. are carefully recorded. I have toned down the identifications of people and places, often simplifying and occasionally even suppressing them; and I have also simplified some descriptions, or replaced technical terms with more familiar approximations — like "veranda." Sometimes I have inserted short definitions or explanations into the text.

The problem of form has to do with the beginnings and the endings of the stories. First, while most collections set the tales out pretty plainly, the *Konjaku* compiler carefully began each tale with a set formula resembling "once upon a time," and ended it with an editorial comment, a little moral or bit of sage advice, and a set closing formula. I left out all these formulas and kept parts of the comments only when I thought they were amusing or particularly appropriate. Beginnings could present another sort of problem. This is where many stories cram in a particularly large amount of background information, and sometimes rhetorical ornaments that the modern reader may not admire. In such cases, I simplified.

The conclusions of the stories are the last thing to mention. Japanese writing has always avoided snappy endings. Even modern novels may seem to fade out gradually, or even to break off in mid-thought. Most of these tales end softly, too. This approach does not produce punch lines, but it has its own virtues and I have not tried to change it.

THE PATTERN OF THE BOOK

The 220 tales are grouped in sets of five, with a few irregular sets of four or six, and each set has its own thematic heading. This arrangement is meant to make convenient units for reading and to allow interesting juxtapositions of stories. The normal pattern for a set — and there are many exceptions — is to start with a short tale, continue with two of medium length, feature a longer story in fourth position, and close with another short piece.

Do not be held back by the themes suggested. Some are very specific, others catch-all. Most stories could easily have been put under other headings, including ones I did not mention at all. In any case, few headings exhaust their announced subject. The presence of two sets on foxes, for example, does not mean that are no fox stories in other sets; and the book is even more full of snakes than of foxes, though there is only one set entitled "Snakes."

J A P A N E S E

T
A
L
E
S

OAK
MELON
GOURD
ANGEL
FLEA

1 .

THE GIANT OAK

In Kurita county of Ōmi province there once grew a giant oak tree. Since the trunk was five hundred fathoms around, the height and the spread of its branches can easily be imagined. In the morning its shade reached Tamba province, and lay over Ise in the afternoon. No storm could move it and no typhoon could set it swaying.

On the other hand, the farmers of Shiga, Kurita, and Kōga counties could not grow anything because the tree blocked the sunshine from their fields. They presented a complaint to the emperor, who sent a party to cut the oak down. The farmers got good harvests once it was gone, and their descendants are working those fields still.

2 .

MELON MAGIC

Late one summer a train of pack horses was on its way up from Yamato province toward the Capital, loaded with melons. North of Uji the drivers stopped to rest under a persimmon tree. They took the melon baskets

073661

off the horses and loafed in the shade, eating some melons of their own which they had brought along.

An old man shuffled up to them, leaning on a cane, and stood there while they ate, weakly fanning himself and staring greedily at their melons. Finally he said he was thirsty and asked for one. The drivers said he would be welcome to a melon but unfortunately the ones in their load weren't theirs to give away — they were just delivering them to the city.

"You boys are mean," the old man complained. "You should be kinder to old people. Well, all right, I'll grow my own."

While the drivers laughed, the old man picked up a stick and began to work a tiny patch of earth into a miniature field. Next he planted some melon seeds the drivers had scattered. The drivers looked on with growing amazement as the seeds sprouted before their eyes and melon vines began snaking everywhere. Soon the flowers had bloomed and the fruit swelled into big, ripe melons.

By now a dread had come over the drivers — the old man surely must be a god. The old man helped himself to a melon. "See?" he said. "The melons you wouldn't share have grown me my own!" He passed out melons to all the drivers and even to people passing by. When all the melons had been eaten he got up. "Well, I'll be going now," he said and wandered out of sight.

It was time to load the baskets back on the horses and get going, but the baskets were empty. The melons were gone! The drivers decided that the old man had somehow confused their vision and gotten all the melons out of the baskets without being seen. They were furious. All they could do was turn around, much to the onlookers' amusement, and set off lamely back to Yamato.

3 .

THE SPARROWS' GIFTS

One warm spring day an old woman was sitting at home picking lice while a sparrow hopped about in her garden. Then a little boy threw a stone at the sparrow and broke its leg. As the sparrow fluttered helplessly along the ground, a crow came circling overhead. "The poor thing!" thought the old woman. "The crow'll get it!" She picked the sparrow

up, breathed on it, fed it, and put it in a little tub to keep it safe for the night.

In the morning she fed the sparrow rice mixed with powdered copper to make it better. Her children and grandchildren made fun of her. "Silly old thing," they said, "now you're babying sparrows!"

She tended the sparrow for a month or two till it could hop again, and the sparrow was as happy as could be. If she went out she made someone watch and feed it for her. The family kept teasing her unkindly. "What's all this fuss over a sparrow?" they grumbled.

"It's such a dear little thing, you see!" she answered.

At last the sparrow seemed mended. "The crows'll never get you now!" she said, taking it outside and lifting it on her open palm. "Let's see how you fly!" The sparrow wobbled into the air and flew away.

Having spent so long fussing over the sparrow, feeding it every day and putting it to bed, she missed it very much. Sometimes she talked about it and even wondered aloud whether it might come back. Mocking laughter was all she got in return.

Three weeks or so later she heard a sparrow cheeping loudly nearby. Sure enough, it was her sparrow back again. "How lovely!" she cried. "You haven't forgotten me!" The sparrow cocked an eye at her, dropped something tiny from its beak, and flew off. It was a single gourd seed. She kept it because the sparrow had brought it to her.

Her children jeered at her for being so happy about a present from a silly sparrow, but she had to plant the seed to see how it would grow. By fall the vine was huge and laden with far more fruit than any ordinary gourd vine. The old woman was very pleased. Though she gave gourds away to all the neighbors there were always plenty more. The family who had mocked her now ate gourd for every meal. Finally, she shared out the gourds with the whole village, then hung seven or eight of the very biggest up inside to dry.

Months later, when the gourds were ready, she began taking them down. How heavy they were! She cut the top off one to make a storage container, and on finding the gourd was full she poured out a little of what was inside it. It was white rice! After she had emptied what seemed like a whole gourdful into a bucket, the gourd was still as full as before.

It was the sparrow she had to thank for this miracle! She was in rapture. The other gourds were just as full, and no matter how much she poured out there was always more left than she knew what to do with. Her family grew rich.

The neighbors could not believe their eyes and were terribly jealous.

"What makes you and her so different?" they complained to their old woman. "She's made them rich. We don't see you doing that for *us*!"

The woman went to her succcessful neighbor to find out how she had done it. "I gather it had something to do with a sparrow," she said, "but I don't quite understand. Please tell me the whole story!" The first old woman admitted cautiously that it had all started with a seed a sparrow had brought her, but when pressed for details she thought it would be petty of her not to tell all. She explained how she had cared for the sparrow with the broken leg, and how she had planted the grateful sparrow's seed. The neighbor begged for just one seed from the bountiful vine, but the first old woman said no, she really could not give out the seeds. She offered rice from the gourds instead.

The disappointed neighbor decided she would find her own injured sparrow and kept a sharp eye out for one, but in vain. Then she noticed the sparrows hopping about at her back door each morning, feeding on the rice grains scattered there, and she tried throwing stones at them. There were so many sparrows and she threw so many stones that she finally managed to stun one.

In glee she broke its leg properly, then fed it food and medicine. As far as she could see, if one would make her rich then more would make her richer, and she would get still more praise from her children than that neighbor woman had gotten from hers. So she scattered more rice and threw more stones at the sparrows till she had hit three. That seemed enough. She put them in a tub and looked after them for a few months till they were better, then merrily took them outside and watched them flutter away. She was ever so pleased with herself. The sparrows, on the other hand, were very unhappy to have had their legs broken and to have been shut up for months.

In ten days the three sparrows came back, and the woman peered eagerly at their beaks. Each dropped a gourd seed and flew off.

"There!" she chortled, and planted the seeds. The vines grew faster than normal and became very large, but they did not bear many gourds — seven or eight per vine, no more. The woman looked on with a big grin. "You told me I was useless," she said to her children, "but I'm doing better than that woman next door!" How the children hoped she was right!

Since there were so few gourds they gave none away and did not even eat any themselves. They remembered, though, that the neighbor woman had shared her gourds with the whole village, and given them some as well. Perhaps they should offer some to other people, since they had three vines. The old woman agreed to give their nearest neighbors some gourds, and even sat down to a meal of gourd with her family. Everyone took a liberal portion, but the gourds turned out to be horribly bitter, and whoever ate any threw up.

The neighbors they had been so generous to besieged the house, shouting, "What kind of stuff was *that* you gave us? Everyone who's even touched it is nearly dead from nausea and vomiting!" But the old woman and her children, writhing on the floor and retching helplessly, were in no condition to answer. Fortunately, the victims recovered in a few days.

What a disaster! The old woman decided she had been overeager and ought to have waited longer for the gourds to turn into rice, so she hung up the rest to dry. Months later, when she judged they were done, she got together enough containers to hold her harvest. Her toothless old mouth gaped wide in a shameless grin as she took down the gourds. Then she poured. Out came horseflies, wasps, centipedes, lizards, and snakes which battened onto her eyes, her ears, and every part of her body and stung her without pity. But she was so sure she was pouring out rice that she never felt a thing. She just kept muttering, "Just you wait, you little sparrows, I'll get some from each of you!"

Swarms of venomous snakes from the gourds bit the children and stung the old woman herself to death. Those three sparrows had enlisted the help of every nasty creepy-crawly in the world and put them in the gourds.

Envy is something to avoid.

4 .

THE MAIDEN FROM THE SKY

One day long ago an old man who made bamboo baskets went to the bamboo grove to cut some more bamboo and saw that one of the bamboo stems was shining. Inside the stem he found a baby girl only three inches long.

Never having come across anything like *that* before, he hurried home to his wife with the little girl in one hand and his bundle of bamboo in the other. He and his wife were very happy. They put the tiny baby in a basket and cared for her tenderly. In three months she was a normal size for a child, and the bigger she grew, the lovelier she became. Meanwhile the old man kept going for more bamboo, and each time he found gold in the stems he cut.

Soon he was rich. He built a palatial home peopled by flocks of servants and retainers, and his storehouse overflowed with treasures of all kinds. He and his wife, who now had their heart's desire in everything, continued to lavish love on their daughter.

She was so dazzling that it was hard to believe she belonged to this world. Rumors about her beauty began to get around and soon many lords were courting her, but she would have nothing to do with them. When they showered her with love letters anyway, she tried to put them off by setting them hopeless tasks. "I'm yours," she wrote to one, "if you'll bring me the thunder from the sky." She told others she wanted the flower that grows in paradise, or the drum that sounds without being beaten. But her beauty had so intoxicated the suitors that they did their best to obey. Off they went to ask people wise in old lore where they should look for such things. Some ended up roaming the beaches like vagabonds, while others wandered homeless through the mountains. Some died, others never returned.

Finally even the emperor heard she was the most beautiful woman in the world, and he decided to go and see her for himself. "If it's true," he thought, "I'll make her my empress." He set out with all his ministers and officials and was surprised to find, when he reached the house, that it was fit for a king. The girl came to him when he called her. No, there was no one like her in all the world. Why, she must have refused everyone just so as to keep herself for him!

"Fine!" he said happily. "We'll go back to my palace and you'll be my empress."

"That would please me very much, Your Majesty," she replied, "but you see, I'm not actually human."

"Well, what are you then? A demon or a god?"

"Neither, Your Majesty. But they'll soon be coming from the sky to take me away. You should go home now."

The emperor hardly knew how to take this. "What's she talking about?" he wondered. "Nobody's coming down from the sky to get her! She's just saying that to get rid of me!"

But a throng soon did descend from the heavens, and they carried the maiden away. They looked quite unlike the people of our world.

Well, it had been true. She had not been of this earth. The heartbroken emperor never forgot her, but not even he could follow her to her home.

What kind of being *had* she been, though? And why had she become the old couple's daughter? It's all a mystery.

5 .

THE FLEA

A wife and her lover were once in bed when the husband came home. Since the lover had no time to run or hide, the woman rolled him up in a straw mat, marched out with the mat under her arm, and announced that she was going to knock the fleas out of it. As she jumped over the hearth, the naked lover slid out and fell thump into the ashes. The husband's eyes widened. "Biggest flea I ever saw!" he exclaimed. He seemed to register nothing else.

The big flea fled on all fours.

S U R P R I S E S

6 .

THE LITTLE SPIDER

A shō is a sort of bamboo mouth organ.

Once there was no one to play the *shō* for the emperor, and so Kanetoshi, the former governor of Chikuzen province, was granted special permission to audition at the palace. He put the priceless instrument they gave him right to his lips and began to blow. Unfortunately, the imperial *shō* had a little spider inside it. The next time he inhaled, the spider shot straight to the back of his throat. The coughing and choking fit that seized him then made the emperor and his officials almost split their sides laughing. Having made a terrible fool of himself, the poor man was never asked to the palace again. He should have realized that an imperial treasure like that is seldom played and tried it out cautiously first.

7

A FLASH IN THE PALACE

Early in his career Lord Fujiwara no Norikuni was a chamberlain of the fifth rank. One day when he was on duty he had to go into the Palace Council Chamber to receive an imperial decree from Minister of the Right Sanesuke, together with some instructions on where to take it.

The room was open to the breezes. As Norikuni approached the minister, he glanced toward the next building (the Great Hall of State) and spotted Lord Minamoto no Akisada, a lieutenant in the Imperial Police, on the veranda of the hall. Akisada had just whipped out his tool. The minister was too far inside the room to see him, but Norikuni, who had a perfect view, could not help bursting out laughing.

"I take it you realize this is a proclamation from His Majesty," said the minister sharply. "I fail to understand why you find it so amusing." He reported Norikuni's mirth to the emperor immediately. Though desperately frightened, poor Norikuni could not very well explain his laughter by revealing that Lord Akisada had exposed his penis at the palace. Akisada must have been very pleased with his joke.

SALT FISH
AND DOCTORED WINE

While governor of Echizen (though he actually lived in Kyoto), Lord Fujiwara no Tamemori failed to contribute his share of the rice stipend due the Palace Guards. The six contingents of the guards responded by rising up as one man and marching to Lord Tamemori's residence where they lined up shoulder to shoulder, seated on camp stools, under awnings they had thoughtfully brought with them. They had the house blockaded, and refused to let anyone in or out.

It was the sixth moon, and the days were long and very hot. The guards had been there since early morning. By midday they were roasting, but they managed to hang on by reminding themselves that they could not leave without satisfaction. Then the gate opened a crack and a senior retainer stuck his head out.

"His Excellency the Governor has asked me to speak to you," the retainer announced. "He says he would like to meet you immediately, but unfortunately that is impossible because your presence has terribly frightened all the women and children. He does realize, though, that in this heat you must all be thirsty, and he thinks he might discuss things with you inside, through a screen, as long as you don't mind coming in in small parties. He suggests some refreshments. We might first have the Left and Right Inner Guards, if you have no objection. The other contingents can follow. His Excellency knows he ought to have you all come in at once, but unhappily his residence is too small and poor to allow that. So please be patient, the rest of you. Will the Inner Guards now be good enough to come in? His Excellency will receive you."

The guards certainly *were* thirsty, and the thought of getting not only a drink but a chance to say their piece pleased them very much. "How kind of him!" they replied. "We'll be happy to go in and explain to him why we're here."

"Fine!" said the retainer and opened the gate. The men of the Left and Right Inner Guards quickly gathered before it.

Long mats had been laid out in the gallery north of the middle gate, and on them stood several dozen individual tables arranged facing each other in two rows. The tables were piled high with sliced sea bream, dried and well salted; slices of very salty-looking salt salmon; salted horse mackerel; and sea bream pickled in *miso*. For fruit there were ten great lacquered bowls heaped with nicely ripened purple plums.

"This way, please!" cried the retainer. "Just the *Inner* Guards now, if you don't mind!"

In they trooped: Kanetoki from Owari province and Atsuyuki from Shimōsa first, followed by all the oldest and most senior officers. "The other contingents will all have their turn!" called the retainer to those left outside, then locked the gate behind him and kept the key.

The retainer pressed the guards politely to step up into the gallery and take their seats, which they did. When they were all in place, in twin rows, the retainer called for wine. In fact, though, the wine was slow to appear, and in the meantime the hungry guards quickly picked up their chopsticks and helped themselves to the victuals.

"What *can* have happened to the wine?" the retainer kept muttering, but still it did not come. At last it was announced that although the governor did so much want to meet with the guards, he was just now suffering from a bout of some stomach ailment and could not be with them quite yet. He would be out when they had finished their refreshments.

Finally the wine came. Two young men brought in a pair of big cups on trays and set them down before Kanetoki and Atsuyuki, who were opposite each other. With generous ladles they then filled the cups full. Kanetoki and Atsuyuki picked them up and drank greedily till wine dribbled down their chins. The wine was a bit cloudy and sour, but having broiled so long in the sun the men had a powerful thirst, and they kept pouring it down. In fact, their cups had to be refilled twice before they would pass them on to the next in line.

Turn by turn the men all drank their fill which, parched as they were, was for some as many as five cups. Next they had the plums. Soon the wine was back again and kept coming round (with plums in between) until everyone had wet his whistle half a dozen times.

Only now did the governor emerge and seat himself on the other side of the blinds which screened the gallery from the interior of the house.

"Ah, gentlemen," he began, "I never imagined that any failure of generosity on my part would set you against me this way and hold me up to shame before all the world! There's been a drought in my province ever since last year, you see, and we've taken in nothing, nothing at all! At least, the tiny amount we *did* harvest was claimed quite persuasively by Their Excellencies at court. They took everything, I'm afraid. There's not a grain left. My own household is out of food, and the serving-girls are going hungry. Well, I suppose I deserved it. But, gentlemen, please understand that I can't offer you a single miserable potful of rice. It's this awful karma of mine that kept me for years from any official appointment, and that now has gotten me a hopeless province so poor that it yields me nothing but embarrassment. I certainly don't blame *you* for anything, I assure you! No, I'm only getting what was coming to me!" The governor sobbed aloud.

Kanetoki and Atsuyuki reassured him that they quite understood his predicament, but they reminded him too that they did not represent only themselves. "We have nothing at the guards' headquarters either," they went on, "and the men are very unhappy. That's why we're all here: the problem affects us all. Naturally we feel for you, sir, and we're sorry to pressure you like this, but at the same time we certainly wouldn't have come if we hadn't felt we had very good reason . . ."

Their stomachs rumbled shamelessly as they spoke, which was particularly embarrassing since they were so close to the governor. For a time some tried covering the squawks and gurgles by tapping their formal batons against their tables, while others tried different dodges to distract attention from their problem. But the governor behind his blind could hear that bowels were in loud rebellion all down the line and could see perfectly well that the men were doubling up with cramps.

"Excuse me a moment!" exclaimed Kanetoki, and he bolted out. Everyone else leaped up and pelted helter-skelter after him. Some cut loose right on the edge of the gallery, even as they were jumping off. Some made it to the carriage house and burst before they got their trousers off. Others got their trousers off and squirted like nozzles. Then there were those who did not even look for a place to hide but shat, oblivious to all else, wherever they happened to be. All the while they were laughing their heads off. "I knew the old boy would pull some-thing!" they chortled. "No, no, we've got no complaint! It's our own fault. We were too greedy for that wine!" And laughing still, bellyache and all, they shat on in chorus.

Meanwhile, the retainer opened the gate again. "Very well," he an-nounced, "you gentlemen may leave. Could we have the next contingent, please?"

"Oh yes," the men chuckled as they left, "by all means get 'em in here and treat 'em to a good shit the way you did us!"

The were wiping at their filthy trousers as they emerged. The men of the other four contingents burst into laughter at the sight and fled.

It had gone exactly as Lord Tamemori had planned. The day was good and hot. He would let them stew for hours under their awnings, then bring them in parched, stuff their empty stomachs with salt fish and plums, and wash it all down for them with plenty of sour, cloudy wine — wine liberally fortified with that trusty medicine for innards in need of encouragement, ground morning-glory seeds. Oh yes, those rascals would shit all right!

Actually, Lord Tamemori was a cagey old scamp and a whiz at making people laugh. This was just his sort of thing. The whole court enjoyed the incident hugely. Those guards had picked a slippery fellow to tangle with!

Perhaps the guards learned their lesson, too, because they never again descended on a provincial governor who failed to make his contribution. Tamemori was very clever to catch them out the way he did. He could never have gotten rid of them by main force.

THE TAPEWORM'S SAD END

Walnuts are still recommended in Japan
against intestinal worms.

Once a woman who had a tapeworm inside her married, conceived, and bore a son. When the son grew up, he began a government career which culminated in his appointment as governor of Shinano province.

On arrival in Shinano the new governor was met at the border by the representatives of the province, as custom required, and welcomed with a banquet. Together, the governor's own men and the throng of local people made a large party.

Gazing out over the gathering, the governor noticed that every single table, his own included, was liberally heaped with walnuts. The sight bothered him intensely. He felt somehow as though he was being squeezed dry. On asking why the guests should be given so many walnuts, he was told that since walnut trees grew all over the province, walnuts were routine at every meal. This news made him feel still worse and the squeezing sensation continued.

He was getting desperate. This was not missed by the deputy governor, a seasoned old hand who found his new superior's behavior curious —so odd, in fact, that he wondered whether the governor might not actually be a tapeworm which had managed to get itself born as a human. The thought inspired him to try a little experiment.

The deputy mixed plenty of ground walnut meat into some aged wine and heated the wine well in a jar. Then he put the cup on a tray, lifted the tray respectfully above his head, and went to present it to the governor. When the governor took the cup, his deputy promptly filled it with wine, which the ground walnut made a cloudy white.

The sight made the governor very nervous. "This wine looks strange," he said. "Why's it all cloudy?"

"It's an old custom of ours, sir, that when we welcome a new governor we offer him wine aged three years and mixed with ground walnut. Then the new governor drinks the wine." The deputy's tone of voice suggested that the custom was not lightly to be ignored.

The new governor looked even more ill than before and trembled uncontrollably.

"You must drink it, sir," the deputy insisted.

Shaking violently, the governor brought the cup to his lips. "I'm really a tapeworm!" he blurted. "I can't take this stuff!" Then he turned to water, slumped to the floor, and flowed away. There was no body at all. The governor's retainers were overcome by confusion and dismay.

"You never realized, did you?" said the deputy. He and the rest of the party from Shinano packed up and went home.

The governor's men could only return to the Capital and report what had happened. The governor's wife, children, and household were very surprised, but everyone who heard the story got a good laugh.

1 0 .

A TOAD TO RECKON WITH

Once a big toad lived in the so-called Guards' Gate into the palace compound and used to trip people up. Every evening at twilight it would come out and sit there looking like a low rock. No one heading in toward the palace would fail to step on it and fall flat, as the toad hopped off into the gloom. The victim might learn his lesson and look out next time, but for some reason he would always step on the toad again anyway and take the same tumble.

Now a certain student at the Academy was a great fool, always braying with laughter or spouting loud abuse. In time he heard about the toad and allowed that it might get him once, perhaps, but not a second time — no indeed, not even if someone were lurking in the shadows to help it with a push.

Darkness was falling. As the student left the Academy, he remarked that he was off to see a lady who lived on the palace grounds. Within the Guards' Gate sat the toad.

"Oh, there you are, are you?" the student sneered. "Well, you may get other people but you won't get *me*!" As he jumped over the toad his hat unfortunately slipped off, hitting his foot as it fell.

"So you'd like to trip me, would you?" the student bellowed. "We'll see about *that*!" He stamped violently on this toad of his, but the hat was the stiff, lacquered kind worn by the gentry, and it resisted being crushed. "Damned toad! Stupid toad! Think you're so tough, huh?" The student summoned all his pitiful strength and stamped like one possessed.

Some gentlemen came out to see what the commotion was about, sending servants ahead to light the way. The student knelt according to etiquette as the servants approached.

Coming upon a disheveled young man, they asked him what he was doing there. The student identified himself in the tone of a warrior on the field of battle. "You have surely heard of me!" he declaimed. "I am a history student at the Academy, Fujiwara no Thingamajig by name, and concurrently charged with visiting justice upon this toad which trips people up at the Guards' Gate!"

"What in the world is he talking about?" laughed the servants. "Get him up. Let's have a look!"

They pulled him roughly to his feet, tearing his cloak and wounding his dignity in the process. When he felt over his head, he found his hat was gone. The servants must have taken it. "What did you steal my hat for?" he roared. "Give it back this minute! Give it back!"

The servants lunged at him and chased him away. As he fled down the avenue outside, he fell flat and scraped his face all bloody, but he picked himself up and ran on, hiding his face behind his sleeve, till he was quite lost. Finally he glimpsed a light. It was a little house. Alas, despite all his knocking at the door the people inside naturally refused to open up. By now it was so late that all he could do was lie down by the ditch till morning.

When the neighborhood awoke at dawn they found him there in his sad state and cried out with surprise. It was only by asking constantly for directions that he managed to find his way home.

There really used to be fools like that in the old days—even in the Academy, apparently, since the fellow was a student there. How odd that he should have been so hopeless, yet so clever in school!

HAUNTS

1 1 .

BETTER LATE THAN EARLY

The staff of the Council of State used to hold what were called "morning sessions," which took place before dawn. The participants would arrive carrying torches.

Once a certain secretary arrived after the controller, who outranked him, had already taken his seat. The secretary had been afraid this might happen, and his fears were confirmed when he got there and saw the controller's carriage by the gate. Rushing to the council building he found the controller's servants waiting for their master by the wall. Next, he ran in panic to the door of the East Council Chamber and peered cautiously into the hall. The lamps were out. No one was there.

This was a surprise. Back he went to the controller's servants, who could only tell him that their master was already inside. The secretary called a guard with a torch and had him light the way into the chamber. At the controller's seat there was only a bloody head. The hair was scattered far and wide. Nearby lay a ceremonial baton, a bloody pair of shoes, and a fan on which the controller had written the procedure for the meeting. The matting was soaked with blood. There was nothing else.

The horror of the scene can scarcely be described. At dawn an excited crowd gathered while the controller's servants left with their master's head.

After that, the morning sessions were no longer held in the East Chamber, but were shifted to the West.

1 2 .

THE RAVENOUS STOREHOUSE

The great lover Ariwara no Narihira made sure he courted every woman known to be a beauty, whether palace lady or common gentleman's daughter. He became especially fascinated with one girl who was supposed to be lovely beyond imagining, but unfortunately her parents had their hearts set on getting her a far more exalted husband than Narihira. He was not even in the running. Somehow, though, he managed to persuade her to run off with him.

But now that he had her, where was he going to hide her? Finally, he remembered an abandoned, tumbledown mansion in the mountains. The door on the big storehouse was lying broken on the ground, but since the house no longer had a floor, he spread a mat in the storehouse after all. He had just lain down on it with the girl when lightning flashed and there was a crash of thunder. Drawing his sword, he got the girl behind him and kept watch through the storm. At dawn it finally passed.

Puzzled to hear no sound from the girl, Narihira glanced behind him. She was gone. Nothing was left of her but her clothes and her hair. He fled, terrified.

Later he learned that that storehouse was known to eat people. It was not the thunder that had gotten her after all, but the demon in the building.

It just goes to show that you shouldn't go near a place you don't know. And as for spending the night there, you shouldn't even consider it!

1 3 .

THE GRISLY BOX

Ki no Tōsuke lived on an estate the regent owned in Mino province. When the regent sent a gentleman to look after the estate, this gentleman came to rely on Tōsuke above all; and it was Tōsuke who was sent to serve the regent during a lengthy period when the regent was on duty at the palace.

Finally Tōsuke got leave to return home. On the way he naturally crossed the bridge at Seta where the river flows from the southern end of Lake Biwa. A woman was standing there on the bridge, holding her skirt in her hand, and Tōsuke as he passed thought she looked rather odd. Just then she hailed him.

"Where are you going?" she asked.

He dismounted politely. "I'm on my way to Mino," he replied.

"I'd appreciate it so much if you'd take something there for me. Would you do that?"

"Certainly."

"Oh, thank you!" said the woman, drawing a silk-wrapped box from the inner fold of her robe. "Please take this to Morokoshi village in Mino. You'll find a woman at the western end of the bridge there. Give this box to her."

By now Tōsuke was uncomfortable about the whole thing. Not that the request itself was difficult, but the woman was awfully strange. In the end, though, he found it impossible to refuse. "What's the name of this woman?" he asked. "Where does she live? Where should I look for her if she isn't on the bridge? And who should I tell her this is from?"

"Don't worry," the woman answered. "Just go to the end of the bridge and she'll come, you can count on that. All you need do is wait. I have to tell you, though, that you absolutely must not *open* the box."

Meanwhile Tōsuke's servants, who saw no woman, could not imagine what their master was doing. Tōsuke took the box and the woman walked off.

He rode on to Mino but forgot all about the box until he was home, even though he actually crossed the bridge where he was supposed to make the delivery. This slip bothered him a good deal when he noticed it, and he decided to make a special trip back to the bridge. But since he could not go right away, he hung the box for the time being high up in an outbuilding.

Unfortunately, his wife, a jealous woman, spotted him hiding the package. She assumed immediately that it was a present for some mistress, and as soon as he was gone she took it down and opened it. It was full of gouged-out human eyes and severed male members with the hair still on them.

Her scream brought Tōsuke running. Remembering with horror what the woman had said about opening the box, he frantically put the lid back on and wrapped the box up again. Then he took it straight to the bridge and waited. Sure enough, a woman appeared. He handed her the package with a short explanation of how he had come by it.

"This box has been opened and looked into," the woman observed as she took it.

"No, no it hasn't!" Tōsuke protested, "I assure you!"

The woman's expression became dreadful. "You've done a terrible thing," she said, but accepted the box nonetheless. His mission completed, Tōsuke hurried home.

Ill now, he took to his bed. His wife bitterly regretted opening the box, but it was too late. Shortly he was dead.

14 .

THE BRIDGE

A governor of Ōmi province had many brave young men in his service. One morning they were amusing themselves playing games, drinking, and telling stories when one of them said, "Have you ever heard of Agi

Bridge? It's right here in Ōmi. People used to use it all the time, but now they say no one can cross it, so nobody takes that way any more."

One of his listeners seemed to have heard of the bridge already (or perhaps he simply did not believe the story) because he quickly declared that *he* would cross the bridge. "I don't care what kind of demon is blocking it," he continued, "I'll get across as long as I'm riding His Lordship's best horse, the roan."

The others thought this a fine idea. "All right, let's find out!" they cried. "Let's see what sort of courage you've got!" The gathering got quite rowdy while they egged him on, till the governor himself heard the noise and wanted to know what it was all about. When he found out he was not impressed with the demon-baiter's good sense, but he did not object to the use of his horse.

"This is crazy!" the daredevil exclaimed. "I'm sorry I ever brought it up!"

"Shame, shame!" the others shouted. "Coward!"

"Getting across the bridge is nothing," the man went on. "What makes me sorry is that I should ever have seemed to covet His Lordship's horse!"

Loud voices objected that the sun was already high and that they were wasting time. The roan was saddled.

Though he wished he had never opened his mouth, the man was determined to see the thing through. He smeared the horse's hindquarters liberally with grease, cinched the saddle on tight, and lightened his clothing, then slipped his wrist through the loop on the whip handle so that he could not drop it and rode off. By the time he reached the bridge his heart was pounding and he was frightened half to death, but there was no turning back.

The sun was sinking toward the mountains and the deserted landscape looked indefinably bleak. Wisps of smoke rose from the houses of a distant village. He gritted his teeth and pressed on. Halfway across the bridge a woman was leaning against the railing, though from further off she had not seemed to be there.

This no doubt was the demon. He looked her over with deep misgiving. Under her pale cloak she had on a dark gown and a long red trouser-skirt, and she was holding her sleeve over her mouth. She looked so pathetic that at first glance it was hard not to feel sorry for her. She might have just been abandoned there.

The demon watched him coming with signs of mingled embarrassment and pleasure, and for a moment he could think of nothing but the desire to lift her up on his horse and take her away; but the thought that she had no business being there let him steel himself to ride on by. She clearly expected him to stop, and when instead he galloped past with his eyes tightly shut she shouted, "Say, are you just going to leave me here? I didn't *ask* to be dropped here in the middle of this bridge! You could at least take me on to the next village!"

Her hair seemed to swell and thicken as she spoke. He only whipped his horse on harder. "You brute!" she screamed, and the earth shook. Now she was after him. "Sure enough!" he thought, and prayed to Kannon to save him. Despite the horse's tremendous speed the demon caught up, but the horse's rump was too thoroughly greased for its clutching hands to find a hold.

Glancing back, he saw a red face with one amber-yellow eye as huge and round as a cushion. The thing was greenish and nine feet tall. The three fingers on each hand had five-inch, knifelike nails, and the hair was like a snarl of weeds. Maddened now with fear he galloped on, calling on Kannon with might and main, till at last he reached the village.

"All right, I'll get you next time!" said the demon, and suddenly vanished.

Panting and exhausted, the man dragged himself back as fast as he could to his lord's mansion and arrived at twilight. He was too weak to answer the barrage of questions that greeted him. All the household could do was try to bring him round. But when the governor, who had been concerned all along, finally asked him to tell his story he did so. The governor scolded him for having risked his life over a trifling wager, then gave him the horse. The man went home well satisfied and told the tale again to his horrified family and servants.

A spirit began to haunt the house after that, and the man called in a yin-yang diviner to find out what the trouble was. The diviner told him to be very careful the next time the day when he had thwarted the demon came round. When the day did come, the man shut his gate to all comers.

Now, he happened to have a younger brother who had gone off with their mother to Mutsu, in the provincial governor's entourage. This was the day when the younger brother came back and knocked at the gate. His older brother refused to talk with him except through a servant, and the only reply he got was, "I'm in strict seclusion. I'll see you tomorrow. Try somewhere else in the meantime."

"What do you mean?" the younger brother protested. "The sun has already set! *I* can go somewhere else, I suppose, since I'm alone. But what am I going to do with my baggage? I only just managed to come at all, and today was the only day I could find. Our mother has passed away, you see, and I wanted to tell you myself."

The older brother had been worrying about his mother for years, both because she was old and because he loved her dearly. When this news was relayed to him, he broke down and in tears had his brother let in.

The younger brother entered, all in black, and first had something to eat on the veranda. Then the older brother came out to talk to him. Both wept. The older brother's wife stayed behind the blinds that curtained the veranda off from the house proper and listened to the two men's conversation.

Suddenly, for no reason she could see, the brothers fell to grappling fiercely and crashed over and over, locked together, on the floor. She shouted at them to stop. When her husband got his younger brother under him, he demanded the sword he kept by his pillow. She answered that he must have gone mad and refused to budge.

"Give it to me!" he barked. "Do you want to get me killed?"

Just then the younger brother turned the tables, got on top, and with one crunch bit off his older brother's head. As he fled he turned back to glance at the wife. *"That's* better now!" he exulted. His face was the demon's. Then he vanished.

There was nothing the distraught household could do. As for the awful intruder's baggage, it turned out to contain only animal bones and skulls. So the man died for a petty wager and everyone who heard the story called him a fool.

After playing a few more tricks, the demon disappeared.

1 5 .

THE ROOTED CORPSE

The elder of two sisters was married and lived in the mistress's apartment toward the back of her late father's mansion. The younger had served for a time in a noble household but now lived at home. She had no husband or accepted lover, only occasional, casual visitors whom she saw in her room at the front of the house, by the double doors in the west wing. The house was near the crossing of Takatsuji and Muromachi streets in Kyoto.

At the age of twenty-seven the younger sister fell ill and died. Her body was left in her room, since there seemed to be nowhere else for her in the house, till her older sister and the rest of the household took her off to the burning ground at Toribeno.

They were about to unload the coffin from the carriage, in preparation for the usual funeral rites, when they noticed that it was oddly light and that the lid was ajar. Why, the body was gone! This was a shocking discovery. The body could not possibly have fallen out on the way, but they retraced their steps to make sure. Of course, they found nothing. But on reaching the house they thought they might as well check the room by the double doors. There she was, lying there as though she had never been moved!

The night wore on while the mourners discussed anxiously what to do. At dawn they put the body back in the coffin and carefully sealed the lid, then waited for night and another chance to proceed with the cremation. But at nightfall they again found the coffin open and were really terrified this time. The body was lying as before by the double doors, and it defeated every attempt to get it back where it belonged. They simply could not budge it. They might as well have tried to move a rooted tree.

There she was, and apparently that was where she meant to stay. "That's what you want, is it?" one level-headed mourner finally said to the corpse. "You like it here? All right, this is where we'll leave you. But we *are* going to have to get you out of sight, you know!"

They took up the floor, and she was as light as a feather when they lowered her through the hole. So they buried her under the floor and built a good-sized mound over her. Then the family and servants all moved away, since no one wanted to stay on in the same house with a corpse. Over the years the house fell to ruin and eventually disappeared.

For some reason, not even the common people seemed to be able to live near the mound. People claimed that awful things happened there. As a result, the mound stood all alone, without a single hut for forty or fifty feet around it. In time a shrine was built on top of it, for one reason or another, and they say the shrine is still there.

1 6 .

AN OLD, OLD GHOST

Demon Hall is in the Capital, north of Third Avenue and east of the East Tōin Palace. The place is haunted.

Long ago, before the Capital ever grew up, there was a great pine tree at the site. An armed rider passing by got caught in a violent thunderstorm, so he dismounted and led his horse under the tree to seek shelter from the downpour. A lightning bolt split him and his mount in two and killed them. That rider is the ghost.

Later on, the Capital came and people built houses all over the area, but the ghost refused to leave. They say it's still around and that that's why awful things have often happened there. It certainly is an old ghost!

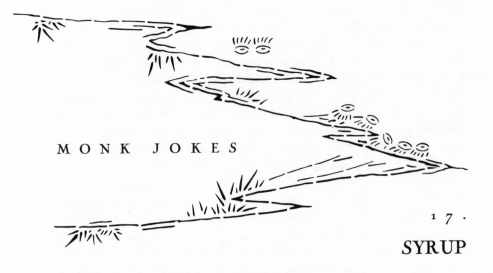

MONK JOKES

1 7 ·

SYRUP

The stingy senior monk of a mountain temple made a batch of sweet syrup, guzzled some all alone, then carefully put the jug up on a shelf. His little acolyte got none. In fact, he warned the acolyte that the stuff would kill you if you ate it.

The boy badly wanted some too, and one day when his master was out he got the jug down. Unfortunately, he spilled some syrup in the process and got it all over his robe and hair, but this did not discourage him from gulping several mouthfuls. When he was done, he smashed his master's precious jug to bits on a rock outside.

The monk came back to find the boy crying as though his heart would break. "What's the matter?" he asked.

"Your jug!" sobbed the boy. "I broke your good jug by mistake and I just didn't know *what* you'd do to me, so I decided I'd be better off dead and I ate a big mouthful of that stuff you told me was poison, but it didn't work. I ate more and when *that* didn't work I tried smearing it all over my robe and hair but I'm still not dead!"

The monk got no more of his syrup, and he lost his nice jug, too. What a clever boy! He'd no doubt have made a fine scholar.

1 8 .

NOT QUITE THE RIGHT ROBE

Once a very great monk was making clandestine visits to an exalted gentleman's residence. The gentleman knew nothing of the affair until one day, late in the third moon, when he went to the palace.

While he was gone, the monk got in and made himself at home with the gentleman's wife. A lady-in-waiting hung his nice, soft robe right on her master's clothes rack. Meanwhile the gentleman sent a servant back from the palace to fetch him a less formal outfit than the one he had on, since he was now off to have a good time with a band of courtiers. "Bring me my hat and my hunting cloak," he ordered.

The lady-in-waiting took the hanging cloak from the rack, put it in a bag with the hat, and sent it off. By the time the servant caught up with the gentleman, he and his friends had already gotten where they were going. The gentleman opened the bag. There was the hat. But where was the cloak? He took out instead a rumpled, brownish robe.

He understood immediately. Of course, all his companions saw the robe too, and he was as embarrassed as he was angry. There was nothing he could do, though. He simply folded the robe up, put it back in the bag, and returned it with a curt verse that let his wife know he now knew. He never went back to his house again.

The lady-in-waiting was a silly woman, and the room had been dark. In her haste she had taken the monk's robe instead of the lord's hunting cloak, since both were on the same rack and felt equally soft.

When the wife saw her husband's letter she was distraught, but there was nothing *she* could do either.

1 9 .

THE NOSE

The monk Zenchin was so learned and holy that people often commissioned prayers from him, which made him quite comfortably wealthy and well able to keep his chapel and his own lodging in very good repair.

There were always offerings on his altar, the altar lamps were always burning, and the small crowd of monks who lived around him kept the place lively. The bath was heated every day, and the bathhouse resounded with cheerful voices. When laymen added their houses to the community, a bustling village grew up.

Zenchin had a long nose. Its five or six inches, reddish-purple with a pimply surface like a mandarin orange, dangled below his chin and itched terribly. Zenchin had a hole made in a square tray, just big enough to put the nose through, to protect his face from the fire while he boiled the nose in a pot of water. When done the nose would be a dark purple. Next, Zenchin would lay it out flat on a pad and have someone trample it. A vaporish sort of stuff would puff out from each pimple, and with diligent pressing a white worm would ooze from each pore. Each pore would yield to the tweezers half an inch of worm. Then Zenchin would put his nose back in the pot and bring the water back up to a good boil. Soon his nose would shrink to about the size of anyone else's, but in two or three days it would be as bad as ever.

So most days Zenchin's nose was big, and to eat he would have to have an acolyte sit opposite him with a sort of paddle, a foot long and an inch wide, to lift his nose up and out of the way till he was finished. Some who did this for him lifted with a bit too much enthusiasm, and then he would get angry and not eat. That is why he made sure that the one acolyte who did it right was always there to help him.

One day this acolyte was ill and failed to appear for his usual duty. Zenchin wanted his breakfast but there was no one to hold up his nose. What a pickle! Finally one of the servant boys piped up, "*I'll* hold up his nose! I can do it just as well as that other fellow!" An older servant reported this to Zenchin, who decided he liked the boy well enough and would give him a try. He called the boy in. The boy picked up the nose paddle, sat very nicely opposite Zenchin, and held up his nose just right, neither too high nor too low. "He's wonderful!" thought Zenchin as he sipped his gruel. "Even better than the other one!"

Alas, the boy felt a sneeze coming on, turned aside, and let out a good a-choo. His hand shook, the paddle quivered, and the nose slipped off and plopped into the gruel. Gruel splashed all over Zenchin's face and the boy's. Zenchin was furious. "You rascal!" he bellowed as he wiped gruel off his face and pate. "A nasty little beggar is just what you are! You wouldn't have done that if you'd gone to hold up the nose of some fine gentleman! Disgusting little idiot! Get out! Get out!"

The boy got out, but on his way he loosed a parting shot. "I certainly *would* go hold up some fine gentleman's nose," he retorted, "if any gentleman in all the world ever had a nose like yours!"

Zenchin's students had to dive for cover before they exploded laughing.

2 0 .

TWO BUCKETS
OF MARITAL BLISS

At a temple in Izumi province, each trip to the bell tower took the bell-ringer monk past a statue of Kichijōten. Everyone knows how beautiful this goddess is. Seeing her day after day was quite enough to drive every other thought from the monk's mind. He took to hugging the statue, pinching it, or even going through the motions of kissing it.

In time he dreamed he was fondling Kichijōten as usual, on his way to ring the bell, when she suddenly moved.

"My dear," said she, "I'm touched by your loving attentions. I'm going to be your wife. Go to Inamino in Harima on such-and-such a date and I'll meet you there."

The bell ringer awoke blissfully happy. He could still see her lovely face before him. The day she had mentioned seemed so far away!

Feverish with anticipation, he could hardly believe the day would ever arrive; but when it did, there he was at Inamino, pacing impatiently up and down. At last he saw a radiantly beautiful woman coming toward him, dressed in brilliant colors. Could she be the one? He was trembling and could not bring himself to hail her.

"How nice to see you here!" she said when she got to him. "Now, make us a house!"

"How am I supposed to do that?"

"Why, there's nothing to it. You just get to work!"

A man came up to them. "Who are you?" he asked, "What are you doing out here in the fields?"

"We're planning to live here," answered the monk, "but we have no house and I don't quite know where we're going to get one from, either. I'm wondering what to do."

"Say no more! You've nothing to worry about as long as I'm here. *I'll* get you your house built. Wait and I'll bring some men."

The man was soon back with a good crew of workers. Each brought a joist or a beam, and everything else they needed just kept coming while they worked. Some of the materials apparently belonged to the workmen themselves, while some seemed to have been purchased by the lady. At all events, a beautiful house quickly rose on the spot. Beside himself with joy, the monk led his lady in and lay down with her.

"I'm your wife now," the goddess reminded him. "If you love *me*, you mustn't get involved with anyone else. For you, I'm the only one. Remember that."

Even if she had been a perfectly ordinary woman he happened to be fond of, he would hardly have objected; but under the circumstances he agreed with all his heart. "Of course!" he promised. "I wouldn't dream of wandering away from you!"

"Thank you, my dear," said the goddess.

He began growing rice and found that the least plot he worked gave more than anyone else's whole farm. Every comfort was his now, and in fact he was the richest man in the whole county. People came from far away just to ask for his help, and he always gave them what they wanted. His herds of horses and cattle were vast. Finally even the governor of the province began to defer to him and listen to his advice.

After several years of this pleasant life, he had to go off for a few days on business to another county. While he was there, a retainer of his just happened to mention a very nice girl he knew of. "You could have her come and massage your feet or something, sir," the retainer suggested.

"Well," thought the goddess's husband, "even if I start getting ideas, I suppose it doesn't really matter as long as I don't actually *do* anything with her."

"Fine!" he said. "I'll try her."

The girl arrived, dressed to kill. He had her begin working on his feet, but one thing led to another and soon they were a lot more intimate than that. Not that he had fallen in love with her, but he did keep her by him as long as his trip lasted.

His business over, he got back home to find his wife looking very put out.

"You swore you wouldn't," she said, "and now you've gone and done it! Oh, how *could* you? I'm leaving. I can't stay here any more."

He started justifying himself and making excuses, assuring her that she was still his only love. She, meanwhile, went to fetch two big buckets of whitish liquid.

"Here," she said, "I've saved it all since we've been together. You can keep it!" Then she vanished.

It was, of course, all the semen he had ejaculated into his heavenly wife.

Life was never quite the same for him after that, but he was still far from poor. So he gave up being a monk for good and lived on simply as a prosperous farmer.

2 1 .

HOME IN A CHEST

At one time Kaishū, the abbot of Gion temple, was paying secret visits to a mansion which belonged to one of the Capital's most prominent provincial governors. The governor caught wind of the affair but for some time pretended not to notice.

Once while the governor was out, Kaishū slipped into the house and made himself right at home. When the governor came back, he noticed that his wife and the other women seemed a bit flustered, and he understood right away what the trouble must be. In the women's part of the house he noted that a long storage chest which normally stood open was now closed and locked. Obviously that was where they had the fellow hidden. The governor called a senior retainer and had him summon two workmen. Then he ordered the chest carried immediately to Gion as a fee for having some sutras chanted there. Off the chest went on the workmen's shoulders, accompanied by the retainer bearing a formal note. Though horrified, the wife and her women kept quiet.

The Gion monks came out to receive the chest and were much impressed with the donor's generosity. "Go get the abbot!" they said to each other. "We can't very well open it without him." But the one who went came back, after a long delay, to report that the abbot was nowhere to be found. The retainer complained that he had no time to wait. "*I'm* here," he insisted. "Nobody's going to accuse you of anything. Just go ahead and open it. I'm in a hurry."

The monks were still wondering what to do when a doleful little voice from inside the chest piped up, "*Any* monk will do, you know!" The monks could hardly believe their ears, but very gingerly they opened the chest. Out popped the head of their abbot. The sight so alarmed them that they all fled, and so did the retainer. Meanwhile the abbot extracted himself from the chest and ran to hide.

Of course the governor could have hauled Kaishū straight out of the chest and given him a few good, swift kicks, but this would not have looked very good. It was wise of him to shame the man instead. Kaishū was always a fast talker, and even in the chest he had something to say.

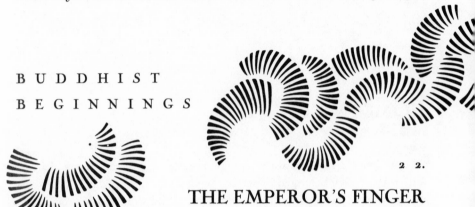

B U D D H I S T
B E G I N N I N G S

2 2.

THE EMPEROR'S FINGER

While visiting a certain shrine at Awazu in Shiga county of the province of Ōmi, Emperor Tenji decided to build a temple. This was about the year 665. But where should the temple stand? The emperor prayed for help. That night he dreamed a monk came to him and announced that there was an excellent spot to the northwest. The monk said he should look that way right now.

Waking up, the emperor saw a light in that direction. The next morning he sent someone to investigate, and the messenger, still following the glow, came to the foot of Mount Sasanami. Far up a ravine he came to a deep cave under a rock face and peered inside. He was face to face with an extraordinary old man who seemed infinitely holy and wise. The messenger announced that the emperor had sent him to find out why the mountain was shining, and asked the old man politely who he was. The old man ignored him. The messenger was upset, but went back to His Majesty to report.

"I'll have to go there and question him myself," said the emperor and set out. His bearers brought his palanquin as close to the cave as they could, and he walked the rest of the way. The old man was still there. He had on a brocade hat and a pale violet robe and looked more like a god than a man. Apparently the emperor did not impress him a bit.

"Who are you, and what are you doing here?" the emperor asked.

The old man brought his sleeves together a little, made a slight gesture of deference, and said, "Immortals have always lived in this cave." Then, after a few more cryptic words, he vanished.

The emperor decided this was a very holy spot indeed, and certainly a good place for the temple.

The temple, Shigadera, was built the next year, with a sixteen-foot-high statue of Miroku. While the construction was under way, the workmen dug up a miniature pagoda that obviously was not Japanese. It could only have been one of the 84,000 pagodas distributed throughout the world, each with a relic of the Buddha inside it, by the great Indian king Asoka some nine hundred years before.

In front of the temple stood a great lantern. For the consecration of the temple the emperor kindled a flame on the tip of his own right ring finger and lit the lantern with it. Then he cut off the finger and buried it under the lantern, in a stone box, as an offering to Miroku.

Having considerable power, the emperor's finger would send any visitor who was the least unclean tumbling down into the neighboring ravine. This discouraged pilgrims completely, and a priest who took over the temple much later got bored with having no visitors. The problem was that finger. The priest decided to dig it up and get rid of it.

As soon as the workmen began, a frightful storm broke, with thunder, lightning, rain, and violent wind. This just made the priest angrier than ever, and he kept his men digging till they got to the box. The finger looked perfectly fresh and gave off a pale glow, but it soon turned to liquid and disappeared.

Soon the priest went mad and died.

2 3 .

JAPAN'S FIRST GOLD

Tōdaiji in Nara is a must for every tourist,
and its Great Buddha is famous. The original Great
Buddha was dedicated in 752, in a magnificent ceremony
attended by monks from all over Asia.

When Emperor Shōmu built Tōdaiji, long ago, he had his workmen cast a huge, seated bronze image of the Cosmic Buddha, and he enshrined it in a correspondingly vast hall. This statue was the original of the Great Tōdaiji Buddha we know today.

For the emperor, this Great Buddha was the priceless jewel that was to draw our land together in the Buddhist faith, and he gave himself to the project heart and soul. When the time came to build the dais for the Buddha to rest on (the dais would look like a lotus flower), the emperor dug the first spadefuls of earth himself, and his empress carried the earth away in the long sleeves of her robe.

The temple was quickly built, with willing support from all, and the Great Buddha was cast. The next thing was to get thousands of sheets of gold foil to gild the Buddha with. But where were they to come from? Japan had never had any gold. The emperor sent an envoy to China, laden with treasure, to buy the gold required, and the next spring the envoy returned. Craftsmen were assembled and started work, but the color of the gold was wrong, and besides, there still was not enough of it even for the Great Buddha, let alone the many smaller images in the other, lesser halls of the temple.

In this desperate situation the emperor called in the greatest monks of the time to ask their advice. They told him about Golden Peak, a mountain in Yoshino county of Yamato province, and said this mountain was bound to have gold. But they reminded His Majesty that a powerful god watched over Golden Peak, and recommended that before taking any gold His Majesty should first speak to this god.

The emperor ordered Rōben, the monk in charge of the whole project, to beg the god respectfully for some of his gold. After praying for seven days and nights, Rōben had a dream. The god appeared as a monk and said to him, "The gold of my mountain was placed here by Miroku, the Future Buddha. It will be given out when Miroku comes into the world, and must be kept till then. My role is only to guard it. But I will tell you what to do. In Shiga county of Ōmi province, along the river that runs into Lake Biwa, there is a spot called Tagami. Nearby is a low, isolated hill whose eastern spur forms Tsubaki Point. You will find there a group of standing rocks. There always used to be an old man fishing from one of them. Build a chapel on that rock and enshrine Nyoirin Kannon, then pray there for your gold. You will get it, I promise."

Rōben reported his dream and the emperor sent him straight off to Ōmi. The hill was there and Tsubaki Point had the strange rocks the god had mentioned. Among them was the one the old man had fished from. Rōben had soon made a Nyoirin Kannon and built the chapel, and he prayed there for gold.

Shortly Mutsu and Shimotsuke provinces in the north sent a gift to the emperor in the form of some gold-colored sand. Metalworkers summoned to melt it found that it really was the most beautifully yellow gold. The delighted emperor sent for more, and it quickly arrived. So much was left over from gilding the Great Buddha that there was plenty for all the other Buddhas too.

That was how gold was first found in Japan.

2 4 .

GYŌGI AND BARAMON

Baramon's name is simply a japanization of
"brahman," meaning an Indian of high caste.

Long ago Emperor Shōmu invited Gyōgi to preside at the consecration ceremony for the Great Buddha of Tōdaiji. This was natural because Gyōgi was a beloved saint: a great teacher, preacher, and builder whose work helped everyone throughout the land.

But Gyōgi declined. "No, Your Majesty," he said, "I'm not worthy. The man you need is on his way here from across the sea." His Majesty let Gyōgi lead a hundred monks and a band of court musicians to Naniwa in Settsu province, where they waited on the shore to welcome the foreign monk.

The monk Gyōgi meant was Baramon, an Indian from Kabirae where the Buddha himself was born. Baramon, who longed to meet the Bodhisattva Monju in person, had learned in a dream that Monju lived on a Chinese mountain named Godaisan. He left for Godaisan immediately, but an old man he met on the way told him that for the benefit of all sentient beings there, Monju had now been born again in Japan. So Baramon went on to Japan. Thanks to divine inspiration, Gyōgi knew he was coming.

When Baramon failed to arrive at Naniwa, Gyōgi set a bowl of holy water afloat in the sea. The bowl sailed off westward, undisturbed by the waves, till it vanished from sight. Then it reappeared, sailing landward this time in front of Baramon's ship. Baramon knew about the consecration and hoped he would be in time.

Baramon and Gyōgi joyfully took each other's hands. It was a wonder how the Japanese and the Indian seemed to have known each other all their lives and talked together like the best of friends. Gyōgi said in verse,

"The love we pledged each other as brothers in truth, before Shaka on Vulture Peak, is still alive; and so we meet again!" And Baramon, who recognized in Gyōgi the bodhisattva he sought, answered, "How rightly we pledged each other love in Kabirae, for now at last I see Monju's face!"

That was how we in Japan found out that Gyōgi was actually an incarnation of Monju.

Gyōgi brought Baramon to the emperor, who was very happy to meet him and immediately appointed him to preside over the consecration. It went off beautifully.

2 5 .

THE OLD MACKEREL PEDDLER

When Tōdaiji had been built and the Great Buddha was ready to be consecrated, Emperor Shōmu appointed the Indian monk Baramon, recently arrived in Japan, to preside over the ceremony. But who should Baramon's assistant be? The emperor could not decide, and he worried till he had a dream in which a holy being came to him and said, "You must appoint as assistant the first man to pass the temple on the day of the consecration. Never mind whether he is a monk, or a layman, or a noble, or a nobody."

The consecration was set for the fourteenth day of the third moon of 752. The emperor made up his mind to do exactly as he had been told and posted guards at the appropriate time to keep watch. Along came an old man carrying a basket of mackerel over his shoulder on a pole. The guards whisked him straight off to the emperor, who dressed him in priestly robes and had almost appointed him when the old man finally protested, "Dear me, Your Majesty, I'm not at all the man you're looking for! I'm just an old mackerel peddler!" But the emperor ignored him.

Soon it was time for the ceremony, and the old man was installed on a throne right next to Baramon with his basket of mackerel beside him. His pole was stuck in the ground east of the entrance to the hall. When the rite was over, Baramon came down from his throne and the old man just vanished.

"I thought so!" said the emperor to himself. "He *was* magic!" Then he had a look at the basket. Those had definitely been mackerel in there, but now they were the eighty scrolls of the Kegon Sutra. The emperor wept and prostrated himself in awe. His vow to build the temple had been well conceived and a buddha had come to help him!

The mackerel peddler's pole is still by the entrance to the hall. It hasn't grown, or burst into bloom, or done anything in particular. It's just there.

2 6 .

KŌBŌ DAISHI

Kōbō Daishi (Daishi means "Great Teacher")
is credited with many extraordinary
accomplishments including the invention of the Japanese
phonetic script, and his temple on Mount Kōya is
still an important pilgrimage center. Women have been
allowed there only since the late nineteenth century.
*   A vajra is a key ritual implement in Esoteric Buddhism.*
The term means "diamond" or "thunderbolt" in Sanskrit.

Long ago Kōbō Daishi braved the voyage to China to study the Teaching and brought back the Esoteric Buddhism which he then spread far and wide. When he was getting old, he gathered his disciples together and distributed among them the many temples he had founded. But there was one temple, the greatest of all, which he had yet to found because he still did not know where to build it. This was the one on Mount Kōya.

Kōbō Daishi had planned this temple even in China. The day before he left China, he stood on a cliff overlooking the sea and hurled a three-pronged vajra toward Japan. As he did so, he prayed that the vajra should land at the right place for a temple — a temple that would last till Miroku comes into the world. The vajra soared high up and disappeared into the clouds.

Now that his disciples were provided for, Kōbō Daishi decided to go looking for the vajra. He set out from the Capital in the sixth moon of 816. Finally, in Uchi county of Yamato province, he met a hunter, an immensely powerful, red-faced man eight feet tall, wearing a greenish coat and armed with a bow and arrows. The hunter had two black dogs, one big and one little. He asked Kōbō Daishi where he was going and Kōbō Daishi explained about his vajra. "I prayed for it to land on a mountain good for meditation," he went on, "and now I'm looking for it."

"I'm a hunter from Mount Kōya," the hunter replied. "I know where your vajra is. Let me tell you the way." He loosed his dogs and they quickly disappeared.

Kōbō Daishi followed the hunter's directions till he reached a large river on the border between Yamato and the province of Kii. There he met a mountain man, who told him that the place he wanted was a basin in the mountains some way to the south. The man went with Kōbō Daishi. "I'm the Mountain King," he told Kōbō Daishi as they walked along. "All this land is my gift to you."

They got to a place that was just like a bowl, with eight peaks all around it. Huge cypresses towered there, as dense and straight as bamboos. One of the trees was forked, and in the fork was the vajra. Kōbō Daishi was overjoyed. He asked the god his name and learned it was Nifu no Myōjin. "And the hunter you met," the god went on, "is Kōya no Myōjin." Then he vanished.

Kōbō Daishi went back to the Capital, resigned all his offices, and settled his affairs. Then he returned to Mount Kōya, where he built the temple and named it, by imperial wish, Kongōbuji, Temple of the Vajra Peak. Finally he prepared the place for his own passing.

On the twenty-first day of the third moon of 835, he sat in a cave, in lotus posture, and passed into eternal meditation as his disciples around him chanted the name of the Buddha Miroku.

Long afterwards his disciples opened the cave, shaved his head (for his hair had continued to grow), and changed his clothes. But they never came back, and it was only much later that someone opened the cave again. This was Kanken, a student of one of Kōbō Daishi's disciples and a high-ranking monk on the mountain.

When Kanken opened the cave, he was met by a thick cloud of dust. When the dust cleared, he saw that it had been from Kōbō Daishi's robe, which had disintegrated and been swept up by the wind as he opened the cave. Kōbō Daishi's hair was a foot long. Kanken, who had washed and put on a fresh robe beforehand, shaved the saint's head once more with a new razor. The cord of the saint's crystal rosary had rotted away, and the beads lay scattered before him. Kanken gathered them up, strung them on a new cord, and put the rosary back in Kōbō Daishi's hand. Finally he dressed the saint in a new robe. As he left the cave he wept, overcome by a feeling of deep personal loss.

No one has ever opened the cave again, but when a pilgrim comes there the doors of the chapel built against it open of themselves, and the mountain is heard to rumble. Sometimes people hear the sound of a small gong. It is also remarkable that here, so deep in the mountains that even birdsong is rare, no one ever feels afraid.

The two gods, Nifu and Kōya, have their shrines side by side below the mountain and still protect it as they vowed to do so long ago. Countless pilgrims still visit Mount Kōya, all men. Women have never been allowed on the mountain.

2 7 ·

THE KANNON IN THE PINE

One hall at Kōfukuji, the great temple in Nara, enshrines a miraculous statue of Eleven-Headed Kannon. This is how the statue came to be there.

On the very first day of 1007, a monk named Chōkon was on his way back to the place called Deer Park, a little way south of the temple, when a small boy came up to him, asking to go home with him and serve him. Chōkon readily agreed.

Six years later, in 1013, the boy lay dying. "I won't last much longer," he told Chōkon. "When my breathing stops, don't disturb my body in any way. Put me exactly as I am in a coffin, then hang the coffin in the pine tree at Deer Park where we first met. After seven days, but not earlier, you may open the coffin and look at me." Then he died as though falling asleep.

Weeping, Chōkon followed the boy's instructions and hung him in the pine. He walked on from there several hours to Hasedera and went into retreat before that temple's own most holy Eleven-Headed Kannon. Now and again he could not help bewailing his advancing age and charging Kannon with having neglected him.

Seven days later he headed back to Nara. A delicious fragrance filled the air around the pine at Deer Park, and when he opened the coffin a blaze of light burst forth. Inside was a life-sized statue of Eleven-Headed Kannon. Astonished and overjoyed, Chōkon regretted all his complaints. He carried the statue on his back to Kōfukuji and enshrined it in its present hall.

After he died an oracle revealed that he had passed on to Fudaraku, Kannon's paradise.

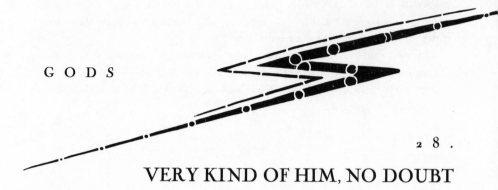

GODS

VERY KIND OF HIM, NO DOUBT

An epidemic sickness that caused a terrible cough was once going round, and everyone from peasant to emperor caught it.

A cook had finished working in his employer's kitchen and left for home late in the evening after the household had retired. At the gate he met a haughty, frightening gentleman in a red cloak and formal head-dress. The cook had no idea who the gentleman was, but since there was no doubting his quality he knelt and bowed.

"Do you know who I am?" the gentleman asked.

"No, sir."

"I used to be a major counselor named Ban no Yoshio, and I died in exile in Iyo province. Then I became a god of pestilence and disease. I'd committed a serious offense against His Majesty, you see, and I was quite justly punished. But I owe my country a great deal for the favor I enjoyed while I still served at court, and when it turned out that this year there was to be a wave of sickenss which would kill everyone, I petitioned to have the epidemic commuted instead to coughing. That's why everyone is down with a cough. I was waiting here because I wanted to let people know. Don't be afraid." When he had spoken, he vanished.

The cook fearfully continued on his way and told others what he had seen and heard. That was how people found out that Ban no Yoshio was now a god of pestilence.

But why did Ban choose that cook to talk to? He could have chosen anyone else. Well, no doubt he had his reasons.

THE DOG AND HIS WIFE

A young man of the Capital once went for a walk in the mountains that rise so attractively north of the city. As the sun sank in the sky, he became more and more lost and ended up with no idea how to get back. There seemed to be no shelter anywhere, a problem which worried him greatly till at last he glimpsed a hut far down in a hollow. It was a human dwelling, at least, and he gratefully made his way to it.

A pretty girl of twenty came out when she heard him, and the sight of her gladdened his heart still more. She, on the other hand, seemed troubled and asked what he was doing there. He explained. "I couldn't find any shelter for the night," he said, "and I was very glad to see your place!"

"No one ever comes here," she answered. "The master will be back soon, and when he finds you he'll be sure you're some boyfriend of mine. What'll you do then?"

"I'll think of something. The thing is that I can't possibly get home tonight. I just have to stay."

"All right, if you must. I'll tell him you're an older brother I haven't seen for years. You were walking in the mountains when you got lost and came here by chance. Remember that. And when you get back to town, don't tell anyone about us."

"I understand," said the young man. "Thank you very much. I won't tell a soul, if that's the way you want it."

She led him inside and spread him a mat to sit on. Then she came very close. "Actually," she whispered, "I'm a gentleman's daughter from the Capital. This creature stole me, and for years now he's done with me as he pleases. He'll be back any minute. You'll see what I mean. Not that he doesn't give me everything I need." She sobbed pathetically.

As far as the young man could tell, this "creature" of hers must be some sort of demon. He was terrified. Night fell. Outside, something howled.

While the young man's insides churned with fear, the girl went to open the door. In came an enormous white dog. Why, the girl was his wife!

At the sight of the visitor the dog stopped short and howled again. The girl hastened to tell her story about the young man being her brother. "I'm so happy to see him!" she cried and burst into tears. The dog seemed to listen. Then he came in and lay down by the fire while the girl sat beside him spinning hemp. Shortly she served a very nice meal. When it was over, the young man lay down to sleep while the dog retired to an inner room and went to bed with the girl.

The next morning the girl brought the young man breakfast and whispered to him again that he must never tell anyone. "Come back sometime, though," she said, "now he believes you're my brother. I'll gladly do anything I can for you." The young man promised silence and said he would return. Then he finished his breakfast and set off to town.

He had no sooner arrived than he began blabbing the story to everyone. The word spread, and some spirited braves wanted right off to go and shoot the dog and bring his woman back. They got the young man to guide them.

A couple of hundred set off, each well armed with bow, arrows, and club. They reached the place soon enough and spotted the hut down in the hollow.

"There it is!" they shouted. The dog heard them, came out to see, and recognized the young man. Darting back inside, he reemerged in a moment, driving the girl before him. Both fled deeper into the mountains. The intruders shot many arrows at them but scored no hits. Next they tried pursuit, but the dog and the girl fairly flew, until the youths decided they must be supernatural and gave up.

Once back in town, the man who had started all the trouble felt ill and lay down. In two or three days he was dead.

The dog was surely a god, and the man who told about him was very foolish indeed. No one ever saw the dog again.

3 o .

AN OLD GOD RENEWED

As soon as Taira no Korenobu reached Mutsu as the province's new governor, he went around greeting all the local gods. By the roadside one day he came across a sparse little grove with a small shrine inside it. There was no sign that anyone ever came there.

Korenobu asked the local officials with him whether any god was present here, and an old man who looked as though he might know many a tale replied, "Yes, sir, there used to be. He was powerful, too. But when General Tamura was governor, a violent quarrel broke out among the shrine priests. It got so bad that even the court heard about it. As a result the governor stopped sending his monthly offerings, and new governors never came to greet the god again. The shrine fell to pieces, and pilgrims practically disappeared. That's what my grandfather told me *he* had heard, and he was eighty at the time. It must have happened a good two hundred years ago."

This was sad news. The quarrel had not been the god's fault, after all. Korenobu declared that from now on he would honor the god just as people had done long ago. He lingered till the weeds could be cleared and the place tidied up, then left orders with the county administration that the shrine should be rebuilt on a generous scale. He had the shrine's name inscribed on the official register of the sanctuaries of the province, and he sent formal offerings every month. He was sure the god would be pleased by all this attention, but during his term of office he noticed no special sign and had no special dreams.

When his term was over, he started back to Kyoto. A few days later the official who had told him about the god in the first place did have a dream. Someone unknown to him entered his house and announced, "He is outside the gate and summons you to attend him. Go now." The old man wondered who on earth could be "summoning" him now that the governor was gone, since no one else in the province could possibly "summon" someone like himself. The whole thing seemed so odd that at first he did not move, but the visitor insisted till the dreamer decided that he *would* just have a look.

A big, beautiful ceremonial carriage, fit for an emperor, stood at his gate, and the gentleman inside it looked extremely distinguished. Rows of attendants stood nearby.

"Perhaps there's something to all this!" thought the old official as he knelt in awed greeting.

"You, my man, come here!" called the gentleman in the carriage. The frightened dreamer froze for a moment, but when the gentleman called again he forced himself to obey.

The gentleman moved the carriage blinds slightly aside. "Do you know who I am?" he asked.

"How could I know Your Worship?"

"I'm the god who was abandoned all those years. The governor gave me such joy that I'm seeing him back to the Capital. When he's safely there I'll return, of course, but not before I've made sure he gets another good post. In the meantime I'll be away. I'm letting you know because it occurs to me that you're the one who originally told him about me."

The old official saw the carriage move off toward Kyoto and awoke in a sweat. When he realized it had been a dream, he was filled with gratitude toward the god, and all those who heard him tell the dream were similarly moved.

In time the new governor arrived, and in the commotion the old official forgot all about his dream. Years later he dreamed again that "he" was at the gate and summoning him. He hurried out, wondering whether it was the same god as before. Sure enough, he saw the same ceremonial carriage. This time it seemed somehow less alarmingly awesome and so did the god. The official knelt as he had years ago and received the same summons to approach.

"Do you remember me?" the god asked.

"I haven't forgotten you, Your Worship."

"Very well. For the last few years I've been with the former governor in the Capital, and I've been able to have him appointed governor of Hitachi. Now I'm back again. I just thought I should let you know."

The old official told the same colleagues as before about his dream, and they were impressed with the god's kindness and power. Meanwhile the list of that year's official appointments reached the province from Kyoto, and the former governor had indeed been posted to Hitachi.

After that the people of the province served the god with increasing devotion, and the god, who was the soul of gratitude, rewarded them richly. The wonders he worked were many, and the old official prospered too.

3 1 .

COME TO MY KASUGA MOUNTAIN!

The god in this story is definitely male,
but the intensely feminine quality of the medium
makes this hard to remember.

The Venerable Myōe had a genius for communication with the divine, and his link with the Kasuga God was truly exceptional. He was staying with relatives in the province of Kii when he decided that this was the time to act at last on his lifelong wish to visit India, where the Buddha lived and taught.

This was a brave idea. Travel to China is dangerous enough, but India is so far from Japan, and the difficulties of the journey are so immense, that few Japanese can have reached it and fewer still, if any, have ever returned. Myōe knew this, and he must have known too that the Buddha's Teaching is almost dead, alas, in the land of its birth. But his only thought was to seek out and honor the source of the Teaching, at whatever risk to himself.

In the first moon of 1202, on the nineteenth day, his uncle's wife began a total fast. She even stopped drinking. Although the family feared she was ill, she looked if anything more radiantly healthy than before. Every day she bathed, read the sutras, and called the Buddha's holy Name. She could give no special reason why she was doing this. "It's just that I'm so full of the perfection of the Teaching!" she said. "The things of this world no longer touch me at all."

At noon on the twenty-sixth, she threw a new mat over the beam under the ceiling of her room, then rose and sat on the beam.

"I am the Kasuga God," she said, addressing Myōe. "Good monk, I'm so sorry about the trip you're planning that I've come to ask you not to go. You're so much wiser than all the others, you see, that I protect everyone who has faith in you. Please visit me sometimes! My home is in Nara."

"I'll give up my pilgrimage, then," answered the awed Myōe.

Although pregnant the lady descended, as she had risen, with the greatest of ease, like a moth fluttering its wings.

Three days later she began fasting and purifying herself as before, then shut herself in her room, from where a marvelous fragrance spread to fill the whole garden. Myōe slid open her door and found her lying down with the covers over her face. She lifted her head and smiled at him. He asked about the fragrance.

"I don't know what it is either," she replied, "but when I noticed it was coming from me I got ready to receive you. Now I want to sit up high again. Please leave a moment and close the door."

Myōe did so. When he opened the door again, there she was up near the ceiling. A ceiling plank had been removed so that she could sit comfortably. The fragrance was stronger than ever. He and his attendants prostrated themselves, saying, "Hail to the Kasuga God!"

The lady began in a kind and gentle voice. "It's rude of me, I know, to set myself above you by speaking from here," she apologized, "but I'm afraid I'm so used to being high up that I've taken the liberty of raising the woman I'm addressing you through. After you've heard what I have to say, I'll be happy to come down. I'm here, you see, because you don't seem to be quite sure you believe what happened at our last meeting."

"You *must* stop prostrating yourselves to me!" she interrupted herself to protest, but Myōe and the others continued nonetheless. She insisted that their manners left much to be desired.

"All the gods protect you, good monk," she then went on, "especially the Sumiyoshi God and I. I'm always with you, you know, deep inside you, so even if you do go to India we won't be parted and I won't personally mind. But I can't think of your trip without feeling sorry for all the people here in Japan whom you might have inspired to faith! I love all those who honor the Buddha's Teaching, of course, but there's no one I love quite as I do you!"

When she was finished, she came down as silently as a swan's feather falling. The fragrance was more pronounced than ever. It was not musk or any other such perfume of the human world, however rare, but it was very fine and rich.

The people present were in ecstasy. They pressed in to lick her hands and feet, which were deliciously sweet. (One woman's mouth had been hurting for days, but when she licked her the pain was gone.) She did not resist. On the contrary, she stayed perfectly still with an expression of pure love on her face. Though her eyes were wide open, rolled up to show far less pupil than white, she never even blinked. In fact, nothing about her was ordinary in any way. She was as clear and bright as crystal.

"I've never come down into human presence this way before, in my true form," she now continued, "and I never will again. Only my love for you, good monk, could have made me do it! It's a wonderful thing, of course, for your own spiritual development, that you should have your heart set on this great pilgrimage of yours. But when you're gone, you see, those you'd otherwise have a chance to touch will lose their opportunity to conceive, through you, their own faith in enlightenment. That's what I find so sad!" She continued in this vein for some time.

"This has been a long meeting!" she finally said. "I'd meant to leave earlier, but I was so happy to be with you that I couldn't bring myself to go." She pressed her palms together and bowed to Myōe. Myōe tried to avoid accepting this homage, but she bowed to him again anyway. Then she spoke briefly of another monk the god loved, an older friend of Myōe's. "It's extraordinary how much I care for him too," she said, "but I can't accept his living as a hermit. Please tell him so from me!"

"Ah, but *you!*" she went on again. "Your ardor to adore the Buddha in the land where he actually lived makes you unique in all the world, and gives me such joy! I love you more than any parent loves an only son. But I *must* go now. Come to my Kasuga mountain! You won't see me, but you can be sure I'll be there and will come to greet you. Oh, it's so late! Good-bye, good-bye!"

She drew Myōe's hands to her, and her fragrance grew still more intense. Everyone, including Myōe, was crying.

"Don't be sad!" she said. "The world has come into a degenerate age when no one follows the Buddha's path heart and soul. Now that people love everything but the Teaching, there's little hope that truth can prevail. Please don't let time slip wastefully by! Study the sacred writings till you grasp their deepest meaning. Good monk, your wisdom is of the highest, but your learning is still not quite mature. If you'll stop allowing your energy to be scattered hither and yon into this worthy task and that, and keep your eyes on the Teaching alone, then you'll come to know what the Buddha knew. Be willing to take on many students, a hundred or a thousand of them, even if all they mean to gain from their study is fortune and fame! And for yourself, simply weep that hearts can't help being base in this present age!" The god's grief and pain showed plainly in the tears that ran down her cheeks. She was pure compassion in visible form.

After a moment of silence she lifted her head again. "Now I *am* going," she said, "but I'll leave my fragrance behind to remind you of me. You must all take comfort from it. Good monk, come soon to my Kasuga mountain! And I promise you this. If you'll gather people together each year on this same night, and pass on to them the Buddha's message, I'll come down to be with you, wherever the place may be."

Of course Myōe never set off for India. Instead, he went to the Kasuga Shrine, which is below the god's mountain. When he rode up, several dozen of the tame deer that roam there bent their forelegs to kneel before him and bowed their heads; and once again that marvelous fragrance floated on the air.

When he returned to Kii, he learned through the same medium as before what had actually happened. "You know," remarked the god in the course of a conversation, "the deer didn't really bow to you, but to *me*. I was in the air over your head, you see. You didn't know it, but they did."

"I had no idea!" answered Myōe. "If I'd realized what was happening I'd have dismounted. It was very rude of me not to. I'm so sorry!"

"Never mind," the god consoled him. "They say a beloved child can do no wrong. I certainly never thought of scolding you for it. Anyway, there was no harm done since I was already higher than you!"

Myōe did hold the meetings the god had asked for. Much given to dreams and visions, and to intense spiritual struggle, he led an exemplary life and became one of the great figures of his time.

3 2 .

PRINCESS GLORY

In the reign of Emperor Yūryaku an old couple lived at the foot of Mount Fuji. Having no child made them sad. Then one day the old man found a beautiful little girl in the bamboo grove behind their house. She seemed to have come from nowhere. He and his wife were very happy, and since she shone with a lovely light they called her Kaguya-hime, Princess Glory.

Princess Glory grew up to be so beautiful that even the governor of that province courted her, and the two were married. When the old couple finally passed away, she confessed to her husband that she was not really from this earth at all. "I'm actually the Immortal Lady of Mount Fuji," she explained, "and I only came down in answer to the dear old people's prayers. Now I'm no longer tied to them, and I must go home to my palace."

The governor was distraught, but she did her best to comfort him. "You'll find me on the top of Mount Fuji," she said. "Come there when you miss me, or look into this box." And she gave him a box of the magic incense called Incense to Recall the Soul. Then she vanished.

Heartbroken now, he missed her so badly that he soon opened the box, but all he could see through the smoke was a shadowy wraith that sometimes faded altogether. In despair he climbed Mount Fuji as she had invited him to do. At the top he found a large pond with an island in the middle. The island seemed to have a palace on it, but through the vapor that rose from the water he could only barely make out Princess Glory's form. Bitterly disappointed, he pressed the box of incense to his heart, jumped from a precipice, and died.

The heat of his burning love set the box aflame, and the smoke from this fire is the smoke of Fuji that so many people have put in their poems about love and longing. Later on he and Princess Glory both appeared as the god of the mountain. The god is one, but may be seen as either a man or a woman.

T E N G U

A N D

D R A G O N S

3 3 .

THE MURMURING OF THE SEA

Once an Indian tengu set off to visit China, and on the way heard these lines in the murmuring of the sea:

> *All things pass:*
> *this is the law*
> *of birth and death.*
> *Once birth and death*
> *likewise have passed,*
> *that peace is bliss.*

The astonished tengu wondered how in the world the sea could be murmuring this deepest expression of the Buddha's Teaching, and he determined to find out what set the sea talking that way. "And when I do," he promised himself, "I'll give it a good dose of trouble!"

He followed the murmuring all the way to China, but since the sea there was still murmuring he went right by and on to the sea off Japan. The sea was still murmuring. He flew over the port of Hakata in Kyushu, and at the strait between Kyushu and Honshu he listened again. The murmuring was a little louder. More astonished than ever, he flew on over province after province until he reached the mouth of the Yodo

River, the river that flows from near the Capital into the Inland Sea. Up the river he flew, and the murmur grew louder still. The Yodo narrowed to the Uji River, and the tengu soared on up to where the Uji empties out of Lake Biwa. Here the rumor of the waters was distinctly loud. He pressed on over the lake to where a brook came tumbling down from Yokawa on Mount Hiei. Here the voice of the waters chanting the sacred verse rose to a roar, and he saw upstream the Four Heavenly Kings and countless other glorious Guardians of the Teaching watching over the brook. Awed and amazed, he dared not go further, but he could not resist hiding awhile to see whether he could find out what this place was.

When a lesser celestial spirit happened past, the tengu plucked up enough courage to ask, "Why is the water chanting this deepest expression of the noble Teaching?"

"There are a lot of learned monks up on the mountain," the spirit replied, "and this brook runs through their privy. That's why its waters proclaim the noble truth, and why we spirits guard it."

The tengu forgot all thought of mischief. "If even the stream that flushes their privy proclaims the deepest truth," he reflected, "then the monks of this mountain must be more holy than I could ever imagine! I'll become a monk on Mount Hiei!" And as he made this vow he passed away.

Next he lodged in the womb of a very great lady, the wife of Prince Ariake who was a son of Emperor Uda, and he was born as the prince's son. In time he did become a monk on Mount Hiei and acquired a great reputation for learning and sanctity.

3 4 .

JAPAN MEANS TROUBLE!

A powerful Chinese tengu named Chirayōju once came to Japan and met one of our local tengu. "In *my* country," he boasted, "there are lots of rough, tough warrior-monks, but now that I've got them all eating out of my hand I thought I'd come and have a look around Japan. They say there are some pretty potent ascetics here. Perhaps I might see what I can do with them. What do you think?"

The Japanese tengu thoroughly approved. "I've got all the good, brave monks of *this* country eating out of *my* hand," he answered, "but if you want to give them a bad time, go ahead. One's just asking for it, in fact. I'll show you. Come on."

Off he went with the Chinese tengu in tow. They flew up to the stone tower on the main peak of Mount Hiei and stood together beside the trail.

"People here know me," said the Japanese tengu. "I'd better not show myself. I'll just hide down the hill a little. Turn yourself into an old monk and wait. Make sure you take care of anyone who comes by!"

The Japanese tengu hid in a thicket and from there kept an eye on his Chinese colleague, who turned into a perfect, bent old monk. The weird gleam in his eye showed he was planning something good, and the Japanese tengu looked forward with pleasure to what would come next.

Along came a palanquin from higher up the mountain. Inside it rode Yokyō, a monk of rank and reputation who was on his way down to the Capital. When he reached the tower, the Japanese tengu glanced over to check on the old monk. He was gone. Yokyō and a crowd of disciples passed by in peace.

Thoroughly puzzled, the Japanese tengu went looking for his Chinese colleague and found him cowering down in the ravine with his behind in the air.

"Why are you hiding?" asked the Japanese tengu.

"Who was that monk who went by?"

"That was Yokyō, a famous wonder-worker. He's on his way down to the palace for a special rite. He's so holy I thought you'd show him up a bit, but you just let him go. Too bad."

"Right, right, I could see he was very holy and I knew he must be the one you were talking about. Well, that was fine, and I was just going to have at him when he disappeared. Instead there was a column of flame rising from his palanquin. I could see I'd get burned if I got too close, so I thought, well, I'll just pass on this one. Then I sort of got myself out of sight."

The Japanese tengu laughed mockingly. "Here you fly in all the way from China," he said, "and you can't even roll a fellow like that over a few times? You just let him by? I'd say you're pathetic. Next time, stop your man and *do* something to him!"

"Absolutely!" said the Chinese tengu. "Just you watch!" He set himself to wait as before by the stone tower while the Japanese tengu crouched in a thicket.

A noisy band came down the path. It was the great prelate Jinzen heading off to town with acolytes running ahead of his palanquin to clear the way. When the acolytes got to the old tengu monk, they just herded him on ahead with merry whacks of their sticks. The old monk put his arms up to protect his head and cleared out. He obviously was going to get nowhere near the palanquin. Those acolytes had gotten rid of him in no time.

The Japanese tengu went after him and heaped ridicule on him again. The Chinese tengu protested. "With all due respect," he complained, "you don't know what you're saying! I wasn't going to get close to those acolytes, not the way *they* looked, and I thought I'd better get out before they caught me and cracked my skull. So yes, I let that monk by. I can fly here from China in a flash, but those acolytes were too fast for *me*. No sir, I hid instead!"

"Well, for pity's sake do something to the *next* one at least! You can't come all the way here and do nothing! Why, you'll be an embarrassment to your country!" Having tried again to shame his colleague into action, the Japanese tengu went off to hide.

Soon a babble of voices rose toward them from a party on its way up. A monk with a red stole appeared first, clearing the path, and behind him young monks bore a ceremonial chest containing the illustrious traveler's monastic robes. The palanquin behind them carried Jie of Yokawa, the abbot of the entire temple complex on the mountain. "Will they get him?" wondered the Japanese tengu, as two dozen boy acolytes passed by on either side of the palanquin. But the old monk was gone. He had hidden again.

"I noticed a suspicious character around here," said one of the boys. "Let's spread out and look!" The fierce boys dispersed on either side of the path, brandishing sticks, and the Japanese tengu prudently stole further down the slope into a deeper thicket.

"Here he is! Get him!" shouted a boy's voice.

"What?" yelled an answering chorus.

"There's this old monk hiding here! He doesn't look right!"

"Hold him! Don't let him get away!" The others dashed off to provide reinforcements.

"How awful!" the Japanese tengu groaned, but he was far too frightened to do anything but burrow deeper into his thicket and flatten himself to the ground. Peering fearfully out, he saw a dozen boys drag the old monk to the stone tower, beat and kick him, and give him a very bad time indeed. The old monk bellowed and roared, but it did him little good.

"Who are you, you old monk?" the boys shouted, whacking him as they spoke. "Tell us! Tell us!"

"I'm just a poor tengu from China, young masters! I thought I'd have a look at the monks passing by. But the first was Yokyō, and he was reciting the Mantra of Fire so there was a huge flame in his palanquin; the next was Jinzen, who was doing the Mantra of Fudō so that Fudō's own minions were guarding him with their iron staffs; and the third, the abbot, was pondering Perfect Meditation. The first two frightened me so I hid, but the abbot didn't seem frightening at all and I was careless. That's how I got caught!"

The boys could not see that he was much of a threat, so they decided just to let him go, but not before each had filed past and given him a swift kick in the behind.

Once the abbot was by, the Japanese tengu crawled up from the bottom of the ravine and went to find the old monk where he lay all battered and bruised. "How'd it go *this* time?" he asked. "Did you get him?"

"Shut up. Just lay off me," the Chinese tengu growled. "I came here all the way from China, innocently believing I'd get a little cooperation from the likes of you, but you wouldn't give me any straight help, no, you had to put me up against men like living Buddhas, and all I've got for my trouble is a bruised backside and a good beating!" And he burst into tears.

"I don't blame you," the Japanese tengu replied consolingly, "but you see, you're a tengu from a great big country, and I thought you'd be able to take care of anyone from a small country like mine. I'm sorry you got your behind kicked!" He took the Chinese tengu to a nice place in the mountains where the poor fellow could soak the sore part in a hot bath and make it feel better, and then he packed the visitor back off to China.

While the two were bathing, a couple of servants from the city came into the mountains to fetch firewood. Passing the bath shed, they noticed smoke rising from the chimney, and decided that as long as someone was already heating water they might as well go in and have a soak themselves. They put down their loads and went in to find two old monks in the big tub. One of them seemed to have some sort of pain in his butt. The monks wanted to know who the two men were, but the men, for their part, noticed that the bath shed stank to high heaven — so horribly, in fact, that they both instantly got a splitting headache. Terrified, they escaped as fast as they could.

Later on the Japanese tengu possessed someone and told the whole story.

3 5 .

THE INVINCIBLE PAIR

In Sanuki province there still is a large body of water named Mano Pond that Kōbō Daishi made out of kindness toward the people who live nearby. It is so big, and the dikes around it are so high, that it looks more like a lake than a pond. Its deep waters harbor countless fish great and small, and at the bottom there once lived a dragon.

One day this dragon came out of the water to sun himself, and slithered around on an isolated section of the dike in the shape of a little snake. Just then the tengu of Mount Hira, far off in Ōmi province, flew over in the form of a kite. He dove at the little snake, caught him in his talons, and soared up again into the sky.

A dragon is, of course, immensely strong, but this one had been taken so suddenly that all he could do was hang in the tengu's claws. The tengu for his part meant to crush the snake and eat him, but that turned out to be impossible since, after all, it was a mighty dragon he had seized and no weakling serpent. Not knowing quite what else to do, the tengu took the dragon back to his lair on Mount Hira and stuffed him into a hole in the rocks so small that the dragon could hardly move. The poor dragon was miserable. Not having a drop of water he could not fly away, and for several days he lay there waiting to die.

Meanwhile the tengu was planning a little foray to Mount Hiei to catch himself a nice fat monk. That night he perched in a tall tree and kept his eyes on the dormitory across the valley on the side of the hill. A monk came out on the veranda to relieve himself. When he picked up the water jar to wash his hands, the tengu pounced, seized him, and carried him off to Mount Hira, where he stuffed him into the hole with the dragon. The terrified monk thought he was done for, but the tengu went off again.

From out of the darkness a voice asked, "Who are you? Where did you come from?" The monk explained what had happened — so suddenly that he still had his water jar — and asked who had spoken. The dragon introduced himself and told his own story. "It's very tight in this hole, you know," he groaned, "but I can't fly away because I haven't a drop of water!"

"Maybe there's some left in this jar," suggested the monk.

"Oh, how wonderful! What luck you're here! If there is, I can save us both. I'll take you back home!"

With joyous anticipation the monk turned the jar upside down over the dragon and a drop of water fell out. The dragon was wet.

"All right," said the dragon, "don't be afraid. Just close your eyes and sit on my back. I'll never forget what I owe you."

The dragon turned into a small boy, took the monk on his back, smashed the rock walls of their hole, and burst forth amid thunderclaps and bolts of lightning. Huge clouds gathered in the sky and heavy rain fell. The monk was frightened but trusted the dragon enough to hang on. He was deposited instantly right where he had started, on the veranda of his dormitory on Mount Hiei. The dragon flew off.

With all the crashing and roaring, the other residents of the dormitory were sure that any second a bolt would destroy them. Then suddenly the thunder stopped and blackness fell. When the sky cleared, they discovered their colleague who had vanished the other night, and he answered their astonished questions by telling them his story.

The dragon pursued the tengu everywhere in search of revenge. At last when the tengu was cruising the streets of the Capital, disguised as a warrior-monk soliciting donations for his temple, the dragon swooped down and killed him with one blow. Suddenly the tengu was a kestrel with a broken wing, and he was trampled underfoot by the passersby.

On Mount Hiei the monk repaid his debt by reading the sutras faithfully on behalf of his friend the dragon. Each had saved the other's life — surely the result of a deep karmic bond between them in lives gone by.

3 6 .

RAIN

In Nara there used to be a temple called Ryūenji, or Temple of the Dragon Garden. The single monk who lived there served the Lotus Sutra, expounding a chapter a day and chanting its text. A dragon, moved by the chanting, would come in human form every day to listen, and when the monk found out who his visitor was the two became fast friends.

Then a drought struck. Without rain the crops withered and died, till nobles and commoners alike faced terrible suffering. The emperor got a petition reminding him about the monk and the dragon (for their friendship had become widely known) and suggesting that the monk be commanded to have the dragon make rain.

The emperor called in the monk and made him a little speech at the end of which he gave his order. "When the dragon comes for your daily sermon," he said, "you're going to direct him to make rain. I'll banish you from Japan forever if you don't."

The monk was very upset. When he got home he explained the situation to the dragon, who said he would gladly give his life for his friend in thanks for all the Sutra had done for him over the years. "But *I* don't govern the rain," he went on. "King Bonden decides these things. If I open the gate of the rains my head will fly. I'll do it, though. Rain will fall three days from now, and I'll be killed. Please, pick up my body, bury it, and build a temple over it. You'll find it in the pond which is up in the hills in the western part of Heguri county. And there are three other places I'll visit on my way there. Build a temple in each one."

Despite his sorrow, the monk could not ignore the imperial order. He agreed to the dragon's last request, and the two parted in tears.

On learning what the dragon had said, His Majesty looked forward with relief to rain. Sure enough, on the promised day the sky clouded over, there was thunder and lightning, and heavy rain fell for three days and nights. Now that there was plenty of water again the crops ripened and all was well. The emperor and his people were very happy.

The monk found the pond in the hills where he had been told to look. The fragments of the dragon's dismembered body floated in its reddened waters. Weeping, the monk buried them and built over them a temple called Ryūkaiji, or Temple of the Dragon Lake; and he expounded the Lotus Sutra there daily for his friend. With the emperor's help he built three other temples too, as he had promised to do. These were Ryūshinji, Temple of the Dragon Mind; Ryūtenji, Temple of the Dragon Heaven; and Ryūōji, Temple of the Dragon King. And all his life the monk chanted the Sutra for the dragon's final enlightenment.

3 7 .

NO DRAGON

Ein, a monk in Nara, had a big, red nose. At first people called him "Ein the Red-Nosed Cleric," but shortened it later to "Ein Red-Nose" and finally to just "The Nose."

Legend has it that a dragon lives in Sarusawa Pond, by Kōfukuji's Great South Gate right on the edge of Nara. In his youth The Nose posted a notice beside the pond, announcing that on such-and-such a date the dragon would rise from the pond in broad daylight. The passersby who read it were intrigued, and the word began to get around. The resulting rumor greatly tickled The Nose, who after all had started it himself, and he was amused at people's foolishness. Resolving to see the joke through, he went on pretending he knew nothing about the notice.

As the day drew near, the rumor about the dragon attracted crowds not only from nearby but even from the neighboring provinces. The Nose was impressed. "What *are* they all here for?" he wondered. "How very strange! Perhaps something really will happen!" But he went on looking as innocent as ever.

On the day, the streets were so jammed that even The Nose began to take the story seriously. Since apparently the dragon *was* going to rise, he wanted to go and watch. Of course it was impossible to get anywhere near the pond, so instead he climbed up on the foundations of the Great South Gate, which stands on a high embankment. Gazing out over the pond and the whole enormous throng, he waited eagerly for the dragon to appear.

The very idea! By sunset there was still no dragon. When night fell, The Nose had to give up. He was crossing a little bridge on the way home when he nearly bumped into a blind man. "Goodness," he exclaimed, "you shouldn't be out in the dark like this! Why, you can't see the hand in front of your face!"

"The nose," the blind man corrected him, "You mean you can't see the *nose*."

It had not been The Nose's day.

PURE
HEARTS

38 .

THINGS AS THEY ARE

The Venerable Shōkū of Mount Shosha had founded a great temple and inspired countless people to faith. He was in fact a saint, and by chanting the Lotus Sutra had gained a wonderful freedom from the tyranny of the senses. But the thought of the Bodhisattva Fugen, who plays in the Sutra so grand a role, still filled his mind, and he knew he would have no peace until his own eyes had seen Fugen in the flesh.

After seven days spent praying for this boon, he finally saw, at dawn on the last day, a divine boy who told him, "Look at the chief harlot of Muro. She is the true Fugen."

This news astonished Shōkū, but he hurried to the little port which, as he well knew, was famous for its whores. It would be odd, though, for a monk in his black robe to enter a brothel, so he changed into a plain white garment. In Muro he found the house, and the harlot came out to greet him. Then she poured him wine and danced to a singing-girl's song:

> *Down in Suō*
> *among the marshes*
> *of Mitarashi*
> *the swift winds blow*

she sang, and her girls took up the refrain,

> *and waves are dancing,*
> *look!*
> *the pretty waves!*

"So this is the living Fugen!" thought Shōkū. Closing his eyes to contemplate quietly the presence of his beloved bodhisattva, he now saw Fugen perfectly real before him, exquisitely adorned, radiating wisdom and kindness, and mounted on his customary white elephant. Fugen was singing:

> *On the great sea of truth unsullied,*
> *how brightly the moon of pure insight shines!*

When he opened his eyes again, there was the harlot singing about waves dancing in the wind; when he closed them, there was Fugen. Deeply awed, he finally took his leave.

He had not gone more than a hundred yards when the harlot died.

3 9 .

THE PORTRAIT

Retired Emperor Kazan thought so much of the Venerable Shōkū that he once took a painter with him to Mount Shosha. The painter was supposed to hide where he could get a good look at the holy man, then paint his portrait while he and Kazan talked. As the painter worked, the mountain rumbled and shook — in response, as the astonished Kazan immediately realized. Kazan confessed his plan to Shōkū and revered him even more after that.

Now, the painter had neglected to put in a few moles on Shōkū's face. One tremor, which almost made him drop his brush, shook several drops of ink off onto the portrait. To everyone's amazement they corresponded precisely to the moles.

The portrait is still in Mount Shosha's treasure hall.

4 o .

WHAT THE BEANS WERE SAYING

Shōkū, the holy man of Mount Shosha, had achieved the highest sanctity by continually chanting the Lotus Sutra, and he took in through all his senses things that ordinary people never perceive. Once in his travels he heard a pot of beans bubbling over a fire of bean husks. "Brutes, brutes," the beans in the pot were saying, "you're brutes to boil us, for we're beans too!" But the husks were crackling back, "We hate to do it but we must! It hurts us so! Oh, don't blame us!"

4 1 .

MERCY

Once a quite ordinary monk, tired of life in the Capital, vowed to make a hundred pilgrimages (one each day) from Kyoto to the Hie Shrine and back. On his way home on the eightieth day, he passed a young woman sobbing as though her heart would break. Her violent sorrow moved him to ask her what was the matter.

"No, no, I can see you're a pilgrim!" she cried. "I can't tell you, I really can't!"

He insisted so kindly that she spoke at last. "My mother was sick for so long," she said, "and this morning she finally died. That's bad enough, but the worst is that I've no idea what I'm going to do with her body. I'm a widow, you see, and I've no one to ask for help. Being a woman, I'm not strong enough to manage it alone. My neighbors talk about how sorry they are, but they're so busy now with festivals for the gods that I'm sure they won't really do anything. I just don't know where to turn!" She burst into fresh weeping.

The monk understood, and felt so much for her that he too had tears in his eyes. He knew the gods enter this dingy world of ours only because they take pity on us, and he did not see how he could simply ignore her plight. "I've never done much in the way of good deeds," he reflected. "Look upon me, O buddhas! O you gods, forgive me now!" And to the girl he continued aloud, "Don't be so sad. I'll help you as best I can. We should go inside, people may wonder about us." Through her tears the young woman smiled assent.

That night, in the dark, they took the body where it had to go. But when the deed was done, the monk could not get to sleep. He kept thinking about the eighty days of pilgrimage he had thrown away, and about what a pity it was to have to stop now. Well, he had never meant to gain anything special by his hundred days anyway, so he might as well go back to the shrine and see how the god felt about it. The pollution of birth or death was superficial enough, after all, and not much connected with one's real state of mind. So the next morning he washed and set out for the shrine. All the way there his heart beat fast because actually he was afraid.

A large crowd before the shrine was listening to a medium deliver oracles from the god. Not daring to go near, the polluted monk hid instead some distance away to pray on his own. He was glad at least to have come and not missed a day.

The medium spotted him leaving. "You monk there, come here!" she called.

It was an awful shock, but there was no escape for him now. Shivering with dread he obeyed, under the suspicious gaze of the whole crowd. The medium brought him very close. "I saw what you did last night!" she whispered.

The hair stood on end all over his body and he thought he was going to faint.

"Don't be afraid," she went on. "I thought it was wonderful! I'm not *really* only a god, you know. It's compassion that brought me here. I want people to believe the Teaching. Taboos are just a way of going about it, as anyone enlightened knows. Don't tell anyone else, though. People are so foolish. They won't understand that you really acted from deep mercy, they'll think they too can break the taboo whenever they want, which means that they'll just get all mixed up and ruin the tiny bit of faith they have. It's not the rules that really count, it's the person."

The monk was moved to tears, and after that was often inspired to acts of special kindness.

4 2 .

AMONG THE FLOWERS

Saigyō, a monk and a wonderful poet, was roaming the East when one night in brilliant moonlight he crossed Musashino Plain. The carpet of flowers he trod was sparkling with dew, and insect murmurs mingled with the sighing of the wind. Far out on the moor he heard a chanting voice.

Heading that way, he came to a hut hedged with pink, nodding *hagi* and yellow valerian, and charmingly thatched with pampas grass, plume grass, and reeds. Inside a hoarse-voiced old man was chanting the Lotus Sutra.

Saigyō asked him who he was.

"I used to serve Emperor Shirakawa's youngest daughter," the old man replied. "She was only twenty when she died, and after that I felt I wanted no more of the world. I took up a life of religion. Longing to live where no one would find me, I wandered off without any goal till I came here, and the flowers were so beautiful that I stayed. That was many years ago. The flowers of fall, my favorites, linger in my mind when all the flowers are gone. Yes, I love the flowers so much that I'd say I have no cares!"

Tears sprang to Saigyō's eyes. "But how do you live?" he asked.

"Oh, I don't waste my time going round the villages begging. People bring me food if they want to. Sometimes I go without for days at a time. I wouldn't want to make a fire here among the flowers, so you couldn't call what I eat proper meals at all."

Was ever a man's heart more wonderfully pure?

MUSIC AND DANCE

43.

FOR LOVE OF SONG

On a festival day at Tennōji around 1202, when the temple's famous relics of the Buddha were to be brought out as usual for the pilgrims, the divine powers refused to let the doors of the reliquary open. Apparently someone in the crowd was unclean. The priests had the people step back a little, but still the doors could not be budged.

"Is anyone here a good singer or dancer?" cried an old priest. "If so, now's the time to show off your art!"

Middle Captain Morimichi came forward and sang a *kagura* song, the kind so often offered to the gods. The reliquary doors opened immediately. It was so like the time when the Sun Goddess pushed open the door of her Heavenly Rock Cave, and light again burst upon the world!

4 4 .

THREE ANGELS

The versatile Makoto, a son of Emperor Saga and the Minister of the Left, was an especially fine musician. On the long, mellow-sounding zither called the *koto*, no one could compare with him. One evening he became so absorbed in his playing that he went on all night, never even closing the latticework shutters that swung up horizontally to open onto the garden. Finally, near dawn, he began a rare and difficult piece. His own heart swelled with the wonder and beauty of the music. Noticing a light over one of the shutters he stole out, mystified, for a look. Three angels, each a foot tall, were dancing on the shutter and the light was their shining presence. They had come down to hear him! He was filled with a tender awe.

What a lovely thing to have happen!

4 5 .

GIVE ME MUSIC!

The monk Rin'e lived in Nara in Emperor Ichijō's time. The god who protected his temple, Kōfukuji, was at the Kasuga Shrine nearby.

One day, after presiding over an especially solemn rite, Rin'e came to the shrine and meditated awhile. He reviewed in his mind as he did so the full range of his sacred learning and offered it all to the god who, he was sure, could only be pleased.

Suddenly the shrine attendants began making music for the god with drums and bells. Rin'e frowned. "This is all very well," he thought, "but I can't have them making such a racket while I'm offering the god the Buddha's own wisdom. If I ever get to be abbot, I'll see that this sort of thing doesn't happen again."

When Rin'e did become abbot he silenced the music, and the shrine became so cold and lifeless that people were afraid to come near it. No one complained because Rin'e was so powerful.

Having reached the pinnacle of glory in *this* life, Rin'e finally began a seven-day retreat at the shrine to pray, with many a heartfelt tear, for the god's protection on the path to enlightenment in the life to come. When the god gave no answering sign, he stayed on another seven days.

At dawn on the last day he dozed off a moment and saw a gentleman in formal court dress emerge from the sanctuary. Tears of gratitude sprang to Rin'e's eyes because this was surely the god coming to grant him his prayer. But when the gentleman had come far enough down the sanctuary steps for Rin'e to see his face, his expression turned out to be an angry scowl. Afraid now, Rin'e hurriedly reminded the god of his blameless life and his countless merits, and he protested bewilderment at this display of divine wrath.

> *The drums' lively beat resounds in the palace of truth.*
> *In wisdom's mirror may be seen the lightly shaken bells.*

And he vanished.

The horrified Rin'e rued his folly. Before leaving, he carefully ordered that the drums and bells should never again be silenced for any reason whatsoever.

4 6 .

THE WEIGHT OF TRADITION

Harutō, a dancer from Nara, belonged to a family that had specialized generation after generation in performing the noble dance *Genjōraku*. Unfortunately, he fell ill and died before he could teach the dance to his successor.

Since it was late summer and still hot, his coffin was hung in a tree in
Hahaso Wood. Two or three days later, a woodcutter passing that way
heard groans from the tree and reported this disturbing incident to the
priests of the nearby temple.

Finding that he had come back to life, Harutō's family took him home
and looked after him. This is what he told them when he regained his
senses.

"I went to King Emma's palace in hell, and while I was being judged
one of the king's officials observed, 'The dancer Harutō, from Japan, has
been called here before he could pass on *Genjōraku*. That means that the
dance will now die out in his country. We should send him back and call
him in again when he's been able to teach it to his successor.' The other
officials agreed, and I realized I was to be sent home. Then I came to."

Once Harutō had taught the dance to his successor, Suetaka, he died
again.

The founder of Harutō's line originally got the mask for *Genjōraku*
directly from heaven. The mask's name is Iburi, and they say it's now
one of the treasures of Nara. Iburi too, like the dance itself, is passed on
from generation to generation. How wonderful that Harutō's tradition
should also be prized at King Emma's royal palace in hell!

4 7 ·

THE GOD OF GOOD FORTUNE

The biwa *is the East Asian cousin of the lute.*

Lord Tadazane wanted so desperately to be appointed regent that he sent
for a monk, a wonder-worker, to do the Dakini rite, hoping its magic
would get him the prize. He told the monk he needed results by a certain
date.

"Don't worry, Your Excellency," replied the monk, "the rite has never
failed me yet. I'll have results for you within seven days, and if I don't
I'll go on another seven. If it hasn't worked by then, Your Excellency,
you can send me straight into exile."

Lord Tadazane provided all the offerings and other necessities, and
the monk began. After seven days nothing had happened, and he let the
monk know he was worried.

"Send someone to observe the rite, Your Excellency!" the monk answered. "I think your man will find there's good reason to be optimistic." Lord Tadazane's representative saw a fox, completely unafraid of the people present, come and eat all the offerings. Since the Dakini rite involved fox magic, this was indeed a hopeful sign.

The monk started another seven-day period, as he had promised to do. On the closing day Tadazane dozed off for a moment and saw a woman walk by him with three feet of her magnificently long hair trailing behind her along the floor. She was so beautiful that without thinking he reached out and grabbed her hair.

"Don't do that!" she cried, turning back to look at him. "What do you want with me?" Her face and voice might just as well have been an angel's, and the enthralled Tadazane only held on harder. With a sharp toss of her head she freed herself and passed on. Tadazane was horrified to find that he still had her hair. Then he woke up. His hand was gripping a fox's tail.

Astonished, he called the monk and described what had happened.

"I told you, Your Excellency, I told you!" the monk burbled. "Oh, I never doubted the rite would work, but I must say, in all my years of experience it's never worked quite like this! You'll have what you want at midday tomorrow. Perhaps you won't have to exile me after all!" Tadazane lost no time in making him the handsome present of a woman's robe.

The next day at noon Lord Tadazane's appointment was announced. He made it his first official act as regent to name the monk to a distinguished ecclesiastical post. As for the fox's tail, he carefully put it away. Then he set about learning the Dakini rite himself and performed it whenever he had a special wish. They say it worked beautifully for him.

Eventually Tadazane enshrined the tail in a hall on Mount Hiei, one already dedicated to a healing spirit. But for one reason or another (perhaps because this sharing of the hall was not a good idea) a special shrine was eventually built for the tail down in the city. The god was given the name Fukutenjin, or Celestial God of Good Fortune. The shrine is still there.

The most curious of Fukutenjin's many wonders occurred in 1229. It involved a man known as Saemon no Jō, the son of a former official in Echizen province.

One evening at twilight Saemon no Jō had just left his master's residence when at a nearby crossroads he stopped and exclaimed, "Oh, what beautiful *koto* music!" Then he just stood there listening. The man with him said he heard nothing. "What a pity!" said Saemon no Jō, rooted to the spot in fascination.

As soon as Saemon no Jō got home, something went very wrong in his chest, and he became terribly ill. He also went completely mad and tried to rush off westward. It took six strong men to stop him. Then he leapt high in the air, came down head first, and hit the floor so hard with his shoulders that it looked as though he would dash himself to pieces.

A gentleman named Takatoki was then renting part of a mansion just east of the sick man's house. When Saemon no Jō now pointed in that direction and again strained to rush off, his father demanded to know where he wanted to go. "Is it Takatoki you want to see?" he asked. The sick man nodded yes. "Then why not just let me call him over?" The sick man looked pleased and again nodded yes.

The father went over to Takatoki's place, explained the strange situation to him, and brought him back. As soon as the sick man saw Takatoki, he left off raving. Very quiet now, he picked up a formal hat, put it on (he wanted to be properly dressed), and bowed deeply to Takatoki. Next, he glared meaningfully at the half-dozen men who were stationed around him. They took the hint and withdrew. The father made himself as inconspicuous as he could in a corner, but when the sick man glared at him in the same way, he left too. The sick man and Takatoki were alone together.

The sick man looked perfectly happy and went on bowing to Takatoki. "Well?" said Takatoki. "What is this all about?"

The sick man bowed even more deeply than before. "You're a neighbor, you see, and I so much wanted your company!"

"So here I am. Tell me frankly what I can do for you."

"I *must* hear you sing, and play the *koto* and *biwa.*"

"Why, of course, I'll be happy to make music for you as long as it'll cheer you up!"

Takatoki had a *biwa* brought over and began to play. The sick man nodded on and on as he listened, and rocked from side to side. He looked as blissful as when he had stood listening to the music at the crossroads. Takatoki went on to sing all sorts of songs as the sick man requested them, and the sick man was in ecstasy.

"Well, now I've played or sung for you practically everything I know," Takatoki finally declared. "Don't hesitate to tell me when you'd like to hear me again, because I'll happily oblige. There's no need to carry on the way you did. Next time, just ask quietly!"

The sick man started bowing again. "Oh, I wouldn't presume to ask you over again till I'm better!" he protested.

"Fine. Then I'll be going. But first I'd like to see you eat something."

When the sick man agreed, Takatoki had him brought some rice and dried abalone. The sick man gobbled up the rice with a great clicking of teeth, then scraped the abalone into a pile which he swallowed easily in a couple of mouthfuls. His manners were not exactly normal. Next, Takatoki offered him wine. Normally Saemon no Jō barely drank at all, but now he downed two large cupfuls in quick succession, then disposed willingly of a third.

"All right, I'll be going now!" Takatoki announced. "Good-bye!"

Near dawn the sick man's father came for Takatoki again. "He went back to raving once you were gone," he explained. "Could you possibly come?" Takatoki arrived to find the sick man in a terrifying frenzy.

"All right," he said firmly, "what's this act you're putting on? I did everything you asked, and I played you all my music. You should have been fine then. What do you mean by carrying on like this instead?"

"Well, you see," the sick man replied, "you *didn't* do everything I wanted! There's that wonderful *te* style on the *biwa,* and I wanted to hear that, too!"

"Fine! Why didn't you tell me in the first place?" Takatoki played a couple of pieces like that and the sick man listened attentively, nodding as usual.

"All right, you've played the *biwa* for me," he said. "How about some *koto* now?"

"Certainly, if that's what you want." Takatoki played a couple of pieces while the sick man listened again in rapture.

Finally day came and sunlight streamed in through a hole in the wall. When a dog's nose suddenly appeared in the hole, sniffing vigorously, the sick man straightened up, paled, and showed every sign of terror. His father and Takatoki realized that the dog must have smelled a fox, and it dawned on them that the cause of all the trouble was Fukutenjin. They chased the dog away.

"Well, I'm sure you feel fine now," said Takatoki, speaking quite consciously to the god. "I think I'll be going. Thank you very much for having had me to play for you! I promise you music at your shrine, too."

Saemon no Jō lay unconscious till late afternoon while Takatoki, very upset over what had happened, took his two sisters to the Fukutenjin Shrine and went on playing the *koto* and *biwa* with them, for the pleasure of the god.

4 8 .

DIVINE APPLAUSE

Three master dancers named Noritaka, Masasuke, and Tokisuke accompanied the new governor of Bitchū when he went down to his province to salute its gods. They danced the traditional offering dances at each shrine.

When Noritaka performed *Ryōō* (always a favorite) at the Kibitsu Shrine, the sanctuary creaked and shook. The crowd was amazed. Masasuke and Tokisuke were equally startled, but glad, too, that the god was so pleased. Then the god threw open the sanctuary doors, though of course he still could not be seen, and the crowd was transported with joy and awe.

Soon it would be Masasuke and Tokisuke's turn to dance. How embarrassed they would be if the god gave *them* no such sign! Both turned toward the sanctuary and prayed, in tears, that their art should be just as enjoyable.

When the time came, they began *Rakuson*. In a moment the sanctuary was shaking so violently that it was quite alarming!

M A G I C

4 9 .

BRING BACK THAT FERRY!

A little crowd of people waiting for the ferry at Kōraki in Echizen province were joined by a mountain ascetic named Keitōbō — a fellow who had done the pilgrimages to Golden Peak, to Kumano, and to every other sacred mountain of any importance in the land.

When the ferry arrived, the people paid their fare and went aboard, but Keitōbō demanded to be taken across free. The ferryman refused and cast off. "How can you do this to me?" Keitōbō shouted, but the ferryman ignored him and rowed away.

Keitōbō clenched his teeth and began rubbing the beads of his rosary intently together, making a buzzing sound. He was casting spells, as anyone could tell. The ferryman glanced back at him from a few hundred yards offshore, showing plainly enough by his look that he thought Keitōbō a pathetic fool.

Keitōbō stared after him and stamped his feet into the sand halfway up his shins. Then, glaring red-eyed at the ferry and almost demolishing his rosary with the fury of his rubbing, he began to shout, "Bring it back! Bring it back!"

The boat kept going. Keitōbō strode to the water's edge. "Guardian spirit," he thundered, "bring that ferry back! I'm through with the Buddha forever if you don't!" Next, he threatened to throw his priestly stole into the sea. The bystanders turned pale when they saw what he was doing.

The boat began gliding back toward the shore even though there was no wind. "That's it, that's it!" Keitōbō roared. "Hurry, hurry, bring it in!" The onlookers turned paler still.

"Fine!" he bellowed when the ferry was less than a hundred yards offshore. "Now, roll it over, capsize it!"

This time the onlookers cried out in protest. "What a horrible thing to wish! You brute! Why can't you leave them alone!"

Keitōbō only rose to a still higher pitch of ferocity. "Turn that ferry over *now*!" he thundered. There was a huge splash as the ferry capsized and the two dozen passengers were pitched into the sea.

Keitōbō wiped the sweat from his brow. "The idiots!" he muttered. "When will they ever learn?" And he stalked off.

5 o .

THE MAN-MADE FRIEND

Saigyō, the poet and wandering monk, was living on Mount Kōya when he ran into an acquaintance of his, a fellow religious wanderer who was staying on the mountain too. They met on a bridge and paused there to chat and admire the brilliance of the moon. Saigyō's friend remarked that he was off to the Capital.

Saigyō was sad to lose this companion and found himself longing for someone else to share his pleasure in moonlight and flowers. Then he heard a man whose knowledge he respected describe how a demon can collect human bones and make them into a human being.

He went straight to a wild moor where people left the dead, put bones together, and made a man himself. At least, it looked like a man, but it had poor color and no heart or spark of life. Its voice (for it had one) sounded like a musical instrument. It is the heart which is essential in man, however pleasing the voice may be. Having nothing more than a voice, the thing he had made was like a damaged flute.

Still, it was astonishing that he had come so close, and he hardly knew what to do with his creation. He considered breaking it up again, but that might be murder. Of course it had no consciousness, and in that sense was just like a plant. Yet it did *look* human. He left it in a deserted spot. No doubt anyone who found it would be frightened and think it some sort of apparition.

Perplexed as he was, Saigyō set off for the Capital too, to see Lord Tokudaiji, from whom he had learned many things in the past. Unfortunately, Lord Tokudaiji was away at the palace. Saigyō decided to visit Lord Moronaka instead.

He explained how his experiment had turned out, and Lord Moronaka asked him exactly what he had done.

"I went into the wilds where no one could see me," Saigyō explained, "and put human bones together to make a complete skeleton. Then I painted the bones with arsenic, and crumbled snake-strawberry and chickweed leaves over them. Next I tied the bones together with thread and vines, and washed them in many waters. On the skull, where the hair would be growing, I rubbed ashes from the leaves of *saikai* and rose of Sharon. Finally I spread a mat on the ground, laid the bones on it, and wrapped them securely so the wind couldn't get at them. Fourteen days later I came back. I burned musk and regular incense and did the Secret Rite of the Soul's Recall."

"That was about right," said Moronaka, "but you did the Rite of the Soul's Recall a bit soon. For myself, it happens that I've made people by the Shijō major counselor's method, but I'm afraid I can't *tell* you the method because if I did, the people and other things I've made would all vanish. You do know a good deal, though, so I'll help you. For one thing, don't burn incense. It's angelic beings, you see, not devilish ones who are attracted to incense. And since angelic beings have a deep horror of the round of birth and death, you aren't going to get any life-spark into your creature that way. You'd do better to burn musk and milk. And then, anyone who does the Secret Rite of the Soul's Recall should have fasted for seven days. If you follow those directions, I guarantee it'll work. You'll see."

But Saigyō thought better of the whole thing and decided to go no further.

THE LAUGHING FIT

When Takashina Shumpei was sent down on an official assignment to Kyushu, his younger brother, who had no government post, went with him. Shumpei's brother soon met a newly arrived Chinese master of *san* magic. The method involved manipulating the hexagrams of the *Book of Changes* by means of six wooden sticks about three inches long and square in section. These were called *san*.

Shumpei's brother wanted to learn *san* magic too. At first the Chinese refused to teach him, but realized when he tried him out a little that he actually had a remarkable talent. "There's no point in your staying here, though," the Chinese warned. "Japan is hopeless for working the *san*. I'll teach you if you'll come back with me to China."

Shumpei's brother agreed right away, promising that he would happily do anything to master the art. "I'll be glad to go to China with you as long as I can serve you," he assured the man. So the Chinese began giving him lessons.

He learned with amazing speed, which pleased his teacher greatly. "There are many *san* masters in my country," he said, "but none of them understand the *san* the way you do. Yes, you *must* come back with me to China!"

"Of course I will," his student answered. "Anything you say."

"In the art of the *san*," the Chinese continued, "there are methods for healing the sick, as there are also methods for killing instantly anyone you may have cause to dislike. I'll give you full knowledge of them all. Only *swear* that you'll come back to my country with me."

Shumpei's brother swore, but not quite wholeheartedly. This did not escape the Chinese, who taught him many things but withheld the technique for killing. "I'll teach you how to kill people when we're on the boat," he said.

One day Takashina Shumpei had to leave for the Capital on urgent business, and his brother prepared to go with him. The Chinese protested, but Shumpei's brother refused to stay behind. "The idea!" he exclaimed. "I can't just let him go by himself! But I'll keep my promise, don't worry!"

"All right," agreed the Chinese, "but come back! I've been planning to leave for China any day now. We'll go together when you return."

With this understanding concluded, Shumpei's brother left for Kyoto. He was thinking he might really go to China after all, but his relations, as one might well imagine, persuaded him to stay on in the Capital instead. Then Shumpei himself got wind of his brother's plans and put a stop to the whole idea. His brother never went back to Kyushu.

The Chinese waited, and when he heard nothing from his student began to send him accusing messages. All he got back were excuses about "my aged parents," and about wanting to see them through to the end of their lives before undertaking so long a journey. The Chinese realized that his student had never meant to keep his promise, and he sailed to China alone.

But before he left he laid a thorough curse on the miscreant. Shumpei's brother had always been highly intelligent but now, under the influence of the curse, he grew vague, forgetful, and stupid. In the end he could only make himself into a sort of monk at a mountain temple, and he spent his life trudging back and forth between this temple and Shumpei's residence. He had become a useless fool.

He was once at Shumpei's house on the night of the monthly Kōshin vigil, when everyone has to stay awake till dawn on pain of suffering some calamity. The young women of the household had gathered to while away the night together, and in the small hours, when they were beginning to feel awfully sleepy, they noticed their master's brother over in a corner, looking as witless as ever. "How about *him*!" cried a particularly high-spirited lady. "Maybe *he* knows a good story or two! Come, sir," she called to him, "tell us a story and make us laugh! Laughing will keep us awake!"

"I can't talk very well," the poor fool answered, "and I don't know any funny stories. But if you just want to laugh, yes, I can make you laugh, I certainly can!"

"You won't tell us a story but you'll make us laugh anyway? What are you going to do? Dance, perhaps? Oh, that'll be even better than a story!" The lady laughed at the very thought.

"No, no, I'm just going to make you laugh."

"Well, *how*? Come then, show us!"

The women watched eagerly as Shumpei's brother moved up to the lamp, untied the bag that held his *san*, and emptied the sticks on the floor.

"What's funny about those things?" the women complained. "Why, nothing at all! Come, come, we want to laugh!"

Shumpei's brother ignored them. Instead, he began making passes with the sticks and arranging them in patterns.

When he was finished, he had one left over, and he held it up before them. "Now, ladies," he said, "you're going to laugh, and let's hope it doesn't hurt too badly. Yes indeed, you're going to laugh!"

"How stupid can you be?" the women muttered. "How could laughing hurt?"

Shumpei's brother added the last stick to the pattern. A spasm of mirth abruptly seized all the women. They laughed and laughed and simply could not stop. Tears poured from their eyes, their sides felt as though they were literally splitting, and they thought they were going to die. Unable even to speak, they wrung their hands before the tormentor who just now had been their victim, begging him to desist.

"I told you!" he said. "Have you had enough?"

They nodded frantically, rolling around the floor and laughing hilariously even as they pleaded. When he thought they had suffered enough, he broke up the pattern. There was a sudden, dazed silence. "I'd have been dead if that had gone on much longer," one woman finally gasped. "I've never had such an awful experience in my life!" They were all lying in a heap, practically ill with exhaustion.

People said it was a good thing that Shumpei's brother had never been taught how to kill people with the *san*. If he had, something *really* awful might have happened.

5 2 .

SMALL-TIME MAGIC

Long ago Emperor Yōzei sent Michinori, an imperial guard, down to the east to collect tax revenues. On the way Michinori stopped off in Shinano province at the house of a county magistrate, who entertained him very civilly before retiring with his retainers for the night.

Unable to sleep, Michinori quietly got up again and began poking about the house. He soon found a beautiful room with fine new matting on the floor and a screened-off space inside. A lamp was burning within the screens, and a delicious fragrance floated on the air. Peeking curiously between two screens, he saw a woman in her late twenties, exquisitely lovely in face and figure, lying there all alone.

The more he looked the less he felt like leaving. No one was around. He thought it over. The magistrate had been very kind, and if this was his wife, he ought not to take advantage of her. On the other hand, he could not resist trying his luck. He slid into bed beside her.

The woman just smiled. Michinori was as pleased as punch. Her scent was delicious. Since it was early fall and the weather still warm, neither of them had much on. He undressed. When he slid his hands under her shift, she put up only token resistance and let him fondle her as he pleased.

Feeling a sudden tickle between his legs, Michinori reached for his member. It was not there. He groped around feverishly like a man trying to catch a bug in his beard, but it was gone as though it had never been. All thought of the woman, who lay there smiling enigmatically, vanished from his mind. Finally he got up, went back to his own bed completely confused, and made another minute inspection. It was hopeless.

Michinori was not too panicked to use his head. He called one of his men, told him about the stunning woman he had found, and mentioned that she was available. The man who went off with high hopes soon came back looking deeply disturbed. "He got it too!" thought Michinori, and passed the tip on to the next victim, who came back in his turn with anguish written all over his face. Michinori sent all eight of his men to the woman, and they all looked the same way when they came out.

The sky paled with the coming of dawn. Considering the night's disaster, Michinori preferred to leave as quickly as possible, despite his host's kind welcome, and he and his men hurried off before it was fully light. They had not gone more than a quarter of a mile when a man galloped up behind them, hailing them urgently and holding aloft a package wrapped in white paper. The rider was one of their host's retainers.

"The magistrate told me to deliver these to you," he said. "How *could* you have left them behind? We had your breakfast all ready, but you were in such a rush that you must have just forgotten them. Anyway, we picked them up for you and here they are." Michinori and his party wondered what he was talking about.

The packet contained a heap of male organs; they looked rather like mushrooms. Dumbfounded, the men inspected them one after another, each counting nine. Suddenly the organs vanished, and the messenger wheeled his horse around and galloped away. Michinori and his men shouted for joy, "It's back! It's back!"

On his return journey Michinori stopped again at the magistrate's house and made him a generous gift of gold, horses, eagle feathers, and the like. He explained to the puzzled magistrate that he hoped to learn just what had been done to him during his last visit. The magistrate felt he could hardly refuse. He told Michinori how in his youth he had had an affair with the young wife of the magistrate of another county, himself an old man, and how suddenly his member too had disappeared. He had done his best to be very, very nice to the old magistrate until he had succeeded in getting himself taught the same magic. But he reminded Michinori that Michinori was presently traveling on imperial business. If he wanted to learn the magic too, he should go straight back to the Capital, conclude his mission, and then come back privately. Michinori readily agreed, and set off.

When he came again he brought this magistrate another suitable present, and the magistrate cheerfully undertook to teach him all he knew. "However," he cautioned, "you don't learn this sort of thing casually. First you'll have to spend seven days fasting and purifying yourself with cold water."

Michinori did as he was told, and on the appointed day the magistrate took him far up into the mountains. They came to a stream beside which the magistrate went through various ritual procedures and made Michinori swear a terribly sinful oath. Then the magistrate set off upstream. "No matter what comes down the stream," he warned, "grab it in your arms. Devil or demon, I don't care, just throw your arms round it!"

Soon a heavy rainstorm blew in from upstream. The sky blackened and the water rose. Down the stream came a colossal snake. Its head alone was big enough to fill a man's arms and its eyes were like great bronze bowls. The snake's back was a deep blue and its belly was red. Michinori knew well enough that he was supposed to throw his arms around it but instead was so terrified that he collapsed on the spot.

The magistrate quickly returned. "How did it go?" he asked. "Did you hold on to it?" Michinori reported what had happened. "Too bad!" said the magistrate. "You won't be able to learn. Well, anyway, let's try again." And off he went.

In no time an enormous boar came hurtling down, bristling with fury, crushing great boulders, and belching fire. Once again Michinori was terrified, but he desperately screwed up his courage and dashed forward to clasp it in his arms. It turned out to be a bit of old log. He was terribly let down, especially when he realized that the snake too must have been a log. He was kicking himself for not having gone after the snake when the magistrate reappeared.

Michinori told him how it had gone this time. "Well," replied the magistrate, "you lost your first chance and that means you can't learn what you wanted. But I think you could manage some other little amusement. I'll teach you one." Michinori learned what he could and returned disappointed to the Capital.

Back at the palace he bet his fellow guards that he could turn all their shoes into puppies, then did it, and the puppies scrambled around all over the place, yapping madly; and he turned an old straw sandal into a great big carp flopping around on a dinner tray. When the emperor heard about these goings-on, he summoned Michinori and got himself taught magic too. His Majesty used it to make the grand procession of the Kamo festival go by over the screen he always sat behind.

People deeply disapproved of the emperor himself learning an art which offended the Buddha's way, and one has to agree that not only was Michinori (who after all was a nobody) very wrong to teach him, but that however rare these sort of tengu tricks may be, His Majesty was a bit crazy to want to learn.

5 3 .

THE LITTLE OIL JAR

Sanesuke, the Minister of the Right, was traveling up Omiya Avenue one day on his way to the palace when he saw a little oil jar rolling and hopping along in front of his carriage. This was so odd that he guessed a spirit must be at work. Eventually the jar turned west off Omiya, and after still another turn rolled up to a certain gate. The gate was locked, and the jar began jumping against it in an obvious effort to get in through the keyhole. After missing time after time, it finally succeeded, and in through the keyhole it went.

Sanesuke left now, but he identified the house to one of his servants and had the man find out as discreetly as possible whether anything unusual had happened there. The man came back to report that the daughter of the house, who had been ill for some time, had just died. Sanesuke realized that the jar had indeed been a spirit, and that it had killed the girl once it got in.

His cleverness greatly impressed everyone who knew him.

THE   SEXES

5 4 .

A HARD MOMENT

Kotōda lived with his wife and daughter in the mansion of Lord Sada-fusa, for all three were in Sadafusa's service. He was very proud of the expert way he saw to all his master's affairs, and he had taken care to provide his daughter with a very fine husband.

Having just spent the night with Kotōda's daughter, the young man woke up one morning to find that it was pouring with rain; so instead of leaving as usual, he stayed where he was. Meanwhile the daughter went to look after her mistress, leaving the young man lying in their bed completely surrounded by screens. The spring rain showed no sign of letting up.

In time Kotōda decided that his son-in-law must be getting rather bored. With a tray of snacks in one hand and a gourd of wine in the other, he headed for the young couple's room. Discretion prompted him to enter not from the garden, as he would normally have done, but from inside the house.

Naked under the covers, his son-in-law was lying staring up at the ceiling, hot for his wife. That sound of a door in the house sliding open obviously meant that she was finally back from Her Ladyship's. Whisking the covers over his face and off everything else, he rubbed up a good hard-on and arched his back to display it. The screens parted.

Kotōda's shocked recoil sent food and drink flying. He fell flat on his back with his beard in the air and hit his head so hard he saw stars.

5 5 .

A NICE MUG
OF MOLTEN COPPER

A chamberlain courting the daughter of the abbot of Daianji in Nara was so much in love with the girl that sometimes he did not even leave her at dawn, as he should have, but stayed on into the day. On one such occasion he was napping in her room when he dreamed he heard the whole household weeping and wailing.

He went to see what was the matter and found them all, from the abbot and his wife (now a nun) on down, holding mugs and sobbing. This seemed very odd till he realized that the mugs were full of molten copper. The most fearful demon could hardly force anyone to take so gruesome a refreshment but, tears or no tears, these people were drinking it; and when in agony they had emptied one mug, some were even asking for more. The servants were drinking up too, every one of them.

When a maid came to call the chamberlain's sweetheart, she got out of bed and went. In horror he watched the maid fill a silver mug with molten copper and give it to his Beloved. The girl took it, uttered a heart-rending little cry, and downed the liquid metal, whimpering pathetically. Smoke poured from her eyes and nose.

"Serve our guest!" commanded the abbot, and the maid approached the chamberlain with a cup on a tray. "Am I going to have to drink it too?" he wondered in terror, and woke up.

On opening his eyes he saw that the maid had brought lunch, and he heard loud slurping and chewing from his future father-in-law's room. Clearly the monk was in fact guilty of a grave sin: he was eating up what rightfully belonged to the temple. Saddened by his discovery, the young chamberlain wanted no more to do with the family, and his love for the girl evaporated. He excused himself with the plea that he felt unwell, left without eating a bite, and never came back.

THE LITTLE BOTTLE OF TEARS

Heichū, the great lover, was quite prepared to feign dramatic sobs when rejected, even if he did not really care for the woman that much; and he went courting with a little bottle of water fastened to his arm so that he could produce tears and wet sleeves whenever he needed them.

One day Heichū's wife noticed him slip something up on top of a beam in their house, and the next time he stepped out she took it down. It was a little bottle of water and a packet of the tiny dried flower buds that people chew to make their breath smell nice. She emptied out the water, filled the bottle with rich black ink, switched the flower buds for mouse turds, then put the bottle and packet back on the beam.

Heichū went off that night as he always did. He came back at dawn in a very sour mood and spat vigorously as he lay down. "Must be some goblin got into that packet!" he muttered. By daylight he noticed his sleeves were all black. Then he looked in the mirror. His smudgy, black face, almost invisible but for two eyes shining out of the darkness, gave him quite a turn. Next he checked the little bottle. Yes, that was ink in there, all right; and he knew a mouse turd when he saw one.

Deeply mortified, Heichū gave up his fake tears and his flower buds.

ELIMINATION

Taira no Sadafun, commonly known as Heichū, was the deputy commander of the Palace Guards. He was a man of respectable rank, handsome and elegant, and in everything he did or said the most amusing fellow of his time. Naturally he courted every wife, every daughter, and above all, every lady-in-waiting within reach.

A certain minister had in his household as lovely and as witty a young lady as ever there was, and her name was Jijū. Heichū knew about her since he often visited the minister, and in fact had been pursuing her for ages, but she had not deigned to answer a single one of his letters.

Much put out, Heichū finally tried a note that begged her at least to answer the one word "acknowledged"; and he ended it, "Yours in ceaseless tears." When he saw the messenger return actually carrying a reply, he ran out and opened it feverishly. The lady had torn the "acknowledged" out of his own letter, stuck it on another piece of paper, and sent it right back to him.

Heichū went wild. "All right, that's enough!" he swore to himself. "I give up."

That was on the last day of the second moon. Heichū sent Jijū nothing between then and well into the fifth moon when, on a dark and dismally rainy night, he found himself brooding over her again.

"If I went tonight it'd surely do *something* to her," he ruminated, "even if she's got a heart of stone." The hour was late, the rain was beating down interminably, and the blackness of the night was final. The helpless Heichū found his way to the minister's residence and called for a little maid who had passed messages for him before.

"Here I am. I can't stand it any more." That was what he sent the maid off to tell Jijū. The maid was soon back with word that Jijū was presently attending His Excellency and Her Ladyship, and couldn't retire just yet because the household was still up. "Wait a bit," Jijū's message concluded. "I'll talk to you in private later on."

Heichū's heart beat fast. "Well, well," thought he, "she really couldn't turn a fellow away on a night like this! I'm so glad I came!"

He waited by the darkened door for what seemed like years. An hour or more later he heard the sounds of people going to bed. Then someone came to his door and quietly opened the latch. With bated breath he tested it: it slid easily aside. He wondered whether he was dreaming. In fact he was shaking with joy, but he managed to calm down enough to steal inside.

A sweet fragrance of incense filled the room. Heichū groped his way toward where he knew the bed must be and found someone was lying there. Yes, it was a woman and she had only one robe on. He felt over her head and shoulders. Her features were fine, and the hair streaming out along the floor was as smooth and cool to the touch as ice. All but delirious now, Heichū was temporarily deprived of speech by a fit of trembling.

"Oh dear," exclaimed the woman, "I've forgotten something very important! I didn't lock the door into this part of the house. I'll be right back."

That sounded all right to Heichū. "Don't be long!" he called after her.

She got up and went just as she was, while Heichū undressed and lay down. A lock clicked. Any moment she would be back. But no, the footsteps faded out deeper into the house. Time passed. With grave misgiving Heichū went to check the door. It was locked, all right — from the other side. He danced up and down and wept with rage, then just stood there in a daze, against the door, pouring as many tears as the rainy skies outside. "What a trap she led me into!" he groaned. "Oh, this is awful! If I'd only realized, I could have stayed with her when she went to lock the door! I suppose she wants to see how far she can push me. She must think me a perfect idiot!" This thought, even more than the missed opportunity, brought Heichū to the last pitch of despair.

"Well, let the day dawn!" his mind ran on. "I don't care, I'm going to sleep right here, and if they come in and find me, so much the better!" But as dawn actually approached and he heard the household waking up, he decided that discretion was the better part of valor and sneaked quickly off while it was still dark.

Forever after, Heichū longed to hear some rumor about Jijū that would really put him off her, but since he never did he went on burning for her instead. Then one day he had an idea. For all Jijū's beauty and wit, the matter she deposited in her chamber pot was bound to be the same as what he left in his own. If by hook or crook he could get hold of some of *that, that* ought to cure him! "I'll ambush her maid when she goes to wash the pot, I'll steal it, and I'll have a good look inside!" he promised himself.

Heichū went straight off to lurk (as innocently as possible) outside Jijū's room. Out came a smart young maid with hair down almost to the hem of her pink and green jacket, which she wore over a purple trouser-skirt casually tucked up. She was carrying a pot (a box, actually, as was the custom then) wrapped in filmy, light-orange silk, discreetly screening it from view with a red paper fan that had some scene or other painted on it. She made a very stylish picture. Heichū shadowed her till she was out of sight of the house, then charged up and snatched the box. She burst into tears and refused to let go, but Heichū tore it ruthlessly from her grasp, fled into a deserted building, and locked the door from the inside. The maid was left crying outside.

Heichū examined the box. It was beautifully lacquered — so pretty, in fact, that he hated to go further. The contents were one thing, but for a chamber pot this was a unique work of art. To think he was going to open it and destroy forever his fond visions of its owner! He could not bear the idea, and for a while just stared at the box instead.

Still, this was no time to turn back. Tremulously he removed the lid. A rich fragrance of incense perfumed the air. What on earth? Golden water half filled the box, and in it swam three brownish, cylindrical objects about the thickness of a thumb. "Well," thought Heichū, "there they are!" But this heavenly scent was not exactly what he expected from them. He speared one with a slip of wood and held it gingerly to his nose. Musk, clove, sandalwood: these perfumes and more mingled in an exquisite blend which floated into his nostrils like a giddying caress.

He was out of his depth. This woman was not of the same order as a common mortal. With awful certainty he saw that the very idea of bringing her round was absurd. He drew the box to his lips and sipped the golden water: it was redolent of cloves. He licked the tip of the round brown object he had speared: both bitter and sweet, it was endlessly fragrant.

Heichū was clever too, and he could see perfectly what Jijū had done. For the urine she had simply boiled cloves and drawn off the water. For the other matter she had ground together yams, incense spices, and sweetvine, and molded the mixture in the cover of a large writing brush. Anyone could do that, of course. But for her to have divined that he would want to contemplate the contents of her chamber pot — *that* was beyond anything. A genius like Jijū was just not of this world.

With these thoughts whirling deliriously through his head, Heichū sickened, suffered awhile, and died.

5 8 .

BUT SHE COULDN'T HELP IT!

Late one evening the future Major Counselor Tadaie was courting a coy and beautiful lady. She was sitting demurely in her room, behind her curtains, while he talked to her from the veranda. The moonlight was brighter than day. Finally Tadaie could no longer stand it. He crawled under the curtains, took her shoulders, and tried to draw her to him. "Oh, don't!" she cried, hiding under her long hair and struggling to escape.

In doing so she let out a loud fart. There was dead silence. She lay very still.

"Oh no!" groaned Tadaie. "This is the end! How can I face the world again? I'll have to enter religion!" Ducking back out under the curtains he sneaked off, fully intending to make himself into a monk. But in a moment he began to wonder why he should have to enter religion just because some woman had disgraced herself, and instead simply got out of there as fast as he could.

No one knows what happened to the lady.

YIN-YANG
WIZARDRY

THE GENIE

Once the famous yin-yang diviner Seimei was watching the parade of gentlemen arriving at the palace in fashionably ostentatious style when he noticed a handsome and elegant young chamberlain alighting from his carriage. The chamberlain had hardly started toward the Great Hall when a passing crow dropped filth on him. "Oh dear," thought Seimei, "he's so young and handsome, and so well received by everyone! What a pity that genie got him — because that bird certainly *was* a genie. Something awful seems to be in store for him!"

He felt so sorry for the young man that he went over to talk to him. "Are you on your way to His Majesty?" he asked. "It's forward of me to speak, I know, but I wonder what your purpose is, because, you see, you mustn't spend the night in the palace. That's quite clear. No, come with me instead. I'll help you as best as I can."

It was about four in the afternoon. The two went to the chamberlain's house in his carriage, and all the way the chamberlain trembled and begged Seimei to save him. After sunset Seimei kept his arms tight around the chamberlain and laid protective spells. He spent the night in endless, unintelligible muttering.

The fall night was long. At dawn there was a knock on the door, and Seimei had the chamberlain send someone to answer. It was a messenger from the enemy diviner. The chamberlain's brother-in-law, who lived in another part of the house, was so jealous of the chamberlain that he had had this diviner set a genie on the chamberlain to kill him. Seimei had spotted the genie. "The gentleman was so strongly protected," the messenger loudly announced, "that the genie came back and killed my master instead!"

"You see?" said Seimei.

The father-in-law drove the villain out of the house, and the grateful chamberlain gave Seimei a rich reward.

6 0 .

ONE FROG LESS

Seimei was visiting a great prelate he knew when a young monk in the prelate's entourage said he had heard that Seimei kept genies, and asked Seimei whether he could kill a man easily. "Not easily, no," Seimei replied. "It would take a big effort. I suppose I could kill a small creature readily enough, but I can't see any point in doing so. Since I wouldn't know how to bring it back to life, I'd just end up committing a sin."

Just then some frogs started jumping across the garden toward the pond. "Try killing one of those for us," said the monk.

"You're wicked, aren't you!" Seimei replied. "A challenge is a challenge, though." He picked up a blade of grass, muttered something, and tossed the grass at a frog. The grass crushed the frog and killed it instantly. The monks looking on turned pale with fear.

6 1 .

THE SPELLBOUND PIRATES

Chitoku, a monk and a professional yin-yang diviner, lived in Harima province. He was an unusual man.

One day a ship came sailing up the Harima coast toward the Capital, laden with a rich cargo. Just off Akashi it was boarded by pirates, who stole everything on board and killed most of the crew. The only survivors were the vessel's owner and a couple of his servants, who plunged into the sea and managed to drag themselves, weeping, up on the shore. When Chitoku happened by, leaning on his staff, he asked them what the matter was. The owner told him how the day before they had been set upon by pirates.

"Why, that's terrible!" Chitoku explained. "I'll bring them to justice and get your things back for you!"

The owner did not take him seriously, but he humored Chitoku enough to say, through his tears, "I'd be very grateful if you would!"

"What time yesterday did it happen?" Chitoku asked, and the owner told him.

Chitoku took the owner out in a small boat to precisely where the attack had occurred, then wrote things on the water and read words aloud over the sea. Back on land he posted warrior guards just as though he meant to arrest someone who was actually present.

On the seventh day after the attack, a ship came drifting in from nowhere, full of armed men. The guards rowed out to meet it, but the men, who looked as though they were dead drunk, made no attempt to get away. It was the pirate ship. Everything the pirates had stolen was still on board, and the cargo was now unloaded and returned to its rightful owner. The local people wanted to seize the pirates themselves, but Chitoku had them turned over to him instead. "Don't you ever do that again!" he warned them. "By rights you should be executed, but that would just be another sin. Remember, there's an old monk in this province that you'd better not cross!" And he sent them packing.

Soon the shipowner was able to begin fitting out another ship.

6 2 .

THE TEST

Many years ago a doddering old monk showed up at Seimei's house on Tsuchimikado Avenue in Kyoto in the company of two ten-year-old boys. Seimei asked him who he was. He answered that he was from Harima province and that he wanted to learn divination. He had come because Seimei was supposed to be a real expert.

Seimei guessed that the old fellow knew more than he let on and had actually come to test him. On his mettle now, he decided to have a bit of fun himself. The two boys seemed to be genies. Seimei prayed silently that if they were, they should vanish; and he secretly cast a spell and made the appropriate passes under his sleeves. Then he promised the monk that he would teach him whatever he wanted if he came back on some other, more auspicious day. The monk thanked him, bowed, and left.

He was nearly out the gate when he stopped and began poking about among the carriages parked there. Then he came back to Seimei. "Those two boys I had with me have disappeared, sir," he said. "I'd appreciate your returning them before I go."

"I'm afraid I don't know what you mean," Seimei replied. "Why should I have taken your boys?"

"I see what you mean, sir, but nonetheless, please accept my apology."

"Very well. You had me worried a moment, coming around with two genies to test me, but I advise you to do your testing elsewhere. You won't catch *me* like that." Then he murmured a spell, and shortly the two boys came running up to their master from somewhere outside.

"It's true, sir," the monk said, "I did mean to test you. It's easy to keep genies, but I couldn't possibly make someone else's genies disappear. Please let me be your disciple."

Seimei accepted him on the spot.

6 3 .

MAN'S BEST FRIEND

A long time ago the Regent Fujiwara no Michinaga built Hōjōji in Kyoto, and after that made a habit of visiting the temple daily. He always brought with him a white dog he particularly liked. One day his carriage was about to pass through the gate as usual when the dog darted ahead, stood in the gateway, and stopped the carriage. Its behavior seemed very strange. Michinaga alighted and tried walking through, but the dog caught the hem of his robe in its teeth and held him back. Clearly the dog had a reason for acting this way. Instead of insisting, Michinaga sat down on a shaft of his carriage and called for Seimei, the diviner. Seimei soon arrived.

Lord Michinaga asked him what he could make of all this. Seimei went through a divination procedure and announced that someone who wished Michinaga ill had buried under the path, in the temple grounds, an object designed to put a curse on His Excellency. "If you were to walk over it," Seimei explained, "something terrible would happen. Your dog's special powers enabled it to warn you."

"Where's this thing buried?" Michinaga demanded to know. "Show it to me!"

"Certainly, Your Excellency." Seimei performed another divination. "Here it is," he said, pointing to a precise spot.

Something *was* buried there, five feet down. It consisted of two unglazed cups bound together, lip to lip, with string made of twisted yellow paper. The string was tied in a cross. The object turned out to be empty except for the character "one" written in cinnabar on the bottom of each cup.

"I'm the only one who knows this kind of magic," said Seimei. "I wonder whether it could be that former student of mine, Dōma. Well, I'll find out." He took out a sheet of paper which he folded into the shape of a bird, pronounced a spell, and tossed the paper into the air. It turned into a white heron and flew off toward the south. Seimei ordered two underlings to mark where it came down, and they ran after it.

The place was an old monk's house. The monk was summarily arrested and brought before His Excellency. He confessed under interrogation that he had been commissioned to lay a curse on the regent by Lord Akimitsu, the Minister of the Left. Michinaga felt he really should send the fellow into distant exile, but instead he just packed him back to Harima province, where he was from, with a warning never to do it again.

After Lord Akimitsu died, he became a vengeful ghost whose further attempts to curse Michinaga earned him the nickname "Ghoul of the Left." As for the dog, Lord Michinaga loved it even more after that.

6 4 .

GENJŌ

In Emperor Murakami's reign the *biwa* Genjō suddenly disappeared. Since the musical instrument was one of the imperial family's greatest treasures, the emperor took its loss very hard. To think that Genjō had vanished during *his* reign! Perhaps it had been stolen, but if so, the thief would never be able to keep it. No, no one would have taken the instrument unless he had a special grudge against the emperor and wanted only to damage or destroy it.

Hakuga no Sammi, the renowned musician, was still grieving over Genjō's disappearance when, late one night at the palace after everyone had gone to bed, he heard it being played somewhere to the south. How extraordinary! He thought his ears must be playing tricks on him and listened again. No, it was certainly Genjō. Sammi could hardly believe it.

Without a word to anyone, he set out with a single page, passed the Gate Guards' headquarters, and left the palace grounds by the Suzaku Gate. Genjō was still somewhere in front of him. He started down Suzaku Avenue. It sounded as though the thief must be playing for his own pleasure in the lookout tower further on, but no, that was still not it. At last Sammi stopped under the Rashō Gate at the other end of the avenue.

Someone was playing Genjō in the gate's upper story. This was another mystery, because in a place like that the player could hardly be human. Why, it must be a demon! The music stopped, then began again.

"Who's that up there playing Genjō?" called Sammi. "His Majesty's been looking for it ever since it was missed, and tonight I heard it all the way up at the palace. I've come to get it!"

The playing stopped again, then with a start Sammi noticed something coming down from up there. It was Genjō, being lowered at the end of a rope. Sammi nervously caught it and took it back to the palace.

The emperor was tremendously relieved, but he certainly found it alarming that Genjō should have been stolen by a demon. As for Sammi, everyone was very impressed with what he had done.

Genjō is still an imperial treasure. It is like a living thing, for when badly played or allowed to gather dust it gets angry and refuses to sound. And once, when the palace burned down and nobody rescued it, Genjō got out into the garden away from the flames all by itself.

6 5 .

THE RASHŌ GATE

Once a man came up from Settsu province to the Capital in order to steal. Since it was still daylight when he arrived, he hid out under the Rashō Gate, the southern gate to the city. Northward, straight toward the palace compound, stretched Suzaku Avenue. At this hour it was still bustling with people, and the man waited patiently under the gate for the city to quiet down. Then he heard a large group approaching the gate from the south. To avoid being seen, he stole up to the gate's top story, which formed a room.

A dim light was burning in the gloom. Strange! He peered in through the latticework windows and saw stretched before him the corpse of a young woman. The light was by her head where an ancient crone was roughly picking out the corpse's hair.

For all the frightened thief knew, the crone could be a demon or a ghost, but he decided to try giving her a scare. He opened the door softly, drew his dagger, and charged in with a shout. The terrified crone wrung her hands in a frantic plea for mercy.

"Who are you, old woman, and what are you doing here?" snarled the thief.

"My mistress died, sir, and there was no one to do the needful for her, so I brought her up here. You see, sir, her hair is longer than she was tall, and I'm picking it out to make a wig. Please, sir, don't kill me!"

The thief took the corpse's clothes and the old woman's, picked up the pile of loose hair, dashed back down, and fled.

Yes, the upper story of the Rashō Gate used to be full of human skeletons. If people couldn't provide a proper funeral they would sometimes just leave the corpse up there instead.

6 6 .

THE SELFLESS THIEF

Having no settled place to live, a Lotus Sutra devotee named Shunchō wandered here and there as the spirit moved him. When he saw someone in pain, that pain became his own; and the same with another's joy.

The sight of the Capital's two prisons, one in the east of the city and one in the west, caused Shunchō deep sorrow. He understood that the prisoners had been sentenced for their crimes, but he still wanted to help them by planting in them the seed of future buddhahood. Otherwise, if they died in prison, they would be reborn among the beasts or the starving ghosts, or even worse, squarely in hell. He would have to commit a crime to get himself arrested and sent to jail so that he could chant the Sutra for the prisoners.

Shunchō broke into a mansion, stole a golden bowl, and went straight to a gambling den to show the bowl off. The gamblers were surprised to recognize it as one that had just been reported stolen, and the tip soon reached the authorities. Shunchō was arrested, interrogated, and thrown in jail. Of course this was just what he wanted. He started right in chanting Sutra for the inmates, who wept to hear him and reverently touched their foreheads to the ground.

When word of his imprisonment reached the lords and ladies of the court, they informed the chief of the Imperial Police that Shunchō was a holy man and urged his release. The chief of police, for his part, had a dream. The Bodhisattva Fugen, shining and riding a white elephant, came to the prison with a bowl of rice. He told the guards that he was bringing rice, as he did every day, to Shunchō who was imprisoned there. On awaking, the chief of police had Shunchō released immediately.

Although he got himself into jail half a dozen times, Shunchō never managed to stay there long. Then one day the police caught him again, and this time had a meeting about him. They were sure by now that he was a hardened criminal and that thanks to repeated release he was simply enjoying free license to steal. He would have to be dealt with more severely. They decided to cut off his kneecaps and make sure he served a good long sentence. A corps of officers marched Shunchō off to one of the imperial riding grounds to execute the punishment, but Shunchō chanted the Lotus Sutra so movingly that they dissolved in tears and let him go.

Again the chief of police had a dream. A beautiful boy in court dress told him that Shunchō stole only in order to get into jail and save the prisoners there. "This is his seventh arrest," the boy reminded the dreamer. "He might as well be the Buddha himself!" The chief of police was even more deeply impressed than before.

In time Shunchō died by the horse stalls on the same riding ground where he had once nearly come to grief. Since there was no one to look after him, his body lay there untended, but the neighborhood began to hear every night a voice chanting the Lotus Sutra. Nobody knew where it was coming from. Then another holy man took Shunchō's skeleton away deep into the mountains, and the voice was never heard again.

6 7 .

AUTHORITY

The seasoned warrior Fujiwara no Chikataka lived in Kōzuke province. Once a robber got caught in Chikataka's house and was clapped in irons on the spot. Then he slipped free somehow, and since escape was impossible, he took Chikataka's little son hostage, dashed into a room, pinned the boy to the floor, and waited with his dagger poised at the child's stomach.

Chikataka was at home at the time. "He's taken the young master hostage, sir!" cried the retainer who rushed to him with the report.

When Chikataka saw with his own eyes how true this was, his sight dimmed and he thought all was lost. If only he could get the dagger away from the man! But the robber had the glittering blade pressed to his son's skin. "You get any closer and I'll run him through!" he snarled. It was not worth the risk, no indeed!

"Stay away!" Chikataka ordered his retainers. "Just keep an eye on him from a distance! I'll go and inform the governor."

The governor was Minamoto no Yorinobu, a very old friend indeed since Chikataka's mother had been Yorinobu's wet nurse. He lived nearby. Chikataka burst in on him in a panic, blurted out the story, and wept.

Yorinobu smiled. "I understand how you feel," he said, "but this is no time for tears. You should be standing up to this fellow, never mind whether he's a man, a god, or a demon. Don't you realize you look an awful fool, carrying on this way like a baby? He's only a little boy, you know! Let him be killed! *That's* the way a warrior thinks. All this tender love for wife and children just drags a man down. Being fearless means not caring about your own life *or* your family's. But anyway, I'll go and have a look."

With his sword at his side, Yorinobu strode off toward Chikataka's house. The robber recognized him when he looked into the room. Far from threatening him as he had Chikataka, the robber simply glowered toward the floor, poked his dagger at the boy a little harder, and made it plain that if the governor came any closer the boy (who was bawling lustily) would die.

"Well? Did you take him hostage to keep yourself alive, or do you plan to kill him?" Yorinobu asked. "Answer me!"

"How could I possibly *mean* to kill him, sir?" replied the robber gloomily. "But I don't want to die myself. I thought taking him might help me stay alive."

"I see. Then get rid of that dagger! You'll do that for me, won't you? I don't want to see you have to kill a child. You know the kind of man I am, I'm sure. Now, drop it!"

The robber thought for a moment. "Thank you, sir," he said. "I really have no choice, do I?" He threw the dagger across the room, lifted the boy to his feet, and let him go. The boy ran off.

Yorinobu stepped back into the garden while one of his men dragged the robber out by the collar. Chikataka assumed the governor would execute the fellow on the spot and let the dogs have his body.

"Fine," said Yorinobu. "He let his hostage go very nicely. Poverty made him steal, and he took a hostage only to survive. We needn't hold any of that against him. When I told him to release his hostage, he did. He's no fool. Let him go."

"Now then," he went on to the robber, "tell me what you need." The robber was too dissolved in tears to answer.

"Give him some food," Yorinobu ordered. "He's already committed crimes, and he may end up killing someone after all. Get a good strong work horse out of the stables, put a cheap saddle on it, and bring it here." Someone went for the horse while Yorinobu sent someone else for an old bow and quiver. When the things arrived, Yorinobu put the quiver on the man's back and set him on the horse, with ten days' worth of parched rice in a bag slung from his waist.

"Now get out of here!" he commanded. The man galloped away at top speed.

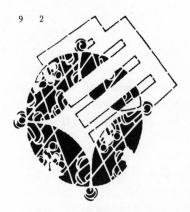

THE WRESTLER'S SISTER

Oi Mitsutō, a wrestler who lived in the province of Kai, was stocky and fierce, immensely strong, and wonderfully swift of foot. In character and physique he was a model for his profession.

Mitsutō's younger sister, a slender, pretty woman in her late twenties, lived a short way from her brother. Once a fleeing robber stormed into her house, drew his dagger, and took her hostage.

A servant ran with the news to Mitsutō, who remained untroubled. "He must be a real champion to have taken *her* hostage," was all he would say. The puzzled servant ran back to the house and peered in through a crack. There lay his mistress dressed in a thin mauve robe and a pink trouser-skirt lined with green. The man, huge and terrible, had her clamped between his legs from behind and was holding the point of his great dagger to her stomach. Her left hand was over her face and she was crying. Her right hand was toying with some arrow shafts which lay scattered on the floor. When she picked up a tough bamboo shaft and ran its end along the boards, the shaft would break like rotten wood. The robber doubted that Mitsutō himself could break an arrow shaft like that, even if he bashed at it with an iron hammer. Afraid he might be torn to pieces too, he timed his move as best he could and fled, only to be caught, bound, and hauled off to Mitsutō.

Mitsutō asked him why he had run and laughed when he heard the story. "You'd never have gotten your dagger into her," he said. "She'd have torn your arm off. You were lucky she didn't. Even I could handle you with ease, but she's as strong as two of me. She looks like a pretty slip of a thing, yes, but I'll never beat her. It's a shame she's a woman, it really is. If she were a man, nobody would stand a chance against her."

The robber almost died. He had picked quite a hostage.

"I suppose I ought to kill you," Mitsutō went on, "and I would if you'd ever been a real danger to my sister. How right you were to get out! She can break a stag's antlers over her knee, you know, like a dead twig." Mitsutō brusquely threw the robber out the door.

6 9 .

TO SOOTHE THE SAVAGE BREAST

A hichiriki *is a small but surprisingly loud reed instrument made of bamboo.*

A musician named Mochimitsu was on his way home from a trip to Tosa province when, at a harbor in Aki, he was attacked by pirates. Having no skill at arms, he was quite unable to defend himself and was sure he was going to be killed.

He had taken refuge on top of his ship's cabin. At the last moment he took out his *hichiriki* and shouted, "You pirates, listen to me! I'm defenseless, as you can see. Help yourselves to anything you want! But I'd just like you to hear this piece on the *hichiriki*. I've been working on it for years. It'll be something for you to remember today by!"

"All right, men!" shouted the pirates' leader. "Hold it! We're going to listen to some music!"

When the pirates had quieted down, the weeping Mochimitsu began to play. This was the last time he would ever make music, and he poured his whole soul into the piece. The beautiful sound of his instrument floated far out over the waves and filled the bay where the ship was moored. It was just like a scene in an old tale.

The pirates listened in perfect silence. When the music was over, their leader loudly declared, "I came because I wanted your ship, but your playing has brought tears to my eyes. I couldn't possibly harm you now!"

The pirates rowed away.

HEALING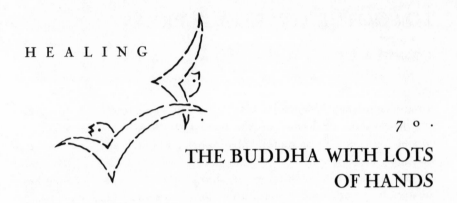

THE BUDDHA WITH LOTS
OF HANDS

In the summer of 1278 an epidemic struck the East and many people died. A boy I knew well caught the sickness. As he lay there he cried out that some children were tormenting him, and complained that he felt awful. Several monks then chanted the Darani of Thousand-Armed Kannon for him. They had only repeated it twenty-one times when he exclaimed, "A buddha with lots of hands came out of the temple and hit those children on the head! They ran away to the north, and they were angry and crying. The buddha chased them away!" Then he was well again.

I saw this with my own eyes.

THE PROTECTOR SPIRIT

Lord Mototsune, the chancellor, once caught an illness that was going round and had healing rites done for himself. All the best-known monks crowded into his mansion, which rang with the din of their chanting.

No monk from Gokurakuji was called, though his lordship had founded the temple himself; but one Gokurakuji monk who knew how much he owed Mototsune, and what a fix he would be in should Mototsune die, went to the mansion anyway with the Sutra of the Benevolent King. Finding the place crowded and noisy, he sat off in a distant corridor and began chanting the sacred text. No one paid any attention to him.

Four hours later His Lordship asked for the monk by name and was told yes, he had been seen out by the middle gate. When Mototsune actually sent for him, his attendants wondered what he could possibly want with such a nobody.

The Gokurakuji monk came in and sat at the edge of the room, behind the rows of prelates, but Mototsune was not content till he had the Gokurakuji monk by him. Since so far he had been too weak even to speak, his attendants were amazed to see him go to so much trouble.

"I dreamed that fiends were after me," Mototsune told the monk, "till a young boy came from the middle gate and beat them off with his staff. They all fled. The boy said he was a protector spirit who served *you*, and he told me you'd been chanting the Sutra of the Benevolent King for me. I woke up feeling much better and I wanted to thank you personally." Mototsune bowed to the monk, called for a robe from a rack nearby, and put it over the monk's shoulders with his own hands. "Be sure you keep praying for me when you get home!" he begged.

The monk, whom no one had noticed while he chanted so devotedly in his remote corridor, withdrew from the mansion covered with glory.

7 2 .

THE FLYING STOREHOUSE

Once a monk from a remote part of Japan went to get properly ordained at Tōdaiji in Nara. Afterwards he decided to stay on, rather than return to his primitive hinterland, and prayed to the Great Buddha of Tōdaiji to help him choose where to live. At that moment he noticed Mount Shigi looming in the distance toward the southwest. He settled there, built a little chapel, and took up the ascetic life. Soon a fine little image of Bishamon materialized for his modest altar.

The monk's begging bowl would fly down every day for alms to a rich man who lived below the mountain, and every day the rich man would fill it. But one day the rich man happened to be working in his big storehouse when the begging bowl arrived. "Bother that greedy bowl!" he muttered, and instead of filling it, tossed it into a corner. The bowl waited patiently, but eventually the man tidied up and left, locking the storehouse door behind him. He had forgotten all about the bowl.

The storehouse began to tremble and shake, much to the household's amazement, till it shook itself loose and hovered, vibrating, a foot off the ground. "Of course!" the rich man realized. "Of course! It must be that bowl! I left it in there!" Meanwhile the bowl squeezed its way out, got under the storehouse, and carried it off a hundred feet up in the air.

There was an uproar below. The rich man could only follow to see where his storehouse would go, and everyone else trooped in confusion after him. The storehouse flew to the top of the mountain and came down with a thud next to the monk's hut.

The rich man was certainly awed, but he still felt he should say something. He reminded the monk how faithfully he normally filled the bowl and explained how today he just happened to have shut it thoughtlessly in the storehouse. He ended with a plea for the return of his property.

"This is all very strange," the monk replied, "but now the storehouse is here I don't see how I *can* give it back. I have nothing like it myself and I can certainly use it. But you're welcome to the contents."

"How am I going to get all that rice back down the mountain? There are a thousand sacks in there!"

"That's easy. I'll do it for you."

The monk had a sack loaded onto the bowl, then sent the bowl flying into the air. All the other sacks followed after it like a flock of geese. "Wait!" cried the rich man. "Don't return them all! Keep a couple of hundred for yourself!"

The monk refused on the grounds that he would not know what to do with so much rice.

"Then keep a couple of dozen sacks anyway," the rich man pleaded, "as much as you can use! They're yours!"

The monk said this was still far too much and refused again. Every single sack arrived in good order back at the rich man's house. The monk's fame spread far and wide.

About that time Emperor Daigo happened to become very ill. All sorts of prayers and rites tried on his behalf brought him no relief. Finally an official thought of the holy man of Mount Shigi. "He never comes down from his mountain at all," the official reported. "He has such extraordinary powers, you see, that he can have his begging bowl fly down by itself to get him food, so he has what he needs without going anywhere. If you summon him, Your Majesty, I think you will find that he can cure you." The emperor agreed and sent for the holy man.

The messenger was awed, too, when he delivered the imperial summons. The monk just asked what His Majesty wanted him for and gave no sign of moving. The messenger explained that the emperor was ill and that his prayers were required.

"I don't have to go to him," the monk said. "I can heal him perfectly well from here!"

"But if you do, how will he know you're the one he has to thank?"

"What difference does it make whether or not he knows who cured him? As long as he's cured, that's all that matters."

"Still," the messenger insisted, "there are a lot of people praying for him and it would be better to be clear about whose prayers worked."

"All right, then," the monk conceded. "I'll send my spirit-helper, the Sword Guardian. If His Majesty sees the spirit in a dream or vision, he'll know that he comes from me. The Sword Guardian wears a cloak woven of swords. As for me, I'm staying here."

The messenger returned to the Capital and reported what the holy man had said. Three days later the emperor was napping in broad daylight when he saw something glitter. He realized it must be the holy man's guardian spirit. Instantly he felt perfectly well. The court was immensely relieved and impressed with the evidence of the monk's powers.

Once again an imperial messenger made his way to Mount Shigi, this time with the offer of rich rewards. "Would you like to be a bishop or an archbishop?" the emperor's message ran. "Would you like an estate to provide income for your temple?" But the monk said he had no use for titles and protested that an estate would be far more trouble than it was worth. "I'll just stay as I am," he declared, till the messenger gave up and went away.

All that was many years ago. The holy man's flying storehouse is still on the mountain, with relics of him still inside, though now it is crumbling with age. Those who are blessed to obtain the smallest fragment of its wood make it into a buddha like the monk's own, and are sure to enjoy good fortune, peace, and ease. The monk's Bishamon, too, is still on the mountain, and countless pilgrims pay homage to it there.

7 3 .

NO RESPECT

Sōō, of Mudōji on Mount Hiei, used to practice regularly at a triple waterfall just north of the mountain, invoking there the fiery Fudō. Once he prayed to Lord Fudō: "Put me on your back, take me to the Tosotsu

Heaven where Miroku, the Future Buddha, lives! Bring me to the Inner Sanctum from where, in the fullness of time, Miroku will be born into this world to save us!"

"That's not easy," Fudō answered, "but I'll take you there if you insist. First, wash your butt."

Sōō ducked under the waterfall, made sure his butt was clean, got up on Fudō's head, and flew off to the Tosotsu Heaven. When they reached the gate to the Inner Sanctum, he saw above it the words, "Lotus of the Wonderful Teaching."

"People go in chanting the Sutra," Fudō reminded him. "The Lotus Sutra, you know, the Sutra of the Lotus of the Wonderful Teaching. You can't get in if you're not chanting it."

Sōō lifted his eyes to the boundless heavens. "Drat!" he exclaimed. "I *read* the Sutra, of course, but I can't chant it now because I still don't know it by heart!"

"Oh. That's too bad. Then I suppose you can't go in. I'll just have to take you home again. We'll come back when you have the Sutra down." Lord Fudō dropped Sōō off again by the waterfall.

Sōō was terribly disappointed, but they say he did master the Sutra in the end and got into the Inner Sanctum. The Fudō who took him was, to be precise, the one he himself had made, life-sized, and enshrined in his temple.

Sōō was known for his miracles. One day the Somedono Empress fell ill, tormented by an evil spirit. When someone suggested Sōō as an outstanding healer ("a disciple of the great Ennin, you know — he lives on Mount Hiei"), the empress sent a messenger to fetch him.

When Sōō arrived, he waited at the middle gate of the mansion: a tall monk more like a demon than a man, wearing rough clogs and a bark-fiber habit and carrying a rosary of big seeds. The empress's attendants found him there. "Goodness!" they whispered to each other. "What a tramp! We can't possibly let him into Her Majesty's presence!" They told him he would have to pray from the veranda outside the empress's room, and word directly from Her Majesty immediately confirmed the order.

Since the empress was some distance away, all Sōō actually had of her was the groaning that came through her curtains. On hearing her, he began loudly working his rites. Lord Fudō himself seemed present, and a shiver of awe gave the attendants gooseflesh. Suddenly the empress shot through her curtains, all wrapped up as she was in two pink robes, and came rolling out to Sōō on the veranda.

There was an uproar. "Oh! My lady! How awful! Oh please, Your

Grace, please put her back! You can go right up to her curtains, of course
you can!"

Sōō would not budge. "Why, I wouldn't think of it!" he said. "A poor
beggar like me wouldn't dare approach Her Majesty!" Furious at having
been denied direct access to the empress in the first place, he had no
intention of moving. On the contrary, right out there on the veranda he
raised Her Majesty four or five feet into the air and gave her a good
whack. Panic-stricken, her attendants hustled the curtains over to hide
her, while at the same time chasing all the bystanders they could get at
—passing servants, ladies-in-waiting, gentlemen of the court—out of
sight. Alas, the damage was already done. Everyone had seen the empress as plain as plain could be.

Sōō gave her a few more whacks and scooted her back to where she
had started out from, so decorously concealed. Then he left. "Oh, do
wait a moment!" the empress's attendants cried out, but he ignored them.
"I've been standing around too long as it is," he grumbled, "and my back
hurts."

The empress found that the evil spirit was now gone and that she felt
perfectly well. Sōō had been so impressive that he soon got an imperial
proclamation appointing him a bishop. "Now what's a beggar like me to
do with a fancy title like that?" he muttered, and sent the messenger
packing.

After that, Sōō was constantly being called to heal people in Kyoto,
but he refused to go. He would always complain that in the Capital you
don't get any respect.

7 4 ·

THE INVISIBLE MAN

There once lived in the Capital, no one remembers just when, a humble
man who was devoted to Rokkakudō, a holy temple dedicated to Kannon. He often went there on pilgrimage.

On the last night of the year he went out alone on a visit and came
home late. Just as he was crossing the Horikawa Bridge westward, along
First Avenue, he saw a troupe of people approaching with torches. No
doubt a great lord was on his way somewhere. The man quickly hid

under the bridge and sneaked a look as the crowd passed overhead. They were not humans at all but frightful demons! Some had a single eye, some had horns, some had lots of arms, and some hopped along on only one leg.

The man forgot whether he was alive or dead and stood rooted, witless, to the spot. Meanwhile the demons passed by — all but one who was trailing behind and who muttered, "There's a man around here!" Another demon said that he didn't *see* any man. "Get him!" shouted a third, and the man thought he was lost.

One demon charged, caught him, and dragged him up. The others agreed that he had done nothing much wrong and decided to let him go, but first four or five of the demons spat in his face. Then they went their way.

The man was happy just not to have been killed. His head ached now and he felt rather strange, but he was so eager to get home and tell his wife all about it that he went on as fast as he could. When he entered his house, his family never said a word to him, though they looked straight at him, and they did not answer when he spoke to them. Even when he went right up to them they seemed not to know anyone was there. At last he understood. The demons' spit had made him invisible.

What a disaster! He could see and hear as well as ever, but no one could see or hear *him*. He even tried eating some of the food his family had left out, but no one noticed. They, for their part, were sure by the time dawn came that he had been murdered the previous night.

Several days later there was still no improvement. The man stayed at Rokkakudō and begged Kannon for help. "Year after year I've visited you and put my trust in you," he prayed. "Now, please, grant me this boon: make me visible as I used to be!" He fed himself from the meals of the others on retreat there and from the offerings they made to Kannon, yet even someone right next to him would never realize he was doing so.

After two retreat periods (seven days each), he dreamed one night, toward dawn, that a holy monk stood beside him. "Leave here early in the morning and do as the first person you meet tells you," the monk ordered. Then the man woke up.

He left at dawn and met at the gate a weird oxherd with a huge ox. "Hey, you!" the oxherd called. "Come with me!" The man was relieved to gather that he was visible again and gladly followed the oxherd as the dream had instructed him to do. After half a mile or so, they came to an imposing gate. It was closed, but the oxherd tethered his ox and started through the crack between the leaves of the gate — a crack much too small for anyone to get through. "Come on!" he ordered. "You too!"

"How am I supposed to get through a crack like that?" the man protested.

"Just do it!" The oxherd took his hand and pulled him through. They were on the grounds of a big, prosperous mansion.

They walked into the house unchallenged. In an inner room a girl was lying ill, with women sitting at the head and foot of her bed watching over her. The oxherd gave the man a small mallet, sat him down by the girl, and had him hammer her on the head and hips. As he did so, the girl half sat up in agony. Her parents, who were there too, told each other the end was near and wept. Someone was chanting a sutra.

A servant went to call a famous healer who shortly arrived, sat down beside the girl, and intoned the Heart Sutra. At the sound of his voice, the hair rose on the man's head and he shivered with awe. The oxherd, meanwhile, escaped as fast as he could and disappeared.

Next, the healer chanted Fudō's Fire Darani. The man screamed and his clothes burst into flames. Suddenly he was plainly visible again for the whole household to see: a miserable wretch seated right beside the patient. He was quickly seized, hustled outside, and questioned; he told his story as best he could. The household had difficulty believing him. On the other hand, they were very happy to find that the girl was now perfectly well.

The healer assured them that the man was not to blame, and that on the contrary he had just been mercifully blessed by the Kannon of Rokkakudō. They were to let him go. So they drove the man from their door, and he returned home to tell his family the whole adventure. Though disturbed by it, his wife was awfully glad to have him back.

The oxherd had been the follower of some god, and it was he who had been persuaded somehow to possess the girl and torture her. Both she and the man enjoyed perfect health after that. How powerful the Fire Darani is!

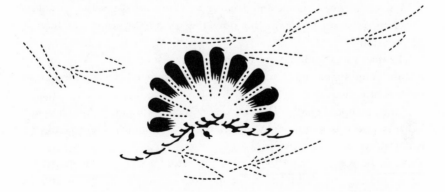

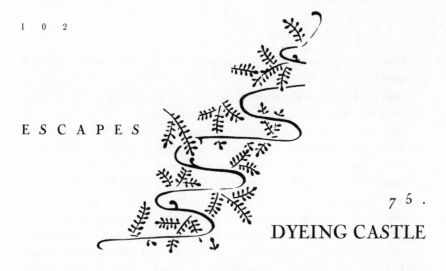

ESCAPES

DYEING CASTLE

Long ago the great master Ennin went to study the Buddha's Teaching in China, so as to pass it on to our own land. In 845 he encountered Emperor Wu-tsung's terrible persecution of Buddhism. Temples were being razed, and monks and nuns were being seized and killed or forced back into lay life.

Ennin was almost caught, too, when he fled into a hall of the temple where he was staying. Soldiers went in after him. Desperate, he hid among the sacred images, and the soldiers were surprised to find a new Fudō among the buddhas on the altar. They were also suspicious, however, and when they lifted the Fudō down it turned back into Ennin. They reported this alarming transformation to the emperor who decided that being a foreign monk, Ennin should simply be expelled from China.

Greatly relieved, Ennin fled for the border. Beyond the distant mountains he came to an isolated compound with a high wall around it, pierced by a single gate. It was good to see a human dwelling. He learned from the gatekeeper that the establishment belonged to a certain rich man. The gatekeeper asked Ennin who he was.

"I'm a Japanese monk and I came to China to study the Buddha's Teaching," Ennin replied. "But now I'm trying to escape this terrible persecution."

The man remarked that hardly anyone ever came there. "Why not stay awhile?" he suggested. "When things have quieted down you can go back to studying."

Ennin accepted gladly. The gatekeeper locked the gate behind him and led him into a bustling compound filled with buildings. He was given a room off to one side.

Next, he went looking for a good place to practice his devotions. He found no sign of Buddhism or of monks, but in the back, toward the mountains, he heard pitiful human groans coming from a building. Peering anxiously through a crack in the fence round the place, he saw people tied up and hung in mid-air, with jars below them to catch their dripping blood. Horrified, he called to ask them why they were being tortured, but got no reply. Then he tried another spot and heard an answering groan.

Beyond the fence people were lying on the ground, deathly pale and emaciated. Ennin beckoned to one and asked again what had brought them to this pass. The victim slipped his wasted arm through the fence and with a bit of wood traced the following message on the ground.

"This is Dyeing Castle," the victim wrote. "People who come here are first given a drug which deprives them of speech, then fed another which fattens them. After that they are hung up and their skin slit all over so that their blood drips out. The blood is used to dye tie-dyed stuffs, which are sold. All of us are being tortured this way because we did not know about the trap. You will find in your food dark grains like sesame seeds. These are the drug that robs you of speech. If they try to feed them to you, only pretend to eat them. Get rid of them, and groan if anyone talks to you. Then escape as fast as you can, but not through the gate because it is locked and impassable."

Ennin returned to his room, and a meal was soon brought him. In the food there were black grains, which he slipped into the fold of his robe and later threw away. When a servant spoke to him, he only groaned in reply. The servant was deceived and gave Ennin next the drug to fatten him. Ennin pretended to eat this too, but did not. When he was alone again, he turned to the northeast and prayed with desperate intensity to all the good powers of Hiei, his home mountain and monastery in Japan.

Suddenly a large black dog appeared, caught Ennin's sleeve in his jaws, and tugged. Ennin thought it best to follow. The dog led him to where a brook entered the compound, a place he would never have found on his own. Once he was outside, the dog vanished.

He ran wherever his legs would carry him till he came to a village beyond the mountains and described to a curious villager who he was and where he had been. "How awful!" exclaimed the villager. "That's Dyeing Castle! No one who goes in there ever returns. Only the Buddha's aid could possibly have gotten you out! You must be a saint!" He immediately prostrated himself before Ennin.

At last Ennin made his way secretly back to the Capital, and in 846 Emperor Wu-tsung died. The next emperor halted the persecution, so that Ennin was able to complete his stay in China profitably and return to Japan with a rich store of holy wisdom.

TAKEN IN

A newly appointed deputy viceroy of Kyushu had many children, but the last of them was his favorite: a bright and handsome son now twenty years old. Though not from a warlike family, the young man was remarkably strong and brave, and his parents were so fond of him that they took him down to Kyushu with them. Meanwhile the deputy viceroy's assistant, the governor of Chikuzen, had a lovely teenage daughter whom he and his wife loved so much that they had taken her down to Kyushu, too.

The deputy viceroy was so eager for the two to marry that his assistant could hardly refuse, and on an auspicious day the pair were happily united. But the groom had always aspired to a government career, and he now planned to go up to the Capital. Parting from his wife was out of the question, so he decided to take her with him — by land, since the sea route seemed a bit risky. He set off with a party of twenty picked retainers, and with a train of pack horses and of servants on foot.

They were making good time when they reached Inamino in Harima province, late on a January afternoon. A stiff wind was blowing, mixed with snow. From the mountains to the north a monk rode toward them, an imposing fellow in a red robe, violet trousers, and straw boots, carrying a lacquered whip. The saddle on his spirited horse was inlaid with mother-of-pearl.

He dismounted and bowed respectfully to the young man. "I have long served His Excellency the governor of Chikuzen," he said. "I happened to hear, sir, that you were on your way to the Capital, and since I live in the mountains north of here I came to offer my hospitality, if you do not mind roughing it a bit." He was ever so polite.

The young man's retainers all dismounted in turn while the young man reined in his horse. "It's very kind of you," he replied, "but I want to get to Kyoto as fast as I can. I may return to Kyushu next year, though, and I'll be happy to visit you then."

But the monk would not take no for an answer. The sun had almost sunk behind the mountains by now, and the retainers were so obviously eager to accept that at last the young man yielded. The monk led the way with a satisfied air, assuring his guests that they had not far to go.

Two or three miles brought them to a compound entirely surrounded by a high wall. The monk took the young couple straight in to what appeared to be living quarters on the south side of the compound, and had refreshments served them while the horses were foddered. The servants and retainers, meanwhile, were given lodgings a good way off.

After a lively and luxurious feast the couple, alone but for a maid or two, loosened their clothes and lay down. The maids had enjoyed themselves freely and were now asleep, but the couple were wide awake. Somehow ill at ease, they had hardly eaten or drunk. As they chatted they assured each other tenderly of their love and wondered, in a strangely gloomy mood, what their journey would yet bring them. Slowly the hours passed.

In the small hours they heard with misgiving footsteps approaching from within the house. Suddenly the door by the head of their bed slid open. The young man jumped up but was seized by the hair and dragged away. Strong though he was, it had all happened too fast. He had not even been able to pick up the sword he kept by his pillow.

The assailant knocked a shutter open and hauled him out of the room. "Kaneomaru!" he called. "Are you ready? See that you take care of the usual!"

"Right!" answered a nasty voice. Hands seized the young man's collar and hustled him off.

There was a fenced area in one corner of the compound, and the gate in the fence opened onto a pit thirty feet deep with hundreds of sharpened bamboo stakes planted at the bottom. Year after year travelers like the young man, on their way back and forth to the Capital, were lured in, given wine that left them dead-drunk, then thrown into the pit while their similarly drunk retainers were stripped of everything they owned. Some retainers were killed, while others, the more promising ones, were pressed into service. This was the trap the young man and his party had fallen into.

Kaneomaru dragged the young man to the fence, opened the gate, and propelled him through it, but the young man clung to a gatepost and could not be budged further. Kaneomaru got on the pit side of him and pulled. There was a slight incline down from the gate. The young man shifted his weight and gave a powerful shove which sent Kaneomaru hurtling into the pit. Then he closed the gate and stole under the veranda of the house.

At last he was able to think. He could try to arouse his retainers, but they were unconscious with drink, and besides, there was a moat between him and them and the bridge was drawn. Instead, he crept under the floor of the room where he had just been. He heard the monk come in to his wife.

"No doubt you'll be shocked to hear me confess it," said the monk, "but in the daylight, when the wind blew your veil aside, I caught a glimpse of your face and now I can think only of you. Forgive me." He slid into bed beside her.

"Before I started up to the Capital, I made a vow to abstain for one hundred days," the wife replied. "There are just three days left. When those three days are over, I'll do anything you say."

"What I have in mind will bring you far more merit than that!"

"The man who was everything to me has vanished before my eyes, and I can't prevent you doing whatever you want with me. I can't refuse you in the end, you know that. You've no need to be so impatient." She was holding him off.

Conceding she had a point, the monk went away.

"That husband of mine won't die a shameful death!" the woman murmured to herself, and the young man under the floor, raging, heard her. He pushed a sliver of wood up through a crack between the floorboards, right in front of her, and when she saw it she knew she had been right. She waggled the sliver and he knew she had understood.

The monk kept coming back to try again, but she always managed to put him off. When he was finally gone, the wife silently opened a shutter and her husband came out from under the floor into the room. Both burst into tears and promised each other that if they were to die they should die together. The young man asked what had happened to his sword. "I hid it under the matting when you were dragged away," she answered, and brought it out. It was a ray of hope at last.

Sword in hand, the young man stealthily made his way toward his retainers. Seven or eight carving blocks stood beside a long fire pit and the monk's men were sprawled nearby amid the scattered remains of their dinner, with their bows, quivers, armor, daggers, and swords beside them. The monk himself was asleep on his armrest. A pair of tables before him bore silver vessels full of the leavings from his meal.

"Help me now, O Kannon of Hasedera!" the young man prayed. "Let me see my parents again!" Since the monk was so unexpectedly sleeping, he decided to attack straight off, cut off the monk's head, and die, for he saw no chance of escape. At the first blow the monk cried out and raised his arms in fright, but the next blow killed him.

The monk's men were certainly many, but Kannon must really have protected the young man because when they saw their leader dead they thought they had been invaded by a large force. Besides, they themselves had all been caught and forced into service by the man, and they had no wish to fight for him. Now he was dead, it did not occur to them to resist. Instead, they all blurted at once, "*I* didn't do anything wrong! I used to serve Lord So-and-So before I fell into this trap!" The young man put on a good show of having ample reinforcements behind him, herded them all off, and locked them up.

It was a long wait till dawn. When day came at last, he aroused his own retainers, who came out dazed and rubbing their eyes to clear away the fumes of last night's wine. They sobered up right away when they heard what had happened and went to look at the pit. The bamboo stakes down at the bottom bristled up through corpses new and old. Kaneo-maru, a lanky youth clad in a single miserable wrap and with the clogs still on his feet, lay there impaled, still twitching a little. The scene might as well have been from hell.

Now the young man called the monk's servants out again, and they confessed all the terrible things they had been made to do over the years. They were not punished since they themselves were not responsible. A messenger was sent with a report for the emperor, who was greatly impressed with the young man's deed.

Finally the young man himself went on up to Kyoto, received an official post, and found that everthing went for him just as he had always hoped. He and his wife stayed with each other through all the trials and joys that came their way, and must often have talked over their memories of that awful night. No one ever discovered any relative or other connection of the robber monk, so for him the matter was closed.

It took a wise and prudent man to do what the young man did! Anyone who hears this story should consider himself warned not to spend the night in a place he doesn't know. Note, too, that the young man could have done nothing without Kannon's help. Not that Kannon ever wishes to kill, but after all, the robber had killed many people himself, and Kannon could hardly approve!

7 7 ·

THE SACRIFICE

In the province of Mimasaka there are two gods, Chūsan and Kōya. Kōya is a snake and Chūsan a monkey. Each year, during the annual festival, these gods used to be offered a live human, and they had always gotten the sacrifice they required: a pretty girl with a handsome figure, long hair, and fine white skin.

One year the choice fell on the daughter of a certain household. Her

parents were heartbroken. After all, the tie of parent to child springs
from a karmic bond already long established in lives gone by, and even
an ill-favored child will always be dear, let alone one as lovely in every
way as this girl. The girl, for her part, knew that soon she would never
see her mother and father again, and she spent her days and nights in
tears.

Then a hunter from the east passed through the village. A strange,
fierce man, he was so immensely strong that his accustomed prey were
wild boar, which he killed and ate at will, thinking nothing of it, though
to ordinary people an angry boar is terrifying. The hunter happened to
stop at the girl's house, and her father mentioned why the family was so
sad. "What did she do in past lives," he groaned, "to have been born here
for this? What a horrible fate! And I don't say so just because she's my
own daughter, you know. She's so very pretty!"

The hunter took all this in. "The gods are harsh," he said. "But don't
offer her at the festival. Let me take care of her instead. She'll die otherwise. You don't want your only daughter cut up alive and set as meat
before the god, that would be too awful. Give her to me!"

The father was convinced. Anything, after all, rather than let his
daughter die so ghastly a death. So the hunter went to the girl. She was
practicing calligraphy, but with a very sorrowful air, and her sleeves
were visibly wet from weeping. When she turned aside at his approach
and hid her face modestly behind her hair, he saw that it too was wet
with tears. How lovely she was! She looked so distinguished that it was
hard to believe she was just a villager's child. He fell in love with her and
decided to take her place at the sacrifice, though it might mean his own
life.

"I have a plan," he told the girl's parents. "Would you be sorry to die
for your daughter?"

"Of course not," they answered. "What good is life to us without her?
Please do as you think best."

"In that case, stretch a sacred rope round your house and tell people
you've begun purifying your daughter for the festival. Don't let anyone
in, and be quite sure also to tell no one I'm here."

He spent the next few days very happily with the girl. Meanwhile he
chose the two cleverest of his dogs, which had all served him well in the
mountains for years, and trained them by setting them day in and day
out to catch and eat monkeys. Since dogs and monkeys are natural
enemies, the two would soon attack and kill any monkey they saw, and
in fact they destroyed a great many. The hunter for his part spent a lot
of time sharpening his murderous dagger and sword. Often he sighed to
the girl, "Ah, what link from past lives can have brought us together, to

make me now offer my life for yours? I'm happy to do it, but the thought of parting from you makes me sad." The girl answered in words of gratitude and affection.

At last the festival day came, and the priests arrived at the head of a large throng to take charge of the victim. They brought a long chest, newly made, which they slid into the girl's room. "Put the offering inside as usual," they ordered, "and send her out to the god."

Instead, it was the hunter who got in, with his dogs. "Listen, you two," he said, "I've given you a good life lately and now it's your turn to look out for *me*. Understand? He patted their heads and they whined back, then lay down on either side of him. Next he had the weapons he had so carefully sharpened laid in the chest too. Finally the lid was secured with strips of cloth, and the knots were sealed. With an expression of suitable grief on his face, the father slid the chest out again, and the priests took it. The procession set off with a great shaking of spears, bells, and branches of the *sakaki* tree dear to the gods, and with a great clamor from those who went ceremonially before it to clear the road.

The girl listened to the commotion and thought once more of the man who had taken her place in the chest. She wondered fearfully what her parents would do if anything went wrong. But they assured her that in the face of the god's harsh command they themselves were quite prepared to die, and that they feared nothing at all.

The offering was carried to the shrine. All the priests lined up in front of it, in order of precedence, and the chief priest solemnly intoned the divine invocation. Then he opened the sanctuary doors, slid the chest inside, and closed the doors again.

The hunter, meanwhile, had carefully pierced a peephole in the chest with his dagger. He now saw before him, in the seat of honor, a giant monkey eight feet tall with a red face and buttocks, and long, glossy white fur. Two hundred lesser monkeys crowded around it on either side, some with flushed faces, some with eyebrows excitedly raised, and all barking and chattering madly. A huge carving board and a long, long knife lay before them; and around the board stood jars full of salt, vinegar, and wine.

While the others all clustered round, the giant monkey approached the chest and undid the knots.

"Get 'em!" the hunter shouted. His dogs burst from the chest, set their teeth in the giant, got him down, and dragged him along the floor. Out leaped the hunter right behind them, his blade glittering like ice. He hauled the giant onto the carving board, put the sword to his neck, and roared: "Scum, this is what you get for killing and eating people! You listen to me! I'm going to cut off your filthy head and feed it to my dogs!"

The giant monkey's red face got even redder. He blinked and great tears rolled from his eyes, while his lips drew back to expose gleaming teeth. Though he rubbed his hands together in abject entreaty, with a ghastly expression, the hunter gave him no quarter. "All these years you've been eating young women and leaving people childless!" he bellowed. "Now your head's coming off for it! Just you try eating *me*!" He struck a savage blow, but the giant monkey's head did not roll quite so easily. Meanwhile the two dogs had chased the others into the trees, where they sat shrieking so frantically that the mountains rang and the earth seemed ready to split.

Next, the god possessed one of the shrine priests. "Never, never make me a live offering again!" he howled. "The practice must stop! I've learned, oh how I've learned not to kill humans! And don't harm the man who did this to me or punish the family that was supposed to provide the offering! I'll protect them and their descendants forever! But quickly now, please, beg this man for my life! I'm in terrible danger!"

The priests and their followers rushed into the sanctuary and pleaded with the hunter to desist. "We understand," they cried, "but please, please release the god! He's promised not to do it again!"

"Don't just let him go!" the hunter retorted. "He's a murderer, and I'm going to teach him a thing or two about suffering!" As he showed no sign of relenting, the monkey's head seemed as good as off. The chief priest made every promise he could think of and the god swore that he would never, never do it again.

At last the hunter gave in. "All right, all right," he said, "just make sure you don't!" The monkey went free.

When it was all over, the hunter returned to the girl's house and lived on happily as her husband. Since he was actually of noble stock, he made an excellent match.

After that, it was boar or deer which served as live offerings to the god.

7 8 .

THE LURE

A fine young man of the highest birth (a captain of the Palace Guards, let us say) once made a secret pilgrimage to Kiyomizu, where he spotted a very pretty girl. She was beautifully dressed, and to the captain she was obviously of gentle birth. She too seemed to be there on a secret pilgrimage.

He watched her worship innocently before the altar. In her early twenties, she was by far the loveliest young woman he had ever seen. Who could she be? He was going to be courting her, there was no doubt about that, and was already deeply in love. When she left the temple, he had a page follow her.

The captain was home again when the page returned to report. "I found out where she lives, sir," he said. "The house isn't in the city at all, but in the hills south of Kiyomizu, just north of Mount Amida. It's a fine, prosperous-looking place. The woman with her noticed me behind them and asked what I thought I was doing. I told her I was just obeying my master, because he'd seen her lady at the temple and had told me to find out where she lived. The woman said next time I came that way I should be sure to stop by."

Greatly encouraged, the captain sent a letter to which the girl replied very sweetly. Several such exchanges followed, and in one letter the girl wrote that living as she did back in the mountains she really could not go into the city. "But do come here," she added. "I'm sure there's no harm in our talking through a screen."

Desperate to see her again, the captain rode off gaily at dusk with just two attendants: a groom and the usual page. Needless to say, he did not advertise his departure.

When they arrived, the page announced them and the older woman invited them to follow her in. The compound was surrounded by a stout earthen wall pierced by high gates and divided by a deep trench with a bridge over it. The woman had the captain's attendants and horses stop at a lodge short of the bridge, then led the captain himself on across. Among the many buildings on the other side was what seemed to be a guest pavilion. The captain entered to find himself in a beautifully appointed apartment, complete with folding screens, a curtain of state, very nice mats on the floor, and blinds dividing off the main room. For a mountain retreat, the place was thoroughly impressive.

The evening was well along by now and the girl herself appeared. The captain went straight in behind her curtains and lay down with her. By the time they had made love he knew she was infinitely more beautiful in his arms than she ever had been at a distance.

As they talked, the captain let her know how much he loved her. But she seemed very downcast and apparently was even weeping, though she tried to hide it. Not understanding, he asked her why. She only answered that she had just thought of something sad, which puzzled the captain still more. "But we love each other now!" he said. "You shouldn't hide things from me! What's the matter? What is it?"

"It isn't that I don't *want* to tell you," she replied, "but oh, I can't bear to!" She wept all the more.

"Speak! Tell me! Am I going to die somehow?"

"Oh, I *must* tell you! You see, I'm the daughter of so-and-so who used to live in the Capital. When my parents died I was left an orphan. The master of this house is a beggar outcaste whom a tremendous stroke of fortune had already brought to live here. He abducted me, and now he sees to my every need and dresses me in the best. From time to time he sends me off on pilgrimage to Kiyomizu, where men see me and fall in love with me just as you did. I lure these men here as I did you, and while I sleep the outcaste thrusts a spear down from the ceiling. I guide the point to the man's chest and the spear runs him through. When he's dead, he's stripped of his clothes. His attendants in the lodge on the other side of the moat are all murdered and stripped too, and the horses are stolen. I've done this twice already, and all I have to look forward to is more of the same. So this time I'm going to take the spear point instead of you and die myself. Run away! I'm sure your attendants are dead. Oh, to think that I'll never see you again!" She sobbed as though her heart would break.

The captain's mind reeled, but he managed to gather enough wits to say, "How horrible! And you talk of dying for me! No, no, thank you, but I can't escape by myself and leave you behind! We'll go together!"

"Yes, I've longed for that too, many times. But if he doesn't feel flesh under his spear he'll be down instantly to see what's wrong. If we're both gone, we'll both be caught and killed. No, please, save yourself and do pious works for the good of my soul. I can't go on committing these monstrous crimes!"

"How can my good works ever repay the debt I'll owe you? But all right, I'll go."

"They'll have taken up the bridge over the trench after you crossed it. Go out the door there and make your way along the narrow bank beyond the trench till you get to a little opening in the outer wall, where the brook comes in. You can squeeze out through that. Ah, it's time! When the spear comes down, I'll put it to my own chest and let it stab me to death."

Already the sound of voices, terrifying now beyond description, could be heard elsewhere in the house. Weeping, the captain drew on a single robe, tucked the skirts up into his belt for ease of movement, and stole out the door. He got along the bank and out through the opening. So far,

so good. But where was he to head now? He simply ran in the direction
he happened to be facing, and as he did so he heard footsteps running
behind him. They were after him! He glanced back in panic. It was his
page.

"Where did *you* come from?" he cried in relief.

"As soon as you were gone they took away the bridge, sir," the boy
replied. "That was a bad sign, so I got out over the wall. When I gathered
they'd killed the groom, I wondered what they might have done with *you*,
so instead of getting away I hid in a thicket to see what might happen.
When I heard someone running, I hoped it might be you, sir, and I
followed to make sure."

"I had no idea such a horror was possible, I just had no idea!" the
captain groaned as they ran on together toward the city.

On reaching the river at about the level of Fifth Avenue, they looked
back and saw a great fire. Having thrust down his spear, the outcaste
had assumed he had killed his intended victim. But he expected the girl
then to say something. Alarmed by her silence, he came down to see what
was wrong. He found the girl dead and the man gone. Obviously there
would soon be people there to arrest him, so he had set fire to all the
buildings and fled.

Once back at home the captain swore his page to silence and never
breathed a word of what had happened. Every year he commissioned
solemn Buddhist rites, and though he never revealed who they were for
they must have been for the girl who had died to save him.

In the end, rumor of the incident did get out and someone built a
temple where the house had stood; in fact, it's still there.

It all goes to show that you shouldn't let a lovely woman sweep you
off somewhere you don't know.

7 9 ·

JUST LIKE A BIRD

As a young man Tadaakira, an officer of the Imperial Police, quarreled
with some local toughs below Kiyomizu Temple. The toughs had their
swords drawn and were out to surround and kill Tadaakira if they could.
He too bared his sword and broke away up to the main hall. When still
more toughs came after him, he fled into the hall.

Now Kiyomizu Temple is built out from a steep hillside and stands on a structure of huge wooden pillars. From the open platform before the temple you look out over the treetops. Tadaakira seized one of the great shutters that protect the temple from wind and rain, dashed out clutching it under his arm, and hurled himself off into the valley below. The wind caught the shutter. He sailed like a bird down to a gentle landing and disappeared with all possible speed.

The toughs watched in a row from the railing above. They could not believe their eyes.

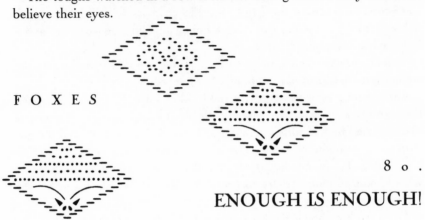

F O X E S

8 o .

ENOUGH IS ENOUGH!

The foxes which infested the house and grounds of Major Counselor Yasumichi's old mansion were always making mischief, but since they never really did any harm Yasumichi let the matter pass. They got naughtier and naughtier as the years went by, though, until one day he angrily decided that enough was enough. Those foxes would have to go.

He announced a grand fox hunt to his household, for the next day. The servants were to bring bows and arrows, sticks, or whatever weapons they could devise, and flush out every last one. They would surround the house, and men would be posted not only on the garden wall but on the roof as well, and even in the space between the ceiling of the rooms and the roof. Every fox that showed itself would be killed.

Near dawn on the fateful day Yasumichi had a dream. A white-haired old man, looking rather like an aged menial, was kneeling under the tangerine tree in the garden, bowing respectfully to him.

"Who are you?" asked Yasumichi.

"Someone who has lived here in this mansion for many years, sir," the old man answered nervously. "My father lived here before me, sir, and by now I have many children and grandchildren. They get into a lot of mischief, I'm afraid, and I'm always after them to stop, but they never listen. And now, sir, you're understandably fed up with us. I gather that you're going to kill us all. But I just want you to know, sir, how sorry I am that this is our last night of life. Won't you pardon us, one more time? If we ever make trouble again, then of course you must act as you think best. But the young ones, sir — I'm *sure* they'll understand when I explain to them why you're so upset. We'll do everything we can to protect you from now on, if only you'll forgive us, and we'll be sure to let you know when anything good is going to happen!"

The old man bowed again and Yasumichi awoke. When the sky had lightened, he got up and looked outside. Under the tangerine tree sat a hairless old fox which, at the sight of him, slunk under the house.

The perplexed Yasumichi gave up his fox hunt. There was no more troublesome mischief, and every happy event around the house was announced by a fox's sharp bark.

8 1 .

THE LOVING FOX

A man was once walking at twilight along Suzaku Avenue in Kyoto when he met an extraordinarily beautiful woman. She seemed happy enough to let him strike up a conversation with her, and from close up he found her even more alluring. Unable even to imagine letting the opportunity pass, he filled her ears with so many sweet nothings that he soon very nearly had what he burned for.

The woman tried to hold him off. "Now that we've gotten this far," she said, "I'd like so much to go all the way! But you see, if we do you'll die."

Much too excited to listen, the man kept pressing himself on her until she gave in. "I really can't refuse you," she said, "since you insist so urgently. Very well then, I'll do whatever you wish and die in your place. If you want to show me gratitude, copy the Lotus Sutra and dedicate it for me."

The man seemed not to take her seriously, and he finally consummated his desire. They lay in each other's arms all night long, chatting like old lovers. At dawn the woman got up and asked the man for his fan. "I meant what I said, you know," she told him, "I'm going to die instead of you. If you want proof, go into the palace grounds and look around the Butoku Hall. You'll see." Then she left.

At daylight the man went to the Butoku Hall and found there a fox lying dead with his fan over its face. He was very sorry. Every seven days after that he finished a copy of the Lotus Sutra and dedicated it for the fox's soul. On the night following the forty-ninth day he dreamed that she came to him, surrounded by angels, and told him that thanks to the power of the Teaching she was to be born into the Tōri Heaven.

8 2 .

TOUCHED IN THE HEAD

Kaya no Yoshifuji lived in the village of Ashimori in Bitchū province. He had made a fortune trading in imported Chinese coins.

In the fall of 896, Yoshifuji's wife went up to the Capital, leaving him all alone. He was far too randy a fellow to stand this for long. One evening at twilight, he was out for a stroll when he spotted a lovely young girl he had not seen before, and wanted her right away. She tried to run when he grabbed at her, but he caught her and asked who she was. Very sweetly, she answered, "Nobody."

"Come to my place," said Yoshifuji.

"Oh no, sir, I couldn't!" She tried again to pull away.

"Then where do you live? I'll go home with you."

"Over there." She set off with Yoshifuji beside her, keeping a good hold on her. It was not far, and the house was lovely. What a surprise to find a place like this so close by! Male and female servants clustered round to greet their mistress, and Yoshifuji realized that the girl was the daughter of the house.

The two slept together that night, to Yoshifuji's delight. The next morning a man whom Yoshifuji understood to be the girl's father came in. "You were always meant to come here," he said, "and now you must stay!" The girl was ever so nice to him, and he was so taken with her that he forgot all about his wife. As for his house and children, he never gave them a thought. He and the girl pledged each other eternal love.

Yoshifuji's household assumed, when he first disappeared, that he was just catting around as usual; but as the hours passed and he failed to return, they began to worry. "What a lunatic!" they grumbled. "We'll have to look for him!" Servants sent in the middle of the night to comb the neighborhood turned up nothing. Yet Yoshifuji could not have gone far since he had been dressed only casually and all his clothes were still at home. By daybreak every likely place had been searched in vain. The household was at a loss. If he were young, he might have become a monk in a moment of folly, or even killed himself, but surely not at his age. It was very strange.

Meanwhile Yoshifuji was comfortably installed in his new home and his lady was pregnant. After she had an easy delivery, the two grew closer than ever. Time flew by. Yoshifuji had not a care in the world.

Back at his old home, they never found him. His brothers and his only son Tadasada, affluent men all, were very upset, and wanting at least to find his body they banded together, felled a tree, and carved an image of Eleven-Headed Kannon just Yoshifuji's height. When the statue was done, they prostrated themselves before it and prayed to find the corpse. Be it noted, too, that from the day of Yoshifuji's disappearance they had been calling the Buddha's Name and reading sutras to guide Yoshifuji's soul toward the next life.

Suddenly a man with a stick arrived at Yoshifuji's new house. While the whole household fled in terror, the man poked his stick into Yoshifuji's back and drove him through a tight passageway to the outside.

This was the thirteenth evening after Yoshifuji's disappearance. The people at his old home were still shaking their heads over what had happened when a strangely dark, monkeylike creature crawled out from under the storehouse nearby. What could it be? Through the jabber of the excited onlookers came a voice saying, "It's me!" It was Yoshifuji. Even Tadasada found it hard to believe, but there was no doubt about the voice. Tadasada jumped down from the veranda and brought his father up into the house.

Yoshifuji explained how desperate he had been for a woman while his wife was gone and how he had married a fine gentleman's daughter. Now he had a little boy. "He's so pretty I carry him in my arms all the time!" Yoshifuji declared. "He's my heir, you know. You're only number two from now on, Tadasada. That's because I think so much of his mother."

"Where *is* this little boy?" asked Tadasada.

"Why, over there," Yoshifuji answered, pointing at the storehouse.

This was strange news. Yoshifuji looked terribly thin and sick, and he had on the same clothes as when he had vanished. A servant sent to look under the storehouse found lots of foxes, which fled in all directions. That was where Yoshifuji had been. Obviously a fox had tricked him. He had married the fox and was no longer in his right mind.

A holy monk and a yin-yang diviner were called immediately to purify

Yoshifuji, but after repeated ablutions he still was not the man he had once been. It was only later that he finally came back to himself, and he was horribly embarrassed. The thirteen days he had spent under the storehouse had seemed to him like thirteen years, and the few inches of clearance between the ground and the floor of the building had looked to him like a stately home. The foxes had done all this. The man with the stick was an emanation of the Kannon Yoshifuji's brothers and son had carved.

Yoshifuji lived on in good health another decade and died in his sixty-first year.

8 3 .

YAM SOUP

In his youth General Toshihito belonged to the regent's household. One year, after the regent's New Year banquet, he and the others who had served the banquet were allowed to eat up all the leavings. Sir Goi, a gentleman in the regent's service, sat with them slurping leftover yam soup. Though the fifth rank (*go-i*) he bore was not much to boast of, Sir Goi thought it very fine. "Ah," he sighed, smacking his lips, "I can never get enough of that stuff!"

"Really?" said Toshihito. "You still haven't had enough?"

"No indeed!"

"Then I'll see that you get your fill."

"Thank you," murmured Sir Goi.

A few days later Toshihito appeared at Sir Goi's lodging and invited him for a bath.

Sir Goi accepted, "I *am* a bit itchy this evening," he admitted. "But I've no conveyance."

"Don't worry," said Toshihito, "I've brought you a nag to ride."

"Wonderful, wonderful!" Sir Goi rose to go. He had on a tattered light-blue outfit with rents and gaps here and there, and not even proper underwear under his trousers. The end of his sharp nose was red, and the drop quivering there showed that he had not wiped it for some time. Though his sash dangled raggedly from under the back of his outer robe, he made no attempt to fix it. All in all he was quite a sight.

The incongruous pair rode eastward toward the Kamo River. Sir Goi did not have a single miserable boy with him, but Toshihito had three: one to carry his weapons, one to lead his horse, and one to do whatever else was needed. They had crossed the river and were nearing the foot of the pass over into Ōmi when Sir Goi finally asked where they were going. Toshihito assured him that they had not far to go and kept repeating these assurances as they passed Yamashina.

"What's going on?" Sir Goi insisted, baffled. "You keep telling me it's just ahead and here we are past Yamashina!"

"Just a little further! It's on just a little!" answered Toshihito as they crossed the pass.

Sir Goi had once been to see a monk whom Toshihito knew out that way, at Miidera, and he thought perhaps they were to have their bath there. But it was crazy to come so far for a bath, and besides, they were nowhere near a bath anyway. "Where is this bath of yours?" Sir Goi demanded to know.

"To tell the truth," Toshihito confessed, "I'm taking you up to the Japan Sea coast, to Tsuruga."

"You're mad! If you'd told me from the start I'd at least have taken some men with me!"

"You've as good as a thousand men," laughed Toshihito, "as long as you have *me*!"

On the shore of Lake Biwa Toshihito spied a fox. "There's my messenger!" he cried and gave chase. The fox ran hard, but Toshihito got it cornered, then dove at it and caught its hind legs. His horse did not look like much but it was a remarkable animal. It had not taken long to catch that fox.

Toshihito held the fox dangling in front of him, and Sir Goi managed to catch up in time to hear him say, "Fox, you're going up to Toshihito's house in Tsuruga tonight and you're going to say: 'The master is bringing a surprise guest home from the Capital. He wants his men to meet him at ten tomorrow morning at Takashima. They're to bring two saddled horses.' If you don't deliver that message, you'll be sorry. You've got magic powers, I know, and you'd better get yourself there right away!" Then Toshihito let the fox go.

"What an odd messenger!" remarked Sir Goi.

"Just you watch," Toshihito said. "He'll go."

Sure enough, the fox ran straight off, glancing back again and again. "There he goes!" cried Toshihito, and the fox vanished as he spoke.

They stopped that night on the road and set off again first thing the next morning. At ten they saw thirty riders approaching. Sir Goi was worried, but Toshihito assured him they were his men. For Sir Goi, it was all a mystery.

The riders dismounted before them. "You see?" they said to each other. "Our master's really coming!"

Toshihito grinned and asked how they had found out.

"In a very strange way, sir," the senior retainer answered.

"Did you bring the horses?"

"Yes, sir, both of them."

Since the men had food, Toshihito and Sir Goi dismounted too and ate. The senior retainer told them about the previous evening.

"Around eight o'clock, sir, Her Ladyship felt a sharp pain in her chest. She was very agitated and wanted to call a healer. Then she suddenly said, 'Don't worry, madam, I'm just a fox. I met His Lordship today on the shore of Lake Biwa, on his way from Kyoto. I tried to run away but he caught me and said to tell you he'll be here tomorrow with a guest. He wants his men to meet him with two saddled horses at ten tomorrow morning at Takashima. He threatened me if I didn't get here before the day was over. I hope the men will leave right away! If they're late, I'll suffer for it.' She was terribly upset, sir, but once she had given the message she came back to herself. We left right away and came as fast as we could."

Toshihito smiled and glanced at Sir Goi, who was feeling terribly confused. Then they hurried on and arrived at dusk. The household was amazed. Sir Goi got off his horse and had a look at the house. It was very nice. Toshihito had already given him a good robe to wear over his thin clothing, but still he was awfully hungry and cold. Now there was a big warm fire, and soft mats to sit on. When refreshments were served, Sir Goi felt entirely comfortable. Then he was brought three pale-yellow silk robes, luxuriously padded, and asked solicitously whether he had not been cold on the road. He was fairly swept away.

After everyone had eaten and settled down, Toshihito's father-in-law came in. "What a way to arrive!" he complained. "The messenger you sent was insane, and your wife was very ill. You're mad!"

Toshihito laughed. "I just wanted to see what would happen," he answered. "The fox did come, didn't he!"

"Mad!" the father-in-law repeated with a chuckle. "Is this the gentleman you brought with you?"

"Yes. He says he's never had his fill of yam soup, so I've brought him here to make sure he gets it."

"Imagine never having gotten enough of a simple thing like that!" joked the father-in-law.

"He told me we were just going to take a bath!" chimed in Sir Goi lightly.

They chatted on till at last Toshihito's father-in-law retired for the night.

Sir Goi went to the room where he gathered he was to sleep, and found laid out for him a night robe several inches thick with padding. His own thin garment was pitiful by comparison, and in any case something else seemed to be living in it because he got itchy spots every time he wore it. So he took it off and put the night robe on over the three pale-yellow ones. Never having known such comfort, he felt as though he were floating.

Soon he was sweating. All at once someone moved beside him. Who could it be?

"I was asked to rub your feet, sir," said a young woman's voice.

She seemed very nice, and he cuddled her against him to keep off any draft.

Suddenly a voice outside shouted, "Listen, you peasants! Each of you, tomorrow morning at six, bring in a yam five feet long and three inches thick!" The order sounded absurd. Sir Goi just snuggled into bed.

At dawn he heard a commotion in the yard, and when he finally got up and opened the shutters, he saw four or five large mats laid outside. He could not imagine what they were for. Meanwhile a peasant came in with what looked like a log over his shoulder and laid it on the ground. Another peasant right behind him brought the same, and then another. The things were three inches thick, all right, and by ten o'clock they were piled as high as the roof. Every peasant around had brought in his yam. Sir Goi's mind reeled.

Next, men marched in shouldering half a dozen huge cauldrons good for hundreds of gallons each. They drove stakes into the ground and set the cauldrons up in a row. Once more Sir Goi's mind was boggled. Then came a crowd of pretty girls, all in white silk and carrying freshly made wooden buckets. They emptied their buckets into the cauldrons. Were they going to heat bath water? No, Sir Goi noticed that the buckets held not water but sweetvine syrup. A dozen young men picked up long knives and set to work peeling and slicing the yams. Sir Goi grasped that they were making yam soup, but he did not want any. In fact, he did not like the thought of yam soup at all.

The yam soup was boiling merrily away and the cooks reported it was ready. "Serve it up then!" cried Toshihito. With a monstrous metal ladle they sloshed a gallon or two into a huge bowl and with a "Please, sir," offered it to Sir Goi.

He could not even get through his first serving and confessed he had had enough. Everyone laughed. "Thanks to you, sir," they said, "we've all had lots of yam soup!"

Just then Toshihito spotted a fox peering at them round a corner. "Look!" he exclaimed. "There's my messenger! Feed him!" So they fed the fox yam soup too, and he ate up all he got.

All in all, Toshihito carried through his prank in a wonderfully open-hearted way. A month or so later Sir Goi left again for the Capital, burdened this time with robes for both daily and formal wear, with leather chests full of bolts of cotton and silk, and, needless to say, with the beautiful bedclothes he had slept in the first night. All this was already loaded onto his saddled horse when Toshihito saw him off.

Toshihito did not have much rank, but it just shows how well a man can do anyway when he is well established and liked in his own locality.

8 4 .

THE EVICTION

The Minister Miyoshi no Kiyoyuki, a man of extraordinary intelligence and learning, was expert even in yin-yang lore. Having no house of his own, he located a ruinous old mansion that stood near the crossing of Fifth and Horikawa avenues in Kyoto and bought the place, even though no one would live in it because it was well known to be haunted. Then, over his relatives' strenuous objections, he prepared to move in on an astrologically suitable day.

The right day turned out to be the twentieth of the sixth moon. Kiyoyuki began his move in an unusual way by setting out in his carriage about six in the evening, taking only a straw mat with him.

The house was so old that you couldn't even guess its age, while its garden was full of pines, maples, and cherry trees so ancient that they certainly must have had tree spirits living in them. Vines, now just beginning to redden with fall, clambered everywhere, and the moss that covered the ground had not been swept for years. Kiyoyuki had the shutters raised. The interior partitions were all warped and torn. He had a corner of the floor cleaned up and spread out the mat he had brought. Then he had a lamp lit and lay down on the mat facing south. When his

carriage had been put away in the carriage house, he dismissed all his
servants and ox-drivers with instructions to come back the next day.

Kiyoyuki dozed off, still facing south. In the middle of the night he
was awakened by a sort of rustling in the latticework ceiling and saw a
face sticking out from each crossing of the lattice. All the faces were
different. When he calmly went on looking, they disappeared. Next, forty
or fifty riders, each a foot tall, clattered across the floor from west to east.
Kiyoyuki kept watching.

A closet door opened and out came a very distinguished though tiny
lady all in dark brown, with her hair down over her shoulders. The
delicious scent of musk filled the air as she knelt before him. A red fan
hid most of her face, but the forehead that peeped above it was white
and the eyes elegantly long. The way just the pupils moved as she glanced
to either side was both dignified and sinister. Watching her, he assumed
that the rest of her face must be very pretty, but as she prepared to go
she moved the fan aside a moment. Lo and behold, her nose was bright
red, and crossed pairs of long silver fangs protruded from the corners of
her mouth! This did give him a bit of a shock, but she meanwhile had
vanished into the closet and closed the door.

It was nearly dawn now, but there was a bright moon. Kiyoyuki was
lying there as alert and untroubled as ever when an old man in a light-
blue robe came in from the dim garden outside, knelt, bowed very low,
and respectfully held a letter forth.

"What have you got to say to me?" asked Kiyoyuki sharply.

The old man answered in a little voice, "I'm here to let you know, sir,
that we consider it very wrong of you to claim possession of a house
which has been ours for many years, and that we wish to register a
vigorous protest."

"You don't know what you're talking about. People often buy houses
from one another. It's perfectly normal. But *you* insist on disrupting this
process by frightening away anyone who wants to live here and by
occupying the place yourselves. You should be ashamed. Real demons
know right from wrong and are perfectly straight about it. That's what
makes them frightening. But all you do is invite the punishment of
heaven. Why, you're only a tribe of old foxes! Give me a single hawk or
dog and I'd have him eat you all. Go tell that to your friends!"

"You're perfectly right, sir, perfectly right. But we've lived here so
long, you see. We wanted you to know how we feel. I'm not in the habit
of frightening people. The culprits, I'm afraid, are a couple of youngsters.
I *try* to control them, sir, but they're always up to their tricks. If you're
going to move in here, though, sir, I really don't know what we're to do.

We've nowhere to go. Or at least, the only place is a vacant lot by the main gate of the Academy. May we have your permission to move there, sir?"

"That sounds like a very good idea," Kiyoyuki answered. "You might as well get started."

The old man shouted an order and forty or fifty voices shouted assent.

After daybreak Kiyoyuki's household came to fetch him home again. He then went about the business of having the house remodeled and made more up-to-date. Nothing special happened while he lived there.

ASCETICS

8 5 .

INCENSE SMOKE

Jōkan, a holy monk on Mount Hiei, had spent every night for years chanting an invocation called the Sonshō Darani. Whoever heard him was struck with awe.

One night an Immortal named Yōshō flew over Jōkan's dwelling, heard Jōkan's voice, and came down to the railing outside his room. Startled, Jōkan asked who it was. Yōshō answered in a thin, reedy voice like a mosquito's buzzing, and Jōkan recognized him as a former disciple. He opened the door and Yōshō flew inside.

The two talked over old times till the Immortal felt it was time to leave. But the company of a mortal man had weighed him down, and he found he could not rise. "Would you move the incense burner over here?" he asked, and Jōkan did so. Yōshō mounted the smoke and sailed up into the sky.

Jōkan had always wondered about his student's disappearance, and now he understood. He wept with emotion that Yōshō should have come to see him again.

8 6 .

THE BLESSING

A devout monk who lived by the Kuzu River, at the foot of Mount Hira, took no grain and ate only wild greens. Once he dreamed a holy being told him, "There's an Immortal on Mount Hira and he chants the Lotus. Go and get his blessing."

Though he climbed Mount Hira right away, it was only after days of hunting that he heard far, far off a chanting voice. He was exhausted, and the day nearly done, when he finally discovered a cave under an overhanging crag. The great pine before it was shaped like a broad, conical hat. Peering in, he saw the Immortal. His bones had no flesh on them and his only robe was moss.

"Who are you?" the Immortal asked. "No one has ever been here before."

"I live by the Kuzu River, and a dream told me to get your blessing."

"Then first keep away from me for a while. The smoke of the human world makes my eyes sting and water. Come to me in seven days."

The monk retreated twenty yards or so from the cave, while the Immortal chanted the Sutra day and night. His voice was deeply moving, and the monk felt as though all the sins he had committed through beginningless time were melting away. The deer, the bears, the monkeys, and all the other creatures of feather and fur brought the Immortal nuts and seeds, and the Immortal had a monkey give the monk some, too. Seven days later the monk approached the cave.

"I used to be a monk and a scholar," the Immortal said, "and I did my best to master the approved doctrines. But I read in the Lotus Sutra, 'He will regret it, who does not take this Sutra to heart,' and I believed it. The Sutra said to practice in a place apart, so I did. Then my karma led me to this cave, and I left the human world altogether. With the eye of the One Teaching I see things far off, and with the ear of Compassion I hear all sounds. I've been to the heaven where the Future Buddha lives, and I've heard the Buddha speak. The pine shelters me from heat and wind. Stay with me, since your own karma has brought you here!"

The awed monk dearly wanted to say yes, but he knew that a life like that was beyond him. Instead, he prostrated himself and started for home. The Immortal's power brought him to the Kuzu River in a day.

ANOTHER FLYING JAR

A hermit once built a small hut on the upper Kiyotaki River, not far north of Kyoto. When he was thirsty, he would send his water jar flying down to the stream and it would bring him back all the water he needed. As the years went by, he often thought proudly to himself that there could hardly be a more accomplished hermit anywhere.

One day he was surprised to see another water jar fly down from upstream, draw water, and leave, and he wondered jealously who else could be performing this feat. When the jar came again, he followed it a few miles upstream to a hut — quite a large one, with a nice little chapel of its own. The place breathed purity, holiness, and peace. Before the hut was an orange tree with a path round it, worn by the inhabitant as he circled the tree chanting his sutras.

Peering in through the window, the hermit saw a desk strewn with sutra scrolls and a room filled with the smoke of perpetual incense. A saintly-looking monk at least seventy years old was sleeping propped on an armrest, with a five-pronged vajra in his hand.

To test this venerable old man, the hermit began the Spell of the Fire Realm. Flames instantly sprang up and licked at the hut. Still asleep, the old man picked up a wand and sprinkled the four directions with holy water. The flames went out, but by now the hermit's own robe was burning fiercely and he howled in terror, at which the old man opened his eyes and sprinkled his visitor as well. The flames vanished.

"What happened?" the old man asked.

The hermit explained himself and described his little test. "Please forgive me!" he begged. "I'll serve you forever as your disciple!" But the old man seemed to have no idea what he was talking about.

The hermit had become puffed up with pride and the Buddha, displeased, had shown him for his edification a far holier saint — or so at least people say.

8 8 .

THE WIZARD OF THE MOUNTAINS

En no Gyōja founded Japan's mountain ascetic
tradition. The Peacock King is an Esoteric Buddhist deity.

En no Gyōja, or En the Ascetic, lived in Emperor Mommu's reign. He was from the Katsuragi region of Yamato province.

He lost his father when he was two and was brought up entirely by his mother at their family home. At the age of thirty-four, he turned the house into a temple and respectfully enshrined there an eight-foot-tall image of Miroku which he himself had made out of earth. Then he gave the temple to the court and went to live in a cave in the Katsuragi Mountains, wearing clothes made of bark and eating pine needles. Though he never went into the world or mixed with people, he practiced nonetheless as a layman rather than as a monk.

From the Katsuragi Mountains you can look southeast across to the Ōmine range. En no Gyōja roamed there, too. One day in Ōmine he glimpsed Shaka Peak from far off and was struck by its unusual form. The mountain clearly had power. Up close it was even more impressive. En no Gyōja found there, hanging from a tree, a nine-foot-tall skeleton with a bell in its left hand and a single-pronged vajra in its right. The skeleton's grip on these two implements was like iron, and En no Gyōja was unable to pry them loose.

So strange a discovery inspired him to vigorous faith. That night he dreamed that the Miroku he so deeply revered (the one he had made for his temple) said to him, "For seven of your past lives you were an ascetic on this mountain. The skeleton you found is your own. If you want the bell and the vajra, chant the Mantra of the Peacock King."

En no Gyōja went away to learn the mantra, and acquired superhuman powers as soon as he began chanting it. He could now fly through space wherever he wanted on a five-colored cloud. When he returned to Shaka Peak, he found the bell and vajra on the ground below the tree. The skeleton was gone.

North of Shaka Peak, in the same range, rises Golden Peak. This sacred mountain is actually the northeast corner of Vulture Peak in India where the Buddha preached the Lotus Sutra. In 552, during the reign of Emperor Kimmei, it broke off and flew thousands of leagues on a white cloud to land here in Japan. When Miroku comes into our world as the next buddha, 5,670,000,000 years from now, the earth will be covered with gold; and all the gold for this purpose is stored in Golden Peak. That is why the mountain's gravel and rocks are gold, and why the mountain bears that name.

Seeing how powerful Golden Peak was, En no Gyōja wanted it to have a god who could help sentient beings toward salvation. After he had prayed for a thousand days, Zaō Gongen rose from the earth. Since Zaō Gongen looked rather like the Bodhisattva Jizō, very quiet and kind, En no Gyōja wondered how a god like that could possibly save deluded beings in the sinful ages to come. As the thought crossed his mind, the peaceful, Jizō-like figure disappeared into the sky.

En no Gyōja prayed anew, and this time Zaō Gongen burst forth in a wrathful form, brandishing a three-pronged vajra in his right hand, and standing in the fierce pose of crushing demons. Finally impressed, En no Gyōja made an image of him and enshrined it on the mountain. In time Zaō Gongen appeared like this on mountains throughout Japan. How great a god En no Gyōja had called forth!

Next, En no Gyōja went into retreat in a cave in these same mountains, and his magic brought supernatural beings to serve him and bring him water and firewood. He also spent years going round Japan, visiting Mount Fuji, Mount Asama, and all the other sacred mountains. Sometimes he also visited the Palace of the Immortals and roamed the Immortals' marvelous realm.

Eventually En no Gyōja decided he wanted a stone bridge from the Katsuragi Mountains to Golden Peak, one that his followers could cross; and he commanded the god Hitokotonushi to build it.

Some two centuries before, when Emperor Yūryaku came to Katsuragi to hunt, Hitokotonushi had ridden beside him all day in the guise of a lordly man; and when the emperor asked his unknown companion who he was, Hitokotonushi replied simply, "the god of Katsuragi," then vanished. Normally, though, the god was so ugly that he was embarrassed to be seen in daylight, and as a result would work on the bridge only at night. This made En no Gyōja angry. He insisted that Hitokotonushi work also during the day. When the god refused, the furious Gyōja bound him with a spell and left him at the bottom of a ravine. That is why the rock bridge never was built.

Soon afterwards, a young attendant of Emperor Mommu began to speak volubly and strangely under the influence of a god who identified himself under questioning as Hitokotonushi of Katsuragi. The god went on to accuse En no Gyōja of using his magic powers to foment rebellion. "If he is not stopped," warned the god, "there will be war!"

The astonished emperor immediately sent the Gyōja an order to appear before him, but the Gyōja ignored it. Next, the emperor sent soldiers to arrest him, but the Gyōja simply flew up and disappeared. The soldiers retaliated by capturing his mother and taking her back to the emperor instead. This brought En no Gyōja to the palace right away, and his innocent mother was released and sent home.

En no Gyōja was exiled to Oshima in the province of Izu, along the coast of Sagami Bay. During the day he behaved himself and stayed where he had been put, but at night he flew through the air and roamed the summit of Mount Fuji. Hitokotonushi got back at him by again possessing the imperial attendant and accusing the Gyōja of wandering wherever he pleased in contempt of the imperial will. Hitokotonushi demanded that the Gyōja be put to death.

The emperor took this denunciation seriously and sent a soldier to execute the sentence. But when the soldier reached Oshima and drew his bow to shoot the Gyōja, the bow broke; and when he lifted his sword to strike the Gyōja, the sword broke too. Next the Gyōja asked for the sword, and the soldier gave it to him. Before handing it back, the ascetic licked it three times. The soldier now read, engraved on the sword, the name of the god of Mount Fuji. Overcome with awe, he returned to the emperor with his report, and the emperor, finally realizing that En no Gyōja was no ordinary man, pardoned him and recalled him to the Capital.

By now, though, En no Gyōja no longer knew what would happen next and was fed up with Japan. So instead, he put his mother in a bowl and set off to China across ten thousand leagues of sky, riding on a five-colored cloud. In China, too, he toured every sacred peak and consorted with the Immortals. In fact, a Japanese monk whom the emperor had sent to China to study Buddhism ran into him and spent some time talking to him. The monk reported this meeting when he got back to Japan, much to the astonishment of the court since it was then almost impossible for anyone to travel to China without imperial authorization.

In the meantime, En no Gyōja's fight with Hitokotonushi was not quite over. The last episode involved the monk Taichō from Echizen province, a great ascetic whose powers were acknowledged throughout the realm. Taichō was the vessel of the god of Hakusan, or White Mountain, in Kaga province; for the god often possessed Taichō and spoke through him.

Taichō too set out on a pilgrimage to all the holy mountains of Japan. Having heard that the Katsuragi and Ōmine ranges were particularly powerful, he first climbed Katsuragi and spent the night chanting sutras there for the god.

When he dozed off, the god took this chance to speak to him. "En no

Gyōja has bound me with a spell," he complained, "and he's left me at the bottom of the ravine. I'm suffering horribly. Please, Your Grace, use your power to free me and heal my pain!" In his dream Taichō saw that the god was imprisoned in a mossy boulder.

On waking he went straight down into the ravine and found the boulder. It was tightly imprisoned by wisteria and other vines. Taichō could see how much the god must be suffering, and felt sorry for him. But when he tried a spell to loosen the vines, the Gyōja, whom rumor placed in China, suddenly appeared, roaring and glaring at him in fury. The frightened Taichō gave up and left the mountain immediately.

Perhaps En no Gyōja stayed on in Katsuragi. At any rate, he was eventually commanded in a dream to go to Mount Minoo in the province of Settsu where, high on the mountain, there is a magnificent waterfall. En no Gyōja was performing his practices by this fall when the legendary Buddhist sage Nagarjuna, whom we in Japan call Ryūju Bosatsu, descended from the heavens, gave him the Water of Pure Knowledge, and sailed up again into the sky again on a cloud. This miracle inspired the Gyōja to build on the spot a temple, which he called Minoodera. He stayed at Minoo a long time, and finally rose into the heavens at the age of 104.

No one ever tried to free Hitokotonushi again.

8 9 .

AN AWFUL FALL

An ascetic at a mountain temple in Yamato province once decided that from now on he would eat only pine needles. He was quite happy to give up rice and the other grains, and in fact much preferred this austere diet, because he had heard that this was the way others in the past had made themselves into Immortals who could fly.

After two or three years of nothing but pine needles, the ascetic really did feel very light. He began telling his disciples that he would soon be an Immortal too, and was so sure of success that he secretly prepared to fly up into the sky. When the moment seemed at hand, he announced his coming ascension and gave away his hut and all his belongings.

He knew that when he took to the air he would find himself clothed in the robe of an Immortal, so he put on nothing but the simplest and most abbreviated wrap; for, he said, he now needed nothing more. Then he strode forth with his water jar (his last and most prized possession) slung from his waist.

A large crowd had gathered to watch him go to the Land of the Immortals. When all the spectators were in place, he climbed to a spur of rock that jutted from the mountainside. "Of course, I'd rather go straight up," he explained, "but since all these people are here I suppose I really ought to give them a good look at a proper Immortal in action. So first I'll glide down from here to those pines and land on a branch."

It was forty or fifty feet down to the tops of the pines. The ascetic dove off head first and the crowd roared. Unfortunately, his body was heavier than he expected, and his strength far less. Missing his target entirely, he crashed to the ground. Though shaken, the crowd remained confident (after all, he must surely have known what he was doing!) that at any moment he would rise again into the air.

Actually he had smashed into a rock. His water jar was in smithereens and so was he, or very nearly. His horrified disciples desperately called his name but got no reply. Since he was at least still breathing, though, they hauled him back to his hut while the crowd dispersed, laughing derisively.

He survived in the end, but was so twisted and broken that he could hardly even stand. He had to take back the hut and possessions he had so bravely given away, and lived on crooked and hopeless.

Not everyone gets to be an Immortal.

9 0 .

THE RICEPOOP SAINT

A holy ascetic in the reign of Emperor Montoku had long ago given up all grain, which was a very difficult and virtuous thing to do. He ate pine needles instead. The emperor heard about him and invited him to come and live in the imperial garden. In time the emperor came to revere the ascetic deeply.

One day some brash young courtiers were joking among themselves when they decided to go and have a look at this famous ascetic. The fellow certainly looked impressive, and the young lords prostrated themselves before him. Then they boldly asked him, "Holy man, how many years has it been since you gave up eating grain? And how old are you, anyway?"

"I'm seventy," the ascetic replied, "and I gave up grain in my youth. That must be fifty years ago or so, I suppose."

One of the young gentlemen now began to wonder what a man's feces would look like if he took no grain. They would have to be a bit unusual. He took his friends off to sneak a peek into the ascetic's privy. What they saw was full of rice. How could this be?

Back they went to the ascetic's hut, and while he was gone for moment, they rolled up the mat he had been sitting on. There was a hole in the floor under it and the earth below had been disturbed. They were onto something. A little digging revealed a sack of white rice. "Well, well!" thought the young lords, putting everything back as it had been.

When the holy man returned they broke into broad grins. "Riceshit saint! Riceshit saint!" they chanted, roaring with laughter. The mortified ascetic fled and was never heard of again.

ODDITIES

WHAT THE STORM WASHED IN

Late one spring, in Hitachi province, there was a terrific storm, and in the course of a furious night a human corpse was washed up on the beach. It was more than fifty feet long, and even though it was half buried in the sand, all you could see of a rider passing by on the other side of it was the tip of the rider's bow. The head was gone, as were the right arm and the left leg. No doubt they had been eaten by the creatures of the deep. What a being this must have been when alive and whole! Since the body lay on its front, it was hard to be sure whether it was a man or a woman, but the overall shape suggested a woman.

The discovery created a sensation. People came from far away to see the prodigy and to offer one theory or another about its origin. One learned monk declared that there was nothing in the words of the Buddha to suggest that the inhabitants of any of the lands in our world are giants; he could only suppose that this impressive specimen must belong to the race of Warring Demons who are said sometimes to live at the bottom of the sea.

Meanwhile the provincial administration had decided they had to report so unusual a find to the court, and they were about to do so when the local people protested. "If we report it," they said, "a court emissary will be down here for a look, and we'll have no end of trouble and expense entertaining him. No, it would be much better to hush the whole thing up." So in the end the governor kept the discovery quiet.

As the days went by, the processes of decomposition set in and people for hundreds of yards around had to evacuate their houses. The stench was just too much.

Of course, the governor told the whole story when he got back to the Capital.

9 2 .

SEA DEVILS

Eight days into the seventh moon of 1171 a ship put in to Oki Island in the province of Izu. The islanders assumed that it had been blown in by a storm and went to have a look.

The ship rode seventy or eighty yards offshore. As the islanders watched, the devils on board let down ropes and moored it on all four sides to rocks on the sea bottom. Then eight devils jumped into the sea and shortly emerged on land. The islanders offered them food and millet wine. Though they never said a word, the devils ate and drank like horses.

The devils were eight or nine feet tall, with wild and tangled hair. Their bodies were blackish and hairless, and their eyes as round as monkeys' eyes. Apart from some seaweed they had wrapped around their waists they were naked, but all sorts of pictures were drawn on their skin, with a sort of outline frame around each. Each devil carried a good long staff.

A devil asked to see one of the islanders' bow and arrows. When the islander hesitated, the devil killed him with one blow of his staff. The devils then struck eight others, of whom four died while four, though wounded, survived. Next, the devils belched fire from their sides. Thinking they were all going to be killed, the islanders took out the bows and arrows belonging to the god of their shrine and prepared to defend themselves. At this point the devils went back into the sea and swam underwater out to their ship. Then they sailed away against the wind.

On the fourteenth day of the tenth moon, a report on the incident was forwarded to the provincial government, together with a sash that one of the devils had dropped. They say the sash is now in the treasury of Sanjūsangendō, the famous temple in Kyoto.

9 3 .

THE DANCING MUSHROOM

Four or five woodcutters from the Capital once went into the mountains north of the city and, as fortune would have it, got lost. They were puzzling over which way to go when they heard people coming down the hillside. Who could they be? Four or five nuns, singing and dancing their way along, as jolly as you please. The woodcutters took fright. Real nuns would never behave this way! They couldn't be human! No, they must be tengu, or demons of some sort!

The nuns made straight for the woodcutters who, despite their alarm, managed to ask the estimable ladies why they were carrying on that way, and why on top of everything else they were coming down from high on the mountain.

"Oh dear, all our dancing and singing must have rather frightened you!" the nuns replied. "You see, we're nuns from such-and-such a convent. We all went into the mountains to pick flowers for the altar and then got completely lost. When we noticed some mushrooms, we realized we were hungry. Of course we realized the mushrooms might be poisonous, but we decided we might as well go ahead and eat them as starve. They tasted good. Then we began dancing. We didn't *mean* to dance, you see, we just found ourselves doing it. We were quite surprised!"

The startled woodcutters now noticed how hungry they were. The nuns had kept their leftover mushrooms. "Why, rather than starve," thought the men, "we might as well beg some off the nuns and eat too!" So they did.

As soon as they had eaten the mushrooms they found themselves dancing. Nuns and woodcutters danced and laughed together, and when the drunkenness passed they went their separate ways, thought by what paths no one knows. Ever since, that mushroom has been called *maitake*, the "dancing mushroom."

All in all, the incident is a bit odd. We have this *maitake* too, in our own time, but the people who eat it don't always dance. On balance the story is dubious, as even they who tell it readily confess.

9 4 ·

THE BEST-LAID PLANS ...

There once lived an old monk who was the abbot of the temple at Golden Peak. In those days (although no longer) the senior monk of the mountain got appointed abbot, and this one had been a monk longer than any of his colleagues.

The next monk in line often wished his superior would hurry up and die, but being a sturdy old fellow the abbot gave no sign of popping off. In fact, at past eighty he was obviously more hale and hearty than anyone had a right to be even at seventy, and the successor knew all too well that he himself was now in his seventieth year. "Why, I could actually die and *never* be abbot!" the successor groaned to himself. "I can't just have him murdered. Someone would be bound to find out. I'll have to poison him!"

Of course the successor was afraid of how the Buddha might feel about this, but the temptation was too great and he began to think about what *kind* of poison to use. What poison was really deadly? Well, there was a toadstool called "great beyond" that was sure to kill anyone who ate it. He would gather plenty of great beyonds, make a really delicious dish of them, and feed them to the abbot as ordinary mushrooms. That would take care of him. "And then *I'll* be abbot," the successor gloated.

It was fall. He went straight off by himself into the mountains, gathered lots of great beyonds, and at dusk brought them back to his hut.

Then he cut them up into a pot, seasoned them nicely, and made them up into a very attractive stew.

The new day had hardly dawned when he sent a disciple to invite the abbot over right away. The abbot arrived, leaning on his cane. "Yesterday I was given some beautiful mushrooms," the successor explained, "so I made a stew of them and thought you should have some. It's when you're old that you appreciate delicacies like this!"

The abbot smiled, nodded, and sat down. His host made rice, heated up the great beyond stew, and set them both before him. The abbot ate heartily. As for the host, he ate mushrooms he had prepared separately.

They ended their meal with a hot drink. "Well, that's it," thought the successor, and waited anxiously for the old boy to start acting crazy and going mad with a headache. But nothing happened. It was very odd. Then the abbot's toothless mouth broke into a grin. "Best batch of great beyonds I ever tasted!" he declared.

He had known! The successor stole speechless from the room while the abbot went on home. The abbot had been enjoying great beyonds for years, though of course the successor had not known this, and had never been poisoned by them. So the whole clever plan went wrong.

9 5 .

REAL FLAMES AT LAST!

When a neighbor's house caught fire and the wind threatened to carry the flames to his own, Yoshihide, a painter of buddhas, ran out into the street. He left inside a painting of Fudō he had been working on, not to mention his wife and children, who at the time were not even fully clothed. He forgot all about them and was quite satisfied to have gotten out himself.

Yoshihide's own house was soon smoking and burning, but he just watched from across the street, ignoring the neighbors who rushed in horror to help him. As he watched his house go up, he nodded agreement from time to time, or smiled. "What a sight! All these years I've been painting them wrong!" he finally muttered.

One of the neighbors told him he was crazy. "Some spirit must have gotten into you!" he said.

"Spirit?" answered Yoshihide. "Oh no, it's the flames. For years I've been painting the flames of Lord Fudō's halo all wrong. Now I see how they burn. What a sight! You're not a painter so you wouldn't understand." He laughed mockingly.

The Fudō he painted next impresses everyone, now as then.

9 6 .

THE PAINTED HORSE

The painter Kanaoka made many pictures for retired Emperor Uda's palace, and the best of all was one of a horse painted on a wall. That horse would get out of the painting every night and eat his way through the neighboring fields. No one could figure out what was doing all the damage until finally someone noticed that every day there was fresh mud on the painted horse's hooves, and put two and two together. Kanaoka promptly scraped off the horse's eyes. Nothing bothered the fields after that.

G O L D E N   P E A K
A N D   T H E   Ō M I N E
M O U N T A I N S

9 7 ·

A MODEL DEMON

Nichizō led the life of a wandering hermit in the Ōmine Mountains. One day on a remote trail he met a seven-foot-tall, dark-blue demon with red hair like flames, a slender neck, a grossly protruding breastbone, a swollen belly, and skinny shanks. The demon turned to Nichizō beseechingly and began to weep.

Nichizō asked it how it had gotten that way. "Four or five hundred years ago I was a man," the demon sobbed, "but then my grudge against someone I hated made me like this. Yes, I murdered him and his sons, his grandsons, his great-grandsons, and his great-great-grandsons too, and now there's no one left for me to kill. If only I knew where they were reborn, I'd murder them all over again. My rage burns as fiercely as ever, but my enemy's descendants are gone! Now I'm alone with the pain of this fire that nothing will extinguish. If I'd never felt this way I might even have been born into paradise, but hate has brought me an eternity of suffering. A grudge against someone else is just like a grudge against yourself. I wish I'd known, I only wish I'd known!"

The demon's tears swelled to a flood as it spoke, and flames leaped from the top of its head. Suddenly it turned and fled further into the mountains.

Nichizō felt sorry for it and prayed the best he knew how that it might suffer less.

9 8 .

THE RIVER OF SNAKES

Nichizō's master, like his disciple, practiced in the Ōmine Mountains, and he never left his remote refuge to visit the profane world. For years he chanted the Darani of Thousand-Armed Kannon in a deep valley toward the southern end of the range.

He had found the valley after a long struggle down slopes thick with dwarf bamboo. After assuming at first that it was waterless, he saw water after all; but the "water" then turned out to be a mass of huge snakes whose undulating backs from a distance resembled a stream. They seemed to have caught the intruder's scent on the wind because they lifted their heads in the air as he approached.

Their backs were dark blue-green and their throats a lustrous crimson, while their eyes glittered like polished bronze bowls and their tongues flickered like flames. The ascetic thought he was lost and scrambled back up the steep slope, pulling himself along as best he could by the tough dwarf bamboo stems. He made such slow progress that hot, fetid serpent breath was soon gusting up at him from below. Any moment he would be devoured, if he did not black out first and die from the horrible smell.

Something was coming down the slope toward him, although he was too dazed by the stench to be able to tell what it was. The thing seized his arm and slung him roughly across its shoulders. Terrified, he felt over the creature with his free hand but found nothing reassuring. It was clearly a demon and would only be hauling him off to eat him. His last thought before he passed out was that today, one way or another, he would die.

The demon raced up hill and down dale till it put down its burden on a distant peak. The ascetic came to and expected the end, but since nothing happened he asked the demon timidly what it was. "I'm the demon Kuhanda," it answered. At last the ascetic opened his eyes. Naked but for a loincloth, the creature was ten feet tall. Its black skin glistened like lacquer and its red hair bristled straight up. Suddenly it turned away and vanished.

The ascetic realized that his own devotion to Thousand-Armed Kannon must have saved him, because only Thousand-Armed Kannon could have come to his aid. The thought brought tears to his eyes and he prostrated himself in thanks.

He set off toward the northeast, all the while chanting the darani, till he came to a waterfall tumbling a good fifty feet from among the crags. It was so beautiful that he stopped awhile to admire it. The moss on the rocks beside it was especially lovely. All at once a boulder many yards across rose from the pool at the base of the fall, thrust twenty feet into the air, then sank again. Shortly it rose and subsided as before. The ascetic watched the cycle several times with mounting astonishment till he saw that the rock was actually a huge snake which filled the pool and which was lifting its head into the pounding waters of the fall. The snake must have been there so long! Despite his fear and loathing, he was touched by compassion for the snake's suffering, and he recited many sutras for it and called often on Thousand-Armed Kannon before he went his way.

9 9 ·

THE WINE SPRING

Once a monk passing though the Ōmine Mountains lost his way and found himself heading down into a totally unknown valley. In the valley was a large village.

He was looking forward to asking where he was, but first he came to a roofed spring. The ground all around it was paved with stone. When he went for a welcome drink, he found that the water was all yellow. It turned out actually to be wine.

While he puzzled over this amazing discovery, a crowd of villagers gathered and wanted to know who he was. He explained how he happened to be there.

"Come with me," one said. The monk followed unwillingly, wondering where they were off to and whether he would be killed. They got to a large, prosperous house and a gentleman came out to meet them. He too asked the monk to explain himself and the monk told his story as before.

The gentleman invited him in, fed him, and turned him over to a young man who was to escort him to "the usual place." Apparently the gentleman was the mayor. The monk quaked to imagine what "the usual place" might be, but there was no escape.

The young man led him to a deserted spot in the mountains where he announced that he had brought him there to kill him. "People have wandered into the village as you did several times in the past," he explained. "We've always killed them because we're afraid they'll talk about us in the world outside. No one out there has any idea our village even exists, you see."

The monk's mind froze, but in tears he managed to remind the young man that being a monk he followed the path of the Buddha and was dedicated to the welfare of all. That was why he had been passing through these mountains in the first place. "You have no idea of the sacrifices I've made, of labors I've performed in pursuit of my goal!" he went on. "And now you're going to kill me just because I lost my way! Of course I'm going to die in the end, I know. Everyone is. That's not what I mind. It's just that it's such an awful sin for *you* to kill a blameless monk! Please, please, won't you let me live?"

"I see," the young man replied. "Yes, I'd like to let you go. But I'm so afraid of what would happen if you talked about us outside!"

"Oh, but I *won't* talk about you, of course I won't. A man values his life more than anything and he never forgets what he owes someone who's saved him!"

"Well, all right. You're a monk. I can see that. I'll let you go, as long as you'll keep this knowledge to yourself. I can just pretend I killed you."

The monk swore every way he knew how that he would keep his mouth shut, and the young man, with many repetitions of his caution, showed him the path back to the outside world. One last time the monk bowed to his benefactor, assuring him that he would never forget his kindness as long as he lived. Then with tears of emotion on both sides the two parted, and the monk followed the trail till it rejoined the normal path through the mountains.

In due course he got back to the village he had started from. Of course he had sworn himself to silence many times over, but he was a great talker and was soon spouting the whole story to everyone. The general reaction was "Tell me another!" but he described the village and the spring of wine in such eloquent detail that some high-spirited youths decided to check. It would be one thing if those villagers were gods or demons, but apparently they were just people. They could not be as scary as all that.

Half a dozen of the strongest young braves set out, each armed with a bow, arrows, and a club, and the monk went with them. Several older, more responsible people tried to stop them, warning them not to engage a completely unknown community on their own ground, but the hotheads paid no attention. The monk's eloquence had fired their imaginations. The parents and relatives who remained behind were very worried.

The party did not return that day or the next. In fact, they never came back at all. No one volunteered to go after them. Amid lamentations, the matter was dropped. No doubt the whole party had been massacred.

That monk had really distinguished himself with all his talk. He would have done better to leave well enough alone, and his audience would have done better still to ignore his prattle!

1 0 0 .

VERY HIGH IN THE MOUNTAINS

The monk Giei spent his life roaming from province to province, visiting every holy site in the land. In his travels he made a pilgrimage to Kumano and from there passed northward into the Ōmine Mountains.

He was headed for Golden Peak, but got so lost on the way that he could no longer tell east from west. A good blast on the conch he had slung at his waist got no answer. Next he climbed a peak for a better view, but all he could see from the top was valley after dim valley.

After ten days Giei was so desperate that he begged the buddha of his portable altar to lead him back to civilization. As he prayed he came to a handsome wood with a pretty little house inside it, surrounded by a broad garden strewn with white sand. The shrubs were as green as green could be, and it was a marvel to see flowers blooming everywhere amid a profusion of ripe berries and fruit.

What a cheering sight! In the house a monk no older than twenty was chanting the Lotus Sutra in a sublime voice that touched the depths of Giei's being. Each chapter was a separate scroll. As soon as the monk had finished one and laid it on his desk, the scroll would rise into the air, roll itself back up cover and all, tie its own cords neatly, and settle back down. Scroll by scroll, the monk went through the whole Sutra. Giei was awed and frightened.

The holy man stood up. He did not hide his astonishment on seeing his visitor. "No human has ever been here before," he said. "I'm so high in the mountains that I seldom even hear the birds singing in the valleys. Who are you?"

Giei explained that he was a monk and lost. The holy man invited him in, and some beautiful acolytes served him a delicious meal that made him forget all about hunger and starvation. He asked the holy man how long he had lived here and why he lacked nothing.

"I've been here eighty years," the holy man answered. "Once I was a monk on Mount Hiei, but I'm sorry to say there was a little trouble between me and my master and he refused to keep me with him any longer. I couldn't think of anything else to do but go roaming. Of course I was young and strong then, and I worshipped at all the holy places. When I got old I took refuge in these mountains, and I've been here ever since, waiting for death."

Giei listened with growing amazement. "You say no one comes here," he insisted, "but you have three beautiful acolytes serving you. Surely you can't be serious!"

"The Sutra itself says, 'Celestial boys will come to serve the one who upholds this Sutra.' Is it really so strange?"

"You say you're old, but as far as I can see you're in the flower of youth. Are you sure you're telling me your real age?"

"The Sutra says, 'He who hears this Sutra will never be ill, nor will he grow old and die.' I'm only telling you the truth."

When the holy man told Giei it was time for him to leave, Giei spoke of the suffering he had just gone through, and reminded the holy man of his starved and weakened condition. He assured the holy man that he wanted to serve him for the rest of his life.

"It's not that I dislike you," the holy man answered. "But I've spent all these years far away from people, and that's why I have to insist that you go. If you want to stay one night and no more, you must promise me you won't move or make a sound." Giei promised and got himself out of sight.

Soon after dark an eerie little breeze sprang up. From his hiding place Giei watched supernatural beings arrive in all sorts of extraordinary forms. Some had the heads of horses, oxen, or birds, while some were shaped like deer. They crowded in with offerings of incense, flowers, nuts, fruit, and drink, and after placing all these good things before the hut they prostrated themselves in perfect order with palms pressed together. Suddenly one among them remarked, "Strange! It's different here tonight! I smell man!" Giei was so upset he moved, but the holy man came to his rescue by intoning the Sutra and kept it up all night long. At dawn he ended by dedicating the merit of his chanting to all beings, and the bizarre company dispersed.

Giei crept out and asked where all the creatures had come from. The holy man reminded him that the Buddha says in the Sutra, "If there is no one to hear the Law, then I will send celestial beings, dragon kings, earth spirits, and demons to be the congregation."

Though ready to leave now, Giei still did not know the way. The holy man told him to go straight south. He put a water jar outside the house, and it rose into the air and headed slowly southward. Giei followed it for hours to a mountaintop, where he looked down and saw a large village below him. The jar soared into the sky and disappeared. Giei realized that he was back where he had started from. He told the villagers, with tears of emotion, how he had met the Immortal, and all who heard him bowed their heads in awe.

No human ever found the Immortal's retreat again.

THE GOD OF FIRE AND THUNDER

*This is a true vision. The statesman Sugawara no
Michizane (845–903) was exiled unjustly by Emperor
Daigo in 901 and soon died, heartbroken. When
disasters began to occur, people believed that his
vengeful ghost was causing them. Within twenty years,
Michizane had been posthumously reinstated and promoted,
and in 959 the great Kitano Shrine, even now a Kyoto
landmark, was built for his spirit. The god's name is
still known as Tenjin. Students pray to him
for success in their examinations.*

This is what the Venerable Nichizō wrote in the *Account of a Visit to the
Afterworld*, which he set down in 941, shortly after the event.

I was born in the Capital. Early in 916 I shaved my head and took
religious vows at a temple in the Ōmine Mountains. I was then in my
twelfth year.

For six years I led an ascetic life, taking no salt or grain, and only left
the mountains when I heard my mother was suffering from a long illness
and calling constantly for me. I went to Kyoto to see her in the spring of
921, then returned to the mountains. Since then I have continued going
into the mountains every spring. This is the twenty-sixth year I have
done so.

Meanwhile many disasters have troubled the realm. I gather that people have noted many strange dreams, and that things have seldom gone
as they should. The movements of the heavenly bodies and the signs of
yin and yang have constantly announced misfortune. That is why I decided to seek divine help. I went deeper than ever into the mountain
wilderness and redoubled my efforts, for my own sake and for the sake
of the peace and prosperity of the realm. I vowed to fast, keep silent, and
contemplate the Buddha for three times seven days.

At midday on the first of the eighth moon of 941, while I was absorbed
in my rite, I began to burn with heat. My throat and tongue dried up and
my windpipe closed. Knowing that I could not speak or call for help, I
wept and simply struggled for breath. Then my breathing stopped and I
died.

I left my cave, carrying my sutra scrolls as I always do when I go into the mountains, and looked around to see what direction to take. As I did so, a hermit monk appeared in the cave. He had a golden jar and poured me some water from it. The water's delicious taste filled me.

The hermit said, "I am Shū Kongō Shin, the Divine Vajra-Bearer. From my cave I guard the Buddha Shaka's Teaching. Your devotion all these years has impressed me, venerable monk, and I brought you this water from the Himalayas."

The celestial acolytes with him brought in all sorts of delicacies, heaped them onto large lotus leaves, and served them to me. The hermit explained that the acolytes were the Twenty-Eight Gods who protect the esoteric adept.

Just then a noble monk descended from a peak to the west and held out his left hand for me to take. He led me straight up the peak, which was thousands of feet deep in snow. From the top of the mountain I saw all the worlds spread out below.

The mountain was very beautiful. Its flat summit was immaculate, and a golden radiance shone everywhere. To the north rose a golden prominence with a throne on it made of the seven treasures: gold, silver, lapis lazuli, rock crystal, jade, coral, and agate.

The monk sat on this throne. "I am Zaō Gongen, a form of Shaka," he said. "This is the Paradise of Golden Peak. You have only a few years left to live. Give your all to build up merit!"

I answered that life itself meant nothing to me. "But having chosen a spot to do just as you say," I continued, "I now find my life is nearly over before I've achieved my goal! Please tell me how many years I have left. What buddha should I serve, what rite should I do so as to prolong my life?"

The monk took a tablet, wrote eight characters on it, and gave it to me. I read, SUN STORE NINE NINE YEARS MONTHS KING GUARD.

"Son of the Buddha," he said, "your life is like a cloud that catches a moment on the mountain, then drifts off and melts into the sky. It is easily lost. But practice in the mountains will lengthen it, while living among men would make you lazy and would cut it short. SUN and STORE (NICHI ZO) mean the buddha and the rite you know. Before, your name was Dōken, but now you must take your new name, Nichizō, which come from this buddha and this rite. NINE NINE is the age you'll live to. YEARS and MONTHS mean time. KING and GUARD mean you'll be protected. Your new master is Gohō Bosatsu, the Protector of the Law. You've already vowed before your first teacher to observe the rules of Buddhist conduct, but the Protector of the Law will administer the vow to you again."

There was a brilliant burst of rainbow light. The monk said, "Behold Daijō Tenjin, the Great Celestial Statesman!"

Instantly a numberless multitude approached from the void above the mountains to the west. It might have been an emperor's enthronement procession. Servants and retainers of species unknown, in unheard-of forms, flocked endlessly past. Terrifying to look at, some resembled vajra guardians, others thunder gods or demon kings. Each was armed to the teeth with quiver and bow, spear, scimitar, and staff.

Daijō Tenjin was going to pass on by when he noticed me. "Come, good hermit," he said to me, "I want to show you my castle. I'll bring you back here afterwards. Will that be all right?"

Zaō Gongen said I could go. I got up behind Daijō Tenjin on his white horse, and after hundreds of leagues we came to a vast lake. In the middle of the lake was a large island a hundred leagues wide, with a square dais on it sixteen feet on a side. A lotus flower rose from the center of the dais, and a jewel-tower above it enshrined the Lotus Sutra. To the east and west hung the Womb-Store Realm and the Vajra-Realm mandalas. Everything was indescribably beautiful.

Then I looked to the north and saw a great citadel brilliant with light. It was Daijō Tenjin's castle. Daijō Tenjin's countless train poured into it and stood guard.

"I am the Sugawara no Michizane who once lived in your land," Daijō Tenjin said to me. "The Thirty-Three Heavens know me as Nippon Daijō Itoku Ten, the Celestial Statesman of Great Majesty from Japan. The pain of parting from those one loves, when I first encountered it, did not leave me unmoved; and that is why I now burn to torment the emperor and his ministers, to wound the people, and to smite the realm. I govern all sicknesses and all calamities.

"I first thought to turn to this vengeful purpose all the tears I shed while I lived, because they would surely overwhelm the land and leave it a faceless ocean. After thirty-two years I established my own land and built a castle for myself. Meanwhile great saints were spreading the Esoteric teachings, teachings which for me have always had a great appeal, and so the rage I once felt largely receded. Then all the enlightened Emanations and Bodhisattvas, in their goodness and mercy, named even me a god. Some of these Emanations live on mountaintops and in forests, others on the banks of rivers or on the shore of the sea, and all bent their supernatural wisdom to calming and comforting me. That is why I still have not visited any dire catastrophe on Japan. But my followers, who number 168,000 evil deities, work their mischief everywhere. Even I cannot restrain them, still less could any other god."

I said to him, "Everyone in my country calls you Celestial God of Fire and Thunder, and we revere you as we do the Buddha Shaka himself. Why are you still so angry?"

"I am your land's implacable enemy," he answered. "Who in Japan honors me? The name of my messenger is Venomous King of the Celestial Essences of Fire and Thunder. Never, never will I forget, till I myself reach enlightenment, the wrongs done me all those years ago! I shall see that whoever held a post at court while I lived is wounded and struck down. But today I acknowledge you my master and I make you this promise. Should anyone have faith in you, pass on my words, make an image of me, call my name and pray devoutly to me, then, good monk, I will grant his desire for your sake. But I see that you are not to live long. Redouble your efforts! Never relax!"

"Zaō Gongen gave me this tablet," I said, "but I don't quite understand it. Would you tell me what it means?"

Daijō Tenjin explained, "SUN (NICHI) means the Cosmic Buddha DaiNICHI, Great SUN. STORE (ZO) means the Womb-STORE Mandala. NINE NINE means eighty-one: eighty-one YEARS and eighty-one MONTHS. KING (O) means ZaO Gongen. GUARD means protection. As long as you devote yourself to the Buddha Dainichi and do the great rite of the Womb-Store Mandala, you will live eighty-one years. If you practice the rite truly, as the Buddha really taught it, your life will be further lengthened to ninety-nine years, while laxity will shorten it by ninety-nine months. At any rate, Zaō Gongen will watch over you. Now adopt your new name, Nichizō, and practice with tireless energy."

When he had finished speaking, I went back to Golden Peak and told Zaō Gongen what I had seen and heard.

Zaō Gongen replied, "I wanted you to know the source of the evils that afflict the world. That's why I sent you there."

Then he went on to repeat that Nippon Daijō Tenjin is Sugawara no Michizane, and that Tenjin's followers number 168,000. He described their many noxious forms and the way they do harm everywhere in the realm. "The older gods are powerless to stop them," he continued. "In the summer of 930, you know, lightning struck the emperor's own palace and killed Lord Mareyo and several others; and it was this messenger, the Venomous King of Fire and Thunder, who did it. He roasted the flesh and viscera of our own Emperor Daigo so that the emperor died, and he set fire to temples like Hōryūji, Tōdaiji, and others. Yes, that too was the Venomous King's work. And all those crimes the evil gods commit, all that murder and destruction, are charged to Emperor Daigo alone as though he were the sea all rivers empty into.

"The power of the King of Fire and Thunder is equal to my own, with all my followers. Sometimes he makes mountains crumble and shakes the earth, or destroys fortresses and wreaks havoc far and wide. Sometimes he makes storm winds blow and sends down torrential rains which cause damage and casualties. Sometimes he creates epidemics and diseases which kill people before their time, or foments treason and rebellion. But the god Hachiman and I keep him in check, so that at least he can't do exactly as he pleases."

When Zaō Gongen had finished, he told me how to get back again, and I returned to my cave. Then I revived. It was four in the mornng on the thirteenth day of the eighth moon of 941. Thirteen days had passed since I entered the gates of death.

I must add, too, that in the vision I had while I was within those gates, Zaō Gongen showed me hell. I came there to an iron cave with a shack woven of grasses inside it. The four men in the shack looked like ashes and embers. One had on a robe that barely covered his shoulders and the other three were naked. They were squatting on glowing coals.

A hell-fiend told me that the one with the robe on was Emperor Daigo, the sovereign of my own land, and that the others were the emperor's ministers. When the emperor saw me, he beckoned to me.

"I am Emperor Daigo of Japan," he said. "I suffer in this iron cave because Daijō Tenjin in his wrath burns temples and hurts sentient beings, and because the retribution for all his crimes falls on me; for I myself am the source of his rage. Daijō Tenjin, meanwhile, has fortunate karma which has made him a god. Yes, there are five major offenses my father and I committed toward him, and countless lesser ones. But above all, I am the one who, by sending him unjustly into exile, aroused the wrath he now visits on the whole land. That is why my agony is endless. O pain! O torment! Take my words back to Japan, tell the emperor what I am suffering, get him to help me! Have the regent and the ministers order purifications on my behalf, have them erect ten thousand holy images for me!"

That is the end of the Venerable Nichizō's account. Many other wonders are attributed to him. For example, he once dug in the earth and found a vajra-handled bell which he recognized as one he himself had owned in a previous life. And once he prayed at the shrine of the god of Matsunoo to know which Buddha the god came from. There was a violent thunderstorm and darkness fell. Then a voice from inside the sanctuary said,

"The Buddha Bibashi." The awed Nichizō went forward and came before an ancient man who had the face of a child.

When Nichizō died he left no body behind.

1 0 2 .

THE GOLD OF GOLDEN PEAK

A man whose trade was beating gold into foil lived on Seventh Avenue in Kyoto. One day he set off on pilgrimage to Golden Peak: the mountain where Miroku, the Future Buddha, is said to have stored all the gold that will make the world shine again when he comes.

At a place on the mountain called Oreslide, he spotted what looked like a nugget and cheerfully hid it under his coat. Back at home he melted it down, and since it was real gold it glittered and gleamed. He was amazed. As far as he knew, there should have been thunder, or an earthquake, or at least a cloudburst when he took the gold, but nothing had happened. "Well," he thought, "I'll use it myself."

The gold weighed nearly two pounds, and the craftsman beat it into seven or eight thousand sheets of foil. They made a thick roll. He was looking for a buyer to take the whole lot when he heard that an officer of the Imperial Police was planning to donate a new buddha to Tōji, and would probably want a lot of gold foil for the statue. So off he went with his gold to the gentleman's house.

The gentleman wanted to know how much foil his visitor had. "Seven or eight thousand sheets," the craftsman replied.

"Are they with you?"

"Yes, sir."

The sheets were perfect and their color was beautiful. But each one, when unrolled, turned out to have "Golden Peak" on it in tiny characters.

"What does this mark mean?" the gentleman asked.

"There's no mark on them, sir. How could there be?"

"But there *is*. Look here!"

Indeed there was. The craftsman was speechless.

"Something's not right," said the gentleman. He had an underling carry the gold while he marched the craftsman off to the chief of police. The chief had the craftsman taken out to the riverbank and put to the question.

They tied him to a post and whipped him till his back was as red and wet as newly washed red silk, then threw him in prison. In ten days he was dead. The gold, they say, was returned to Golden Peak and put back where it had come from. No one ever thought of making off with it again.

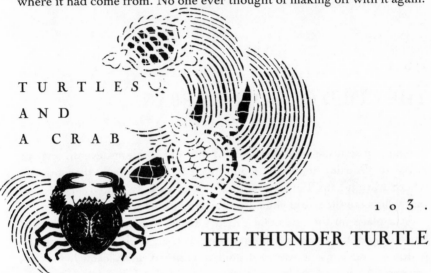

TURTLES
AND
A CRAB

1 o 3 .

THE THUNDER TURTLE

In the spring of 930, the monk Jōsū was in his room at Tōji, reading a sutra, when a large turtle came in. Jōsū thought this odd, but was so absorbed that he hardly gave the turtle a second glance. Suddenly there was a flash of lightning and a clap of thunder, and the turtle rose up into the sky.

The next day the God of Fire and Thunder appeared to Jōsū. "I wanted to talk to you yesterday," he said, "but you wouldn't even look at me! I was quite annoyed."

"All I saw yesterday was a big turtle," answered Jōsū. "I had no idea the turtle was a god. I admit, though, that I was surprised when it rose into the sky."

"I'm suffering for my evil attitude in the past," the god said. "Now look at my real form!"

He showed himself as he really was. The upper part of his body precisely resembled the thunder gods you see in paintings, but from the waist down he was a salmon.

"Below the waist I always feel as though I'm burning," said the god. And he added, "In the sixth moon I think I'll go to the palace." Then he disappeared.

Lightning did strike the palace in the sixth moon of 930 and killed several gentlemen.

1 0 4 .

THE CATCH

A poor man from Kōga county in Ōmi province had no livelihood at all, but his wife managed to make a living by hiring herself out as a weaver. In time, having finally managed to weave a bolt of cloth for herself, she told her husband to take it to Yabase harbor on Lake Biwa and trade it there for fish. In their own village he would be able to exchange the fish for seed rice. "That way," she said, "we can cultivate a little land this year."

The man took the cloth to Yabase and asked the fishermen to catch him some fish, but all they got was one big turtle. They were going to kill it, but the man was sorry for it and asked to buy it instead of the fish he had ordered. The fishermen gladly accepted the bargain.

"Turtles live a long time," said the man to the turtle, "and like all living things, they certainly value their lives. I know I'm poor, but I'm giving up this cloth anyway to save you." Then he let the turtle go in the lake.

He came home empty-handed, and when his wife found out why, she scolded him mercilessly. Soon he fell ill and died, and his body was abandoned by the roadside. Three days later he revived.

The governor of Iga happened to be passing by just then, on his way to his province. Seeing the man showing signs of life, he kindly brought him water and poured it into his mouth before going on. When the man's wife heard what had happened, she came to carry him back home.

This is the story he told. "When I died," he said, "officers seized me and marched me off to a broad plain where we came to the gate of the officers' headquarters. The space in front of the building was crowded with people, bound and helpless. I was terribly frightened. But then a very nice-looking little monk came out. He said he was Jizō and told the officers that he owed me a debt of gratitude. 'To benefit sentient beings I was in Lake Biwa,' he said, 'in the form of a large turtle. A fisherman who had caught me was about to kill me when this man took pity on me. He bought me and put me back in the lake. You must let him go.' And they did.

"The little monk told me to go home now, and to do good and shun all evil. While he was showing me the way out, a very pretty young woman stumbled by with her arms tied behind her. Two demons were beating her and driving her along. I asked her where she was from. She wept as she told me her father was the chief priest of a shrine in Munakata county in the province of Chikuzen. She had suddenly been separated from her parents and had started all alone down a dark path, driven on by demons. It was such a sad story, and I asked the little monk whether something couldn't be done for her. 'My own life is half over,' I said. 'I don't have too many years left. But this girl is still young and has a long future ahead of her. Can't she be released instead of me?' The little monk told me I was very kind to sacrifice myself the way I did for others, and that it was a wonderful thing. He said he would ask to have us *both* released, and at a word from him the demons let the girl go too. The girl cried for joy and thanked me gratefully, then went her way."

Soon the man went to look for the young woman he had met in hell. He found the shrine she had mentioned, and the chief priest really did have a daughter who, according to the servants, had recently died and then come back to life again. On receiving the man's message about his experience in hell, she came out as fast as she could. She was the same girl, and she recognized him too. Both wept as they talked over their experience.

The man went back home then, but both he and the young woman continued to serve Jizō with grateful devotion.

1 o 5 .

THE GRATEFUL TURTLE

Fujiwara no Yamakage, who lived in Emperor Daigo's reign, loved best among all his children a beautiful little son. The boy's stepmother seemed to love him even more than his father did, and this pleased Yamakage so much that he often let her take care of the child.

In time Yamakage was named viceroy of Kyushu, and he set sail in a little convoy of ships, with all his family, to take up the post. It did not worry him that he and the boy were traveling in different ships since the boy was with his stepmother. Actually, though, the stepmother had been wondering all along how to get rid of the child. Along the Kyushu coast she finally picked him up, held him over the gunwale as though to let him relieve himself, and then, pretending to adjust her hold, dropped him into the sea. The convoy was moving briskly under full sail and had gone some way before she cried out that the young master had fallen overboard.

Yamakage nearly jumped overboard himself. He sent men in a dinghy
to look for his son, then stopped the convoy and swore he would go no
farther till he knew whether he was to have the boy back, dead or alive.

The men rowed about all night in vain. Then at dawn, as light was
beginning to spread over the sea, they saw something small and white
bobbing far off on the waves. It looked like a gull, and they were surprised that it did not fly away as they rowed closer. They found it was
the boy, riding the back of a huge turtle and merrily splashing at the
waves with his hands. With sighs of relief they lifted him into the dinghy,
and the tortoise slid into the deep.

"Here's the young master, sir!" they cried in triumph when they got
back to Yamakage's ship and handed the boy back to his father. Yamakage wept for joy. The stepmother wept too, in dismay, though she put
on the best show of happiness she could. She disguised her feelings so
well that it never even occurred to Yamakage to suspect her.

Exhausted, Yamakage lay down in broad day while the convoy sailed
on, and dreamed that a huge turtle lifted its head from the sea. It seemed
to want to speak to him. When he reached the side of the ship, it said,
"Have you forgotten? A year or two ago a cormorant fisherman caught
me on the coast not far from the Capital, and you bought me from him
and let me go again. I'd been wondering ever since how to repay your
kindness, and when you sailed I thought I might at least see you to where
you were going. Last night I saw the young master's stepmother pick him
up, hold him over the railing, and drop him into the sea. I caught him on
my shell. Watch that woman carefully in the future!"

The turtle drew its head back into the water and disappeared, and
Yamakage woke up. He remembered how he had gone on pilgrimage to
the great shrine at Sumiyoshi and had seen a cormorant fisherman coming toward him in a boat. The head of a large turtle had been sticking up
over the gunwale and the turtle's eyes had met his. He had pitied the
creature so much that he had traded his own cloak for it and let it go in
the sea. This was the same turtle! He was very touched. Then he recalled
with loathing how the stepmother had made such a spectacle of her grief.
He hastily brought the little boy aboard his own ship and was careful
even after he arrived to keep the stepmother away from him. The stepmother realized to her sorrow that he had understood.

When Yamakage returned to Kyoto, he made the boy into a monk and
gave him the religious name Nyomu, "As Nothing," because having already died once, as it were, that was what the boy was. Nyomu served
Retired Emperor Uda and achieved a high ecclesiastical rank. He ended
up looking after his stepmother, who had no son of her own, for the rest
of her life. How embarrassed she must have been!

URASHIMA THE FISHERMAN

Young Urashima lived in Tango province, in the village of Tsutsugawa. One day in the fall of 477 (it was Emperor Yūryaku's reign), he rowed out alone on the sea to fish. After catching nothing for three days and nights, he was surprised to find that he had taken a five-colored turtle. He got the turtle into the boat and lay down to sleep.

When the turtle changed into a dazzlingly lovely girl, the mystified Urashima asked her who she was.

"I saw you here, alone at sea," she answered with a smile, "and I wanted so much to talk to you! I came on the clouds and the wind."

"But where did you come from, then, on the clouds and wind?"

"I'm an Immortal and I live in the sky. Don't doubt me! Oh, be kind and speak to me tenderly!"

Urashima understood she was divine, and all his fear of her melted away.

"I'll love you as long as the sky and earth last," she promised him, "as long as there's a sun and a moon! But tell me, will you have me?"

"Your wish is mine," he answered. "How could I not love you?"

"Then lean on your oars, my darling, and take us to my Eternal Mountain!"

She told him to close his eyes. In no time they reached a large island with earth like jade. Watchtowers on it shone darkly, and palaces gleamed like gems. It was a wonder no eye had seen and no ear had ever heard tell of before.

They landed and strolled on hand in hand to a splendid mansion, where she asked him to wait; then she opened the gate and went in. Seven young girls soon came out of the gate, telling each other as they passed him that he was Turtle's husband; and eight girls who came after them told each other the same. That was how he learned her name.

He mentioned the girls when she came back out. She said the seven were the seven stars of the Pleiades, and the eight the cluster of Aldebaran. Then she led him inside.

Her father and mother greeted him warmly and invited him to sit down. They explained the difference between the human and the divine worlds, and they let him know how glad this rare meeting between the gods and a man had made them. He tasted a hundred fragrant delicacies and exchanged cups of wine with the girl's brothers and sisters. Young girls with glowing faces flocked to the happy gathering, while the gods sang their songs sweetly and clearly and danced with fluid grace. The feast was a thousand times more beautiful than any ever enjoyed by mortals in their far-off land.

Urashima never noticed the sun going down, but as twilight came on the Immortals all slipped away. He and the maiden, now alone, lay down in each other's arms and made love. They were man and wife at last.

For three years he forgot his old life and lived in paradise with the Immortals. Then one day he felt a pang of longing for the village where he had been born and the parents he had left behind. After that, he missed them more each day.

"Darling," said his wife, "you haven't looked yourself lately. Won't you tell me what's wrong?"

"They say the dying fox turns toward his lair and the lesser man longs to go home. I'd never believed it, but now I know it's true."

"Do you want to go back?"

"Here I am in the land of the gods, far from all my family and friends. I shouldn't feel this way, I know, but I can't help being homesick for them. I want so much to go back and see my mother and father!"

His wife brushed away her tears. "We gave ourselves to each other forever!" she lamented. "We promised we'd be as true as gold or the rocks of the mountains! How could a little homesickness make you want to leave me?"

They went for a walk hand in hand, sadly talking it all over. Finally they embraced, and when they separated their parting was sealed.

Urashima's parents-in-law were sad to see him go. His wife gave him a jeweled box. "Dearest," she said, "if you don't forget me and find you want to come back, then grip this box hard. But you mustn't open it, ever."

He got into his boat and they told him to close his eyes. In no time he was at Tsutsugawa, his home. The place looked entirely different. He recognized nothing there at all.

"Where's Urashima's family — Urashima the fisherman?" he asked a villager.

"Who are you?" the villager answered. "Where are you from? Why are you looking for a man who lived long ago? Yes, I've heard old people mention someone named Urashima. He went out alone on the sea and never came back. That was three hundred years ago. What do you want with him now?"

Bewildered, Urashima roamed the village for ten days without finding any sign of family or old friends. At last he stroked the box his divine lady had given him and thought of her; then, forgetting his recent promise, he opened it. Before his eyes her fragrant form, borne by the clouds and the wind, floated up and vanished into the blue sky. He understood he had disobeyed her and would never see her again. All he could do was gaze after her, then pace weeping along the shore.

When he dried his tears, he sang about her far, cloud-girdled realm. The clouds, he sang, would bring her the message of his love. Her sweet voice answered him, across the vastness of the sky, entreating him never to forget her. Then a last song burst from him as he struggled with his loss: "My love, when after a night of longing, day dawns and I stand at my open door, I hear far-off waves breaking on the shores of your paradise!"

If only he hadn't opened that jeweled box, people have said since, he could have been with her again. But the clouds hid her paradise from him and left him nothing but his grief.

1 0 7 ·

THE GRATEFUL CRAB

A girl in Yamashiro province had served Kannon faithfully ever since she was a child, devoutly fasting on Kannon's special day (the eighteenth of each moon) and chanting the Kannon Sutra. She was so sweet and kind that when she saw a man about to kill a crab she took pity on the creature, bought it, and let it go.

Meanwhile her father went out to work his field and found a snake beginning to swallow a frog. He did his best to get the frog away from the snake but was disappointed to find that he could not get it out of the snake's mouth. "Let that frog go!" he commanded. "I'll give you my daughter if you do!"

The snake looked him in the eye, then disgorged the frog, which hopped away into the bushes. The farmer wished he had kept his mouth shut, because the snake seemed to have taken him at his word, but it was too late.

That night a gentleman came to the door. "I'm here for what you promised me this morning," he said. The horrified farmer hardly knew what to say, but he managed to ask the man to come back in a few days.

The man agreed and went away. When then the farmer told his daughter, she was so frightened that she hid at the bottom of her bed and refused to come out.

A few days later the snake was back, this time as a snake and not as a man. It knew perfectly well where the girl was, and it slithered to her room and beat on the door with its tail. The poor girl desperately chanted the Kannon Sutra till a little Kannon a foot tall appeared to her and told her not to be afraid.

In the middle of the night hundreds of crabs invaded the house, went for the snake, and tore it to pieces with their claws. Then they vanished. Kannon's protection had allowed the crab the girl had saved to express its gratitude.

DESIRE

108.

YOUNG LUST

In Owari province a girl of eleven or twelve was out gathering greens in the fields when a farmer working nearby noticed her flat on the ground. He thought he had better investigate. A five-foot snake was about to wrap itself around her. The farmer ran for his hoe to beat it off with, but the snake, now very close to the girl's head, suddenly flinched, slithered away, and vanished. When the farmer got back, the girl was unconscious. He kept calling her till she came to and he could ask what had happened.

"Such a wonderful, handsome boy was just here!" she said. "He told me to lie down and I did. I'd have done anything he asked! But then for some reason he got frightened and ran away."

The farmer wanted to know whether she had an amulet on her. She said no, but he searched her all the same. In the end he found she had tied up her hair with a bit of paper that had the Sonshō Darani on it.

This is supposed to have happened in the 1260s or early 1270s.

1 0 9 .

THE PRETTY GIRL

A young monk served a very distinguished master. One day he went with his master to Miidera, the great temple near Lake Biwa. It was a summer afternoon. He soon felt sleepy, and in the spacious residence his master was visiting he had no trouble finding a quiet spot for a nap.

He dreamed that a beautiful girl came and made the most wonderful love to him. When he woke up, he discovered a five-foot-long snake next to him, and was on his feet in fright before he realized the snake was dead. Its mouth was open. Next, he saw he was wet in front where he had ejaculated. The beautiful girl who had made love to him must have been the snake. Horrified, he peered into the snake's mouth and saw traces of the semen which the snake had apparently spit out.

He must have had an erection while he slept, and the snake had seen it and taken his penis in its mouth. That was when he had had the dream about the girl. His ejaculation had been too much for the snake and it had died. What a weird and awful thing to have happen! He went right away to wash his penis thoroughly, in secret.

He wanted to confide in someone, but kept quiet because he knew that if he did he would end up being known as "the monk who did it with a snake." Still, he was disturbed enough by the incident to talk about it to a monk who was a close friend of his. His friend was very sympathetic.

Clearly you shouldn't fall asleep where there's no one else around. It's true, though, that nothing special happened to the monk afterwards.

They say a creature will die if it swallows a man's semen, and apparently it's true. The monk was not quite himself, either, for some time.

The story was passed on by the friend the monk talked to.

1 1 0 .

MESMERIZED

One summer day a young woman walking west along Konoe Avenue in Kyoto, on the south side of the street, apparently felt a sudden urge to relieve herself, for she squatted against the earthen wall she was passing and did just that. Her little girl attendant paused discreetly to wait.

It was fairly early in the morning. The little girl knew her mistress must have finished, but time kept passing and the young woman never moved. An hour went by. The girl called to her mistress in vain. Another hour. The sun was climbing toward noon. Nothing the little girl could say got any reply. Finally she burst into tears.

A man riding by with a large company of followers saw the little girl crying and sent someone to ask her what was the matter. The girl told him, pointing to her mistress who was still there with her skirts tucked up, squatting against the wall.

"How long have you been here?" asked the rider himself.

"Since early morning, sir," the girl sobbed. "She's been like that for hours."

It certainly was strange. The rider dismounted and examined the young woman's face. She was as pale as death.

"What is it?" he asked her. "Are you sick? Has this ever happened to you before?"

The woman said nothing, but the girl assured him that this was the first time.

The rider could see the woman was not of the commonest class, which made him feel all the more sorry for her. He tried lifting her to her feet, but she was rigid.

Happening to glance over at the wall, the rider noticed just inside a hole the head of a large snake which was staring straight at the woman. It must have seen her relieving herself, felt lust for her, and mesmerized her. That was why she was stuck.

Having grasped this, the rider drew his sword and planted it before the hole with the cutting edge toward the snake. Then he had his men pick the woman up bodily and carry her away. Suddenly the snake hurled itself like a spear from the hole, cut a foot of its length in two on the sword, and died. What strange and frightening creatures snakes are!

The man remounted his horse while a follower retrieved his sword. Still worried about the woman, he assigned some of his men to stay with her. In a little while she began to be able to walk again, with someone supporting her, just like a person who has been very ill.

1 1 1 .

RED HEAT

A pair of monks, one old and one young and handsome, were on their way to Kumano. On reaching Muro county, not far from their goal, they found lodging with a young widow who lived all alone, aside from the company of a few maids.

The widow noted the younger monk's good looks, and desire made her treat him well. After dark the two monks retired, but in the middle of the night she stole to the younger one's bed and lay down beside him. When he woke up in alarm, she did her best to calm him. "I don't normally have people to stay," she said, "but I knew I wanted you as soon as I saw you today. That's why I asked you in and that's why I'm here. I'm a widow, you see. Please be nice to me!"

The monk jumped up, protesting that he had vowed long ago to remain chaste, and he reminded her that he had come a long way to make this pilgrimage. "If I suddenly break my vow, we'll both suffer for it!" he cried. "Stop! Please forget your desires!"

His refusal only stung her to anger. All night she twined herself round him, though he managed both to humor her and to put her off. "It's not that I really want to refuse you," he explained. "As soon as I've spent a few days at Kumano I'll be back, and then I'll do whatever you want, believe me!" Finally she accepted his promise and went away. At dawn the monk and his companion set off.

The love-struck widow counted the days and prepared to receive the handsome monk on his return, but he was frightened and took care to go

back another way. She got worried when he failed to come and began
questioning the people passing outside on the road. One pilgrim said yes,
a pair of monks like that, one old and one young, had left Kumano several
days before. The widow panicked when it dawned on her that they had
avoided her house altogether. She rushed home in a rage, shut herself up
in silence in her room, and quickly died. Even as her maids were mourning her, a foul snake, immensely long, suddenly issued from her room,
left the house, and slithered down the road away from Kumano. The
travelers it passed were terrified.

Up ahead, the two monks heard that a huge snake was racing their
way over hill and dale and catching up with them fast. They knew right
away who the snake really was, and they fled for their lives to seek refuge
at Dōjōji. Having heard their story, the monks of the temple decided to
help. They held a council, then let down their bell over the young monk
and barred the gate.

The snake soon came, got easily over the barred gate, slithered a few
times around the compound, then went straight for the hall with the bell.
When the door collapsed under its furious blows, the snake darted inside
and wrapped itself round the bell. It stayed that way for hours, beating
on the top of the bell with its tail, till despite their fear the monks
surrounded the hall and opened the doors on all four sides to watch. The
snake lifted its head. Its tongue flickered and tears of blood streamed
from its eyes. Then it fled in the direction it had come from. The bell
glowed red-hot from its foul, burning breath, and the monks could not
even get near it till they had dashed it with water to cool it down. When
they finally lifted it they found that nothing, not even bones, was left of
the monk inside. There was only a little heap of ashes. The monk's older
companion wept as he took his leave.

Later on, the abbot of Dōjōji dreamed of an even larger snake. "I am
the monk who hid in the bell," it said. "Once that evil woman had become
a snake she took me prisoner and made me hers. Now I suffer horribly
in this awful snake body and I can't save myself from my pain. When I
was alive, I devoted myself to the Lotus Sutra. Please, Your Grace, show
me mercy and put an end to my torment. Purify yourself, copy the
'Revelation of the Buddha's Eternal Life' chapter of the Sutra, and dedicate it for both of us snakes. Oh, save us from this agony!" The snake
then went away and the dreamer awoke.

The abbot copied the chapter in question and called the monks of the
temple together for a day-long ceremony to dedicate it for the two snakes.
Soon he dreamed again. This time a monk and a woman came to Dōjōji
together, all smiles. They prostrated themselves before the abbot and told

him that thanks to his kindness they were rid now of their snake bodies and happy at last. "For," said the woman, "I have been born into the Tōri Heaven." "And I," said the man, "have gone up to the Tosotsu Heaven." And with these words they flew up into the sky.

The Tōri Heaven is where the great god Taishaku has his palace at the top of Shumisen, the cosmic mountain; and the Tosotsu Heaven is the even higher realm where Miroku, the Future Buddha, waits to be born into our world.

1 1 2 .

LOVESICK

Sick with love for a boy, a girl in Kamakura confessed her trouble to her mother. The mother, who knew the boy's parents, immediately arranged for him to visit her daughter sometimes, but he all but ignored the girl and hardly ever came. In the end the girl died. Her grieving parents put her ashes in a box and prepared to send them off to a certain temple in Shinano.

Next, the boy became ill too, and went so thoroughly mad that he had to be shut up in a little room. Hearing him talk in there, his parents peeked in through a crack. He was talking to a large snake.

When the boy died, his body was placed in a coffin, for burial on the mountain nearby. At the funeral a large snake was found coiled around his body, right in the coffin, and the two were buried together.

Before sending their daughter's ashes to Shinano, the girl's parents opened the box to take out some which they wanted to deposit in a temple in Kamakura. They discovered that their daughter's bones had turned into little snakes, or were in the process of doing so.

They told the whole story to the priest they asked to pray over the remains, and the priest passed it on to his colleagues. It happened in the 1270s, within the last ten years. I know the names of the people involved but would rather not record them here.

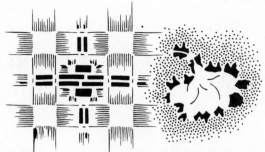

1 1 3 .

GONE, BODY AND SOUL

A monk named Yakuren once lived in Nyohōji, a temple in Shinano province. Not being formally ordained he had a family, but he still spent his life continually chanting the Amida Sutra.

One day he told his son and daughter that he would need to wash and put on clean clothes because tomorrow he was going to be born into the Land of Bliss. The children quickly got things ready for him and at nightfall, fully prepared, he entered his chapel alone. "You may open the chapel door at daylight tomorrow," he warned them, "but not before."

Weeping, they spent the night by the chapel in vigil. Near daybreak a music not of this world sounded from within the chapel, and they thought they must be dreaming. When the sky lightened, they opened the door. Their father's body was gone and so was his copy of the Amida Sutra.

The news brought the neighbors running, and the grieving children told them about the music. Finally it dawned on everyone that Yakuren had gone to paradise in his own body. They all shed tears of joy and awe.

Now, rebirth into the Land of Bliss is not unknown, but those who achieve it leave their bodies behind as a sign. Since Yakuren's body was gone, one might conclude that he had just slipped off to some mountain temple; yet his children had been there all the time and could testify that the door of the chapel had never opened. In other words, Yakuren really had reached paradise in the flesh, as the unearthly music seemed to confirm. Some people, though, have wondered whether the earth gods didn't just make off with the body on their own and leave it in the sort of pure spot where the body of a saint might properly belong.

PARADISE IN THE PALM
OF THE HAND

Two scholar-monks named Chikō and Raikō once lived at Gangōji in the old capital of Nara. Although they had always lived and worked together, Raikō in the end stopped studying and never picked up his books again. He just lay there in silence. Chikō, for his part, was a deeply wise man who loved scholarship, and in time his learning was recognized by all.

When Raikō died, Chikō mourned his old friend. It disturbed him that Raikō had been silent and idle for so many years, and he wondered what his next life would be; but he witheld judgment on Raikō's fate because he knew that good and ill are hard for our limited minds to fathom. In time he decided to try to find out where Raikō had gone.

He dreamed he found Raikō in a place so beautiful that it seemed like paradise, and asked Raikō in surprise where they were. "This is the Land of Bliss," Raikō replied. "Your prayers have brought you here, but now that you've seen me you'll have to go back. This is no place for you."

"But I want to be born into paradise too," Chikō protested. "Why must I go back?"

"Because you've done nothing to deserve staying."

"Yet you yourself, when you were alive, did nothing at all! How did *you* get here?"

"Don't you see?" Raikō explained. "My longing for birth here was perfectly pure. Having no other thought, I said nothing. In every phase of daily living I saw the countenance of Lord Amida and the beauty of his paradise, so I just lay quietly, thinking of nothing else. And here I am. You know all about the scriptures but your mind is in turmoil and you hardly deserve a birth like this."

"Then what can I do to be sure of paradise?" cried Chikō in tears.

"It isn't for me to say. Ask Lord Amida himself." Raikō led his friend before the lord.

Chikō prostrated himself and reverently repeated his question.

"You must contemplate the Buddha's countenance and the beauty of paradise," Amida said.

"But the splendor of all I see here is more than my eyes or my mind can take in! How can I contemplate these things with the eyes of an ordinary man?"

Lord Amida lifted his right hand, and Chikō saw in the palm a tiny paradise. Then he woke up. He immediately had a painter transcribe what he had seen, and all his life he contemplated that image till he too passed on to the Land of Bliss. Later, his dwelling was renamed Goku-rakubō, or Paradise Hall, and the painting still hangs there in great honor.

1 1 5 .

NO COMPROMISE

Gendayū, who lived in Sanuki province, was a fierce hunter and killer. Dawn or dusk he was out in the wilds after deer and fowl, or fishing; and the day rarely passed when he did not chop off someone's head, arm, or leg. He knew nothing about karma or religious faith, and naturally only hated and shunned holy men. In a word, he was a menace, and people were terrified of him.

He was coming home one day from hunting deer in the mountains with some of his band when he noticed a crowd in front of a building and asked what the people were doing. His men told him the place was a temple and that a monk was preaching there. "Preaching," they explained, "means offering the buddhas a sermon on the holy sutras, for the benefit of all beings."

"Oh yes, I've heard about that," said Gendayū, "but I've never actually seen it. I'll go and hear what he's got to say. You wait here."

He and his men dismounted. The men hated to imagine what their master was up to and were afraid he was going to torment the preacher.

When Gendayū came into the temple, some of the congregation simply fled. He shoved his way through the rest, with the people parting before him like grasses in a gale, till he came to the preacher and glared into his eyes.

"Preacher," he said, "I want to know what you've been saying. And talk sense. If you don't, you'll wish you had." He brandished his dagger.

The frightened preacher thought he was lost and his mind went blank, but he was wise enough to call on the Buddha for help before he answered.

"Westward from here," he answered, "beyond many other worlds, is the place where a buddha lives. This buddha's name is Amida. His kindness is wide and deep. You may have been the worst of sinners, but if you repent and call his Name just once he'll come to fetch you and you'll be reborn into his Land of Bliss where you'll be a buddha too."

"If this buddha of yours is as kind as all that, then I suppose he wouldn't turn me away either."

"Of course not."

"So if I call his Name he'll answer?"

"Yes, if you call him sincerely."

"What people does this buddha like best?"

"He doesn't reject anyone, but parents can't help loving their own children most and so he does slightly prefer his own disciples."

"What's a disciple?"

"Any monk who's shaved his head like me. Laymen and laywomen can be his disciples too, but it's even better if you're a monk or a nun."

"Then shave my head," commanded Gendayū.

"Oh dear!" the preacher exclaimed. "It's wonderful to hear you say that, but you see, I can't just do it all of a sudden. If you're serious you should first go home, talk it over with your family, and put your affairs in order."

"You call yourself a disciple of this buddha and you claim he tells only the truth," Gendayū growled. "You say he loves his disciples. What do you mean by turning around now and telling me to do it *later*? You don't seem to understand, do you?" Gendayū drew his dagger and cut off his own topknot at the roots.

The preacher was speechless and a clamor burst from the congregation. Gendayū's men heard it. Obviously their master had done something, and they rushed to the temple ready to fight. Gendayū stopped them with a roar.

"How dare you come between me and paradise!" he bellowed. "This morning as usual I was wanting more men, but now, as far as I'm concerned, you can all get out and go wherever you please. I'm not keeping any of you!"

The men decided their master had gone mad. Some spirit must have possessed him. They sobbed and howled and rolled on the floor, but Gendayū quickly put a stop to their noise. Then he offered his topknot to the Buddha, heated water as fast as he could, washed his head, and came to the preacher again.

"Shave me properly!" he ordered. "You'll be sorry if you don't."

"Since you insist," the preacher replied, "I'm sure I'd be wrong not to shave you. Yes, it'd certainly be a sin." Though still afraid, he came down from his seat, shaved Gendayū's head, and administered the appropriate vows. Gendayū's men shed unrestrained tears of grief.

Having put on a monk's stole, Gendayū traded his quiver and bow for the devotee's little gong, which he hung around his neck. "Now I'm going to go west," he said. "I'll keep calling Amida and beating this gong till he answers. No moor, no mountain, river, or sea will turn me back." And off he went shouting, "Hey, Amida Buddha! Hey, hey!" When his men moved to follow him, he accused them of getting in his way and kept beating his gong till they gave up.

Gendayū did just what he said he would: he went straight west, calling Amida and beating the gong. When he came to a river he did not look for a ford, and he did not try to find a way round when a mountain rose in front of him. Stumbling, falling, he pushed straight ahead till at sundown he reached a temple, where he explained to the priest what he was doing. "Now I'm going over those mountains to the west," he continued. "Come and find me in seven days. I'll tie the grasses together as I go to mark the way. Do you have anything to eat? If you do, just give me a little."

The priest gave him plenty of parched rice, but Gendayū, protesting that it was too much, took only a tiny amount, which he wrapped in paper and put in the fold of his robe. Then he started off. "But the sun is down!" the priest called after him. "Stop here for the night, at least!" Gendayū seemed not to have heard.

Seven days later the priest set out. The trail was marked and led over the mountains, beyond which rose still another range. Looking westward from a peak, the priest saw the sea.

At last the priest came to a forked tree overlooking the ocean. Gendayū was sitting up in the fork, beating his gong and calling, "Hey, Amida! Hey, Hey!" He told the priest that he had meant to go on west to the sea. "But Amida answers me here," he explained, "so I stayed and now I just keep calling to him."

"What do you mean, he answers you?" asked the priest, who could make nothing of this.

"Well, I'll call. You'll hear him for yourself." And Gendayū shouted, "Hey, Amida! Where are you?"

"Here I am!" replied an awesome voice from the depths of the sea.

"Did you hear that?"

The priest had heard it and dissolved, overcome, in tears of joy and awe. Gendayū wept too. "Hurry home now," he said, "and come back in seven days to see what's happened to me."

"Don't you want anything? I brought you some parched rice."

"No, no, thank you, I still have the rice you gave me." The priest could in fact see the little packet of rice, wrapped just as it had been when Gendayū left his temple. He went away.

When he came again, Gendayū was still in the tree facing the west, but this time he was dead. A beautiful lotus flower had bloomed from his mouth, and the weeping priest picked it. It occurred to him that he should bury Gendayū, but he decided after all to leave him since Gendayū probably would have preferred simply to feed the birds and beasts.

Gendayū had certainly gone to paradise.

1 1 6 .

THE FAILURE

Once a holy man decided to trade his body for paradise by plunging into the waters of the Katsura River near Kyoto. He prepared himself for this by doing the Lotus Confession rite for a hundred days at Gidarinji, a temple in the city. Pilgrims flocked from far and near to worship him, and a constant stream of gentlewomen's carriages rolled toward the temple past an equally constant stream leaving.

The holy man, a slight fellow of about thirty, would not look anyone in the eye. Instead, he kept his eyes half-closed as though falling asleep. Now and again he would call Amida's Name aloud, but otherwise only his lips moved. Apparently he was repeating the Name then, too. Sometimes he would heave a sudden sigh and sweep his gaze over the faces around him. Having come precisely in the hope of looking into his eyes, the pilgrims at such moments would push and shove ruthlessly so as not to miss any chance of doing so.

Early in the morning on the appointed day the holy man, wearing a paper robe and stole, entered the temple's main hall. All the monks, who were already inside, filed out ahead of him. He got into a waiting cart and the procession moved off. Though his lips were moving, it was impossible to make out what he was saying. He would not look anyone in the eye, and from time to time he would heave a big sigh.

The crowd along his way kept showering him with good-luck rice, which made him cry out now and again, "Ow! It's getting in my eyes and nose! If you want to be kind, put your rice in a bag and send it to my temple!" At this the most ignorant onlookers would rub their hands in pious worship, but those with a little more wit would mutter, "What's he talking about? He's about to give up his body and go to paradise, and he's complaining about rice getting in his eyes and nose? Isn't there something funny about that?"

Finally the cart reached the Katsura River. More people had gathered to witness the holy man's passing, and to share its blessing, than there were stones on the riverbed. The cart drew up to the water and stopped.

"What time is it?" the holy man asked. The monks with him told him it was nearly six. "Then it's a bit early for going to paradise," the holy man replied. "I'll wait till sundown."

Those of the spectators who had come from the farthest off could not wait and left. The crowd thinned out. But some were determined to watch to the end. One of them, a monk, remarked what a strange idea it was that there should be any proper time for going to paradise.

Finally the holy man, naked except for a loincloth, turned to the west and walked into the river. He instantly tripped on a mooring rope and floundered about without even being able to plunge all the way in. When a disciple disentangled him, he tumbled in head first, making desperate glub-glub noises. A man standing in the river himself, to get a better view, seized his hand and pulled him up.

The holy man just stood there, wiping his face and spitting out all the water he had swallowed. Then he turned to his savior and wrung his hands abjectly. "How can I ever thank you?" he murmured. "I'll sing your praises in paradise!"

When he climbed back up onto the bank, the crowd and all the young scamps who had joined it picked up the stones that lay so thickly under their feet and began pelting him with them. Still naked, he fled downstream, but the crowd poured after him and stoned him till his head was all bleeding.

1 1 7 .

LETTERS FROM PARADISE

A holy man in Tango province desired rebirth into the Land of Bliss. Not that he was alone in this wish, but he aspired so fiercely to paradise that others' piety paled in comparison.

On the last day of the year he would write on a piece of paper: "Come to me before the day is over. Do not fail!" Then he would have an acolyte deliver the letter to him the following dawn, before he got up for the early morning litany.

"Knock on my door," he would tell the acolyte. "I'll ask who's there, and you'll say, 'A messenger from Amida Buddha in the Land of Perfect Bliss, with a letter for you!'" Then he would go to bed.

At dawn the obedient acolyte would knock at the door of his hut. "Who's there?" the holy man would call.

"A messenger from Amida Buddha in the Land of Bliss, with a letter for you!"

The holy man would stumble forth, weeping with joy. "What does it say?" he would cry, and reverently inspect the writing. Next he would collapse, overcome with devout emotion.

This happened every year. The acolyte who played the messenger got quite good at the part.

Eventually a new governor was posted to the province and came to revere the holy man deeply. One day the holy man visited him to enlist his help in a new and worthy project: a pageant of Amida's welcome to the soul. There would be musicians, and dancers costumed and masked as Amida, the bodhisattvas, and all the saints. The governor gladly pledged his support, gained the cooperation of other locally influential people, and set about getting musicians and dancers from the Capital. His enthusiasm pleased the holy man very much. "At the pageant I'll really believe Lord Amida is coming for me," he declared, "and I'll die!"

"Well, well, perhaps you will, who knows?" murmured the governor, who did not quite know what to say.

The day came and the beautiful pageant began. The holy man himself lit the incense. The two bodhisattvas Kannon and Seishi came forth, with a drummer behind them leading the joyous host of celestial musicians, and approached the holy man: Kannon to offer his soul a golden throne to ride to paradise on, and Seishi to shelter the soul with a jeweled canopy on the way there. Heavenly music filled the air.

The holy man was seen to weep and call Amida's holy Name while they came on, but when Kannon held forth the golden throne he did not respond. He seemed too overcome to move. Actually, though, he had just died. Of course the cast did not realize this, what with the music and the excitement, and they went on vainly offering him the canopy and the throne in the hope that he would say or do something. When they finally went away, the holy man stayed as motionless as ever. His alarmed disciples shook him and found he was already stiff.

At last everyone understood that he had actually gone to rebirth in the Land of Bliss, and they wept.

1 1 8 .

NOT EXACTLY THE LAND
OF BLISS

A hermit whose only practice was calling Amida's Name had lived for years in the Ibuki Mountains of Mino province. He was calling the Name one night when he heard a voice from the heavens saying, "You have devoutly trusted me and have called my Name countless times. Early tomorrow afternoon, at the hour of the Sheep, I promise I will come and welcome you into my Western Paradise. Do not stop calling upon me!"

The hermit redoubled his devotions. He washed, lit incense, scattered flowers, and sat down with his disciples facing the west so they could all call out the Name together.

When the time came, there was a gleam in the west. Amida appeared in glory like the full autumn moon breaking through clouds, and the hermit was bathed in the sublime rays that streamed from between his eyebrows. Flowers floated down from the sky. The hermit prostrated himself with such fervor that when his forehead touched the ground his behind rose high in the air. The cord of his rosary all but snapped with the vigor of his invocations. Then Kannon advanced among downy purple clouds to offer him a lotus throne. The hermit crept reverently forward, mounted the throne, and sailed away westward. His disciples wept with joy and awe as they watched him go.

A week or so later, the servants at the hermitage decided it was time to make the monks a bath and went into the mountains to cut firewood. When they came to a great cryptomeria growing over a waterfall, they heard cries from high in the tree. A monk was up there, tied naked to a branch. One particularly good climber discovered that the monk was their master who had sailed away to paradise. He was tied to the tree with vines.

"Master!" the horrified servant cried as he began working on the vines. "What happened?"

"He promised he'd be back for me any minute," the hermit babbled, "and he told me to stay right here! Don't you go untying me!" The servant untied him anyway. "Amida Buddha!" his master screamed, "this man is killing me!"

In the end they got him down and took him back to the hermitage. It was a tragedy. He had completely lost his mind, and two or three days later he died. Simple as he was, a tengu had tricked him.

TENGU,
BOAR,
AND
BADGER

1 1 9 .

ONE LAST SHOWER OF PETALS

In Emperor Daigo's reign, long ago, there was a big persimmon tree near the shrine on Fifth Avenue. When a buddha appeared in the tree, shining and scattering the loveliest flowers, all Kyoto crowded round for a look and a reverent bow. You could not get in one horse, carriage, or spectator more.

After a week or so, it occurred to the Minister of the Right that no genuine buddha would appear in these latter, degenerate days. He decided this must be some sort of tengu mischief and thought he would have a look for himself.

He got himself up in full court dress and went in a ceremonial carriage with a whole train of attendants. The crowd parted at his approach. He had the ox unhitched and the carriage shafts propped up for a long stay, then sat there staring at the buddha's branch. He never blinked or glanced aside. After a couple of hours the buddha let go a little shower of flower petals and a burst of light, but in the end the minister's relentless gaze was too much. Suddenly a big kestrel with a broken wing fell off the branch and lay helplessly flapping on the ground. Some boys dashed up and killed it.

"Sure enough!" said the minister to himself as he left. The people were deeply impressed.

INSPIRING, UNFORTUNATELY

The people of Emperor Reizei's reign were buzzing over a spate of tengu mischief when a monk from Mount Hiei started home after a little trip down to the city. Walking back toward the mountain along Kitaōji Avenue, he came to a pack of boys beating a fierce-looking old kite they had caught. He scolded them sharply. "Why do you want to hurt the poor bird?" he asked. They said they were killing it for its feathers.

The monk felt so sorry for the kite that he traded his fan for it to the boys and let it go. The good deed made him rather pleased with himself.

A bit farther on, where the path started up the mountain, a funny, monkish-looking old fellow popped out of the bushes and came panting after the monk. Though the monk did his best to avoid him, the old fellow insisted on accosting him and thanking him effusively for having saved his life.

"I don't know what you're talking about," the monk answered cautiously. "Who are you?"

"You remember me, of course you do! I'm the one the boys were busy murdering on Kitaōji Avenue! How can I ever thank you? If there's any wish of yours I can make come true, any little wish at all, just tell me. I've got a few magic powers, you see, and I'm sure I can do something nice for you!"

Confused by this astonishing offer, the monk hesitated, but the old fellow insisted till he finally replied, "Well, I don't really *have* any special wishes any more, you know. I'm seventy now, after all, and I've lost any interest in fame or fortune. I hate to think where I'll be born next time, yes, but I don't suppose there's anything you can do about *that*. So I don't quite know what to say. Still, I often imagine how wonderful it must have been when the Buddha preached the Lotus Sutra on Vulture Peak, and I wish I could have been there too. Could you perhaps give me a vision of the scene?"

"Of course I can!" the old fellow cried. "I'm a veteran at shows like that!" He led the monk some distance up the hillside. "Now," he said, "close your eyes and open them again when you hear the Buddha preaching. But be careful! Don't get carried away and imagine that it's all real! I'll be in terrible trouble if you do."

The old fellow climbed farther up the hill. In a moment the monk heard the Buddha's voice proclaiming the Teaching and opened his eyes.

The ground he stood on was lapis lazuli blue; the trees were all made of gold, silver, and jewels; and straight in front of him sat the Buddha, flanked by Monju and Fugen, on his Lion Throne. An infinite host of adoring saints, bodhisattvas, and gods clustered around the Buddha, before whom sat all the great disciples who appear in the scriptures. Sixteen kings, each the sovereign over a vast realm, were touching their jeweled crowns to the earth in homage, while flowers of four kinds floated down from the sky, exquisite fragrances perfumed the air, and angels filled the heavens with celestial music. The Teaching that poured from the Buddha's mouth was immeasurably stirring and profound.

At first the monk was simply awed by the old fellow's amazing skill; but every wonder, every miraculous touch, conspired to persuade him that this vision really was the moment long ago when the living Buddha preached, and he was quickly swept away. Tears of ecstatic joy sprang to his eyes. Then, lost in adoration, he pressed his palms together, greeted the Buddha aloud, and threw himself prostrate on the ground.

Suddenly the mountain roared, and the vision vanished as thoroughly as a dream when the dreamer wakes. The monk, almost in shock, found himself as before on the wild mountainside. All he could do was to start walking again.

He had not gone far before the old fellow was back, complaining bitterly. "I *told* you not to get carried away!" he scolded. "You *promised*! Oh, how *could* you go back on your word like that? Your faith was so strong that it brought all the Guardians and Protectors down, and when they saw my show had taken in a true believer they gave me an awful beating. All my colleagues who were helping me were frightened to death and got away as fast as they could. Oh, I wish I'd just left well enough alone!"

Then he disappeared.

1 2 1 .

NO FOOL, THE HUNTER

A seasoned hermit, devoted to the Lotus Sutra, once lived on Mount Atago just northwest of Kyoto. Though he never left his hut, he did not starve, for a hunter who lived nearby and revered him often brought him food.

The hunter had not been around for a long time when one day he turned up with a sack of dried rice, and the relieved hermit mentioned that he had been getting worried. Then he told the hunter about something wonderful that had been happening. "Perhaps it's because I've been honoring the Sutra so faithfully all these years, I don't know," he said, "but the Bodhisattva Fugen has been coming here every night on his white elephant. Stay this evening and adore him with me!"

The hunter was impressed enough to say he would, but he took the trouble to question the hermit's boy servant. "What's the hermit talking about?" he asked. "Have you see Fugen too?"

"Yes, certainly, half a dozen times," the boy replied.

Waiting eagerly behind the hermit, the hunter wondered whether he too would see Fugen. It was the twentieth of the ninth moon, well into fall, and the night was long. At last, past midnight a radiance as of the rising moon shone over the peaks to the east, an eerie wind blew down the mountain, and the hut was filled with light as though illumined by rays from afar. The Bodhisattva Fugen, mounted on his elephant, rode toward them and halted before the hut.

The hermit worshipped this vision with tears of joy. "And you," he asked the hunter, "do you see him too?"

"Indeed I do," replied the hunter, "and so does the boy. This is extraordinary!"

Still the hunter was puzzled. He quite understood that the hermit, with all his years of devotion to the Sutra where Fugen figures so prominently, might be given such a blessing. But he could not understand why the boy, and why he himself who knew so little about these things and who above all killed animals for a living, should see the vision too. So he decided there was no reason why he should not test this Fugen.

Fitting an arrow to the string, he took aim over the hermit (who was prostrate in adoration), drew to the full, and let fly. The arrow seemed to strike the bodhisattva's chest and the light went out. Something went crashing downhill through the brush.

"What have you done?" cried the hermit in an agony of distress.

The hunter explained. "If it really had been Fugen," he said, "the arrow couldn't have done any damage. So it must have been some monster."

At dawn they followed a trail of blood a hundred yards to the bottom of the ravine, where they found a huge badger lying dead with an arrow through its chest.

Saintly though he was, the hermit was ignorant too, and so had been open to deception. The hunter, on the other hand, having his wits about him, had killed the badger and exposed its hoax.

THE HAIRY ARM

A man named Sukeyasu was on his way down from the Capital to Tamba province when, after a day of hunting, he sought shelter in an old chapel. A villager from nearby warned him that the chapel was haunted and that people who stayed there disappeared, but Sukeyasu paid no attention and made himself as much at home as he could. What with the blowing snow and the spooky story, however, he did not feel too comfortable.

There was a babble of eerie voices outside. Peering through a hole in a sliding panel, out into the garden white with snow, he saw the dark, indistinct shape of a monk as tall as the roof. Then a skinny, hairy arm snaked in through the hole and felt over his face. Sukeyasu jumped and the arm withdrew.

Sukeyasu lay down in a ball to wait, facing the hole. The next time the hairy arm came through he grabbed it, and proved too strong for whatever was now struggling to get its arm back. Lifting out the whole panel, he stepped out on the porch of the chapel with the panel still between him and the owner of the arm. Then he tipped the panel away from him and jumped onto it. The creature may have looked as tall as the roof, but it had to be very small indeed to fit under the panel, especially with Sukeyasu sitting triumphantly on top of it! The arm was skinnier than ever.

Finally the creature let out a squeak. Sukeyasu had one of his men strike a light, and he found he had caught an old badger. He gave it to his men to look after until he could show it off to the villagers in the morning, but the men just roasted it and ate it. By morning only the head was left. Sukeyasu exhibited it to the villagers anyway.

Nothing haunted the chapel after that.

EXPERT HELP

An ascetic traveling in the north once came at sundown to a mountain village and asked for lodging. No one would have him, but the villagers told him about an old chapel down in the valley where he could go if he wanted. "They say tengu live there, though," the villagers remarked.

Being a master of spells, the ascetic was sure he would come to no harm and went down to the chapel. Actually, though, he *was* afraid, and he took care to hide up on the altar behind the buddha. Late that night he heard people coming down the mountain and was frightened enough to make the pass of invisibility. Then he held his breath and watched.

In came two or three dozen young acolytes carrying a palanquin with a plump and distinguished monk inside. When the young fellows had put their superior down, he told them to go outside and play. They all clattered noisily out and began wrestling, dancing, and cavorting about.

"Hello there, reverend!" called the monk cheerily.

"Oh no!" groaned the ascetic, for despite his pass of invisibility he obviously could still be seen.

"You didn't do your pass right, I'm afraid. That's why I can still see you. Come here. I'll show you."

The ascetic came out, a tiny bit reassured, and the monk showed him how to do it properly. "I didn't want those idiots to see this," he said, "that's why I sent them outside."

The ascetic went back behind the buddha and tried again.

"You're doing fine!" called the monk. "I can't see you any more!" He called the acolytes back in, and they amused themselves in the chapel awhile. Then the whole party started back up the mountain.

HEALING II

124.

RICE CAKES

A healer and his medium were called to take care of someone who had been possessed by a spirit. As soon as the healer had gotten the spirit over into the medium, it explained, "Curses aren't really my line at all! I'm just a fox who happened to come by. I live with my little ones over among the tombs, and they're hungry. I came because I thought you might have food here. If you'll give me some rice cakes I'll be on my way."

The household served up a nice platter of rice cakes, which the medium ate with happy exclamations about how delicious they were. "That woman!" the people grumbled. "She just faked the possession to get those cakes!"

"Now if you'll be kind enough to give me some paper," the fox continued, "I'll wrap up the rest and be off with them to my family."

The medium carefully wrapped up the cakes and put them into the front fold of her robe, where they made a good bulge all the way up to her bosom.

"Now dismiss me," said the fox. "I'll be going."

"Be gone then, be gone!" the healer ordered.

The medium stood up and instantly collapsed. When she got up again a little later there was nothing in the fold of her robe.

It was very strange how those rice cakes had disappeared.

1 2 5 .

A MEMORABLE EMPRESS

The exquisitely beautiful Somedono Empress was the regent's daughter and the mother of Emperor Montoku. At one time she was persecuted and made ill by an evil spirit, and although the holiest monks and most powerful healers were called in to intervene, nothing they did brought her any relief.

Now a certain hermit lived high in the Katsuragi Mountains of Yamato province, on a peak named Kongōsen. When he was hungry, he had his begging bowl fly down to the foot of the mountain to get him food, and he sent his water jar to the stream to fill itself when he was thirsty. The wonders he worked spread his fame far and wide till it reached the ears of the emperor and his father-in-law, the regent. They decided that the hermit should pray for the empress and issued an order that he be brought to court.

The hermit did his best to refuse, but it was hard to turn down a direct summons from the emperor and he finally went. His prayers certainly worked, because he had no sooner begun than one of the empress's ladies-in-waiting went quite mad and began uttering strange cries. Next, a spirit possessed her and she ran about screaming. The hermit redoubled his efforts, bound the woman with his spells, and threatened the possessing power till an old fox staggered out from the breast of her robe, in no condition to run away. The hermit had the fox tied up and informed the regent, who was enormously relieved. In a day or two the empress was perfectly well.

The regent was so pleased that he insisted on having the hermit stay awhile longer at court. It was summer. One day when the empress was wearing no more than a nearly transparent gown, a gust of wind lifted her curtains and the hermit caught a brief glimpse of her. This was not the sort of sight he was used to, and the vision of so lovely a woman made his heart pound and his innards crumble to dust. In a word, he fell hopelessly in love with the empress.

Passion burned in him like fire and caused him terrible agony. Unable to think of anything else, he at last lost his reason, seized an unguarded moment, darted to the empress through her curtains, and held her tight. The horrified empress broke into a sweat of terror but was not strong enough to resist.

While the hermit strove with might and main to consummate his offense, the ladies-in-waiting saw him and raised the alarm. The physician assigned by the emperor to care for his wife happened to be in attendance nearby and the clamor brought him running. He arrived just as the hermit came out again, and caught him. Next he informed His Majesty, who of course was furious and threw the hermit into prison.

The prisoner would speak with no one. He only lifted his eyes to heaven, sobbing, and prayed to die and become a demon. "In that form," he continued, "may I achieve with this empress, while she still lives, the intimacy I crave!" His jailers heard him and warned the regent, who, in a fright, reported the matter to the emperor. His Majesty thought it safest to pardon the hermit and simply return him to his mountain.

Far from forgetting his lust, the hermit back on Kongōsen pleaded with the buddhas to bring him and the empress together. When he realized that such a thing was impossible in this life, he resolved to become a demon after all. After fasting for over ten days, he died at last of starvation. Instantly he changed into a demon: naked, bald, eight feet tall, and with black, glistening skin. His eyes were like brass bowls and his gaping mouth bristled with knifelike teeth, while short tusks crossed each other from the corners of his upper and lower jaws. Stuck in the red loincloth that was his only garment, he carried a demon's mallet.

In this guise he suddenly stood by the empress's curtains, in broad daylight and plainly visible to anyone. People cowered in terror or fled, while the ladies-in-waiting fainted or simply groveled on the floor and hid under their robes.

Meanwhile he addled the empress's brains so thoroughly that she welcomed him with smiles and led him to lie down with her behind her curtains. All the ladies-in-waiting could hear was the demon telling their mistress how fiercely he had wanted her, and their mistress giggling in reply. Then they all ran away.

When the demon left, around sundown, the ladies-in-waiting rushed back to their mistress wondering what had become of her. She looked the same as ever. In fact, despite the odd gleam in her eye she seemed not to know that anything special had happened.

On hearing of this fresh incident, His Majesty was less frightened by the demon than worried about what might have happened to his wife. The demon now came daily in just the same way. The empress never showed any fear, although she certainly was in no ordinary state of mind, and she treated him each time simply as a lover. The palace ladies and gentlemen who saw what was going on were very sorry.

Next, the demon possessed someone to declare that he was "going to get that physician for what he did to me." The terrified physician soon dropped dead, and all four of his sons also went mad and died.

By this time the emperor and the regent were beside themselves and called in the holiest men they could find to subdue the demon. Perhaps this worked, because for some time the demon stopped coming and the empress recovered a little of her former self.

The emperor was of course kept informed, and he was so pleased that he decided to go and see her. Since it was an unusually touching visit, the whole court attended him as he went. He sat with her and told her, in tears, how sorry he was about the whole affair. She herself was moved and in fact seemed quite her old self.

Just then the demon burst in and made straight for the empress's private, curtained enclosure. The empress hurried to join him as usual, as though it was the most natural thing in the world. In a moment the demon rushed out again, striking terror into every minister, noble, and official present. The empress followed. And there, in the sight of them all, the pair brazenly performed an unspeakable act. When it was over the demon left, and the empress stood up and withdrew. At a loss for what to think, say, or do, the emperor returned to his palace.

Let noble ladies then take heed and allow no such hermit to approach them! This sad story should serve as a dire warning to all.

1 2 **6** .

QUITE A STINK

Emperor En'yū had been ill for a long time, and since a spirit was causing the trouble, all the greatest healers of the time had been called in to do their best. Nothing had worked, though, and the emperor was beginning to be afraid.

Finally someone told him about an ascetic who had been practicing for years on Kōzen, the mountain near Nara. "He's built up such power that he can stop wild animals in mid-run with his spells, and bring down birds from the sky," the informant went on. "Summon him, Your Majesty! *He'll* help you!"

The ascetic came as fast as he could. All the way to Uji, about half the journey, flowers floated down on him from the sky — a sight that boggled the mind of everyone who saw it. (After Uji there were no more flowers.) The emperor called him in as soon as he got to the palace and had him begin his incantations. In almost no time His Majesty felt perfectly well.

Some of the great monks and healers whose intervention had failed found this instant success a bit odd. Among the doubters were five men who had just worked together in a particularly powerful Fudō rite.

"For years we've trusted in the Buddha and practiced his Teaching," one of the five complained. "Day after day we've prayed with heart and soul for His Majesty, and still we've failed. Who *is* this ascetic? What's *he* done to get such quick success? Perhaps he really is more powerful than any one of us, but he can't be more powerful than all five of us put together! It doesn't make sense!"

Having some more rites to perform, the five took the occasion to get near the ascetic from Kōzen and to direct some special incantations right at him.

The ascetic was seated by himself, entirely surrounded by curtains. In a moment they heard a vigorous scrabbling and scratching noise from inside the curtains, and a disgusting stink of dogshit filled the room. The nobles present were horrified, and so was His Majesty, but the five monks could tell that the truth about that ascetic was now beginning to come out. They redoubled their efforts.

Suddenly the ascetic hurtled out through his curtains and crashed to the floor, where he lay sprawled on his back. "Help!" he shrieked. "Good sirs, save me, please! All these years on Kōzen I've worshipped the tengu and prayed to them to make me famous. And it worked, you know, because I *was* called here to the palace! But what an awful mistake it was! I've learned my lesson now, yes I have! Please save me, oh please!"

The five monks were quite satisfied. As for the emperor, his first thought was to arrest the man and throw him in jail, but he changed his mind and only ordered him banished from the Capital. The ascetic was glad enough to make himself scarce. Some laughed to watch him go, while some just wished they could get their hands on him. He had been treated like a Buddha in person when he cured the emperor, but he made a very sorry sight as he fled.

THE MASTER

Though expert in scholarship and in the mysteries of the faith, the monk Yōshin from Mount Hiei found himself passed over for promotion year after year in favor of younger and less experienced monks, and became so disappointed that he eventually left the mountain and wandered off toward Iyo province. On the way he stopped at Akashi, a harbor in Harima.

An epidemic had affected every household around Akashi. Yōshin found the villagers scurrying about. They told him about the sickness, and explained that a monk and strolling diviner had come by and promised them he could stop it. They were now hurrying around, on his instructions, to distribute the things everyone would need to take part in the rite.

Yōshin was shocked that such a charlatan should prey on these poor gullible people, but he decided to join them to see what would happen.

The rite was to be the next morning. At dawn Yōshin dressed in his servant's clothes (for no monk of his station would travel alone) and helped the villagers carry the supplies to the beach. These included half a dozen new buckets, white and glutinous rice, soybeans, cowpeas, fruit and nuts, ginger, small and large earthenware bowls, clean straw mats, handwoven cloth, stout cryptomeria poles, fine paper, oil, and many other things. When all the supplies were at hand, the diviner prepared the ritual site on a fine broad stretch of sand.

He sewed several widths of cloth into a curtain, which he hung on the poles so as to screen off a fairly large space, then planted *shikimi* branches (which are always offered to spirits) around the inside of the curtain. Next, he laid out four mats in a square so that they faced in the four directions, leaving a smaller square of sand in the middle. After carefully smoothing this square he drew on it, with a long thin stick, a beautiful picture of the complicated Womb-Realm Mandala. The earthenware bowls were lined up on the mats, filled with holy water or heaped with fruit, nuts, and rice. He ended by lighting lamps at the four corners of the enclosure, cutting paper streamers, and attaching eight of them to each of the enclosure's four sides. Finally he and his assistants put on pure white ritual robes.

With everything now ready the diviner began the dedication rite for the Womb-Realm. He was very precise. Assuming that no one present would understand what he was doing, he did not bother to conceal the officiant's normally secret hand gestures, and Yōshin could tell he knew exactly what he was doing.

For Yōshin, the very existence of such a man was a revelation. Every detail was perfect. Each of the hundred villagers attending was properly bathed and purified. Even the children had their rosaries and were completely absorbed in invoking the buddhas. Yōshin had witnessed many such rites on Mount Hiei, but he had never seen one so meticulously done. He was so fascinated that he decided to become the diviner's disciple.

When the Womb-Realm dedication was over, the diviner gathered up everything in the enclosure and put it aside, including even the paper streamers and the *shikimi,* then took a new set of the same things and made exactly the same preparations as before. On the smoothed central square of sand he drew another mandala, this time the Vajra-Realm, and dedicated it just as carefully. At the end he dismantled everything including the curtain, heaped it all on the first pile, and set the pile on fire. Soon even the buckets and water dippers were ashes. There was nothing left except the white garments the diviner and his assistants had on. The awed villagers saw clearly that the diviner wanted nothing for himself.

Yōshin was determined to meet the man and waited after everyone had gone for the right moment to approach him.

Having finished tidying up, the diviner put on a straw cloak and started off, for he was not staying in the village. Yōshin chose that moment to accost him and ask him who he was.

"I'm not a peasant," the diviner replied "though out here in the country they all assume I'm one!" A disturbed expression came over his face as he spoke, and he suddenly turned and fled. In his hurry he even left his baggage behind.

Yōshin was very sorry. Back in the village he found out that as soon as the rite was over, everyone lying sick in the houses had shaken off the fever and recovered. The villagers were running around excitedly with the news. In fact, the epidemic disappeared that day not only from the village but from the whole province. The diviner had worked a miracle. Yōshin hunted for him everywhere, but never found him again.

1 2 8 .

A SIMPLE CURE

Lord Kinsue was still relatively junior at court (though later he became chancellor) when he was stricken with malaria. Having heard of a Lotus Sutra ascetic named Eijitsu who lived near Kyoto and was said to be expert at curing such fevers, Kinsue agreed to go and seek his help. Alas, he had not quite reached Eijitsu's temple when his fever returned, earlier than expected. It was too late for him to turn back. He struggled on, brought up his carriage under the temple eaves, and asked to see the ascetic.

Through an acolyte Eijitsu protested that he had been eating a lot of garlic lately, but Kinsue answered that he wanted to see the acolyte's master, garlic or no garlic, and that he was in no condition to go home. Eijitsu had his shutters opened and new mats spread on the floor, and Kinsue was led inside.

Meanwhile Eijitsu cleansed himself and soon came forth, tall, gaunt, and distinguished, to meet his guest. He explained that having caught a bad cold he was eating garlic on a doctor's advice. "But the Lotus Sutra is above considerations of purity or impurity," he added, "so my breath won't matter. I'll chant the Sutra for you. You'll be all right."

Kinsue was lying down. Eijitsu rubbed the beads of his rosary together as he approached him, and his whole manner inspired confidence. Then he took Kinsue's head in his hands, laid it on his lap, and began chanting. Kinsue was awed. He had never known so holy a feeling. Eijitsu's resonant, slightly hoarse voice was deeply moving, and as he chanted great tears streamed from his eyes. Kinsue's fever vanished and he felt renewed. Before he left he pledged Eijitsu enduring gratitude and devotion, and after that Eijitsu's healing powers acquired widespread fame.

1 2 9 .

A BELOVED WIFE, A BOW, A WHITE BIRD

Once a man had a kind and beautiful wife whom he loved very much. One night they were sleeping side by side when he dreamed his dear wife said to him, "After all this time we've been together, I'm going far away and won't see you any more. But I'll leave you something to remember me by. Love it instead of me!"

When he woke up, he was very upset. His wife was gone, really gone. It was a catastrophe. By his pillow lay a bow which had certainly not been there before. It must be the memento she had spoken of. Would she ever come back? He waited, but no, she never appeared. How he missed her! And the bow — it might well be some demon in disguise and he was afraid of it. But in the end he decided he had nothing to lose and began keeping it by him, stroking it as his memory lingered on his wife.

Months passed. One day the bow, which was by him as usual, suddenly turned into a white bird, which flew away toward the south. Astonished, he set out to follow it as it skimmed the clouds. When he reached the province of Kii, the bird turned into a human.

"Just as I thought!" said the man to himself. "That was no ordinary bow, it was a magic form of something else!"

Then he went home again, with on his lips a song about the strangeness of it all.

THE UNKNOWN THIRD

Tsunezumi no Yasunaga, who served Prince Koretaka, was once sent up north to Kōzuke province to collect taxes from an estate the prince owned there. Months later, on his way back to Kyoto, he stopped at the Fuwa barrier in the province of Mino.

Yasunaga had left his young wife at home and had missed her all the time he was gone. Now he suddenly yearned for her more sharply than ever and wondered whether something might have happened to her. Resolving to hurry on first thing the next morning, he lay down in the shelter provided at the barrier and went to sleep.

He dreamed he saw a man of the servant class coming from the direction of Kyoto, carrying a torch. He had a woman with him. When the pair reached the shelter, he saw the woman was his wife. What a shock! There she was on the other side of the wall.

Peering through a hole in the wall, he saw them bring over a kettle, cook rice, and eat. His wife had apparently taken up with this man in his absence. Yasunaga's stomach churned, his heart pounded, and his mind went into turmoil, but he kept watching. After their meal they lay down in each other's arms and began making love. The sight drove him wild and he rushed out. There was no fire. There was no one there at all. He woke up.

It had been a dream, then. Really worried now about his wife, Yasunaga set off at dawn with all possible speed. To his great relief he found his wife safe and sound at home.

She greeted him with joy. "You know," she said, "last night I dreamed a man I'd never seen before came and talked me into going off with him. I don't know where it was we went, but anyway, at nightfall we lit a fire and cooked rice. After dinner we went into some sort of cabin and lay down together. Then suddenly *you* burst in, and he and I both panicked. That was when I woke up. I've been wondering about that dream ever since, and now here you are!"

Yasunaga told her about *his* dream and what it had done to him. "You wouldn't believe how fast I got here!" he said.

How extraordinary that they should have dreamed, simultaneously, complementary dreams!

1 3 1 .

AN IMAGE IN A FLAME

Kochūjō, a young lady who served the empress, was very pretty and graceful, and so nice too that all the other ladies loved her dearly. Though she had no regular gentleman friend, Fujiwara no Takatsune, the governor of Mino, did visit her a good deal.

Once while Kochūjō was looking after the empress, dressed in pale violet over a pink underrobe, a precise image of her appeared in the flame of a lamp nearby. Her costume, her hair, her face, her look as she held her hand before her mouth — each detail was perfect. The other young ladies were amazed at the resemblance and clustered round to chatter and stare. Not one of them was experienced enough to know what needed to be done.

Kochūjō took it badly when she was told. "Ugh!" she cried. "You didn't put it out? You just kept staring at it? How embarrassing!" But when the older ladies of the household found out, they were worried. Those girls should have let someone responsible know right away! Instead, they had just trimmed the lamp as usual and left it at that.

Three weeks or so later, for no apparent reason, Kochūjō began to run a fever. For a day or two she kept to her room, then felt so ill that she went home.

When Lord Takatsune came by to let her know that he would be going away briefly, a little kitchenmaid told him where she had gone. He went straight to her house. The moon was sinking toward the west. When Kochūjō came out to him, he found her curiously pathetic, while she too seemed constrained and acted a little distant. Takatsune went in and lay down with her, but actually he felt like leaving.

They talked all night. By dawn Takatsune found it hard to say good-bye, and he worried about her all the way home. As soon as he got there, he sent her a note to tell her how concerned he was and promised he would be back to see her soon. Then he lingered to wait for her answer.

Her reply consisted of one word, "Toribeno." Why, that was the name of the burning ground where the dead were taken! Deeply troubled, Takatsune slipped the note in under his clothing, against his heart. Then he started off. He kept taking out the note all the way along to examine it. What beautiful writing she had! After being detained at his destination for some time, he got away as soon as he could and hurried back, thinking of her constantly. On reaching the Capital, he went directly to her house.

She had died the previous night and they had take her to Toribeno. Lord Takatsune's feelings can easily be imagined.

Yes, when someone's image appears in a flame, the thing to do is to trim off that part of the burned wick and have the person swallow it. And it's a good thing to pray hard, too. The young ladies hadn't known how dangerous a sight they had seen, and their ignorance caused Kochū-jō's death.

1 3 2 .

THE FORSAKEN LADY

Fujiwara no Moroie was involved with the meekest and sweetest of ladies. No reproach he might have deserved ever passed her lips. Though he did his best to avoid hurting her, official duties sometimes kept him busy, and then there were those inevitable evenings when a passing affection would detain him. In the end he did not actually spend many nights with her, and she came in her innocence to assume that he did not really love her. She began keeping her distance, and the more she did so the more they drifted apart. Not that they disliked each other, but the gulf between them kept widening until Moroie stopped visiting her altogether.

Six months later Moroie happened to pass her house. One of her women, on her way back from an errand, noticed him and told the lady he had just gone by. "Ah, when was it that he used to visit us?" the woman went on to muse. "It brought back so many memories to see him!"

The lady sent a messenger after Moroie. "Ask him to come in for a moment," she said. "I have something to tell him."

When he got the message, Moroie realized with a start where he was. He alighted from his carriage and entered the house.

The lady was seated before a box of sutra scrolls, chanting the Lotus Sutra. She was too beautifully dressed to have just tidied herself up in a hurry to receive him. Moroie saw her with new eyes and could not imagine why he had dropped her. Oh, to make her stop chanting and whisk her off to bed! But the months of separation had made him a little shy, and he tried instead to engage her in conversation. She did not respond, though her looks suggested she would talk with him as much as he liked when she had finished. Her face was simply entrancing. If only he could bring back the past, he thought, he would certainly do so.

Hopelessly in love now, and swearing to himself a thousand times over that he would never neglect her again, Moroie waited. He kept assuring her that he had never wanted to lose her, but she still would not answer. When she got to the seventh scroll, she began repeating the Medicine King chapter until she had been through it almost three times.

Moroie lost patience. "What's the meaning of this?" he complained. "Be done with it! I have so much to tell you!"

As he spoke she came to the passage that promises salvation to women, even in these latter, unhappy days: "She will go, when her life is over, to the Land of Bliss where Amida reigns among his saints, and she will dwell in a blue lotus, upon a jeweled throne." Tears were streaming from her eyes.

"What *is* this?" Moroie cried. "Have you gone pious or something, like a nun?"

She turned her brimming gaze to his, as though dew had touched her frost, yet a shadow seemed to fall between them. How cruel she must have thought him all these months! Moroie too broke down. What if he should never see her again! Could he live without her? The question would not leave him, and he shivered with foreboding.

Her sutra done, the lady began fingering an aloeswood rosary trimmed with amber, and lost herself in prayer. When she lifted her head again, so strange a look came over her face that Moroie flinched. "I asked you in," she began, "because I wanted to see you one more time. Now my anger and hurt . . ." Her voice stopped. She was dead.

Moroie could not believe it. The first time he called, nobody heard him. Finally a maid looked in and asked what was the matter. Moroie simply sat there. The maid quickly lost her composure too, and no wonder. As a single strand of hair breaks, the lady was gone. Moroie could not very well stay on because if he were to do so the pollution of death would oblige him to go into seclusion afterwards. As he left, her face was all he could see.

It was not long before Moroie sickened and died. Some supposed it was the lady's ghost that took him. In fact, those close to Moroie may even have had reason to be sure.

Other people assumed that since the lady had all but died with the Lotus Sutra on her lips, she must have gone on to paradise. But it's also true that she died with deep resentment against Moroie in her heart, and while looking straight at him. Surely the sin of both was very grave.

1 3 3 .

SHE DIED LONG AGO

A Kyoto man, too poor to make ends meet, learned one day with surprise that a gentleman he knew had been appointed governor of a distant province. He went straight to the new governor's residence, explained his situation, and offered his services in any capacity whatever. The gentleman was pleased to engage his old acquaintance on the spot.

The man and his lovely young wife had always been inseparable, despite the hardships of poverty; but now that he was going so far away he left his wife for another, richer one, who not only provided for his journey but came with him and took very good care of him in his province.

In time, however, he began to miss his first wife badly. He could hardly stop himself from rushing back to the Capital, and he tormented himself endlessly with speculation about how things might go if he did. Meanwhile his master's term of office ended, and he set out with his master for Kyoto.

How bitterly he now regretted having left his first wife! He promised himself that he would go directly to her when he reached the city. The way seemed unbearably long. On arrival he rushed to her house, found the gate open, and went in.

Everything had changed. The house seemed uninhabited and was falling to ruin. A wave of anguish swept over him as he gazed at the desolation, lit up as it was by an autumn moon just five days off the full. The night was chilly, too. He felt very sad.

In the house he found his wife lying all alone, just where she had lain in the old days. She showed no sign of anger when he came in, greeting him instead with joy. "How did you get here?" she asked. "When did you get back?"

He told her how he had longed for her and promised that from now on they would live together again. "I'll get all the things I've brought with me delivered here tomorrow," he said, "and I'll get my men moved here too. I just wanted to let you know right away, tonight." She looked very happy. After talking till late about the past, they finally lay down in each other's arms. "Have you no servant at all?" he asked. She explained that she had been too poor to keep one. He knew that her plight was his fault, and pity for her mingled in his thoughts with disgust at what he had done. It was nearly dawn when they fell asleep, with the shutters still open.

Sunlight streaming full into the room woke the man up. The woman in his arms was dried skin over dead bones. In horror he leaped to his feet, desperately hoping it was a hallucination. But no: what had once been a woman was now a long-dead corpse.

He dressed in frantic haste and burst into the neighbor's little house. "Where's the woman who used to live next door?" he shouted. "There's no one there!"

"She? Oh, her husband left her and went off to some province, and she was so hurt she got sick," the neighbor replied. "She had no one to take care of her and this past summer she died. Of course, there was no one to dispose of the body either, so she's still there. People are afraid to go near the place. That's why it's empty and going to ruin."

Terrified though he was, there was nothing further he could say or do, and he went his way.

1 3 4 .

I SAW IT IN A DREAM

Magari no Tsunekata lived in Owari province with his wife and was very comfortably off. After many years of marriage he fell in love with another woman. His wife made quite a fuss about this, as a woman might be expected to do, but he could not give his mistress up. He tried all sorts of dodges to keep seeing her in secret, but his wife had spies out after him, and any report that he was with his mistress would literally give her fits.

Once Tsunekata had business in the Capital and spent some time preparing for his trip. The day before he was due to leave he was overcome by the desire to see his mistress. Since his wife's fierce jealousy made it impossible for him to go openly, he announced instead that he was wanted by the provincial administration.

At his mistress's house, he and his mistress talked awhile in bed. When they eventually fell asleep, he dreamed that his wife burst in on them. "Ah, there you are with that woman again!" she screamed. "That's all you ever do nowadays, lie around with her! You with your innocent face and your smooth lies!" She went on like that for a while, then fell on him and thrust herself violently between him and his mistress. At this Tsunekata woke up.

Frightened and confused, he started home as soon as he could, and by daybreak was back with his wife. "It's really too bad!" he complained. "Here I'm about to leave, and they had to call me in for a meeting! I couldn't get away and so I had no sleep at all. What a thing to do to me!"

"Eat your breakfast," rasped his wife. Her hair was bristling straight up, then lying flat, then bristling skyward again.

"That's sort of scary," he remarked.

"You're disgusting!" his wife retorted. "You were over at her place last night, loving her up. It's written all over your face."

"Who told you that?"

"I saw it clear as a bell, you pig. I saw it in a dream."

"You *did*? You saw *what*?"

"Oh, I knew when you left yesterday evening that that was where you were headed. During the night I dreamed I went to her house. There you were snuggled up with her, chatting away. I listened. 'So you've given her up, have you?' I thought. 'Well then, what are you doing in *bed* with her?' Bah! I dove in between you and both of you jumped up in a panic."

Tsunekata was dumbfounded. "Well, what did I say?" he asked.

His wife repeated every word he had said. Tsunekata himself had dreamed the whole thing, very precisely. He was terrified. He kept his own dream to himself, however, and only revealed the whole awful incident later on, to a friend.

Just think what kind of spiritual state the wife must have been in! Jealousy is a very grave sin. Some suppose she must have ended up turning into a snake.

S N A K E S

1 3 5 .

THE SNAKE CHARMER

The musician Sukemitsu was imprisoned for neglect of duty in a store-house belonging to the Minister of the Left. The assortment of creatures and creepy-crawlies that inhabited the place frightened Sukemitsu quite enough already, but then in the middle of the night (this was exactly what he had been most afraid of) a huge snake appeared. Its head was like a lion's, its eyes were like bronze bowls, and its tongue, three feet long, flickered menacingly. Already the snake's vast jaws were yawning wide to swallow him when, half dead with fear, he managed to pull out his flute and play a passage from the dance *Genjōraku*.

The snake stopped, lifted its head high in the air, and listened awhile. Then it slithered away.

THE TUG-OF-WAR

The wrestler Ama no Tsuneyo lived in Tango province. In the summer he liked to stroll by the river that ran near his house, and was doing so one day, with a small boy beside him, when he paused under a tree by a deep pool.

The pool was blue-green and frightening because you could not see the bottom. Tsuneyo was gazing at the rushes around it when he noticed a large ripple dart from the opposite bank straight toward him. What could it possibly be? When the ripple reached his side, a snake lifted its head from the water. It was a very big one indeed, judging from the size of the head, and it stared at Tsuneyo so hard that he nervously stepped back a little. Then it vanished again into the pool.

The ripple darted off to the far side and a swell of water came rolling back. The snake's tail rose from the pool and thrashed its way toward Tsuneyo, who waited, calmly now, to see what it would do. When the tail had wrapped itself twice around his legs, the snake began to pull. It wanted to drag him into the pool! Tsuneyo planted his feet more firmly, but the snake was so strong that the teeth of his high clogs broke and he felt sure he would be dragged down. Once more he dug in his feet, but the snake tugged so hard that they simply plowed through the earth, leaving a furrow several inches deep. Tsuneyo was just putting up a last, desperate effort, when the snake snapped in two and blood stained the surface of the pool. He pulled up the tail half, unwound it, and washed his legs in the pool. The attack had left indelible marks.

By this time Tsuneyo's servants had rushed up, and he had them wash the wounds with wine. Then they inspected the snake's tail half. Huge was the only word for the creature. The body was a good foot thick where it had broken. It turned out that the snake had wrapped its head end, on the opposite bank, around a thick tree-root to give itself a better hold. Even so Tsuneyo had proved the stronger, and the snake had snapped instead. The head end, still clinging as tightly as ever to the root, seemed not to have realized what had happened. Imagine how it must have been feeling!

But how strong had the snake really been? Tsuneyo's men tied a rope round their master's legs and ten of them pulled on it. Tsuneyo said the snake had tugged harder than that. Three men were added, then five, but they still were not enough. Finally sixty men took the rope, and Tsuneyo decided that yes, that was how the snake had pulled. In other words (considering that Tsuneyo had *not* been dragged down by the snake) Tsuneyo had the strength of about a hundred men.

That was the kind of wrestler we used to have in the old days.

1 3 7 .

AS DEEP AS THE SEA

A professional keeper of hawks once followed an escaped bird deep into the mountains till he spied a hawk's nest in a tall tree. This was a welcome find. He marked the place, went home again, and returned at the right time to get the young hawks.

It was a wild and desolate spot, and the tree leaned over a bottomless ravine. The nest of young hawks was high in its branches, and the parents were circling round it. What specimens the parents were! No doubt the young would be just as impressive. Bent on catching them, the man hardly even knew he was climbing the tree.

Just short of the nest, a branch broke under him and he plummeted into another tree growing straight out of the cliff below. He hung on there, more dead than alive, between a yawning chasm and a sheer wall of rock.

Though his servants assumed he had fallen into the ravine and been killed, they thought they had better make sure. Clinging precariously to the edge of the cliff, they peered over into the depths. All the leaves in the way hid their master from them, and they got nothing for their trouble but a spell of dizziness. They could only go home and inform their master's wife and children, who wept at the news. The family wanted at least to see for themselves where the body lay, but the servants cried, "No, no, we can't even remember the way, and besides, it's no use your going! Goodness knows how deep that ravine is! We did our best to find him down there, but we couldn't see anything at all!" So no one even went back to look.

The man sat on a tiny ledge about the size of a dinner tray, clinging to the tree and keeping very still. The slightest movement, and he would be dashed to pieces on the rocks below. There was nothing he could do. But although his business was raising hawks, he had chanted the Kannon Sutra ever since his childhood and he trusted in Kannon's mercy. Now he called on Kannon to save him and began to chant.

When he got to the passage, "His vow to save suffering beings is as deep as the sea," he thought he heard something rustling up from the bottom of the ravine. What could it be? With infinite caution he peered down and saw an enormous snake at least twenty feet long slithering straight up toward him. It was going to eat him, or at least that was the only explanation that made sense. Now he was *really* frightened, and begged Kannon from the bottom of his heart to save him from this awful danger.

The snake made no attempt to swallow him when it reached his seat. On the contrary, it just kept going. Its only thought seemed to be to climb up and out of the ravine. Perhaps he could hang on to it somehow and go up with it! He drew the dagger from his belt, plunged it into the snake to make a handhold, and let himself be drawn up and over the edge of the cliff. As he slid off he tried to take out the dagger, but it was too firmly planted. The snake pulled away from him and slithered off toward the next ravine with the dagger still stuck in its back.

Delirious with relief, the man tried to run home, but sitting motionless for several days, without food or water, had made him so weak that in fact he could only barely drag himself back to his house. The household was in the middle of a memorial rite for him when he staggered in, causing momentary pandemonium. He wept as he told them his extraordinary experience. Then he ate and slept soundly.

The next morning he got up early, washed his hands, and opened the text of the Kannon Sutra he always read. His dagger, the one he had plunged into the back of the snake, was planted in the text at the words "His vow to save suffering beings is as deep as the sea."

1 3 8 .

WHAT THE SNAKE HAD IN MIND

A woman on her way up to hear the monthly preaching at Urin'in, a temple in northern Kyoto, had come to a stone bridge — just a small slab over a tiny brook — when another, younger woman walking along the brook stepped on the slab as she crossed and overturned it. Where it had been the first woman was surprised to see, all coiled up, a little spotted snake.

The snake slowly unwound itself and set off after the young woman who had overturned its stone. This was intriguing. Perhaps the snake was angry at having been disturbed and wanted to get even. The older woman was curious enough to set out after it.

The young woman the snake was following did look round sometimes, but seemed to suspect nothing. No one passing by did either. Apparently only the older woman could see the snake.

In time they reached Urin'in. The young woman climbed the steps and sat down on the wooden floor while the snake too got up the steps and wriggled to her side. Still no one saw it or raised the alarm.

When the preaching was over the young woman left, and the snake with her. The older woman stayed behind them on the way back. In the southern district of the city the woman entered a house that seemed to be hers, and the snake followed.

The snake was unlikely to do anything during the day, but the older woman was determined to be on hand for whatever might happen that night. She went up to the house, explained that she had just arrived from the country and had nowhere to stay, and begged for a night's lodging. She had assumed all along that the young woman was the owner, but in fact it was an old lady who invited her in. She found the young woman sitting on the raised floor with the snake coiled at the foot of a pillar, gazing at her. The young woman was talking about "the mansion," and it seemed clear that she was in service somewhere.

When the sun set and darkness fell, the visitor could no longer see the snake, so she proposed spinning hemp in exchange for the old lady's hospitality. For this she would need light. The old lady gladly accepted her offer and lit a lamp. As the visitor spun, she looked around her. The young woman seemed to have lain down to sleep. No doubt the snake would go to her now — but it did not. The visitor felt she ought to mention the snake, but decided she would only make trouble for herself if she did and so kept silent. The evening wore on till at last the lamp went out. There was nothing to do but go to bed.

Next morning the visitor woke up with a start, anxious to know what might have happened during the night. After getting up quite normally, the young woman told the old lady she had had an odd dream, and the old lady insisted on hearing it.

"Last night," said the young woman, "I dreamed somebody stood by my pillow. She was human from the waist up, but from the waist down she was a snake. She was beautiful, though, and this is what she said to me. 'Once I hated someone so much that I turned into a snake and spent many long and lonely years under the stone slab of a bridge. Yesterday you overturned the stone and saved me. I felt so gloriously free that I wanted to thank you properly. That's why I followed you to the temple and heard the Buddha's most rare and wonderful Teaching. That in turn canceled my sins, and now I'll soon be reborn in human form. You've made me so happy! In return I'll make sure that your life goes well and you find a good husband.' And that was the end of my dream."

Both listeners were astonished, and the visitor confessed who she really was and why she was there. She and the young woman became fast friends and saw each other often.

The young woman did do well, too, because she married a very wealthy man, a junior steward in a great household. Everything went for her exactly as she wished.

1 3 9 .

RED PLUM BLOSSOMS

In the west of the Capital lived a man of some rank in the world. His only daughter, a sweet and lovely girl, wrote a beautiful hand by the time she reached her teens, and her skill at poetry was peerless. Not only that, she was also an expert musician and played the *koto* particularly well.

The family's large mansion included several bark-thatched pavilions, curiously and handsomely made. Pretty streams ran through a garden which was always beautiful, if not with spring flowers then with the leaves of fall. And while the girl's parents thought only of her, the girl herself was lost in delight over the flowers and leaves.

The garden had places where cherry blossoms opened in the mists of spring, and where the weeping willow fronds' new green swayed deliciously in the breeze; while elsewhere the colored autumn leaves hovered in layers of brocade, and chrysanthemums of many hues leaned under their burden of dew beneath the tall *hagi* plants' feathery curves. Yet the girl loved above all the red-flowering plum.

She planted a red plum tree near her room, and when it bloomed she opened her shutters to gaze on it rapturously, all alone. The fragrance intoxicated her so much that she stayed there all day. She let nothing else grow near her plum and would not have birds nesting in its branches. When the flowers fell, she gathered the fallen petals in a lacquered bowl to enjoy their scent awhile longer; and on windy days she even spread mats to collect them as they fluttered down, so as to make sure they were not blown away and lost. When the petals were withered at last, she mixed them into her incense to save the very last of their sweet smell.

In time she fell ill and grew rapidly worse, despite her parents' lamentations. Before long she was gone. Her mother and father had to bid her farewell forever, and could never look at the plum tree after that without a pang of sorrow.

One day a little snake appeared under the tree. Though it seemed ordinary enough, it came again the next spring and stayed wrapped around the tree. When the petals began to fall, it picked them up one by one in its mouth and heaped them together. Realizing that it could only be their daughter herself, the parents grieved afresh. All they could do was to call in two holy monks and have them expound the Lotus Sutra under the tree, one chapter a day in the time-honored fashion, for the good of their daughter's soul.

The snake, which never left the spot, heard all the preaching. On the fifth day the monks spoke on the chapter in which the Serpent Princess offers the Buddha a priceless pearl and passes straight into Nirvana. Under the plum tree, the little snake died. Those who saw its passing wept.

Later the father dreamed about his daughter. At first she was dressed in torn and filthy clothes and looked very downcast. But a holy man came to her and had her take off her rags. Her skin underneath was golden and glowing, like the skin of a buddha, and the holy man dressed her in rich robes and a priestly stole. Finally he raised her up and they floated away together on a purple cloud.

That was the end of the dream. The girl's salvation was the Sutra's gift.

R O B B E R S   I I

1 4 0 .

THE ENIGMA

Once a thief got into a shop in the Western Market and the Imperial Police surrounded the place, intent on capturing him. Their commander rode among them fully armed, in formal headdress and pale grey cloak.

When a freed convict bearing a spear was posted to stand at the door of the shop, the thief signaled to him through a crack that he should come closer. "Go tell your commander to get off his horse and come here," the thief said. "I have something to tell him in private."

The freed convict reported this message, and the commander moved to obey, over his men's strenuous objections. "No, I'd better look into this," was all he would say as he dismounted and started for the door.

The thief opened it and invited the commander in, closing and bolting it again when he was inside. The men were furious. "Here we've got him surrounded!" they sputtered. "We can't possibly miss him! And now His Lordship has to walk right in and get himself shut up for a nice little chat. This is insane!"

Shortly the door opened again. The commander emerged, got back on his horse, and rode up to his men. "There's more to this business than meets the eye," he announced. "We'll have to hold off till I give a report to His Majesty." He headed straight for the palace, leaving his men to stand guard.

"That's right," he said when he returned, "we can't arrest him. Go back to headquarters. Those are His Majesty's orders."

The men obeyed. Their commander stayed on alone until finally, after dark, he went to the door and announced the emperor's decision. The thief burst into loud and unrestrained sobbing.

After the commander was gone, the thief stole out and disappeared into the night. No one ever found out who he was or why he had been pardoned.

1 4 1 .

WASPS

A quicksilver dealer in Kyoto had gotten rich from his business. He traveled regularly back and forth to Ise province with a train of a hundred horses or more, all loaded with silk and cotton cloth, thread, rice, and other such goods, and he never took with him more than a few boys to drive the animals. As old age approached, he had never suffered a single loss from fire or flood and, still more remarkably, had never lost a single sheet of paper to thieves.

This was extraordinary because the people of Ise are perfectly capable of robbing their own parents. Friend and foe, rich and poor spend their time scheming to bilk each other, and they do not hesitate to plunder the weak to add to their own fortune. For some reason the quicksilver merchant was about the only victim they had not yet despoiled.

Now, there was a robber band one hundred strong which lurked in the Suzuka Mountains on the western border of the province and year after year preyed on all who passed that way. They would seize everything of value (private or imperial property, it made no difference), then kill the unhappy travelers. Even the government in Kyoto had been unable to suppress them.

During the height of their depredations the quicksilver merchant came that way again, traveling out of Ise toward the Capital with his usual train of a hundred well-laden horses and protected only by his youthful drivers. He even had women with him, and all the food, etc., that they required.

The robbers spotted the caravan with glee. Its leader was obviously soft in the head, and they intended to appropriate the riches he was so innocently parading before them. In the depths of the mountains they ambushed him from front and rear. The terrified drivers fled. After rounding up the pack horses, the robbers stripped the women of all their clothes and shooed them off into the wilds. As for the merchant, who was riding a mare, he barely managed to get away and scramble up a high hill. The robbers watched him go but decided he was a hopeless case anyway and not worth chasing. Instead, they headed down into the valley to divide the booty. Everyone was well pleased and felt he had come easily enough by his share.

Meanwhile the merchant on his hill was staring aloft and bellowing, "Where are you? Where are you? Hurry!" In an hour or so a huge, murderous wasp three inches long came droning down from the sky into a tall tree nearby. The merchant redoubled his exhortations to haste. Then a long, thick, reddish cloud appeared in the sky.

The robbers were just putting away their spoils. The cloud descended into their valley and the wasp in the tree followed. The cloud was wasps. Hundreds of wasps overwhelmed each robber and stung him to death. Then the cloud gathered once more, rose, and vanished into the distance.

The quicksilver merchant went down into the valley in his turn and found there the whole hoard of booty the robbers had stored up over the years: a huge number of bows, quivers, horses, saddles, articles of clothing, and many other things. He returned with it all to Kyoto, even richer than before.

His secret was that he brewed wine at home and fed it all to his wasps, which in many other ways too he treated with the greatest consideration. Most robbers knew this and left his property alone. These marauders had been done in by their own ignorance.

1 4 2 .

WITHOUT EVEN A FIGHT

Sakanoue no Haruzumi, a veteran warrior, lived in the province of Kii. Having business in the Capital he set off, but not without being fully armed and accompanied by equally well-armed retainers, for he feared an attack by a particular enemy of his.

Late that night he was passing through the southern district of the Capital when he met a party of court nobles on horseback. Servants were going ostentatiously before them to clear the way. There was no doubt about what had to be done. Haruzumi dismounted. "Lay down your bows!" he orderd his men, who promptly obeyed. Then they all waited with their foreheads pressed to the earth.

Haruzumi was just thinking the lords must have gone by when he, like every one of his men, felt a heavy hand on his neck. He twisted his head round in surprise. The riders he had taken for nobles were instead half a dozen armed and armored men with arrows ready to the string. "Move and you're dead!" one barked.

They were bandits, and Haruzumi had fallen straight into their trap. He was furious with himself, and miserable too, but under threat of instant death he could only do as the bandits ordered. They stripped him and his men of every garment they had on, of their bows and quivers, of their horses and saddles, of their swords and daggers, and even of their shoes.

Haruzumi knew that if he had been on guard against them they would have had to kill him to get away with this, and he felt sure he would have put up a good enough fight to capture the bandits somehow himself. But they had tricked him with their charade into laying down his own arms and waiting politely, with bowed head, to be robbed. It was too much. His fighting career was cursed. Haruzumi gave up the profession of arms.

1 4 3 .

THE TEMPLE BELL

One day an ancient monk turned up at Koyadera in Settsu province and explained to the abbot that he was on his way up from the western provinces toward the Capital. "But I'm so old that I'm all worn out," he continued. "I just can't go on! Perhaps you won't mind if I rest at your temple for a while. Do you suppose there's anywhere I could stay?"

"I can't think of a place offhand," the abbot replied. "If you stay in the gallery around the main hall, you'll be exposed to the weather and you'll get sick."

"Well, how about the bell tower. It's completely enclosed, after all."

"Fine, that's a good idea," said the abbot. "It's all yours. And it would be nice if you'd ring the bell, too."

The old monk looked pleased, and the abbot led him straight to the bell tower. "Here's the bell ringer's mat," he said. "Make yourself at home."

When the abbot ran into the regular bell ringer, he told him about the old monk who had come wandering in and described how he had installed the fellow under the bell. "He says he'll take care of ringing it," the abbot went on, "so you can take it easy while he's here." The bell ringer did not complain.

For two days the ancient traveler rang the bell. On the morning of the third day the bell ringer thought he would just go and see how the fellow was doing. "Hello!" he called at the base of the tower. "Are you there?" And he squeezed inside.

The old monk, amazingly tall, lay sprawled out full length, wrapped in a miserable garment. He was dead. The bell ringer beat a fast retreat and went to find the abbot.

"The old boy's dead," he stammered. "What are we going to do?"

The abbot went straight to check this awful news. It was true. The monk was dead. He closed the door to the bell tower and warned the rest of the temple's monks.

"Congratulations!" they growled back at him. "It was so thoughtful of you to let him stay! Now you've got the whole temple polluted!" But it was too late now to be angry. They saw they would have to get some villagers to come and take the body away.

Unfortunately, the village's shrine festival was near, as the villagers quickly pointed out. "We just can't go and get ourselves polluted now," they said. No one would touch the corpse, and noon came while the monks went on fretting about what in the world to do.

Out of nowhere, two men appeared, about thirty years old and dressed in light grey cloaks that darkened toward the bottom, with broad, conical hats hanging round their necks against their backs. Their skirts were tucked up for easier movement, and they had swords stuck in their belts. Certainly they were humble men, but they seemed alert and pleasant. They went straight to the monks' dormitory and asked whether by any chance an old monk was stopping nearby.

The monks told them a tall old monk had spent the last couple of days in the base of the bell tower, but said they gathered that this morning he had just been found dead. The two men burst into tears of shock and grief. They explained that the old monk had been their father. "He'd gotten stubborn in his old age," they said, "and we had a little quarrel. It was nothing, really, but he stormed off and disappeared. We're from Akashi county in Harima. After he'd gone we split up to find him, and we've been looking for him ever since. We're not penniless, you know. We own a good deal of rice land and you can find retainers of ours even in the neighboring county. We'll have a look for ourselves, and if he's really dead we'll bury him this evening."

The abbot took them to the bell tower and waited outside while they went in. "Oh father, here you are!" they cried when they saw the old monk's face. Then they rolled on the ground and wept aloud. The sight was too much for the abbot, who was soon weeping too. "Our quarrel was nothing," they mourned, "but you were an old man and just wouldn't give in! Off you went to hide from us and ended up here, in the middle of nowhere. And we weren't even with you when you died!" This thought brought on a fresh paroxysm of tears. Finally they said they would go to prepare for the funeral and closed the door of the bell tower behind them. When the abbot described the scene to his colleagues, they wept too.

Well along in the evening some forty or fifty people arrived, with much noise and commotion, and brought out the old monk's body. Quite a few were armed. The monks kept well away from the bell tower. Far from going to watch the proceedings, they were all so afraid that they shut themselves up in their rooms. As a result, they only heard the mourners carry the body to a pine wood several hundred yards off, up against the hillside behind the temple. The mourners spent the night beating gongs and chanting the Buddha's Name, dispersing only at dawn.

For the thirty days the pollution lasted not even the bell ringer rang the bell, and no other monk went near the bell tower either. At last, when it was finally safe to do so, the bell ringers returned to the tower to clean up. The great bell was gone.

The bell ringer ran to spread this latest outrage to the rest of the temple, and the monks trooped out to see for themselves. It was a fact: the bell had been stolen. Why, those people must have planned the whole funeral just so they could steal the bell! The monks thought they had better check the funeral site.

Off they all went, with some people from the village, to the pine wood. The thieves had chopped up a big pine tree to make a fire around the bell and melt it down, and there were bits of bronze all over the place. They had brought off quite an operation! Unfortunately, there was no way to find out who they had been. The monks could only resign themselves to their loss.

Ever since, Koyadera has been without a bell.

1 4 4 ·

THE DEAD MAN WAKES

Being a professional, the robber Hakamadare naturally ended up in jail. He was released under a general amnesty. Having nowhere to go then, and nothing else to turn his hand to, he went up to Osaka Pass and played dead, stark naked, beside the trail. The passing travelers clustered round and, noticing that he was not wounded, chattered to each other about how he might have died.

Along from Kyoto came an armed warrior on a good horse, followed by a troupe of servants and retainers. The warrior saw the crowd, stopped, and sent one of his men to find out what they were gawking at. The man reported that they were puzzling over a dead man without a wound on him. The warrior ordered his followers back into proper formation and rode on. He stared at the corpse as he passed.

The crowd clapped their hands and laughed. "A fine warrior *you* are," they taunted him, "with all that train of yours, to be squeamish about a body!" The warrior ignored them.

In time the crowed dispersed. There was no one left around Hakamadare when another warrior came along. He had no train of servants and retainers, but he was well armed. He went right up to the body. "Poor man!" he said. "I wonder what you died of. I don't see any wound." He poked at the corpse here and there with the tip of his bow. Suddenly the dead man seized the bow, leaped up, pulled the warrior down from his horse, drew the man's own dagger, and killed him.

"Better be more careful next time!" said Hakamadare.

In no time Hakamadare had the slain man's clothes off and was wearing them himself. Next he seized the warrior's weapons, jumped on his horse, and galloped away toward the east. He had already arranged a rendezvous with a dozen or two of the convicts who had been released with him, and he took any latecomer on as a servant. The band swept along, robbing everyone they met of clothing, mounts, and weapons. These were distributed among the naked bandits until it was twenty or thirty well-armed desperados who rode eastward along the road, and no one they encountered could stand against them.

That's what a man like that will do if you give him half a chance. Just get close enough for him to touch you, and watch out! The first warrior, the one who rode resolutely by, turned out to have been a fellow named Taira no Sadamichi. Everyone who heard the story nodded approval of his action. It had been wise of him to pass on, despite his large train. And what a fool he had been, the one who, without a single follower by him, had gone right up to the body!

1 4 5 .

COWED

Late one fall Hakamadare, the notorious bandit chieftain, felt he needed some new clothes and decided to go looking for them. It was the middle of the night and the town was quiet. You could barely see the moon. Along came a man wearing a complete, first-class outfit. He was sauntering down the path playing the flute.

"That's the one!" thought the bandit. "He's come to give me his clothes!"

Hakamadare was about to jump his victim when he suddenly felt afraid, and followed the man instead. The man gave no sign of knowing anyone was behind him. He just strolled along playing his flute. To test him, Hakamadare started running with heavy steps.

The man turned around but did not stop playing. Hakamadare retreated, unable to bring himself to attack. He tried the same thing over and over, but the man never got flustered. "This is an odd one!" thought Hakamadare.

Half a mile or so further on, Hakamadare decided he had to act. He drew his sword and charged. The man stopped playing, stood still, and turned to face him. "Who are you?" he asked. Hakamadare was cowed. In spite of himself he plopped down on the ground.

"Who are you?" the man repeated. Hakamadare could tell it was useless to run.

"I'm a bandit," he answered.

"What's your name?

"Hakamadare."

"Oh yes," said the man," I've heard of you. You're tough. Come with me." He went on again, playing his flute. Hakamadare followed like a demon caught by some god.

They came to the man's house. He turned out to be the famous warrior Yasumasa, the former governor of Settsu province. Yasumasa invited Hakamadare in and gave him a thickly padded coat. "When you need clothes," he said, "just come to me. Don't go attacking people you know nothing about. You could make a big mistake."

The awestruck Hakamadare told this story the next time he was arrested.

LOTUS

TALES

1 4 6 .

THE BLOODY SWORD

A mountain temple in Tajima province was over a century old. No one went near it because it was haunted by demons, but one day a pair of monks, one old and one young, happened by just after sundown, and since they did not know the place they decided to stay there.

After dark they settled down on opposite sides of the altar. In the middle of the night something bashed its way through the wall. The creature stank horribly and wheezed and snorted like an ox, but in the darkness they could not see it. It attacked the younger monk, who, in his fright, recited the Lotus Sutra and fervently prayed to be spared. Suddenly it dropped him, fell on the older monk, and began devouring him. The victim screamed horribly, but no one saved him and the demon ate him up.

The younger monk was sure the demon would now be back for *him*. He clambered up on the altar (there being no other refuge), threw his arms round one of the divinities, and begged for help, then went on inwardly reciting the Lotus. When the demon did come after him, he nearly fainted with terror but his concentration never wavered. He heard the demon crash to the floor in front of the altar.

There was dead silence. The monk assumed the demon was waiting for him to betray himself by some slight noise, so he hardly dared even to breathe. With his arms around the statue, and still mentally reciting the Lotus, he waited for dawn. It seemed like years. When day came at last, he found he had been embracing the divine guardian Bishamon. Before the altar an ox-headed demon lay cut in three, and the blade of Bishamon's spear was red with blood.

¹ 4 7 ·

A PLEA FROM HELL

Tateyama, a mountain in Etchū province, has been known since antiquity for its hells. The rugged, sweeping landscape there is desolate, and countless boiling springs gush from deep fissures in the ravines. Even a huge boulder resting on one of these cracks may be set rocking by the water that surges up irresistibly around its base. The heat is terrible, and you come eventually to a column of endless fire. In one valley of this hellish waste there is a waterfall over a hundred feet high that looks like a vast expanse of white cloth.

One peak of the mountain is named Mount Taishaku because they say that is where Lord Taishaku and the officials of the underworld gather and judge the deeds of sentient beings. People have always believed that most of the sinners in Japan end up falling into the hells of Tateyama.

Once a monk of Miidera came to Tateyama in the course of a difficult pilgrimage to the holy places of the realm, and while he was walking among the hells he met a young woman. The sight of her frightened him because in a remote spot like that she could only be a demon, and he

began to run away. But she called to him, assured him that she was not
a demon, and told him that he need not be afraid. She had something to
tell him.

"My home," she said, "was in Gamō county of Ōmi province, where
my parents still live. My father makes his living carving buddha-images
out of wood. When I was alive, my food and clothing came from these
images, and that's why after death I fell into a hell where I suffer horrible
agony. Please, in your compassion, tell my mother and father what's
happened to me! Have them copy the Lotus Sutra for me and save me
from these torments!"

"You say you're suffering in hell," the monk replied, "but apparently
you're still free to appear to me. How is this possible?"

The young woman explained that this was Kannon's day, the eighteenth day of the moon. "When I was alive," she went on, "I meant to
serve Kannon and read the Kannon chapter of the Lotus Sutra. And even
though I kept putting off actually doing it, just once on an eighteenth day
I did purify myself and call on Kannon. That's why each moon, on the
eighteenth day, Kannon comes and suffers in my place for a day and a
night. Then I can leave my hell and wander freely." When she had
finished speaking, she vanished.

The monk went straight to Ōmi to find out whether all this was true.
In Gamō county he found the young woman's parents, and they wept to
hear the news he brought them. When he had gone, they lost no time in
copying and dedicating the Sutra for their daughter.

Later the father dreamed that she came to him beautifully dressed,
greeted him with her palms pressed together, and told him how she had
left the hell on Tateyama by the power of Kannon. Now, she said, she
had been born into the Tōri Heaven. The monk had just the same happy
dream.

1 4 8 .

THE VOICE FROM THE CAVE

Having one morning some urgent business to look after at the office, a
secretary in the Higo provincial government rode off first thing, all alone.
He normally covered the half-mile or so quickly, but this time he got lost
and came out on a broad plain. He had no idea where he was.

By sundown, after crossing the plain all day, he still had not seen a single house where he might spend the night. How he longed for a village! At last he glimpsed, from the top of a rise, the corner of a well-made roof.

"Is anyone home?" he shouted when he reached the house, for the place seemed awfully quiet. "Please come to the door! What's the name of this place?"

"Who are you?" called a woman's voice from inside. "Come on in!"

Her voice frightened the secretary. He called back that he was lost, and in too much of a hurry to stop. "I just want to know where I am!" he went on. "Won't you please tell me?"

"Wait a minute! I'll be right out!"

Terrified, the secretary wheeled his horse round and galloped away as fast as he could.

"Hey!" shouted the woman as she emerged. "Wait!"

He glanced back. She was as tall as the roof and her eyes were gleaming. "That's it!" he thought. "It was a demon's house!" He frantically whipped his horse on.

"Where do you think you're going?" she bellowed. "Stop right there!"

The secretary nearly went mad with fear because she was after him now, ten feet tall and with eyes and a mouth that spouted dazzling flashes of fire. The mouth gaped wide to swallow him. He almost fainted and fell off his horse, but still managed somehow to pray, "Kannon, save me, oh save me now!"

When his horse stumbled and fell, he was thrown clear. No doubt he would be eaten any second. Without even knowing what he was doing he dashed into a burial cave nearby, and the demon came pounding after him. "Where are you?" it roared. "You were there just a moment ago!" Then it halted and began devouring his horse. Obviously he would be next, unless by any unlikely chance it really did not know where he was. He went on praying to Kannon with all his heart.

Having finished the horse, the demon came to the mouth of the cave. "All right," it said, "this man was supposed to be *my* meal for today. Why have you taken him away from me? You're always playing me nasty tricks like this and I've had enough!" It knew where he was, all right.

"Oh no, he's mine and I'm keeping him," growled a voice from further back in the cave. "You got the horse. What more do you want?"

It was all over now, the secretary was quite sure of that. Not only was that horrible demon right outside the cave, but an even more horrible one was inside it. All his prayers to Kannon were in vain, and in a moment he would be dead. Well, he probably had nothing to blame but his own awful karma from past lives.

The demon outside kept pleading and complaining, but to no avail. Finally it left, still grumbling. Now the secretary expected to be dragged into the monster's lair and eaten.

"You were going to make a meal for that demon today," said the voice, "but you prayed so devoutly to Kannon that you've been spared. Keep up your faith after this and chant the Lotus Sutra. Do you know who I am?"

The secretary said no.

"I'm no demon. A holy man once lived in this cave. On top of the mountain nearby he built a tower and enshrined the Lotus Sutra in it. The tower and the Sutra itself have long since crumbled away and there's nothing left but *myō*, or 'wonderful,' the first word of the Sutra's title. I'm that *myō*. I've already saved nine hundred and ninety-nine people from that demon and you're the one-thousandth. Go home now. Never give up your faith in the Buddha and your devotion to the Lotus!"

A divine boy came out of the cave to see the secretary home. Weeping, the secretary prostrated himself in gratitude and adoration, then followed the boy to the gate of his own house, where the boy vanished. The secretary prostrated himself once more before walking in. It was the middle of the night. He told his family everything that had happened to him, and they were very, very glad to have him back!

¹ 4 9 ·

INCORRIGIBLE

Toshiyuki, a respected poet and calligrapher, had such beautiful handwriting that people were always asking him to copy the Lotus Sutra for them. They took it for granted that Toshiyuki's elegant rendition of the sacred text would help them toward a better life next time. Toshiyuki had copied the Sutra two hundred times this way when he suddenly died.

Not realizing what had happened, he only knew that he had been abruptly seized and dragged off. He was outraged and could not understand how anyone, even the emperor, could do such a thing to a man of his standing.

"What have I done to deserve this?" he asked the officer who he thought had arrested him.

"Who knows?" the officer replied. "I was ordered to go and get you, and that's what I'm doing. Come to think of it, have you been making copies of the Lotus Sutra?"

Toshiyuki said he had.

"How much of this copying was for yourself?"

"None. It's all been for other people. I must have done a couple of hundred Sutras."

"That's it, then. There have been complaints and I suppose the case has come up."

That was all Toshiyuki could get out of him. They marched on in silence.

Soon they met a force of two hundred warriors, wearing grim battle armor and riding strange, terrible horses. The eyes in their ghastly faces flashed like lightning and their mouths were like fire. Toshiyuki almost fainted with fear, but the officer forced him back to his feet and they went on, with the soldiers before them.

"Who are *they*?" Toshiyuki managed to stammer.

"Don't you know? They're the people who had you write out the Sutra. They were counting on the merit getting them reborn in heaven or at least giving them another try as humans. But you — you were eating fish and enjoying women all the time you did your copying. You never purified yourself. On the contrary, you had your mind on nothing but the ladies. So they had no merit whatever from your work and were born instead into these fierce, warlike forms. They're so angry they want revenge, and that's why they've been demanding that you be called in. To tell the truth, it wasn't actually your time yet, but they insisted."

Toshiyuki felt as though a knife had gone through him and his heart froze. "What are they going to do to me?" he asked.

"Obviously they're going to cut you up with those swords and daggers of theirs into two hundred little pieces, and each of them is going to keep one. Every piece will be you, fully conscious, so you'll suffer horribly any time any one of them tortures the piece he's got. Oh yes, you'll find it worse than anything you can imagine!"

"What can I do to be spared?"

"I've no idea," the officer replied. "I can't see what would save you."

Toshiyuki was nearly out of his mind with terror.

On they went till they came to a great river running as black as the blackest ink. Toshiyuki asked what these strange, inky waters might be.

"Don't you understand?" the officer answered. "This is the ink from all the Lotus Sutra copies you made. A sutra copied with pure heart is accepted instantly into the palace of the Dragon King who guards the Buddha's Teaching. But copies made like yours, with defiled mind and filthy body, are thrown away in the fields, and the ink washes off in the rain till it makes a river."

"Oh please, please," sobbed Toshiyuki, "is there no help for me, nothing I can do?"

"I'm sorry, I might possibly be able to do something for you if your sin were a commonplace one, but I'm afraid it's unspeakable. You'll get no reprieve."

Just then a frightful fiend charged up, growled at the officer that he had been slow bringing the prisoner in, grabbed Toshiyuki by the neck, and marched him off. They came to a great gate through which countless others, dragged like Toshiyuki, or bound, or in irons, were pouring from every direction till it was hardly possible even to pass. Inside the gate, the two hundred warriors whom Toshiyuki recognized all too well were glaring at him with fiery eyes and licking their lips in grim anticipation. Toshiyuki was frantically cudgeling his brains for a way out when the fiend who was dragging him whispered in his ear, "Make a vow to copy the Sutra of Golden Light!" As they went in through the gate, Toshiyuki vowed to copy the Sutra of Golden Light by way of atonement.

He was hauled in to stand before the court of Emma, the king of hell. "Is this Toshiyuki?" a bailiff growled. Another bailiff demanded to know why, considering the huge number of complaints lodged against him, Toshiyuki had been so slow to appear.

"I brought him straight here, sir, after I seized him," said the arresting officer.

"What was it you did up there in the world?" they asked Toshiyuki.

"Nothing, really. I just wrote out the Lotus Sutra for people who asked me to. I made two hundred copies."

"Actually," they told him, "your life-span had a little more to run, but you've been brought in because of complaints that you copied the Sutra while you were unclean. Our orders are to deliver you to your accusers so they can dispose of you as they see fit."

The two hundred soldiers prepared to take charge of their victim.

"But I made a vow," protested Toshiyuki, shuddering with fear, "to dedicate to the Buddha a copy of the Sutra of Golden Light, and I was seized before I could fulfill it. It'll be a terrible sin if I don't go through with it, one I could never atone for."

This brought the bailiffs up short. They declared that if this were true the whole arrest had been a mistake, and they ordered Toshiyuki's claim checked in the great Register of Deeds. The secretary of the court of hell leafed through the register and read off every last deed of Toshiyuki's. They were all sins. Only at the last split second, when he had gone through the entire list, did he finally announce, "Yes, it's true. The entry is here at the very end."

"Well, then," they told Toshiyuki, "we'll have to set you free. Go accomplish your vow and continue your life as you think best."

The grim host of two hundred, that just now had felt their hands nearly on him, suddenly vanished. Toshiyuki returned to life.

For two days his wife and children had been mourning him when all at once he opened his eyes and was back. Joyfully they gave him something hot to drink, and it was only then that he finally understood he had been dead. In his mind he saw again everything he had just witnessed as though reflected in the clearest of mirrors, and he resolved to copy and dedicate the Sutra of Golden Light, properly purified this time, just as soon as he should be himself again.

In time he recovered fully and hurried to have a craftsman prepare a scroll of paper to receive the sutra. But at the same time his thoughts began wandering again, and it was not toward the Buddha and the scriptures that they roamed. He was quickly absorbed in romantic visits and fancies, and worried only about how to write the nicest possible verses. So the months and years flew by without his ever copying the sutra until his life reached its allotted term and he passed away.

A few years later the poet Ki no Tomonori had a dream. There came to him one whom he understood to be Toshiyuki, although fearfully changed from what Toshiyuki had once been and terrifying to look at. "A vow I made to write out and dedicate the Sutra of Golden Light gained me a reprieve," the apparition said, "and I was returned to life. But my heart stayed as frivolous as before and I finally died without ever copying the sutra. For this I'm now suffering the most horrible tortures. Have pity on me, find the paper I had prepared for the sutra, take it to a certain monk at Miidera, and have him make the copy and the dedication!" Then it screamed.

Tomonori awoke soaked in sweat. Dawn had barely broken when he hurried off on his errand. He found the paper and soon was knocking at the monk's door. The monk was glad to see him because, as he explained, he had been on the point of sending a messenger to Tomonori's house. Tomonori asked why, concealing for the moment his own reason for having come, and the monk related the precise counterpart to Tomonori's dream. Toshiyuki had appeared to him, told him that Tomonori would be able to find the paper, and asked him to copy and dedicate the sutra. The monk's dream, like Tomonori's, had ended with a horrible scream. Tomonori and the monk wept bitterly over Toshiyuki's awful fate, and Tomonori produced the paper with an explanation of how he had come to bring it.

The monk did exactly as Toshiyuki had asked. When the two dreamed of Toshiyuki again, he seemed in far better spirits. He told them that the merit they had gained for him had greatly lightened his suffering.

1 5 0 .

THE PIRATE'S STORY

A very old and pious monk who lived in Settsu province once heard someone mention an encounter with pirates, and this inspired him to tell his own story.

"When I was young," he related, "I had a very good life. I had all the food and clothing I could possibly want and every day I sailed the sea. 'Admiral Rokurō' they called me. I was a pirate.

"Once I was out among the islands off the coast of Aki and there wasn't another vessel in sight, when up rowed a ship. A nice-looking fellow in his mid-twenties seemed to be her master, and all I could see beside him were a couple of sailors. Well, I thought, there must be some pretty women on board too. I could see a bit round the blinds over the cabin windows, and I could make out piles of trunks. Oh, she was certainly loaded, and all but defenseless. A young monk was up on the cabin roof chanting the Lotus Sutra.

"No matter how I maneuvered, that ship stayed with me. They seemed to have no idea what I was. That made me wonder more than ever, so I hailed her. The master said he was bound for the Capital on urgent business, having put out from the province of Suō. He had attached himself to me because he feared pirates. He must have been a bit soft in the head.

"'I'm not going the Capital,' I shouted back. 'I'm here to rendezvous with another ship and then I'm heading for Suō myself. You'd better find a vessel bound your way!' He said all right, but he wouldn't find one till tomorrow, and meanwhile he'd just stick with me. He anchored right by us in the lee of an island.

"The opportunity was golden and my men were determined to get their hands on that cargo. You can imagine their amazement and horror when we boarded. We were tossing everyone over the side, men and women alike, when the master of the ship began pleading with me, shedding great big tears. 'Take everything I have,' he begged, 'but please, please spare my life! My old mother in the Capital is dying and she's sent me word she wants so much to see me again! That's why I'm on my way as fast as I can go!' He was looking me straight in the eye as he spoke, and wringing his hands. But I told my men they weren't to take any sob stories. 'Over he goes with the rest!' I ordered. He still kept his eyes on mine, though, while big tears rolled down his cheeks, and I felt sorry for him. Yes, I knew it was cruel, but I had my ways, and I couldn't see why I should do him any favors. Overboard he went.

"Over the side too went that little monk from the cabin roof, frantically clutching the Sutra he had in a bag slung round his neck. But he stayed afloat, lifting the sutra bag high out of the water. In fact he was floating higher and higher, and it seemed he would never sink. He should have drowned by now. We started bashing him over the head and jabbing him in the back with the steering oar, but he still floated as high as ever, holding the Sutra in the air. I couldn't understand it. Then I saw several beautiful children in the water with him, fore and aft, each carrying a slender white staff. One was holding his head up while another supported the hand that carried the Sutra.

"My men insisted they saw no children, but *I* could see them. They were keeping him afloat. I was beginning to feel like saving him, now, so I gave him the end of a pole and hauled him back to the ship. My men grumbled a bit, but I got him aboard. The children weren't there any more.

"When I questioned him, he said he was on his way to the Capital because at home he'd never been able to get properly ordained. The master of the ship had offered to take him along and had promised to have him ordained by a monk friend of his. I asked him who those children had been, the ones who had held him up, but he said he had no idea what I was talking about.

" 'Well,' I told him, 'one was supporting the hand you were holding the Sutra with. Anyway, why were you so busy holding the Sutra up when you knew you'd soon drown?' 'I knew I was going to drown,' he answered, 'but that didn't really matter. I just wanted to keep the Sutra dry as long as I could. It's true my arm didn't get tired, in fact it felt very light and seemed to get longer and longer. Even then I realized it was somehow the Sutra's power that was doing it. Thank you for saving my life.' And he wept.

"I was deeply impressed. I asked him whether he would turn back now or whether he would go on to the Capital and get his ordination, and I promised to take him if he was going on. He said no, he didn't feel like getting ordained any more, he just wanted to go home. So I offered to take him that way, too. But I had to ask again who were those beautiful children I'd seen, and I was so overcome that I was crying myself. 'I've chanted the Lotus Sutra constantly ever since I was six,' he answered, 'even when I was badly frightened, so I suppose the gods who protect the Sutra must have been with me.'

"That was when my eyes were opened to the Buddha's noble truth. Right there I dropped my quiver, my dagger, and my sword and resolved to go with that monk and lead a holy life. I got a little food together for us to take, but the rest of the spoils I left to my men. They thought I'd gone mad, of course. They were convinced some demon had gotten into me and they did their best to make me forget the whole thing, but I paid no attention. Off I went with the monk to the mountain temple where his teacher lived, and there, inspired by the memory of my crimes and of those divine children, I became a monk myself. Ever since then I've chanted the Sutra too."

1 5 1 .

A LITTLE LESSON

Two holy men once lived at a mountain temple. One, Jihō, was devoted to the Lotus Sutra and the other, Jikon, to the Sutra of Diamond Wisdom. Their huts stood a few hundred yards apart.

Jikon had visibly put the power of his sutra into action, because his meals came to him all by themselves and he never had to give them a thought. Jihō, on the other hand, got all his provisions from the faithful who visited him and was far from well off. Puffed up with pride at his success, Jikon assumed that thanks to the sutra he served, and thanks to the superiority of his own practice, the angels and protector gods were watching over him day and night; whereas that Lotus fellow was wasting his time on a sutra of lesser stature and had in any case less merit, so that the protectors could not be bothered with him.

Jikon was entertaining these ugly thoughts when Jihō's acolyte happened by. Jikon took the opportunity to advertise his own power and virtue. "And what are *your* master's powers?" he inquired.

"He doesn't have any," the boy answered. "He just manages with what people bring him."

Jihō's only comment was, "He's quite right of course, quite right."

There came a day when Jikon got no food. He got none the next day either. By sundown on the third day he was not only hungry and frightened, but also angry with Subhuti, the Buddha's chief disciple in the sutra he served. That night he dreamed that an old monk, with his right shoulder bare in the Indian fashion, came to him and said, "I'm Subhuti. You may serve the Diamond Wisdom Sutra, but so far you're no model of what it teaches. That's why the angels bring you nothing. What makes you think you've any right to complain?"

"But then, who's been providing my food?" asked Jikon.

"Your food? Oh, that's from Jihō. He's kind enough to take pity on you and he sends you the food which the protector gods of the Lotus bring him. But you're so stupid you've gotten all puffed up about it and you've slandered Jihō instead. You'd better go to him right away and confess your fault."

When Jikon woke up, he bitterly regretted his behavior. He went straight to Jihō's hut, prostrated himself, and begged his pardon. "But why," he asked, "have you sent me no food just these last few days?"

Jihō smiled. "I'm afraid I simply forgot to ask the protectors to bring you any," he answered. And his acolyte set the dinner he had just made before Jikon.

Once Jikon was home again, the meals came as before. Jikon gave up his pride and became Jihō's follower. In time the two passed away together and were welcomed by all the saints into paradise.

BOYS

1 5 2 .

HEROIC PATIENCE, ALMOST

One evening some monks on Mount Hiei decided it would be fun to make rice dumplings. A young acolyte pricked up his ears at their talk, but thought he had better not look as though he were waiting up for the dumplings. Instead, he went off into a corner and pretended to go to sleep. Eventually a flurry of activity announced that the dumplings were ready.

The boy felt pretty sure they would wake him now, and at last, thank goodness, a monk did call him. If he answered right away, though, they would know he had been lying awake all the time. Bravely, he steeled himself to be patient till they called him again.

"Now, now, don't bother him!" chided another voice. "He's just a child and he's fast asleep!"

What a letdown! There was no second call. All he heard was chewing and the smacking of lips. Finally he could stand it no longer. Ages after the one call he piped up, "Yes? What is it?"

The monks roared with laughter.

1 5 3 .

THE POT-HEADED DEMON

The boy acolytes at the great Buddhist temples are popular with the monks, who are sometimes sorry to see them ordained and their beauty tarnished by plain, dull robes.

At a sort of farewell party before an acolyte's ordination, one of the monks became very drunk. In his befuddled gaiety he reached for a three-legged cauldron that happened to be handy, then stuck his head into it so that he could dance as a three-horned, pot-headed demon. His nose was a bit in the way but he squashed it down, got his head in, and performed to the company's uproarious applause.

When his dance was over, he tried to get the cauldron off. The festive mood was dampened when he discovered he could not, and the monks began wondering what to do. They tried coaxing and tugging the cauldron, but blood just ran down the fellow's neck, which swelled till he could hardly breathe. The could not break the cauldron, either, and the awful clanging inside it when they tried was more than the fellow could bear.

Finally they gave up, threw a cloth over the cauldron's projecting legs, gave the monk a staff to lean on, and led him by the hand to a physician in town. All the way there the people stared and stared.

He looked very peculiar sitting there in front of the physician. When he tried to talk, his voice was so muffled that no one could make out what he was saying.

"My books have nothing about a case like this," the physician declared. "There's no oral tradition on the subject either."

So they took him back to the temple, where his relatives and his aged mother gathered with tears and groans at his bedside. It was impossible to tell whether he even heard them or not.

Finally someone pointed out that the monk's life at least could be saved, though he might lose his ears and nose in the process. The idea was simply to pull as hard as possible. They carefully lined the cauldron with straw, to keep the metal away from his face, and pulled till they practically tore his head off. Off came the cauldron with the nose and ears, leaving only blank holes.

1 5 4 .

RIOTOUS LIVING

Zōyo, the fifth son of Major Counselor Tsunesuke, was such an impressive monk that people thought him a living buddha. He had done the great pilgrimage through the Ōmine Mountains twice, and in some of his rites he conjured up visions of snakes, dragon-horses, and other bizarre creatures. You could hear actors and musicians carrying on at his house from two hundred yards away, and young guards from the palace or from private households were always wandering in and out and making a great noise. Peddlers would come around selling saddles, swords, and practically anything else, and since Zōyo paid whatever price they asked, the area outside his gate was a veritable market. Every luxury in the world was his to enjoy.

Zōyo was deeply involved with a young wizard whom he had once seen dance, to loud applause, at a rice-planting festival. Hopelessly in love, he had quickly decided that if he wanted the boy with him all the time he would have to make him into a monk. "I don't know," the boy said, "I'd rather stay as I am for a while." But Zōyo, incapable of letting the matter drop, kept after him till very reluctantly he agreed.

Now, it was a dreary day and the spring rain was pouring endlessly down. Zōyo asked a servant whether the boy's old clothes were still around somewhere.

"Yes, Your Grace, they're still in the storeroom," the servant replied.
"Then bring them here."

The clothes were brought and Zōyo told the boy to put them on.

"But I'll look funny in them now!" the boy protested.

"Put them on!" repeated Zōyo in a tone that discouraged argument.

The boy went off into a corner and changed. He came out wearing his dancer's bird headdress, and in fact looked exactly as he had before Zōyo made a monk of him. Zōyo's face crinkled up at the sight as though he was going to cry; and the boy too, standing before his master, suddenly looked very serious.

"Do you remember the steps of your *Hashirite* dance?" Zōyo asked.

"No, I'm afraid not. But I do remember a little of *Katasawara* because I rehearsed it so much."

The boy began to dance, leaping gracefully about the little room like a bird. Zōyo let out a howl of anguish and burst into tears.

"Come here," he commanded. The boy came, and Zōyo fondled him tenderly. "Why, oh why did I ever make a monk of you?" he groaned.

"I told you!" said the boy. "I told you you ought to wait!"

Zōyo made him undress and led him into the next room. Goodness knows what happened after that.

1 5 5 .

THE BOY WHO LAID THE GOLDEN STONE

A monk on Mount Hiei was a fine scholar, but having no patron he was so poor that he finally found it impossible to stay on the mountain. Instead, he moved to a temple named Urin'in in the northern part of Kyoto. He did not even have any parents to turn to for help. All he could do was go each month to Kurama, a mountain sanctuary not far away, to pray for divine aid. He made these pilgrimages faithfully for several years.

One day in the middle of the ninth moon, he went to Kurama as usual, accompanied by a single, miserable little acolyte. On his way back he reached the outskirts of the Capital just as the sun set, but the moon was so bright that he hurried on. As he came down a little street north of First Avenue, a handsome boy of about sixteen, wearing a casually belted white robe, fell in beside him. The boy looked as though he must be from some temple and the monk found it odd that he had no monk with him.

"Where are you going, Your Reverence?" asked the boy.

"Home to Urin'in," the monk replied.

"Please take me with you!"

"Well, I don't even know you and I'm afraid I really shouldn't. Where are *you* going, anyway? To your master's house? To your parents? I'd be happy to take you home with me, of course, but I hate to think what trouble I could get into for it later on!"

"I understand how you feel, Your Reverence, but you see, ten days ago my master and I quarreled, and I've been wandering in a daze ever since. I don't have any parents because they died when I was young. So I decided that if I could just find someone to love me, I'd follow him anywhere."

"Well then, I'll be glad to have you. It won't be my fault, after all, if there are repercussions. But I've no one living with me, you know, except this poor child here. I'm afraid it'll be a very dull life for you."

Despite these and similar dutiful protestations which he made as they walked along, the monk found the boy so beautiful that he loved him already, and he was determined now to go ahead. When they reached Urin'in he lit a lamp and looked the boy over more carefully. With his white skin and his prettily rounded face he was really adorable, and extraordinarily distinguished-looking. What amazing good fortune! This was no commoner's son. But the boy refused to answer any questions about his father.

The monk prepared the bed with special care, had the boy lie down, and lay down himself next to him. After chatting awhile both fell asleep. In the morning all the neighboring monks came to admire the boy, but the monk was not anxious to display him and did his best to keep him out of sight. His growing passion for the boy surprised him.

That evening the monk cuddled up to the boy and began fondling him. Then a startled look came over his face. "I've never touched any woman's body but my mother's since the day I was born," he said, "so I'm not quite sure what a woman feels like, but you're very different from the temple boys I've been with before! I don't know what it is, I just seem to melt toward you. *Are* you a girl? Tell me if you are. I've wanted you ever since I first saw you, and I just can't understand it otherwise."

"What if I *were* a girl?" said the boy, smiling. "Wouldn't you want me any more?"

"If you're a girl and I keep you, people are going to talk a lot and I don't like the thought of that one bit. And how is the Buddha going to feel? That's even worse!"

"I suppose it *is* pretty bad, as far the Buddha's concerned, if it's my being a girl that makes you so fond of me! But anyway, other people won't see you with anything but a boy. You must always talk to me and behave with me as you would with a boy." The young person seemed highly amused.

"So he *is* a girl!" thought the monk, frightened now and wishing he had never gotten himself into this. He could not send her away, she was just too dear, but he avoided sleeping too close to her and made sure there was at least some clothing between them. In the end, though, he could not help being a man, and they became a loving couple in every sense of the word. The monk was so happy that he could hardly believe it, while his neighbors could not imagine how a destitute fellow like him could ever have gotten himself so delicious a young man.

In time the "boy" began feeling unwell and stopped eating. The monk could not understand it. "I'm pregnant, you see," she explained.

The monk's face fell. "Oh no!" he groaned. "This is awful! For months now I've been presenting you to everyone as a boy. What are we going to do when you have a baby?"

"Just behave as though nothing had happened. Don't tell anyone anything. And when the time comes, keep quiet."

The monk spent the next months in an agony of apprehension. When the moment was finally near, the "boy" looked very sad and cried all the time. The monk cried too.

"Oh, I hurt down there!" she exclaimed. "I think the baby's coming!"

The monk went into a paroxysm of agitated distress.

"Don't get flustered," said the "boy." "Spread me a mat in a shed somewhere."

The monk spread a mat in a storage shed and she went in to lie down. Soon she gave birth, and when it was over she put her outer robe over the child and nursed it. Next, she simply vanished. The astonished monk crept to where the baby lay and removed the robe.

It was not a baby at all but a big stone. Despite the wave of fear and revulsion that swept over him, he brought up a light for a better look. The stone gleamed gold. In fact, it *was* gold! The "boy" was gone and he missed her with all his heart, but he realized that the whole thing had been planned for his benefit by the Bishamon of Kurama. After that he broke off bits of the gold to sell, a little at a time, and lived as comfortably as he wished.

CHERRY BLOSSOMS

A little acolyte on Mount Hiei, fresh from the country, arrived when the cherry trees were in full bloom. When a cruel wind sent the petals flying, the boy burst into tears.

"What makes you cry so, my dear?" a monk gently comforted him. "Are you sorry to see the flowers fall? But flowers never last, you know. They always fall. You shouldn't cry!"

"Who cares whether they fall or not!" the boy sobbed. "Not me! But if the barley flowers in Daddy's field blow away there'll be no crop and that'd be *awful*!" He bawled all the harder.

So much for *that* sweet child's sensitive feelings.

P A R A D I S E   II

THE THIRST FOR PARADISE

A gentleman who longed ardently for rebirth in paradise was afraid of what his body might do to confuse him when the time came, since the body is treacherous at best. "If I'm very ill," he reflected, "my last moments won't go the way I hope and I won't get to paradise. It'll be much easier to keep my mind steady if I die in perfect health." So he decided to burn as a human lamp, the way the Bodhisattva Kiken did in the Lotus Sutra.

Unsure whether he could actually bear the pain, however, he first devised a test: he pressed two red-hot shovel blades against his body with his arms. Since the pain was bearable, he continued his preparations. Then he realized that this course would actually be all too easy. On the other hand, he doubted that he could ever achieve in this life the wisdom and virtue simply to go to paradise without trying, and he was still worried about what doubts might assail him when he came to die naturally.

At this point he remembered Mount Fudaraku, Kannon's paradise. Mount Fudaraku really exists in this world and is accessible in this body. That was where he should go! He gave up treating his burns and set out instead for the coastal province of Tosa, where he got a new boat and practiced sailing.

When he felt ready, he asked a seaman to warn him as soon as a steady breeze should set in from the north. When the day came, he hoisted his sail and started south alone. There was no stopping him. His wife and children could only watch him go. They wept as he vanished over the horizon.

His unbending resolve aroused great admiration at the time. People felt sure that he must have reached his goal.

1 5 8 .

THE CHANTING SKULL

In Empress Kōken's reign the monk Eikō lived in the village of Kumano in Kii. He had moved there to bring the blessings of the Teaching to that remote shore, and the villagers revered him as a bodhisattva. Even the empress recognized that he was a saint.

Eventually another monk arrived but said nothing about where he had come from. His only possessions were a Lotus Sutra in tiny writing, a silver jug, and a rough string chair. For years he worshipped by Eikō's side till one day, as mysteriously as he had arrived, he announced he was leaving. He was going over the mountains to Ise, he said, and he left Eikō his chair. Eikō was touched. He gave the monk a generous parting gift of parched rice and sent two men with him to keep him company on the trail. After the first day, the monk gave the men his Sutra, his rice, and his begging bowl and sent them home. All he kept was his silver jug and a long rope.

Two years later, some villagers were in the mountains along the Kumano River to cut timber for a boat when they heard a far-off voice ceaselessly chanting the Lotus Sutra. The awed villagers look for where it was coming from but found nothing. Half a year later, they were back to bring out their boat and heard the voice again. They left their boat where it was and went to tell Eikō, who came straight back to the mountains with them.

After a long search Eikō discovered a skeleton hanging against a cliff. The man had thrown himself off the cliff after tying each foot to the top with a rope, by now practically rotted away. Nearby lay a silver jug, which Eikō recognized at once. This was how the monk had chosen to flee the sorrows of mortal life. Eikō wept.

After three years Eikō went back to the mountains and heard the voice again. This time he found the skull. Still uncorrupted, the tongue was chanting as it had when the monk lived. Eikō prostrated himself before it and took the lesson to heart. He often remembered his friend in his prayers after that, and gave himself entirely to chanting the Lotus.

1 5 9 .

THE LITTLE GOD SAILS AWAY

Dōkō, a monk and Lotus devotee who lived at Tennōji, confined himself each year for the summer retreat at Kumano. He was on his way back from Kumano when, one evening at sundown, he found himself passing along the shore in Minabe county of the province of Kii; so he camped on the spot under a large tree.

In the middle of the night a lot of horsemen rode up nearby. Who in the world could they be? Dōkō heard one call out, "Are you there, you old man under the tree?"

"Here I am!" answered a voice.

Dōkō was surprised to learn that someone else was under the tree too.

"Hurry up, then! Come with us!" the rider called again.

The voice under the tree declined. "Not tonight, I'm afraid," it said.

"My horse's legs are broken and I can't ride him. I'll have to fix him tomorrow or find another horse. And I'm just too old to walk, you know."

The horsemen rode away. At dawn the worried Dōkō checked all around the tree. He found nothing but the crumbling image of a road god, obviously very old. Images like this were supposed to have a man part and a woman part, but the woman part was missing. In front of the god was a votive plaque with a picture of a horse on it. The legs were broken off. Dōkō realized that it was the god's voice that he had heard last night. He tied the piece with the legs on it back in place with some string so that the picture was whole again, then stayed to see what might happen next.

That night he lay under the tree again and the riders came as before. This time the god got on his horse and rode off with them. Toward dawn Dōkō heard him come back.

In a moment an old man came to Dōkō and bowed. "Holy man," he said, "your curing my horse allowed me to do my duty. I owe you more than I can ever repay! I'm the road god under this tree. All those riders were gods of disease. Normally I clear the way for them as they go through the land, and if I don't go with them they beat and abuse me cruelly. But now I'm sure that thanks to you I can cast off this poor shape of mine and be reborn in some far nobler form."

Dōkō expressed his wonder and protested he could not possibly bring about any such happy change. "Holy man," the god replied, "stay under this tree for three days, chanting the Lotus Sutra. I'll listen, and by the power of the Sutra I'll leave this suffering body and be reborn into the Land of Bliss." Then he vanished.

Dōkō complied. For three days and three nights he chanted the Lotus Sutra and on the fourth day the old man appeared again. "By your compassion, holy man," he said, "I'm leaving this body forever and taking on a much better one. I'm going to be reborn far away to the south, on Mount Fudaraku where the blessed Kannon lives, as a follower of the bodhisattva. This is because I've heard the Lotus. If you want proof that I speak the truth, make a little boat out of branches, put my wooden image in it, and launch the boat on the sea. Then watch what happens." And once again the old man disappeared.

Dōkō made the boat and laid the image in it. The sea was perfectly calm when he put it in the water, and there was not a breath of wind, but the boat sailed straight toward the south. Having watched it go, Dōkō prostrated himself toward it till it faded from view. Meanwhile an old man in the village nearby dreamed he saw the road god, now decked in glory, flying amid strains of heavenly music toward the south.

THE UNEARTHLY FRAGRANCE

Being all alone in the world, a nun in Chikuzen province, in Kyushu, sought out a mountain temple where she cooked year after year for the saintly monk who lived there. She never stopped calling Amida's holy Name, and not discreetly either, because she did it in a voice so piercing that it was more a shriek than a chant. The monk's disciples came to hate the noise and lost no opportunity to slander her to their master, who eventually sent her away.

Having nowhere to go she wandered the plain, still calling Amida, till a good woman invited her in. "We have a large house here," the woman told her, "and large grounds — plenty of room for you to stay and go on calling the Name!"

The nun accepted gladly, and was so grateful to be fed and kindly cared for that she asked for some flax to spin in return. At first the woman would not hear of the idea, but the nun insisted. The thread she spun was so fine that the woman was deeply touched. "Here I'd been glad just to give you a place to call the Name," she exclaimed, "and now you're spinning for me so lovingly!"

Years later the nun said one day to the woman, "The day after tomorrow I'm going to die. May I bathe in preparation? You've been so kind to me all this time, and I want to show you what our last moments can be. But don't tell anyone!" She wept as she spoke. Though saddened by this news, the woman kept the secret.

On the day, the nun bathed and put on a clean robe, then sat down facing the west and began calling the Name as loudly as always while the woman watched her, respectfully, from a few feet away. Darkness fell. Late in the night an unearthly light shone over the fields nearby and the woman felt afraid; but when the air was filled with an indescribable fragrance and a purple cloud floated down from the heavens to envelop the house, the woman joined her voice to the nun's in calling the lord. Then the nun quietly touched her hands to her forehead and passed away. The woman had never seen anything so moving, and wept as she prostrated herself in love and awe.

A certain worthy monk who later lived on Mount Kōya was part of the household at the time, being only about twelve years old. The woman told him the story, assuring him that although she had not seen Amida Buddha and all the saints and bodhisattvas coming to greet the nun's soul, she certainly had seen the light and the purple cloud. In fact, the fragrance of the nun's passing had perfumed her, and stayed with her forever after.

Yes, it's true that those who are to be reborn in paradise always know beforehand when they are to go and are able to let others know. May you too, who hear this story, be filled with faith and devoutly call the Name, so as to pass when your time comes into the Land of Bliss!

1 6 1 .

A TWINGE OF REGRET

Not many years ago a holy man called Rengejō realized that he was growing weaker and weaker with age, and that death was not far off. Since his greatest hope was to die with his thoughts on Amida (for then he would go to Amida's paradise), he decided that when he felt ready he would take no chances but end his own life by drowning.

Tōren, an old and experienced friend, immediately disapproved. "You'd be a fool to do that!" he warned. "On the contrary, you should keep calling the Name just as long as you possibly can because every day then will mean more merit for you."

When Rengejō remained unconvinced, Tōren gave in and promised that he would stop objecting. "What will be, will be!" he sighed, and helped Rengejō get ready.

The news of what Rengejō was going to do had quickly spread, and a large, pious crowd was waiting by the Katsura River to worship and to share in the blessing of his passing. Rengejō found a deep stretch of the stream, called the Name loudly, and a moment later plunged in. Tōren, standing nearby, wept for a friend he knew he would miss.

A few days later Tōren was taken ill, apparently under the influence of a spirit, and his state caused great alarm until finally the spirit declared itself. "I am Rengejō," it said.

"I don't understand!" Tōren exclaimed. "We were friends for years and you never had anything against me! You died such a holy death! I never imagined you'd come back!"

"You tried to stop me, you see," the spirit answered, "but you hadn't realized how determined I was. Now it's all over. What I did was just for my salvation, not for anyone else's, and I don't mean to say that when the time came I had any wish to pull back. I really don't know *what* happened. But at any rate, I was about to go in when suddenly I didn't want to go through with it. There was such a crowd, though, that I didn't see how I could very well change my mind. I looked at you and our eyes met. What my look meant was, 'Please stop me!' But you didn't understand and you just seemed to urge me on. I was so angry as I went under that I couldn't possibly have gone to paradise. Now I'm wandering in a region I never wanted to see. It's all my fault and I'm not blaming you, but it's that last twinge of regret that's brought me back to you."

What happened to Rengejō should stand as a warning. The human spirit is elusive, and one never knows which way it will turn.

YIN-YANG
WIZARDRY II

1 6 2 .

DADDY,
WHO WERE THOSE PEOPLE?

The yin-yang diviner Kamo no Tadayuki was the equal of the greatest masters of the past, and incomparable in his own time. His advice and services were valued highly both by the court and by private patrons.

Tadayuki was just setting out to do a purification when fatherly affection made him decide to take along his nine-year-old son Yasunori, who sat beside him all through the rite. While they were riding home in Tadayuki's carriage, little Yasunori said, "Daddy?"

"Yes?"

"Daddy, during the purification I saw lots of people. They looked like people but they weren't, and they were very scary. They ate up the food offerings, then they got on the little boats, carriages, and horses you'd laid out and they all went away. What were they, Daddy?"

Tadayuki was amazed. He knew he had an unusual gift for the art, but *he* had never seen supernatural beings when he was a child. He had come to see them only gradually, as his study progressed. "Yasunori must be a genius if he can see them just like that, even now," he thought. "He must have the same gift that people had in the Age of the Gods, when supernatural beings and men mingled quite freely."

Tadayuki was right. Yasunori grew up to be a great master, and his children and grandchildren flourished in the same way.

1 6 3 .

THE CURSE

Ōtsuki no Mochisuke, the son of the Budget Bureau director, belonged to a distinguished line of such officials. He was also extremely talented and would certainly have attained unusual prominence if he had lived. Unfortunately, he had rivals who felt that he stood in the way of their own advancement and therefore wanted to be rid of him. After an oracle, delivered in his own home, told him he had an enemy, he consulted a yin-yang diviner for a list of days when he should take special precautions. On the days indicated by the diviner he barred his gate securely to the world.

His enemy secretly commissioned another diviner to secure his death by magic. "Naturally we'll have to be cautious while he's in seclusion," said the enemy magician, "but if we work together and lay a curse on him on one of those days, it's sure to work. Take me to his house and get him to come out. He won't open his gate, of course, but I only need to hear his voice. If I can just hear him talk, we'll get him."

Off they went to Mochisuke's house, where his enemy pounded furiously on the gate. He insisted to the servant who answered that he had urgent business with Mochisuke and that, seclusion or no seclusion, he should be allowed to slip inside. The servant reported this to Mochisuke, who adamantly refused. "Everyone has a right to look out for his own safety," he said, "and I don't want that fellow in here. Tell him to go away."

"All right," said the enemy, "but if he won't open the gate, at least he could put his head out the little window there."

Perhaps it was just Mochisuke's karma to die, because that is exactly what he did. He put his head out the little window and asked his visitor what he wanted. As he did so the diviner heard his voice and saw his face, and laid on him the most powerful curse he could summon. Since the visitor actually had nothing to say, he could only answer that he was going down to the country and thought Mochisuke should know.

"He must be mad to have called me out just to hear *that*," Mochisuke fumed as he drew his head back in.

Soon his head began to ache, and in three days he was dead.

They say that the man who commissioned the curse died shortly afterwards under unfortunate circumstances. It was frightening how his curse turned right back on him.

1 6 4 .

THE HARMLESS HAUNT

As a scholar, Ki no Haseo was so magnificently learned that he had no rival in all the world. However, he knew nothing of yin-yang lore.

A dog kept jumping over the wall to piss in Haseo's garden, and Haseo was puzzled enough to consult a yin-yang diviner about it. He hoped to learn whether the dog's doings boded well or ill.

The diviner divined. "Well, there'll be a demon in your house on such-and-such a date," he announced. "Don't worry, though. This demon doesn't hurt people or put curses on them, or anything like that. The thing to do is to shut yourself up in seclusion on that day."

By the time the day came, Haseo had forgotten all about it. Seclusion was the last thing on his mind. Instead, he had his students over to his house to compose Chinese poetry. Learned meters, metaphors, and rhymes were blossoming on every page when suddenly a lugubrious howl issued from the closet nearby. The assembled scholars quaked where they sat. Then someone cracked open the closet door. A demon burst forth. It was two feet tall, with a white body and legs and a black head, and it had a single black horn. They were all frightened out of their wits.

But one among the company, a wise and brave man, kicked at the demon's head as it darted by. The black thing fell off. Why, the creature was a white dog, barking and yapping like mad! The thing on its head had been a bucket. During the night the dog had gotten into the closet and ended up with its head stuck in the bucket, which was why its howl had sounded so weird. The relieved scholars burst into laughter.

So it hadn't been a demon after all, but the diviner had seen it as a demon because that's what the people first thought it was. Everyone admired how the diviner had even specified that the demon wasn't going to do any harm or lay any curses. What a masterly insight *that* had been! On the other hand, no one thought much of Ki no Haseo. No doubt he was very learned, but it hadn't been very clever of him to forget all about the diviner's advice.

1 6 5 .

IN THE NICK OF TIME

A moderately pious old nobleman, now a monk, lived in the southern part of the Capital. He was wealthy enough to have everything he wanted in life. On receiving a cryptic oracle in his own house, he sent for a yin-yang diviner named Kamo no Tadayuki to find out whether the oracle boded well or ill. Tadayuki determined that on such-and-such date the nobleman should stay strictly secluded at home, or risk being killed by robbers.

When the day came, the frightened nobleman barred his gate and admitted no one. Finally toward evening there was a pounding on the gate. At first the nobleman did not answer, but when the pounding continued he sent someone to find out who it was and to let the visitor know that the master of the house was in strict seclusion. The visitor identified himself as Taira no Sadamori, just back from the far northern province of Mutsu.

Sadamori was an old and close friend. He protested (through the servant) that night had overtaken him on this last stage of his journey home from the north and that in any case a taboo made it important for him not to arrive home that night. "Where else am I to go?" he asked. "What is this seclusion of yours about?"

The nobleman answered that he was keeping shut up on a diviner's orders because otherwise he risked being murdered by robbers.

"In that case," replied Sadamori, "you should be happy to ask me in. How could you even consider turning me away?"

This made sense. "All right," the nobleman agreed, "but just you. You'll have to send all your servants and retainers away first. I'm not taking any chances."

Sadamori complied willingly. He sent his host word that under the circumstances he would not expect his host to greet him personally to-night. He would make himself comfortable in the guest wing and would see his host in the morning. Sadamori then ate dinner and went to bed.

In the middle of the night Sadamori heard someone try the gate. The robbers must have come. He armed himself and went to hide by the carriage house. Yes, it certainly *was* the robbers. They got the gate open with a sword, crowded inside, and went round to the south, front side of the mansion. Sadamori slipped in among them. He kept them away from where his host's valuables were stored, steering them instead toward an empty part of the house.

"Here, here!" he cried. "This is the place to break in!" The robbers of course had no idea who he was and were about to begin when Sadamori realized his friend might really be killed. He would have to shoot them before they got inside. A tough-looking, armed robber was right next to him, but despite his fear he had to act. He shot the fellow from behind. The arrow went all the way through and stuck out the other side.

"They're shooting from behind us!" shouted Sadamori. "Let's get out!" He dragged the body inside.

"No, that was one of *us* shooting!" another robber cried bravely. "Never mind! Come on, let's go in!"

Sadamori dashed up behind him and shot him straight through the middle. "They're shooting, I tell you!" he shouted. "We have to get out of here!" He dragged the second body inside too and left it sprawled by the first.

From inside the house he began shooting the humming arrows that hunters use to start game. The robbers fled pell-mell toward the gate. Sadamori kept shooting at their backs and laid three robbers low before they even reached it. The rest of the band, which had started out as ten men, kept traveling. In the end four men lay dead within the range of Sadamori's arrows, and a fifth, shot in the lower back and unable to run, lay collapsed in the ditch a few hundred yards beyond it. The next morning the remnants of the band were arrested.

That nobleman was very lucky to have had Lord Sadamori stop by. It would have been the end of him otherwise. Just think what would have happened if he had really kept up his seclusion!

1 6 6 .

ASTRIDE THE CORPSE

A man once abandoned his wife of many years and left her so grief-stricken that she fell ill and died. Alas, since the poor woman had no parents and no close friends there was no one to take her body away. She just lay where she was. The neighbors who peeped in through a crack were frightened to see that her hair did not fall out and her bones stayed firmly knit together; and when they noticed that there was always a light in the house, and a sound of groaning, they got so afraid that they ran away.

The husband felt half dead with fear when he heard about all this. "How am I to avoid the ghost's curse?" he wondered. "She died hating me and she's bound to get me." In his difficulty he sought help from a yin-yang diviner.

The diviner agreed that this was a bad situation, but he promised to do his best. "Please be aware, though," he cautioned, "that the procedure is really terrifying. I want you to understand that clearly at the outset."

At sundown the diviner led the husband to the corpse's house. Just listening from outside was enough to make the husband's hair stand on end, and the thought of going in was really more than he could bear, but under the diviner's guidance he went in after all. It was true: his wife's hair was still in place and her skeleton was still intact. The diviner sat him down on the skeleton's back, gave him the hair to hold, and warned him at all costs not to let go of it. Then he read some spells, announced he would have to leave, and reminded the husband again to expect a terrifying experience. The husband, more dead than alive, was left alone astride the corpse clutching its hair.

Darkness fell. In the middle of the night the corpse suddenly said, "Oof! What a weight!" Then it stood up and began to run around. "Now to go look for that brute!" it went on, and charged off. The husband never let go of the hair, and the corpse eventually returned to the house and lay down again. There are no words to describe the husband's terror, but he kept hold of the hair and stayed on the corpse till the cocks began to crow and the corpse fell silent.

At dawn the diviner came back. Having made sure the husband really had kept hold of the hair, he read some more spells over the corpse, then took the husband outside and told him he had nothing more to fear. The husband thanked him with tears of gratitude. Nothing ever did happen to him.

This happened not all that long ago, because the husband's grandchildren are supposed to be alive still, and so are the diviner's.

DEMONS

1 6 7 .

TWINLEAF

The legendary musician Hakuga no Sammi spent one brightly moonlit night wandering up and down in front of the Suzaku Gate, near the palace, playing his bamboo flute. As he did so another man appeared, dressed just like Sammi himself, and began to play too. Sammi could not imagine who the fellow was, but the tone of his flute was truly divine. Neither man said a word.

The two met and played that way every moonlit night. The sound of the other's flute was so extraordinary that Sammi, devoured by curiosity, at last suggested that they try exchanging their instruments. The other man willingly did so. Sammi found that his flute was of a quality unknown in the world.

The two saw each other often enough, but since the other never said anything about wanting his flute back, Sammi simply kept it. After Sammi's death, His Majesty took possession of the flute and had all the best players of the time try it. Not one of them could get a note out of it.

In time His Majesty had the great flutist Jōzō try the flute. Jōzō played it as beautifully as Sammi himself. "This flute's former owner is supposed to have gotten it at the Suzaku Gate," said His Majesty, deeply impressed. "Go and play there yourself, Jōzō, and see what happens!"

The next moonlit night Jōzō went to the Suzaku Gate and began to play. "Aha, another one!" cried a pleased voice from high in the gate's upper story. Jōzō reported this to the emperor, who realized that the flute had belonged to a demon who lived in the gate.

The emperor called the flute Twinleaf because it had two leaves on it, one red and one green. Legend has it that every morning the two leaves had fresh dew on them.

Later on the flute became the property of Lord Michinaga and was eventually deposited in the Sutra Hall of the Byōdōin in Uji. Someone who saw it more recently noted that the red leaf had fallen off and that, alas, there was not a trace of dew.

1 6 8 .

NO NIGHT TO BE OUT COURTING

In Emperor Daigo's reign a certain Minister of the Right had a son named Tsuneyuki. The young man was both major counselor and commander of the Left Inner Guards, a very promising combination that clearly destined him for the highest posts in the imperial government. He was also handsome and amorous, and absorbed like no other in dreams of women. Every night he was off on one romantic expedition or another.

The minister's residence was in the western part of the Capital. Tsuneyuki was in love with a woman in the eastern part of the city and his constant visits to her worried his parents a great deal because the streets were unsafe after dark. Again and again they tried in vain to keep him at home.

One night he rode off as usual, accompanied by a single mounted page. As they traveled east past the Bifukumon'in Gate, one of the southern gates into the palace compound, they saw a noisy crowd approaching with torches. "Who can they be?" the young lord asked. "Where can we hide?"

"I noticed when I came this way today that the north gate to the Shinsen Garden was open," the page replied. "Let's go in, my lord, and close the gate. You can wait there till they've gone by."

Tsuneyuki hurriedly dismounted and crouched beside a gatepost.

The crowd started past. The two had kept the gate cracked open, and when they spied not people but demons they all but lost their wits with terror. Through the confusion of their own panic they heard a demon say, "Hmm. I smell a man! I'll go catch him." Something hurtled toward them and Tsuneyuki thought he was lost. Then it ran away again.

"What happened? Why didn't you get him?" another cried.

"I couldn't!" shouted Tsuneyuki's would-be assailant.

"Why not? All right, *you* go after him!" Another demon rushed the gate, only to turn and flee.

"Well? Where is he?"

"I couldn't touch him either!"

"What's the matter with you? All right, *I'll* do it!" With this boast the speaker charged. He got closer than the others, and his hands were almost on Tsuneyuki (who thought this *was* the end) when he too suddenly fled.

"What's wrong?" a chorus greeted him.

"The Sonshō Darani! He's got the Sonshō Darani on him!"

Suddenly all the torches went out. Footsteps ran off in all directions, then there was silence. The dark and quiet were even more eerily frightening than the demon's assault, and the hair rose on Tsuneyuki's head. Then he fainted.

At last, more dead than alive, he remounted his horse and set out for home. By the time he reached his room he was ill, and he collapsed with a high fever. His father sent someone to find out where Tsuneyuki had been, but learned only that the young master had been out late last night. Finally the minister came himself and found his son lying helpless in bed.

"What is it?" he asked, feeling Tsuneyuki's body. It was burning hot.

"Oh sir," cried Tsuneyuki's nurse, "I just don't know what the matter can be!" But when Tsuneyuki had told his story the nurse exclaimed, "Gracious! Last year my brother, who's an exorcist, had me write out the Sonshō Darani and sew it into the collar of the young master's robe. So it really has power, then! If it hadn't been there, what would have become of the young master?" She pressed her hands to Tsuneyuki's forehead and burst into tears.

After several days of a fever which caused his parents anguished worry, Tsuneyuki began to mend. A glance at the calendar showed that it had been the night when demons are known to walk abroad, and when for safety's sake you should be careful to stay at home.

Obviously you should always have the Sonshō Darani on you. Why, Tsuneyuki had not even known it was there!

1 6 9 .

LUMP OFF, LUMP ON

An old man had a big lump on the right side of his face, as big as a big tangerine. It made him so ugly that he avoided other people and instead worked alone in the mountains cutting wood. Once he got caught in an awful storm and had to stay in the mountains overnight.

No one else was around. He hid, wide awake and terrified, in a hollow tree. Feeling as lonely as he did, he breathed a sigh of relief when he heard other people coming. Then he peeked outside. The crowd, a hundred strong, was a horrible sight. Some in it were red dressed in green, some were black with a red loincloth, some had one eye or no mouth, and most were just indescribable. They built a fire as bright as the sun and made a circle round it, right in front of the old man's tree. He was frightened nearly out of his wits.

One monster, apparently the chief, sat down by the fire in the place of honor, and the rest sat in twin rows to his right and left. Next, they all began drinking and carrying on the way people do. As the wine jar went round and round, the chief got awfully drunk. When a young monster with a tray made his way slowly up to the chief, mumbling something or other, the chief burst out laughing and waved his cup. They really were just like people! The young monster danced, and when he had finished another began. Each one took his turn, right on up to the senior monsters, and if some danced badly others danced well. The old man could hardly believe his eyes.

"This is the most fun we've ever had!" the chief declared. "Now let's have something really special!"

Goodness knows what got into the old man then — perhaps some god or buddha put him up to it — but he suddenly wanted to get out there and dance. At first he checked himself, but the monsters had a fine rhythm going and the temptation was just too much. Out he burst from his hollow tree, with his hat down over his nose and an axe dangling from his belt, right before the chief.

The monsters jumped up. "What's this?" they cried. The old man leaped high and squatted low, he twisted and wriggled all around with hoots and shouts of "Ei!" and "Ho!" till everyone burst out laughing.

"We've been having these parties for years," chuckled the chief, "but no one like *you* has ever joined us! Be here every time from now on!"

"Say no more!" cried the old man. "I will! But it was all so sudden this time that I forgot how to end my dance right. If you liked me tonight, just wait till you see me dance properly!"

"You were wonderful!" the chief insisted. "Make sure you come again!"

One of the chief's lieutenants was not quite convinced. "The old fellow's full of promises," he objected, "but I'm not so sure he *will* be back. We'd better keep something of his as security."

That sounded like a good idea. The chief asked what they should take.

There was a buzz of voices. "What about the lump on his face?" the lieutenant suggested. "A lump's good luck and he'll miss it."

"Oh please," the old fellow begged, "take my eyes or my nose, but not my lump! I've had it for years! You're too cruel!"

"Aha!" said the lieutenant. "You see? That's what we need!"

A monster stepped up to the old man and twisted the lump off painlessly. "Be sure you're at our next party!" he warned.

Soon it was dawn and the birds were singing. The monsters went away. The old man felt his face and found that the lump he had had for so long was gone. He forgot all about cutting wood and hurried home to his astonished wife.

Now, the old man next door had a lump on the *left* side of his face, and when he saw his neighbor's was gone he wanted to know how the old fellow had done it. "What doctor did you go to?" he asked. "Please tell me! I can't stand mine!"

"It wasn't a doctor, it was a monster."

"Well, either way, I'll just do whatever you did. So what did you do?"

The first old man told his story and the second listened carefully. He went to hide in the hollow tree, and sure enough the monsters came. They sat in a ring, drank and carried on, and roared, "Where's that old man?"

The second old man was terribly afraid but he staggered out anyway. "Hurray!" the monsters shouted, "Here he is!"

"All right!" said the chief. "Now, dance!"

He danced, but his faltering steps had nothing in common with his neighbor's gleeful zest.

"That was terrible," the chief grumbled. "Give him back his lump!"

Up stepped a junior monster. "Here's your lump back," he said and stuck it on the other side. The old man had gotten himself two lumps instead of one.

1 7 0 .

TAKE A GOOD LOOK!

Late one night a man was sleeping with a prostitute in a room under the festival reviewing stand on First Avenue. The wind was howling, the rain was pouring down, and the atmosphere was definitely spooky. Suddenly a passerby outside on the avenue sang, "Nothing lasts, no, all things pass . . ."

"What's *that*, I wonder," thought the man and cracked open the shutter to peek out. It was a horse-headed demon as tall as the roof. Frightened, he hastily closed up again and backed as far back in the room as he could, but the demon raised the shutter and stuck its face in. "That was a good look you got at me, yes, a very good look!" it growled.

The man drew his sword and got ready to strike if the demon came in, while the woman cowered beside him.

"Well, take another good look!" said the demon and went its way.

The man decided every fiend in the world must have been abroad that night. He never slept under the reviewing stand on First Avenue again.

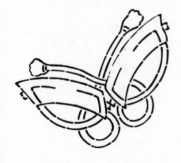
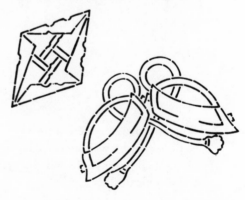

P L E N T Y

171.

CHERISH-THE-AGED SPRING

A poor man of Empress Genshō's reign, in Mino province, gathered wood in the mountains to support his old father. Since his father constantly demanded wine, he often went off with a gourd at his belt to buy him all he wanted.

One day the man, out in the mountains as usual to cut wood, slipped on a mossy rock and fell flat on his face. Looking up again, he noticed a spring running from the rock. The water was the color of wine. He scooped up some and tasted it: it *was* wine, and delicious too. After that he came every day for more, much to his father's delight.

News of the spring reached the empress, who came to see it herself in the ninth moon of 717. The gods of sky and earth had obviously recognized the man's perfect devotion to his father and had made the spring for him as a reward. The empress took the hint and appointed him governor of Mino.

The spring was named Yōrō, or "Cherish-the-Aged" spring, and in its honor the name of the reign-period too was changed to Yōrō.

172.

THE BOTTOMLESS SACK

Ikue no Yotsune, a junior provincial official in Echizen, started out in life so poor that he was almost starving. But when he prayed for relief to the Goddess Kichijōten he ended up rich — in fact, rich far beyond his needs or even his desires.

Soon after Yotsune turned to Kichijōten for help, he heard that a beautiful woman was at his gate asking for him. He wondered as he went out to her who in the world she could be. She *was* beautiful, and she gave him a dish heaped with cooked rice.

"I gather you're starving," she said. "Eat this!"

Yotsune took the rice gladly. Just a little satisfied him right away, and he hardly even felt hungry again for several days. He put the bowl away and ate the rice as slowly as he could, but when it was all gone at last he remained as destitute as before. Again he prayed to Kichijōten, and the woman returned to his gate. He hurried out to her as fast as he could go.

She told him she was awfully sorry but this time she could not help him directly. "Take this requisition slip instead," she said, and handed him a piece of paper.

Yotsune read: "Rice: three bushels."

"But where am I supposed to *get* this rice?" he asked.

"Cross the mountains north of here till you reach the highest peak. Climb to the top and call 'Shuda! Shuda!' Someone will answer you and come out to give you the rice."

Yotsune did as he was told. At the top of the highest mountain he called "Shuda! Shuda!" and a frightful voice answered him. Then something came toward him. It was a demon with a single horn in the middle of its forehead and a single eye, wearing a red loincloth.

The demon knelt before Yotsune. Though it was a terrifying creature, Yotsune plucked up all his courage and announced that he had a requisition slip. "I'm supposed to get some rice," he explained.

"I'm sure you are," said the demon and looked over the document. "It says three bushels," he went on, "but *one* bushel is the quantity I've been told to give you." He put a bushel of rice in a sack and gave it to Yotsune, who took it home.

When Yotsune helped himself from the sack, the sack filled itself back up again. It never ran out. Soon Yotsune was rich.

Having heard about Yotsune's sack of rice, the governor of the province sent Yotsune word that he wanted to buy it immediately. As a resident of the province Yotsune could not refuse. The delighted governor gave him one hundred bushels of rice for it. At its new owner's home the sack refilled itself as before, and the governor was sure he had acquired a priceless treasure. But when he had taken out a full hundred bushels, the rice gave out and the sack never filled up again. The governor was very angry, but there was nothing he could do about it. In the end he decided he would have to give the sack back to Yotsune.

At Yotsune's the sack refilled itself again the way it had always done, no matter how much rice was taken from it. How foolish the governor had been! How could he possibly take almost by force from Yotsune the reward that Yotsune had merited for his devotion to Kichijōten, and then expect to enjoy its bounty himself?

1 7 3 .

THE SOLID GOLD CORPSE

A humble man of the Capital had lost his parents, and having no lord to look to either, was very poor. But he knew that the Kannon of Hasedera answers people's prayers, and he could not believe that he alone would be excluded from Kannon's grace. Despite his difficult circumstances, he set off on foot to Hasedera.

This was his plea to Kannon. "O Kannon, grant me, in your compassion, a little ease in this life! It is not high position I crave, or boundless wealth. I only beg for a modest income. Surely my karma from past lives has brought this poverty on me. O Kannon, they say your vow to help sentient beings is supreme among the vows of all the buddhas. Help me, oh help me, please!" In this spirit he prayed at the temple for several days but went home in the end disappointed, without even having had a dream.

Though he went on making the same pilgrimage each month, he still got no dream. "Why do you insist on going there?" his wife complained. "The life we lead is miserable enough! They say a buddha helps only those who somehow have a link with him. You never get the least response, no matter how often you go. Obviously you have no link with this Kannon. You might as well give up!"

"I expect you're right," her husband answered, "but I've decided to keep up my monthly pilgrimages for three years. My present life may be a loss, but at least I can pray for salvation in the future."

At the very end of the third and last year he went on his final pilgrimage, from which he returned weeping at the thought that his reward in this life, for whatever he might have done in the past, was to be beyond the reach of Kannon's kindness. By sundown he had reached Ninth Avenue. As he continued on, gloomy and depressed, he met a band of freed convicts, the kind who do the lowest jobs for the Imperial Police.

They seized him without warning and informed him, over his protests, that they wanted him for coolie labor. They marched him north toward the center of the city.

This was a nasty shock. At Uchino, near where he lived, they came across a dead boy. The man was ordered with threats and curses to get rid of the body on the dry riverbed. Exhausted as he was from walking all day, this really was too much. Even on his way back from the last of three years' worth of pilgrimages, *this* had to happen. Awful karma was the only possible explanation. His wife had been absolutely right. He and the Kannon of Hasedera had nothing to do with each other. He felt awful. And the corpse was so heavy that he could not get it off the ground, till the freed convicts snarled at him so menacingly that he just managed to pick it up after all. They followed right behind him so that he had no chance to drop it and run.

The corpse was amazingly heavy. He could *not* carry it to the riverbed by himself, and that was final. Perhaps he could get it home instead, so that during the night he and his wife could both take it where it had to go. The freed convicts said they had no objection. So, much to his wife's surprise, he arrived home from Hasedera with a dead body and shed bitter tears as he explained how he had come by it.

"I told you so," said his wife. "Well, now we'll have to do something with it." Though they tried to lift it, its weight was so extraordinary that no effort of theirs could make it seem manageable. Besides it was, as they now noticed, oddly hard. They poked at it with a stick. The surface was gold, for goodness' sake! Next they lit a lamp and banged on it with a stone. The inside was gold too. The whole corpse was gold! They were speechless. The Kannon of Hasedera had taken pity on them after all.

They hid the corpse in their house, and the next day scraped off a little gold and sold it. At last they began doing well. Soon the young man was wealthy. Since he now had property he got a good post and served the court very capably. How wonderful Kannon's blessings are!

After acquiring the golden corpse the man devoted himself to Hasedera more faithfully than ever. He never saw the freed convicts again. Perhaps they had been emanations of Kannon.

A FORTUNE FROM A
WISP OF STRAW

A poor young man had no parents, lord, wife, or children and so was completely alone; and this meant he had no support or comfort. So he sought the aid of Kannon and went on a pilgrimage to Hasedera, where he prostrated himself before Kannon's holy presence. "If my life is to go on this way I'd rather starve to death now, here before you!" he declared. "But if by chance there's hope for me, I won't leave till you have told me so in a dream."

The monks of the temple wanted to know what he was doing. "You don't seem to have any food," they said. "If you go on just lying there you'll pollute the temple" — for they saw that he might die — "and that would be a disaster. Who's your spiritual adviser? Where do you eat?"

"I've nothing and no one," the young man answered. "How do you expect me to have a spiritual adviser? I've nowhere to get food from and no one to pity me. I eat what Kannon kindly provides, and for what spiritual advice I get I rely on Kannon too."

The monks decided that the young man was a nuisance who might make trouble for the temple. Since he was determined to throw himself entirely on Kannon's mercy, they thought they had better take turns bringing him food.

He ate the food but stayed where he was until three seven-day retreats were almost over. Just before the dawn of the twenty-second day he dreamed that someone came from behind Kannon's curtain. "You have some nerve, you know," the person said, "appealing to Kannon this way without even considering that your own past karma is what's made your life so miserable. But your plea is touching, and Kannon has a little remedy for you. Clear out of here immediately. On the way, take whatever your hand closes on and keep it. Now, go!"

The young man gathered that he had been dismissed. He struggled to his feet, went for a final meal with the monks, and left. On his way out the main gate he tripped and fell flat on his face.

He picked himself up and examined what he somehow had in his hand. It was a single wisp of straw. This was a bit disappointing, but who was he to question Kannon? He walked on, twirling the straw between his fingers.

Soon a big horsefly came buzzing round his face. Although he tried shooing it off with a branch, it kept coming back. So he caught it, tied one end of the straw round its middle and the other end to the branch, and went on with the captive fly buzzing before him.

A carriage full of ladies happened by just then, on the way to the temple. A pretty little boy was peering out the window. "What's that the man's got?" cried the boy to the servant riding beside the carriage. "Go and get it and give it to *me!*"

The servant approached the fly-tamer. "Give me that thing you've got there," he said. "The young master's asking for it."

"This is a present to me from Kannon," the young man answered, "but if it strikes your little master's fancy he's welcome to it." He handed the servant the branch.

The ladies liked the way he had parted with his toy. "Here," they called to him, "eat these when you feel thirsty!" They wrapped up three big tangerines for him in fine Michinoku paper and had the servant deliver them.

The wisp of straw was now three big tangerines which the young man carried tied to a branch over his shoulder.

Next, he met a band of mounted servants looking after an apparently distinguished lady who was on foot, having no doubt made a humble vow to do the pilgrimage that way. At the moment she was exhausted and begging her servants in vain for water. The servants were scurrying around looking, but there was simply no water to be found. "What's happened to the supplies?" one of them shouted, but the supply horses were still far behind, out of sight. When the lady fainted dead away, the alarmed servants tried everything to revive her.

The young man came quietly up. "You," they called, "you must know where there's water! Is there any drinkable water nearby?"

He asked what the matter was and the servants explained.

"I'm sorry," he said. "The water's a good distance off and it'll take time to get it here. How about these?" He offered them his three beautifully wrapped tangerines.

The servants fed them eagerly to their mistress, who eventually opened her eyes and asked what had happened.

"You were thirsty, madam, and you asked for water. Then you fainted. We looked everywhere but we simply couldn't find any drinking water. Then this man came along. He understood and gave us three tangerines, which we fed to you."

"So I fainted from thirst, did I? I remember asking for water, but after that my mind is a blank. Without these tangerines I might just have died here in the fields. What a kind man! Is he still there?"

"Yes, madam."

"Tell him to be patient. I'd like to do as much for him as his generosity has done for me, but it's so hard like this on the road. Do we have any food? Give him something to eat!"

The servants told the young man to stay put and promised that when the supplies got there he should have a meal.

Finally the supply horses arrived, and their drivers got roundly scolded for having dropped so far behind. A cloth enclosure was put up and mats were spread. Since the lady badly needed rest, the company decided to stop there awhile, although the place was quite inconvenient. Men were sent to fetch water, food was prepared, and the young man got a very good dinner.

As he ate he wondered what the tangerines were going to turn into. All this was Kannon's idea, and he could not imagine that he would come away empty-handed. Sure enough, the servants soon brought out three bolts of fine white cloth.

"Give him these," said the lady, and sent him this message: "The joy your tangerines have brought me is more than I can describe, but here on the road I cannot do for you all I would wish. These are only a token of my thanks. I live in the Capital at such-and-such a place. Come there, and when you do you will have your full reward."

The young man accepted the gift with pleasure. His wisp of straw was now three bolts of cloth, which he put under his arm as he continued on toward Kyoto.

At sundown he found lodging at a house by the road, and rose the next morning with the birds to pursue his journey. As the sun began to climb in the sky he saw a man riding a beautiful horse. "What a marvelous animal!" thought the young man. "It must be worth a fortune!"

Suddenly the horse toppled over, obviously dying. The astonished rider stood vacantly beside it while his retainers rushed to get its saddle off and tried to think of what to do. But alas, the horse was now quite dead, and none of their voluble grief could remedy that.

Their master mounted a poor substitute which happened to be at hand. "Well," he said, "there it is. I'm going on." He left a servant behind with instructions to do something about getting the carcass out of sight.

The young man thought he knew why the horse had died. His wisp of straw had turned into three tangerines, the tangerines had turned into three bolts of cloth, and now, apparently, the cloth was going to turn into a horse for him.

He learned from the servant that the horse was from somewhere up north. People had offered huge sums for it but the servant's master had kept hesitating to part with it. Now it was dead, a total loss. "I thought I might at least take its hide," the servant went on, "but on the road like this I don't even know what I'd do with it."

"I see," said the young man. "It was a beautiful horse. What a pity! You certainly couldn't very well dry its hide while you're traveling, but *I* can. Why not let me have it?" He gave him a bolt of cloth and the servant, glad of this windfall, ran off with it without looking back, before the hide's purchaser could change his mind.

The young man watched him go, then washed his hands, turned toward Hasedera, and prayed for the horse to revive. When it opened its eyes, lifted its head, and tried to get up, he gently helped it to stand. How pleased he was! But some straggler from the former owner's party might still find him, or the former owner himself might come back, so he led the horse into hiding and waited for it to recover fully. Then he went on to a house, traded another bolt of cloth for a bridle and a cheap saddle, and rode his new mount on toward the Capital.

Sunset found him near Uji, where he paid for dinner, lodging, and fodder with the last of his bolts of cloth. The next morning he once more rose early and went on his way.

Near the southern edge of the city he passed a house alive with bustle and excitement. The owner seemed to be setting out on a long journey. The young man had already realized that if he took the horse right into town someone might recognize it and accuse him of theft, and had decided accordingly that he should sell it. This man might need a horse. Dismounting, he ran up and proposed the sale.

The gentleman *had* been wanting another horse and when he saw this one he got so excited he hardly knew what to do. "Just now I've no silk to pay you with," he said. "Would rice and some rice land in Toba do instead?"

These sounded fine, but the young man feigned indifference. "It's silk and cash I need," he answered. "As I'm traveling I don't know quite what I'll do with rice land, but if you really need the horse I'll be glad to oblige."

The gentleman put the horse through its paces and declared that it was as impressive to ride as to look at. He gave the young man rice and over six acres of rice fields, and even entrusted him with the care of his house. "Keep it as long as I'm gone," he said. "You can give it back if I ever return to the Capital, and if I die it's yours. I've no children so no one will come around to make any claims." And off he went.

The young man settled in and hired a few laborers from the neighborhood. Since it was about planting time, he rented out half his land to someone else and had the other half cultivated for himself. The tenant's half did perfectly well, but his own yielded an immensely rich harvest. Then property gathered to him as though blown in on every wind and he became a very wealthy man. Even the house became his, since he never heard from the owner again.

His descendants flourished too, or so they say.

"DOG'S HEAD" SILK

The two wives of a county magistrate in Mikawa province raised silkworms which yielded plenty of silk thread. Then for some reason all the silkworms in the senior wife's care died, and she never managed to raise any more. As a result her husband ignored her, and his retainers naturally imitated him. Without visitors she lived a sad life in her poor, dreary house, alone but for a pair of maids.

At last she found a single silkworm eating a mulberry leaf and adopted it. It grew larger and larger on the mulberry leaves she piled into its box, and ate all she gave it. Since she had had no silkworms for several years now she could not help being fond of it and looked after it tenderly, though there was little she could actually do with just one.

One day her white dog was sitting in front of her wagging its tail while she heaped leaves into the box and watched the silkworm eat. Suddenly the dog jumped up and ate the worm. The woman was both angry and heartbroken, but it had happened so fast that she made no attempt to punish the dog. Instead she wept over the strange fate that made it impossible for her to keep silkworms.

Meanwhile the dog sneezed and an inch or two of white silk filament came out each nostril. In surprise the woman pulled on them. They got longer and longer — so long that she had to begin winding them on a reel. When the reel filled up, she took another and then another. Two or three hundred reels later the filament was still coming. She wound it onto bamboo poles and onto buckets till she had a tremendous weight of silk. The filament only gave out when the dog at last collapsed and died. She decided that the gods and buddhas must have taken the form of the dog in order to help her, and she buried the creature under an old mulberry tree in the field behind her house.

It was impossible to make this silk finer than it already was, but she was fussing over it anyway when her husband, off on an errand somewhere, happened to ride by her gate. Seeing how deserted the house was, he felt sorry for her after all and dismounted. He found no one in the house but his wife, working over an enormous quantity of silk. The silk obtained at *his* house was dark, lumpy, and altogether poor in quality, but this was as white as snow and almost luminous — far superior to any he had ever seen. When she told him how she had gotten such marvelous silk, he saw how wrong he had been to treat poorly a wife on whom the gods and buddhas smiled, and decided to stay with her. He never went back to his other wife again.

The mulberry tree the dog was buried under soon bore cocoons of the same exquisite silk. The magistrate reported this to the provincial governor, who reported it to the court. After that the silk known as "dog's head" has been offered regularly to the emperor. It is used to weave his robes.

Some people think the second wife killed the senior wife's silkworms on purpose, but no one knows for sure.

ODD PATHS

TO

SALVATION

176.

A VERY SURPRISED
BODHISATTVA

Tsukuma Spring in Shinano province used to be popular for its hot, medicinal waters. Once a villager there dreamed that Kannon would come the next day at noon to bathe in the spring.

"How shall we recognize him?" the dreamer asked, and got the answer: "He will be a warrior thirty years old with a black beard, a conical hat, and a dark cloak. His quiver will be black and his bow wrapped in leather, and his chaps will be made of the spotted hide taken from a deer in summer. He will be riding a roan horse. That is how you will know the bodhisattva."

First thing next morning the dreamer told everyone he knew. The word spread, and soon a huge crowd had gathered at the spring. They made sure the bathing water was fresh, cleaned and tidied carefully, stretched a sacred rope round the pool, offered flowers and incense, and finally settled down in pious patience to wait.

Noon came and went. About two a warrior rode up, precisely like the one in the dream. The crowd rose as one man and prostrated themselves before him, touching their heads to the ground.

The astonished warrior could not image what was going on. He tried asking people, dozens of them, but all they did was keep bowing to him. No one would tell him a thing. Then he spotted a monk who was bowing and prostrating himself like the rest.

"Why are you all bobbing up and down at me like that?" he asked in a rich country brogue.

The monk told him about the dream.

The warrior explained that the other day he had fallen from his horse and broken his right arm, and had come to heal his arm in the spring. People poured after him wherever he moved, bowing and carrying on like mad.

At his wits' end, he finally decided that he must actually be the bodhisattva and might as well become a monk. Throwing down his bow, quiver, sword, and dagger, he cut off his hair and entered religion. The crowd wept with devout emotion.

At last someone who knew him by sight cried, "Heavens, that's Master Kan from over in Kōzuke province!" So they gave him the name Kannon, the blessed bodhisattva's own.

¹ 7 7 ·

THE AWAKENING

A young monk on Mount Hiei had *meant* to study after entering religion, but ended up so busy having a good time that he never actually applied himself at all. He had only barely learned a bit of the Lotus Sutra. Since he still planned to study *some* day, he often went to pray for scholarly success to the Kokūzō of Hōrinji, a temple just west of the Capital, but his pilgrimages never inspired him to do anything in particular. He really was a proper dunce.

He knew this perfectly well, and it bothered him so much that one day in the ninth moon he went again to Hōrinji. Just before starting back, he fell into conversation with an acquaintance there, and the sun sank low while the two monks talked. He walked as fast as he could when he did set off, but at sundown he was still in the western part of the city. A friend he thought he might be able to stay with in the neighborhood turned out to be away in the country, and there was no one home but a maid left to watch the place. Then he remembered another acquaintance and went looking for his house.

On the way he came to a Chinese-style gate with a pretty young woman standing beside it. She was wearing several layers of casual clothing against the chilly air. He told her who he was and where he was going, explained that the sun had set, and asked if he could have a night's lodging.

She had him wait and promised him an answer shortly, then went into the house. Soon she was back to tell him he was welcome. His room in the semidetached guest wing contained a pretty screen, and the floor was spread with several elegantly trimmed straw mats. The lamp was already lit. He finished off to the last crumb and the last drop of wine the nice dinner the young woman brought him, and was washing his hands afterwards when he heard sounds from the neighboring room in the main building. A door slid open and curtains were being set up. Apparently the lady of the house wanted to talk to him.

Sure enough, a woman's voice called over to ask him who he was. On hearing his answer, the lady pressed him to stop at her house every time he should visit Hōrinji. When the door between him and her slid shut again, a bit of curtain got caught in it so that it did not close properly.

At nightfall the monk went outside. Pausing before the shutters on the south side of the house, he noticed a hole in one of the panels and peered through. A woman whom he took to be the lady was lying with a low lampstand by her, reading a book. She looked about twenty years old and was extremely beautiful. Her robe was of figured stuff, light mauve and green, and he could see that her hair was long enough to trail along the floor behind her. Two ladies-in-waiting were lying beside her curtains, with an ordinary maid a little further off. Apparently it was the maid who served the lady's meals and who generally fetched and carried. The room had every touch of comfort and elegance. A gold-sprinkled lacquer comb box and an inkstone box rested with easy informality on a two-tiered set of shelves, while exquisite incense smoke rose from a burner.

Gazing at the lady who was mistress over all this, the monk forgot everything else. How on earth, he wondered, could his karma have brought him here to see her like this? Suddenly the thought of living on without loving her made no sense at all.

Once the household was in bed and the lady herself apparently asleep, he opened the door which had never quite shut, slipped into the room, and lay down beside her. She was sleeping too soundly to notice. Her fragrance was indescribably delicious. Afraid to wake her up and tell her his feelings, though that is what he really wanted to do, he instead said a prayer, pulled her robe open, and fondled her breasts.

Now she *did* wake up and demanded to know who he was. He told her.

"I thought you were devout," she said. "That's why I let you stay. I'm certainly sorry I did."

He kept trying to snuggle up to her, but she clutched her robe around her and would have nothing to do with him. This drove him wild, but he did not force her because he feared being heard.

"I don't necessarily mean to refuse you," the lady went on. "You see, my husband died in the spring of last year. A lot of men have courted me since then, but I've decided not to encourage anyone unless he has some-thing special about him. That's why I live alone like this. If I'm to give myself to a monk like you, I want him to be particularly accomplished. I *might* say yes to you, you know. Can you chant the Lotus Sutra by heart? Do you have a good voice? I could give people the impression that I'm deeply devoted to the Lotus and all the time be in bed with you. What do you say?"

"I've *studied* the Lotus Sutra," the monk replied, "but I don't have it by heart yet."

"Is it difficult to memorize?"

"No, not really. No doubt I'll master it sooner or later. I'm sure it's my fault that I haven't managed it yet. I've just spent too much time having fun when I should have been studying."

"Then hurry back to your mountain and come again when you have the Sutra by heart. Then we can be as intimate as you like."

At this the young monk's desire vanished. As soon as the sky began to lighten, he said good-bye to the lady and stole out of her room. She made sure he was properly fed before he set off.

Home again on Mount Hiei he found he could not forget her, and he resolved to memorize the Sutra as quickly as possible so he could visit her again. It took him only three weeks. Meanwhile he wrote her often, and received with each reply a hamper containing food or a robe. As far as he could tell she really cared for him, and this made him very happy.

Now that he had the Sutra by heart he set out as usual for Hōrinji, and on the way back stopped, as before, at the lady's house. Again she had him served a meal, then came out to speak with him herself. Late in the evening the monk washed his hands and began intoning the Sutra. Although his voice was stirring, in his heart he hardly knew he was chanting at all because he could think of nothing but the lady.

In the night, when everyone seemed asleep, he again slid open the door into the lady's room. No one saw him. The lady, who must have been expecting him, woke up when he lay down beside her. Eagerly he began insinuating himself under her robe, but she hugged her clothing to her and kept her distance.

"I've something to ask you," she said, "so listen to me first. This is what I think. You have the Sutra by heart now, and we could say that's enough and go ahead and make love. If we did, and if we went on being fond of each other, you could hold your head high before anyone; and I, for my part, would be stained far less by taking *you* for a lover than by choosing any ordinary man. But I'd be sorry to think that my lover was one to be satisfied simply with having memorized the Sutra. I'd much rather you at least went through the motions of becoming a proper scholar. From now on you ought to be getting yourself invited to look after nobles and princes, but they won't call in a monk who can't do more than chant the Sutra, or keep him in their service either. It's lovely having you here with me, and *that's* the way I'd like you to be when we're together. Now you see how I feel. If you really love me, stay on the mountain for three years, study hard, and make yourself a scholar. Come back after that, and I'm yours. But until then we really can't be lovers. I'd rather die. I'll keep writing to you while you're on the mountain, and I'll take care of you as long as you're poor."

The monk was moved. He knew it would be wrong to force heartlessly a woman who spoke so thoughtfully of his own future, and with her material support he would in the end command recognition. These thoughts prompted him to renew his assurances of love and then to withdraw. In the morning after breakfast he returned to Mount Hiei.

He tore into his studies and never faltered again. The thought of seeing her drove him on like fire. By the time two years had passed, his sharp intelligence had already gained him recognition as a scholar. After three years no one doubted his exceptional learning. In every scholastic debate at the palace, for example, and in every set of formal discourses on the

Lotus Sutra, he completely outshone all his colleagues. On Mount Hiei the word spread that he was by far the most talented scholar of his generation.

During those years the lady asked after him constantly, and her support meant that he lived for the most part an untroubled life. When the three years were over he went as before to Hōrinji and at dusk, on the way back, stopped at her house.

He had already let her know he was coming and was shown to his usual room. The lady talked with him indirectly, through one of her women, about the last three years. Apparently she had never told a soul about her earlier, private encounters with him, for she presently let him know, in a rather formal tone, that she would speak to him in person.

The monk's heart beat faster but he gave the message only a polite acknowledgment. The messenger asked him to follow her. Outside the curtains that surrounded the lady's bed, near her pillow, was a pretty mat with a round straw cushion on it. A lighted lamp stood behind a screen. As far as the monk could tell there was one lady-in-waiting sitting at the foot of the lady's bed. He sat down on the cushion.

"I've wondered so much all these years how you've been getting on," the lady began. "Are you a scholar now?" Her lovely voice conveyed warm affection.

The monk trembled with nervous excitement as he answered, "Well, I can claim no great achievement, but yes, it's true I've been praised when I've debated or lectured here and there."

"That's wonderful. Now I have some questions for you. I'll ask them because I feel you're now a real teacher. I wouldn't dream of putting these questions to someone who could do no more than *chant* the Sutra."

She went through each chapter of the Sutra, from the beginning, posing difficult queries on the points she felt she did not quite understand, and he answered her as his studies had taught him to do. When hard pressed he developed interpretations of his own, or brought in apt quotations from the ancients. The lady was entirely satisfied. "How could you possibly learn so much in so few years?" she exclaimed. "You must be a genius!"

The monk for his part was amazed by the lady's own learning. "She may be a woman," he thought to himself, "but she certainly knows the Teaching. I'd never have believed it possible! She's going to be worth knowing! Anyway, she's made all the difference for my own studies."

They chatted till the monk finally lifted her curtains and went in. She did not protest as he lay down beside her.

"Just stay like that awhile," she said; so they lay there holding hands and talking some more. But having walked that day from Mount Hiei to Hōrinji and part of the way back, the monk was tired. He soon drifted off and fell fast asleep.

When he woke up, his first thought was that he had slept and that he still had not told her how much he loved her. Then he opened his eyes. He was lying on a clump of pampas grass which his weight had crushed. What a shock! A quick glance around told him he was alone in the middle of a moor, he had no idea where. There was no one in sight. His heart beat wildly and his stomach churned with terror. When he stood up he discovered, scattered around him, the clothing he had taken off the night before. Clutching it to him, he stood staring at his surroundings. He now recognized the waste which forms the eastern part of Saga Moor.

It was nearly dawn and there was a bright moon. The air was very chilly since it was still only early spring, and shivering had soon driven every other thought from his mind. He hardly knew where to go, but if Hōrinji was as close as he thought, he could spend the rest of the night there. Starting off at a run, he forded the Katsura River at Umezu, though he had to be careful not to be swept away by the current, which came up to his hips. Finally he reached Hōrinji, shaking with cold. He went straight to the main hall, prostrated himself before the altar, announced his plight, and prayed for help. Then he fell asleep.

He dreamed that a small and very proper monk with a blue-shaven head came from behind the curtain that screened off the image of the Bodhisattva Kokūzō. "It was no fox or badger that concocted what happened to you tonight," said the monk, "but I myself. You're very bright, you know, but you were so addicted to your little pleasures that you never studied and showed no sign of ever becoming a scholar. At the same time you were dissatisfied with yourself and often came to me to pray for scholarly talent and achievement. For some time I was unsure how best to answer you, but I saw you were drawn to women and I thought I'd use *that* to inspire you. You needn't be afraid. Hurry back to your mountain and study harder than ever. This is no time for you to rest on your laurels." Then the dream was over and he woke up.

It dawned on him that for years Kokūzō had been appearing to him as a woman in order to save him, and he was profoundly embarrassed. At daylight he returned to Mount Hiei, weeping with remorse for his own wanton behavior, and dedicated himself more singlemindedly than ever to his studies. He really did become a famous scholar.

What Kokūzō plans will come to pass. Ah, the beautiful and noble deed!

THE LITTLE GOD'S BIG CHANCE

The monk Dōmyō, a great lover, was having an affair with the famous lady poet Izumi Shikibu. Dōmyō also happened to chant the Lotus Sutra very impressively.

Once he was spending the night with Izumi Shikibu when he woke up and decided to chant the Sutra. He had gone through all eight scrolls and was just dozing off again when he glimpsed someone outside.

"Who is it?" he called.

"The old man who lives at the crossing of Fifth Avenue and Nishi-no-tōin street," a voice replied.

"What are you doing here?"

"I'll never forget, through all the lives I'll live, how you chanted the Sutra tonight!"

"But I chant the Sutra all the time. What was so special about tonight?"

The little road god — for that is who he was — answered, "Well, you see, when you chant the Sutra all clean and pure, the great gods crowd in to hear and an old man like me can't get anywhere near you. But this time you didn't even wash before you began, so there was no one else around. That's how I got to hear you. I'll never forget it!"

PIOUS ANTICS

Though originally from a line of yin-yang masters, the imperial secretary Yoshishige no Yasutane had been adopted into a family of scholars. Both kindly and peerlessly talented as a youth, he matured into a scholar who served the court for many years until, as old age approached, he began to long for the religious life. In the end he shaved his head and became a monk, a disciple of the saintly Kūya. He took the religious name Jakushin.

Being a holy man now, and naturally wise as well, Jakushin wondered

what might be the most virtuous thing to do next. He decided to make
the Buddha accessible to all by building a temple. Since he knew he
could not do this without help from his brethren in the faith, he started
going around soliciting contributions, and when he had enough to think
about buying lumber he picked Harima province as the place to look for
a site. He felt sure that in Harima he could get the work done well by
people sympathetic to his aim, and he did in fact get a very good response
there.

He was roaming the province one day when he came to a dry, pebbly
riverbed and saw a yin-yang diviner in a paper hat performing a purification rite. He dismounted in haste.

"What are you doing?" he shouted.

"A purification!" the diviner called back.

"I can see that! But what's your hat for?"

"Well, the gods who rule over purifications shun monks, so during the
rite I wear this hat in order not to look like a monk."

Jakushin let out a howl and jumped on the man, who could only drop
what he was doing and splutter ineffectual protests. The fellow who had
commissioned the rite sat looking on in dismay.

Jakushin snatched the paper hat from the diviner's head and tore it to
pieces. "How *could* you?" he cried, in tears. "How could *you*, a follower
of the Buddha, break the Buddha's commandments and wear that hat
just because the gods of purification will be injured if you don't? Don't
you think you'll go to the lowest hell for this? Oh, how awful! Here, kill
me, just kill me!" He tugged at the diviner's sleeve all the while, weeping
pathetically.

"You're completely mad!" the diviner answered. "Stop crying! Yes,
you're right, of course. But I've got to make a living somehow and that's
why I learned this yin-yang business. How would I feed my family and
keep myself alive without it? I've no real interest in religion and I'll never
be a holy man. I just *look* like a monk. Sometimes I think it's too bad,
yes, but what can I do?"

"If you're that poor I'll just have to give you the money I've collected!
I suppose helping one man toward enlightenment is just as good as
building a temple." Jakushin sent his disciples straight off to fetch the
funds. When they got back, he gave the yin-yang diviner everything and
left for the Capital.

Later on Jakushin was living at Nyoi, in the hills east of the Capital,
when he received an urgent summons from the Rokujō Palace. Borrow-
ing a friend's horse, he set out early the next morning. Now, most riders
keep their mount moving purposefully ahead. Not so Jakushin, who let

the horse go on or not as it pleased. Naturally the horse soon stopped to graze. Jakushin simply waited, and since the horse never did get a move on, he ended up stuck forever in the same spot. The groom who came with the horse was so irritated by this performance that he finally gave the beast a whack on the rump. In a flash Jakushin had dismounted and seized hold of him.

"What did you do *that* for, eh?" he roared. "Do you think an old man like me riding him makes this horse look silly? This horse, I'll have you know, has been mother and father to me life after life for ages past. Perhaps you don't think he's been mother and father to *you*, perhaps *that's* why you're so mean. But this horse has been *your* mother and father as much as he's been mine. Why, it's just *because* he's loved you with a parent's love that he's now an animal! Sometimes he's even suffered down among the starving ghosts and in hell. Yes, that's exactly why he's a horse in the first place: because as a parent he always loved *you*, his child. And there the poor thing was, *so* hungry, trying to crop the lovely green grass that looked too good to miss, when *you*, you lout, had to go and hit him! Myself, I'm just so grateful for all he's given me through all those lives . . . But yes, it's true, my legs won't carry me any more as I'd like, and if I have to go somewhere a little far off I can't very well walk. And so here I am, presuming *again* on the poor beast's kindness. Who am *I* to object if he wants to eat the grass along the way? You're a brute, that's what you are, a brute!" Jakushin burst into loud sobbing.

The groom thought all this rather funny, but he did not like to see the old man cry. "You're quite right, sir, quite right," he answered. "I must have been mad to hit the horse. But what can you expect from a poor groom like me? I had no idea why the horse was born a horse, you see! From now on I'll give him the respect we owe our parents, and be properly grateful."

Finally Jakushin got back on the horse, still sniffling and muttering, "Oh, the poor, dear creature!"

On they went until they came to a rotten, warped old grave-marker standing by the path. Jakushin got all excited and dismounted as quickly as he could. The groom, who could make nothing of this, rushed up to take the bridle. Jakushin had him lead the horse on a little further. Looking back, the groom saw Jakushin prostrated full length in a spot where the pampas grasses grew a little less thickly. When Jakushin got back to his feet, he let down his trouser-skirt (he had hitched it up for traveling) to present a correct appearance, then put on the priestly stole which a servant had been carrying for him. Next, he adjusted his collar, swept his palms ceremoniously together, and bowed till he was nearly doubled over — not straight toward the grave-marker, however, but a bit to one side, like a guard bowing to a great personage whom he dare not face directly; and he threw only sidelong glances toward the object of his deference. Finally he went up to the grave-marker, brought his hands piously together once more, and prostrated himself repeatedly till his forehead knocked against the ground. All in all, his behavior was quite odd.

Jakushin would not remount until the grave-marker was out of sight. And since he did exactly the same thing for every grave-marker he came across, he was getting on and off his horse the whole way along. As a result, a trip that should have taken an hour or so took instead from early morning to late afternoon. By the time they arrived at the Rokujō Palace, the groom was swearing to himself that he would never, never go any-where with *that* old fellow again.

Another time, while Jakushin was living at Iwakura, he caught a chill and got a case of very loose bowels. While he was in the privy the monk in the neighboring hut heard a sound like water squirting from a nozzle and felt sorry for the old man. Then he heard Jakushin talking, and stole up to spy through a hole in the privy wall.

An old dog was sitting across from Jakushin, apparently waiting for him to get up. Jakushin was talking to the dog. "You got your animal body," he was saying, "because in past lives you betrayed others or made them eat nasty things. Yes, and you coveted what you were never meant to have, and thought much too much of yourself. You belittled others, you treated your parents as no one ever should, and you did nothing but awful things. And that's why you're a dog, you see, and why you wait around to eat such filth. When I *think* how in past lives you've been my mother or father, time after time! And these days especially, when my insides aren't right and it's coming out just like water, you mustn't eat it, no, you simply mustn't! It hurts me too much! Tomorrow, you'll see, I'll give you something really nice and you'll have as much as you want!" Great tears rolled down his cheeks as he talked.

The next day the neighbor spied on Jakushin again, curious to see what feast the dog would get. Ordering his disciples to prepare a meal for a guest, Jakushin had them pile a great quantity of rice into an earthenware dish and garnish it generously with vegetables. Then he had them spread a mat in the yard and set the dish out on it.

"Come!" called Jakushin, sitting down beside the dish. "Dinner's ready!" The dog came and ate while Jakushin rubbed his hands together in glee, weeping for joy and muttering how it did his heart good to see the dog tuck in. Alas, the big young dog which soon arrived did not go first for the rice. It attacked the old dog instead, bowled it over, and sank its teeth into it. Jakushin jumped in horror. "Oh no!" he cried. "Don't do that, *please*! I'll bring you some, too! *Please* just eat together nicely!" And he tried to stop the fight. Naturally the dogs paid no attention. The rice was scattered and trampled into the mud, and all the gobbling, snarling, and snapping brought more dogs running in from everywhere until a furious mêlée ensued. Jakushin fled back to his hut, unable to bear the sight of naked ignorance, anger, and greed.

The neighbor monk chuckled. "He may be wise," he thought to himself, "but he doesn't know dogs. He respects them for what they may have been in past lives, but what does he think the dogs themselves can make of his respect?"

1 8 0 .

THE REPRIEVE

On his way once to Kyoto, the Tōdaiji monk Zōman happened to meet a physiognomist. Since Zōman wanted to have his fortune told anyway, he was in luck. The physiognomist declared that Zōman would excel in his studies but that he would not live past forty. "If you want to live longer than that," he said, "arouse a sincere thirst for enlightenment. Nothing else will work."

The disturbed Zōman immediately left Tōdaiji and retired to a cave on Mount Kasagi, where he began a strict regime of ascetic practice. Early each morning he would be sure to call the name of the Bodhisattva Jizō.

In the fourth moon of his thirtieth year, Zōman fell ill and weakened slowly until the soul left his body and he died. Several angry officials, dressed in green, came to seize him. Zōman cried out that he was a blameless ascetic whose actions and senses were thoroughly pure. "In China there was a hopelessly evil man," he protested, "and when he died the flames of hell suddenly changed into a cool breeze, just because he had called Jizō's name! The Buddha even came to welcome him into paradise! I've called the name too, and I've entrusted myself to Jizō's compassionate vow. Doesn't that mean anything? If it doesn't, then the compassionate vows of Jizō and of all the buddhas of past, present, and future are worthless!"

"So *you* say," growled the officers from hell, "but we've no proof that you've any claim on the buddhas' compassion."

"The compassionate vows of the buddhas and bohisattvas *mean* something! But if you won't grant I'm right, then all the sutras' talk about the buddhas being real is just empty chatter!"

At this point a small monk, very distinguished-looking and giving off a beautiful light, suddenly appeared. Half a dozen equally diminutive monks were around him, and some three dozen more were ranged to either side. They pressed their palms together solemnly in greeting. "Well, that's different!" cried the officers. "Jizō and his host of saints have come to fetch him! We'll have to give him up!" They saluted the holy company and went away.

"Do you know me?" asked the little monk. "I'm the Jizō you've invoked each morning. I protect you with all my power. You were called down to hell because your karma required it, but now you can hurry back to the world of the living, put behind you all the cares that burden men, and fulfill your hope for rebirth in the Land of Bliss. You'll never come back here again."

Zōman returned to life after having been dead a day and a night. He went on to practice with ever greater faith until at last when he was ninety years old, light of step and in perfect health, he knew his time had come. He sat facing the west with palms pressed together in prayer, chanting the Buddha's Name and called on Jizō until he passed into Nirvana.

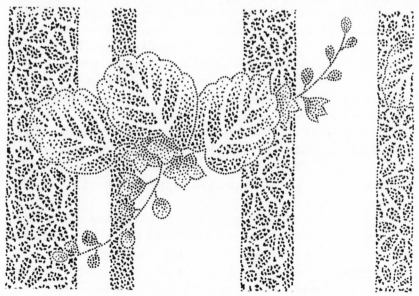

WATER

THE WATER SPIRIT

Retired Emperor Yōzei's palace compound was very large, and after he died the street we now know as Reizei'in Lane was put through it. The northern part was rapidly built over with houses. Only the southern section kept a few reminders of the garden that had once been there, and one of these was a pond.

One summer night a man stretched out on the veranda of the former palace's west wing, the building itself having survived only to pass into the hands of commoners. As he lay there, an old man three feet tall came and felt over his face. Too frightened to move, he pretended he was asleep until the old man softly got up and walked away. By the bright light of the moon and stars he watched the old man go to the edge of the pond and vanish. Not having been dredged or cleaned within living memory, the pond was choked with waterweeds and looked thoroughly evil. Once more the man shivered with fear.

Night after night now the old man came back and felt over the faces of those who were sleeping nearby. Everyone who even heard the story was terrified. Finally another man spoke up. "All right," said he, "I'll catch that fellow!" He lay down alone on the veranda with a length of stout rope beside him.

It was a long wait. Past midnight, when he had actually begun to doze off, he felt something cold touch his face. He leapt up, bound whatever it was with the rope, and tied it to the railing round the veranda.

Next, he called for light. There the creature was, a little old man three feet tall and dressed in pale yellow, blinking in the glare. He seemed about to expire. No questioning got any answer out of him, but after a while he smiled, glanced around, and said in a thin, sad little voice, "Would you please bring me a tub of water?"

When they put a big tub before him, he stretched out his neck to see his reflection. "I'm a water spirit, you see," he said, and collapsed with a splash into the tub. There was nothing left of him, though the tub was suddenly full to overflowing. The rope floated, still knotted, in the water.

The astonished people carried off the tub, taking care not to spill a drop, and emptied it into the pond. The old man was never seen or felt again.

1 8 2 .

THE MASTER OF STREAMS AND FALLS

The remarkable Chūsan, a monk of Kōfukuji in Nara, was said by some to be supernatural. People believed he had actually been born from a stream.

Once Chūsan and several companions set off in a time of terrible drought on a pilgrimage to the East. Even the springs which never failed had all gone dry, and many people were dying of thirst and starvation. People came from far off to get water from one spring in Ōmi province which still ran clear and sweet. When a woman on her way back from this spring, with a jar of water on her head, passed Chūsan on the trail, he asked her for a drink.

"You're a proper holy man," she answered. "Why don't you make a spring right here and get your drink yourself? I've carried this water a long way and I've a lot farther to go. I don't see why you should have to beg any off *me*!"

"You're right," said Chūsan, "I'll do that." He strode to a rock on the hillside, drew his sword, and struck off a chunk. Clear, cool water gushed out. The local people were amazed at their new spring.

Chūsan also went to the Nachi waterfall, where holy men have practiced since time immemorial. The mountain torrent there tumbles gleaming white, four hundred feet down a cliff to the valley floor. When

Chūsan chanted the Heart Sutra amid the roaring and the spray, the waters reversed their flow, and the living Thousand-Armed Kannon appeared on the rocky lip of the falls.

Years later he went to the Minoo waterfall where En no Gyōja, the wizard of the mountains, once met the Indian sage Nāgārjuna. Then Chūsan himself turned into Thousand-Armed Kannon, went straight up through the falls, and vanished forever.

1 8 3 .

THE DRAGON CAVE

The Dragon Cave at Murō in Yamato province is where the Dragon King Zentatsu lives. His first home was Sarusawa Pond in Nara, but a long time ago an imperial concubine drowned herself in the pond and the dragon had to escape to the pool at Kōzen in the Kasuga Hills. Then someone dumped a corpse in the Kōzen pool and the dragon had to flee again, this time to Murō.

Eventually the Venerable Nittai went into the cave at Murō to worship the dragon. After three or four hundred yards of pitch darkness, he came out into light as bright as day and saw a palace. Dazzlingly brilliant, jeweled blinds swayed gently in the breeze along its south side, and he glimpsed behind them a jade desk with a copy of the Lotus Sutra on it. A voice from behind the blinds asked him who he was and what he wanted. Nittai gave his name and said he had come to worship the Dragon King.

"You mustn't look at me," replied the Dragon King. "Leave the cave and I'll meet you three hundred yards beyond it."

Nittai obeyed and went to wait. The Dragon King rose from the earth before him, fully adorned and crowned, till Nittai could see his whole body down to the waist. After Nittai had contemplated him for a while, the Dragon King disappeared.

Nittai built a shrine on the spot and made a statue of the dragon. They say it is still there. When the monks of Murōji, the temple nearby, pray for rain, they chant sutras at this shrine. When their prayers work, a black cloud rises over the Dragon Cave and soon covers the whole sky. Then it rains.

1 8 4 .

GOLD FROM THE DRAGON PALACE

A poor young man of the Capital was so unable to make a decent living that every moon on Kannon's day, the eighteenth, he worshipped Kannon and visited as many temples as he could to pray for help. This had been his custom for years.

One year, in the ninth moon, he was going from temple to temple as usual when he passed through southern Yamashina, which was little inhabited in those days. In a deserted stretch of hills he met an older man carrying a foot-long spotted snake on the end of a pole. As the young man walked by, the little snake moved.

"Where are you going?" the young man asked. The older man replied that he was on his way to the Capital and asked the same question back. The young man explained his pilgrimage and inquired about the snake.

"I've a purpose for it," the older man answered.

"Won't you let me have it? Killing's a sin. Give it to me, for love of Kannon. This is Kannon's day, after all."

"You may talk of Kannon, but Kannon protects people as well as snakes. I need this snake. I don't particularly want to kill it, but I have to live somehow."

"What do you want it for?"

"Well, you see, I make the *nyoi* wands that monks carry when they preside at a rite. The head of a *nyoi* is curled like a fern shoot and made of ox horn. I need the oil from this little snake to work the horn into the right shape."

"What do you do with your *nyoi* then?"

"What a question! I sell it to a monk! That's my trade!"

"I see. You need the snake, and I certainly can't ask you to give it to me for nothing. Would you take my coat for it?"

The man agreed and the exchange was made.

"Where'd you get the snake?" the young man asked, and learned that it was from a pond nearby. After the older man had gone on, he took the snake to the pond, scraped the sand of the bank down a little to where it was cool, and let the snake go. The snake went right into the water. With his mind now at rest, he continued his pilgrimage.

A few hundred yards further on, a pretty twelve-year-old girl, very nicely dressed, came toward him. He could not imagine what she was doing in so lonely a place.

"You're so kind!" she said. "I've come to thank you."

"Kind? What do you mean?"

"Why, you saved my life! When I told my parents they said I should go straight to thank you and tell you how grateful they are. That's why I'm here."

He realized this must be the snake, and though touched he was also afraid. "Where are your parents, then?" he asked.

"Over there. I'll take you to see them!" She led him toward the pond.

He was so frightened that he would gladly have run away, but when she promised that no one would hurt him he instead followed her reluctantly to the water's edge. She asked him to wait while she announced he was coming, then vanished. His mind reeled.

"I'll take you now," said the girl, suddenly back. "Please close your eyes."

He did so and was just feeling himself drifting off when she told him to open them again. A magnificent gate, far finer than any palace gate in our land, stood before him. Having let her parents know he was there, she came out again and asked him to follow her.

He obeyed timidly. Inside the gate rose a dazzling palace made of every precious metal and stone. She led him to a central pavilion built all of shining multicolored jade, with the most beautiful floors and curtains. The place seemed like paradise.

Out came a gentleman in his early sixties, so distinguished that the young man was quite overawed. "Please come in," he said.

For a moment the young man wondered who he was talking to. "You're too kind, sir," he finally replied. "May I?"

"Of *course* you may! I didn't come to greet you for nothing! Come in!"

With great hesitation the young man did so. His host told him what a joy it was to welcome him, in view of the outstanding kindness of what he had done.

"But I've done nothing, sir!" the young man protested.

"The world knows well enough how parents love their children," the gentleman went on. "I've a good many children myself, and the youngest is this girl. Today she wanted to play in the pond. Oh, I tried to stop her, but she wouldn't listen! Then she came back and told me how she'd been caught and was going to be killed when you came along and saved her. I can't tell you how grateful I am!"

Finally the young man grasped that this was the girl's father.

Next, the gentleman had some overpoweringly splendid servants serve a feast. As he ate, he pressed his guest so insistently to do so too that the nervous young man let himself be persuaded. It was a delicious meal.

"I'm a Dragon King," the gentleman began when the dishes were finally cleared away, "and I've lived here since time out of mind. What I'd really like to give you in thanks is a Wishing Jewel, but I'm afraid the people of Japan are too evil at heart and can't be trusted with one. I've something else for you instead, though." He had a servant fetch a box from which he took a rice cake three inches thick, made of pure gold.

He broke the cake in two and gave the young man half. "Don't use this up all at once," he warned. "If you break off a little as you need it, you'll be quite comfortable the rest of your life."

The young man put the cake in the fold of his robe. At the appropriate moment he excused himself, and the girl took him back to the gate. Again she told him to close his eyes. When he opened them, they were both standing by the pond. The girl said she would have to go now and promised him she would never forget his kindness. Then she disappeared.

When he got home, his family clamored about how long he had been gone. What he had thought an hour or two had actually been several days!

He told no one about his golden cake but quietly broke off bits and exchanged them for what he needed. Since the cake always grew back to its old size, no matter how much he broke off, he became very rich. All his life he served Kannon faithfully, and after he died the golden cake disappeared. It did not pass on to his children.

1 8 5 .

THE POND GOD TAKES A WIFE

A woman in Shimōsa province often took her stepdaughter, a girl of twelve or so, to the edge of a large pond and announced to the god of the pond that the girl was his to marry. She did this once when a gale was blowing and the pond was very rough. The girl was so frightened that her hair stood on end; and what with the wind and waves, and the ominous darkness of the day, she fled home again as fast as she could go with the awful feeling that something was behind her.

Dashing panic-stricken into the house, she clutched at her father and began telling him what had happened. Next, her stepmother ran in just ahead of a huge snake. The snake stared at the girl, the tongue in its huge head flickering.

The father was no great lord, but he was still quick-witted. "She's *my* daughter," he told the snake. "This woman here is just her stepmother and she's got no right to give her away. I'm the only one who can do that and I refuse. No, a wife's bound to do as her husband says, and as far as I'm concerned *she's* the one who's yours, if you want her. Go ahead, take her!"

While father and daughter made their escape, the snake slithered toward the stepmother instead and coiled around her. They say she went mad and began turning into a snake herself.

The story was going around one summer ten years or so ago, which would be about 1270. Rumor had it that on a certain day that fall, both snakes would rise from the pond during a tremendous storm. There really was a storm on that day too, but I never heard whether or not the snakes appeared.

C L O S E D

W O R L D S

1 8 6 .

THE ISLE OF MAN AND MAID

A poor farmer once lived in Hata county of Tosa province, along the southern coast of Shikoku. His rice field was in the neighboring province, not in his own, but he raised the seedlings at home and when planting time came he prepared to take them to his field by boat. He also loaded aboard everything else he needed: a plow, a hoe, a spade, cooking pots, and food to feed himself, his wife and children, and the laborer he meant to hire.

When the boat was ready to sail, he and his wife went to find a willing laborer, leaving their little son and daughter fast asleep on board. They never bothered to make the boat fast, since they planned not to be gone long, but only pulled it up a bit on the shore.

The boat floated on the rising tide. Then a breeze sprang up and blew it, as the tide ebbed, far out to where the wind was strong. Now the boat ran as though under sail. When the children woke up and saw how far they had drifted from land they began to cry, but they could not stop the wind taking them wherever it wanted to blow.

The parents brought their laborer to the shore only to find the boat gone. Thinking it might have caught in the lee somewhere, they called and called, and searched every inlet and cove when they got no answer. In the end, though, they had to give up.

The boat was blown onto an island far away to the south. Still crying, the children disembarked and tied it up. There was no one on the island. "We'll just have to do the best we can," they told each other. "We can eat a little food every day for as long as it lasts, then we'll just see. Anyway, let's plant these seedlings before they die."

They found a nice place for a field, with a brook nearby, and made good use of the spade and hoe that had come with them. Next, they cut wood and built a shelter. Since one kind of tree or another was always in fruit they easily survived till fall, when their luck brought them a much richer harvest than they could have hoped to get in Japan. They carefully laid this harvest by.

Once the two had grown up, they saw they really had no choice but to marry. Their many children married each other in turn till despite its generous size the island was dotted with fields. In fact, that first pair had so many descendants that their island can scarcely hold them any more, or so people say.

Imose-jime, the Isle of Man and Maid, is supposed to be out in the ocean south of Tosa.

1 8 7 .

THE SNAKE AND THE CENTIPEDE

A band of seven men in Kaga province chose to live by fishing on the sea, rowing together in the same boat. Although fishermen, they always went well armed with bows and arrows.

They had rowed out of sight of land one day when a sudden gale hit them and blew them farther still. All they could do was pull in their oars, groaning that they would die, and let the wind take them where it would. Eventually they sighted a large island ahead. "An island!" they cried. "If we can reach it we can at least survive!" They succeeded with a tremendous effort, disembarked, and drew their boat safely up on the shore. There was a stream, and apparently plenty of fruit on the trees. They had just started looking for something to eat when they saw a handsome man coming toward them. It was a surprise and a relief to find the island inhabited.

"Do you realize I brought you here?" the man asked.

"I don't know what you mean," one of the fishermen answered. "A gale blew up while we were fishing and swept us out to sea. We were very glad to find this island, I can tell you!"

"Yes, you see, I'm the one who made the wind blow."

The fishermen realized this was no ordinary human.

"But you must be tired," said the man and shouted toward the woods, "Come! Bring it all down!"

With a clatter of footsteps, bearers arrived carrying a wine jar and two large chests full of delicious food. The exhausted fishermen ate hungrily and drank their fill of wine. When they had finished, the leftovers were put back in the chests and set aside for the next day.

"Now," said the man of the island when the bearers had left, "I'll tell you *why* I brought you here. There's another island beyond this one, and the fellow who lives there is always attacking me. He wants to kill me and take over this island too. I've fought him off so far, but tomorrow he's coming again and our battle will be decisive. One of us will live and the other will die. I brought you here to ask for your help."

"How much of an army does he have?" the fisherman asked. "How many ships has he got? We'll fight for you to the death if need be, since we're here."

The man was pleased. "My enemy doesn't have human form," he explained, "and I won't either when I fight him. You'll see tomorrow. Every time he's attacked here before, I've come down this slope to keep him below the waterfall over there. I've alway tried to turn him from the beach. But tomorrow I'm counting on *you*, so I'm going to let him up. He'll be only too eager to climb, since he gets stronger as he gets higher. Just watch us fight at first. When I can't take any more I'll signal to you with my eyes. Then shoot all your arrows into him, and please don't miss! Be ready tomorrow morning. The battle will start about midday. Make sure you get plenty to eat! And stand on this outcrop of rock because he'll be coming from up here." Having given these careful instructions, the man withdrew into the depths of the island.

The fishermen cut saplings and built themselves a shelter, then sharpened their arrows and readied their bowstrings. They spent the night talking around a fire. Dawn came, and after a good breakfast they looked toward where the enemy was supposed to come from. A steady gale was blowing, and the strangely menacing sea now began to glow. Inside the light they saw two large masses of fire. The mountain behind them looked just as ghastly. The grasses were bending low, the trees were whistling in the wind, and on the mountainside as well they saw twin masses of fire.

A centipede a hundred feet long came swimming in, shining blue on its back and red along its sides. Above them an equally huge snake was beginning to descend, its tongue flickering. The snake let his enemy climb, as he had said he would, and watched with his head alertly raised as the centipede seized his chance. Then the two frightful monsters paused, fixing each other with a furious glare.

The seven fishermen on the rocky outcrop fitted arrows to their bowstrings and waited, their eyes on the snake.

The centipede charged. Both creatures tore at each other till they were covered with blood, but the centipede, with all its legs, always seemed to be winning. After several hours the exhausted snake finally gave a look that clearly meant "Now!" The seven shot their arrows deep into the centipede, from its head to its tail, then they hacked at its legs with their swords till the monster was helpless. Once the snake had disengaged itself, the fishermen attacked still more savagely and killed it. The snake meanwhile slithered away.

Shortly their host returned in a sad condition, limping, bleeding, and wounded all over; but he brought them food and thanked them again and again. They cut up the centipede's body, felled trees for a huge bonfire, and after burning the grisly remains threw the ashes and bones far away.

When the job was done, the man thanked them again. "There's no one now to dispute my ownership of the island," he said, "and that makes me very happy. Plenty of places on the island would make good rice paddies, and even more would do for dry fields. And there are so many fruit trees! Yes, it's a fine island. Come and live here!"

"That's a good idea," the fishermen answered, "but what about our wives and children?"

"Bring them too!"

"How can we get them here?"

"When you cross to the mainland I'll send you a following wind. And when you come back, well, the Kumata Shrine in Kaga province is my sanctuary too, and if you worship there before you set out you'll get back here quite safely."

He sent them off with enough food for the trip. As they cast off, a wind blew down from the island and in no time they had crossed to the mainland.

They all went home and told their families where they were going now and why. Then in secret they got themselves ready, each party preparing a boat loaded with seeds for all the crops that would grow. Finally they visited the Kumata Shrine to report their journey to the god. As soon as they had boarded their boats a following wind arose, and all the boats crossed straight over to the island.

On the island they cultivated paddies and dry fields, and multiplied till it was hardly possible to count them any more. The island is called Neko-no-shima, Cat Island. Once a year, they say, the islanders sail to the mainland and worship at the Kumata Shrine. The villagers there know there are coming and why, and would gladly visit with them; but they never actually meet the islanders because the islanders come in during the night. The villagers find only their offerings the next morning, by which time the islanders have left again. These annual visits still occur regularly. You can see the island, rising green on the western horizon, from Omiya in Noto province.

Once a Noto boatman was blown out to the island. Although the islanders would not let him land, they allowed him to tie up on the shore and brought him food. A week or so later a favorable wind brought him back to Noto. From what he had been able to see, there were a lot of houses on the island, with streets between them just as in the Capital, and many people coming and going in the streets.

For that matter, lately Chinese sailors have been putting in to this island first, on their way to Japan. The islanders bring them food, and they stock up on fish and abalone before going on to Tsuruga in Kaga province. Apparently the islanders forbid them even to tell other people the island is there.

1 8 8 .

THROUGH THE WATER CURTAIN

A wandering monk came to the province of Hida where, deep in the mountains, he got lost. Following a faint track buried in dead leaves, he finally came to a wide, high waterfall that cascaded like a great curtain down a cliff. He could not go back since he had no idea where he was, and in front off him rose a two-hundred-foot wall of rock. While praying to the Buddha for guidance, he heard footsteps behind him. It was a man with a load of wood. Though the monk was relieved to see him, the man looked surprised and upset. "Who are you? Where does this path go?" asked the monk, but the man walked straight past him into the waterfall and vanished.

Apparently he had been a demon, not a man. The frightened monk decided that before the demon ate him he would plunge into the waterfall too, and die. "Then it won't bother me if he does eat me!" he said to himself.

Praying for a happy rebirth, he walked straight ahead till water pounded on his face. Then he was through. He supposed drowning came next, but in fact he still seemed to be conscious. The waterfall really *was* a thin curtain, and the narrow path on the other side led on under the mountain. He was glad at last to reach a large village.

The man who had passed him now came running toward him, ahead of a gentleman in light blue-green formal dress. The gentleman hastily invited the monk to follow him home. On the way people joined them from all directions and each one asked the monk home. What could they all want? The gentleman silenced them. "We'll go to the mayor and let him decide who gets this fellow!" he said.

The crowd swept the monk on to a large house, where an agitated old man came out and asked what was going on. The first man the monk had seen complained, "I'm the one who led him here from Japan and now this man has taken him over!" He pointed at the gentleman in blue-green.

Without discussion the old man awarded the monk to the gentleman, who began leading the monk away. The crowd dispersed.

The monk could only think they were all demons, and that this one was taking him away to eat him. He began to cry. "Japan!" he thought in despair. "Where *is* this place if Japan is so far away?"

The gentleman noticed his expression. "Please don't worry!" he said. "It's very peaceful here, you know. I promise you you'll be comfortable. You won't have a care in the world."

The gentleman's house turned out to be a little smaller than the one they had just left, but very nice and with a large staff of servants and retainers. The monk's arrival caused a great stir. When the gentleman invited him in, his pack, straw cloak, hat, and straw boots were politely taken from him and put away.

"Food, please!" the gentleman ordered, and a meal was served. But despite the wealth of beautifully prepared chicken and fish, the monk did not eat. Instead he only sat and stared.

His host asked him what was the matter.

"I've been a monk all my life, you see, and I've never eaten anything like this. Looking is all I can do."

"I understand. But you're with *us* now, you know. You'll have to eat up! And another thing. I have a daughter I love very much and she's ready to be married. So you should start letting your hair grow, because I want her to marry *you*. You can't leave, anyway. Just remember to do as I say!"

The monk thought he might be killed if he showed any sign of resistance, and there certainly was no escape. "I'm just not used to this sort of food," he answered, "but all right, I'll eat it." As the two ate, the monk wondered what the Buddha could be thinking of him now, since he had vowed never to eat the flesh of any living creature.

At nightfall a very pretty girl came in, beautifully dressed. Her father pushed her gently toward the monk. "She's yours," he said. "From now on you must love her as much as I do. She's my only daughter, you understand, so you can imagine how deeply I mean that." With this little speech he withdrew.

No argument was possible. The monk (from now on he will have to be "the young man") welcomed the girl, and after that they were man and wife. The young man was actually very happy. He was dressed in the best and served whatever food he wanted. This new life was so unlike his old one that he put on a good deal of weight. When his hair was long enough for a topknot he did it up properly, and with a respectable hat on he cut a fine figure. His wife thought the world of him and he loved her in return.

After eight months like this, the young woman grew sad. Her father, on the other hand, only redoubled his attentions. "Good, good, we've gotten some flesh on you!" he would say. "Fatten up all you like!" He fed his son-in-law so often that the young man kept putting on weight. As he did so his wife began to have fits of weeping. When the young man asked her why, she would answer only that she felt sad, but wept more and more. The baffled young man put up with it as best he could.

One day his father-in-law entertained a visitor. Listening in discreetly, he heard the visitor say, "That's a nice young man you've got! You must be pleased to have your daughter so well provided for."

"I certainly am!" the gentleman answered. "If I didn't have him, I don't know how I could stand it by now."

"I just wish I could get one myself," said the visitor, rising to go. "I'm sure I'll be miserable by this time next year."

Having seen his guest off, the gentleman asked solicitously whether his son-in-law had eaten and made sure a meal was served. The young man's wife wept while he ate. The puzzled young man kept thinking about what the visitor had said, and although he did not quite understand it he was afraid. His wife resisted every effort of his to coax an explanation out of her, though she clearly wanted to speak.

The village was bustling with preparations for a festival. Depressed as she was, the young man's wife now did little more than cry, and she seemed so estranged from him that he finally reproached her. "I thought we'd always be together in joy and sorrow," he complained, "but you've gotten so far away! You're too cruel!" He burst into angry tears.

His wife sobbed aloud. "What ever made me think I could keep silent till the very end?" she cried. "There's so little time left! Oh, if only I didn't love you!"

"Am I going to die? Well, so are we all, some time or other. There must be something else! Tell me!"

"You see, we have a sacred obligation here to give our gods living human sacrifices. That's why everyone was so anxious to have you when you came. They all wanted you for the sacrifice. Each year it's another household's turn to provide the victim, and if no one from outside can be found the household head has to provide his own son or daughter. I'd have been the victim if you hadn't come. Oh, I wish I could take your place after all!"

"Don't cry!" said her husband. "Perhaps it could be worse. Tell me, is the victim carved up *before* being offered to the gods?"

"No, I don't think so. The victim is laid out naked on a cutting board and carried inside the inner sanctuary fence. Then everyone leaves. I hear the gods carve up their victim themselves. If the victim is thin or displeasing in any way, they're very angry. Then the crops fail, people get sick, and we villagers do nothing but quarrel. That's why my father has been feeding you so often and making you gain weight."

At last the young man understood all the care that had been lavished on him. "But these gods," he said, "what shape do they have?"

"They're supposed to be monkeys."

"All right, I have an idea. Can you get me a good dagger?"

"Of course I can," his wife answered, and quickly did so.

The young man sharpened it carefully and hid it on his body. He got much livelier now, ate with unfailing appetite, and went on fattening nicely. His father-in-law was pleased, and everyone in the village looked forward to a good year.

Seven days before the festival, ceremonial ropes were stretched around all the houses to mark the sacred occasion, and the young man was made to fast and undergo purification. Though his wife counted the days with tears and groans, he himself seemed untroubled. In fact, he comforted his wife so well that even she took heart a little.

On the festival day he was made to wash and put on a beautiful robe. His hair was combed and tied up, and his sidelocks carefully dressed. A messenger came from the shrine again and again, more impatient each time. Finally the young man and the gentleman rode out on horses together while the young wife stayed behind, hiding under her robe and weeping in silence.

The shrine was a row of sanctuaries composing a single large structure inside an impressively fenced sacred enclosure. The crowd before the fence was eating a festive meal. The young man was led to a high seat among them and served food too. After the company had eaten and drunk freely, there was dancing and music.

At last the young man was called on to rise. He was undressed, his hair was unbound, and he was laid on the cutting board with a final, strict order neither to move nor to speak. Green sprigs of the sacred *sakaki* tree were planted at the board's four corners, and a sacred cord with white streamers fluttering from it was strung from sprig to sprig. Having carried the board ceremoniously through the fence and laid it before the sanctuaries, the bearers withdrew and closed the gate behind them. The young man was all alone. He stealthily reached for the dagger hidden all this time between his thighs.

When the door of the chief sanctuary creaked open, the young man's hair stood on end. One by one the other doors opened too. Next a monkey as big as a man came round from behind the shrine and chattered at the chief sanctuary. The sanctuary curtain was swept aside and out came another monkey with gleaming white teeth, larger and fiercer than the first. "They're just monkeys after all!" thought the young man with relief. More monkeys came from the other sanctuaries, and when all were present the messenger monkey received chattered orders from the monkey of the chief sanctuary. These instructions obviously concerned the victim because the messenger monkey now came to the cutting board, picked up the large cooking chopsticks and knife that were laid out for him, and prepared to carve.

The young man leapt up and attacked the chief monkey who, taken completely by surprise, toppled over backwards. A dagger pinned him to the ground. "Are you a god?" the young man roared. The monkey wrung his hands beseechingly while all the others fled and sat chattering furiously in the treetops.

The young man tied up the monkey with some vines that came to hand and bound him to a post. Then with his dagger to the pit of the monkey's stomach he cried, "Why, you *are* just a plain monkey! And all these years you've been calling yourself a god and eating people! *Now* what have you got to say for yourself? All right, call out your sons! Call them out! You're dead if you don't. Of course if you're a god my knife won't hurt you. Perhaps I'll just stick it in your belly and see what happens!" A little pressure on the blade made the monkey scream and wring his hands again. "All right," said the young man, "call out your sons!"

The monkey chattered and the messenger monkey came back. Sending him for more vines, the young man first tied up the chief monkey's three sons, then the messenger monkey too. "You were going to carve me up," he said, "but I'll let you live if you stay quiet. I will kill you, though, if you ever curse those poor, ignorant people again or eat them!"

He led the monkeys out the gate through the shrine fence and tied them to trees. Next, he set fire to the shrine with embers from the recent cooking fires. The village was so far off that no one knew, though when flames leaped from the spot the villagers saw them and worried. No one went to see what was happening because people were supposed to stay at home for three days after the festival.

The gentleman was particularly upset and feared something had gone very wrong. His daughter too was afraid because she knew better than her father what might have caused the flames. Then the victim himself appeared in the village, carrying a staff and driving the tied-up monkeys ahead of him. He was naked but for a belt of vines with a dagger stuck in it, and his loose hair flowed over his shoulders. People peeped at him through every gate along the way. "He's got the gods bound and he's driving them along!" they cried to each other. "Why, our sacrificial victim was more powerful than the gods! And if he can do this to the gods, just think what he can do to *us*! Maybe he'll eat us!" The villagers were terrified.

At his father-in-law's house the young man shouted for the gate to be opened. Silence met his demand. "Open up!" he shouted again. "I won't hurt you! But if you don't open up there *will* be trouble." He kicked at the gate.

The gentleman had his daughter go out to meet her husband. "He's stronger than the gods," he said, "and I'm afraid he may mean you harm. But open the gate and talk to him."

Fearful but happy too, the girl cracked the gate open and the young man pushed it wide. "Let me have my clothes," he said. She fetched him his trousers, his cloak, and his hat, and after tying the monkeys fast to the house he dressed. He also had her bring him a quiver and bow. Then he called out his father-in-law.

"It's horrible!" he said. "These are *monkeys* you've been calling gods and feeding people to all these years. Look! This is Mr. Monkey. You can keep him tied to your house, and if anyone does any tormenting it's *you*, not Mr. Monkey. But you've had it all backwards! Well, you can be sure these monkeys won't trouble you any more as long as I'm here!"

He pinched one of the monkeys' ears. It did not react. The whole thing was rather funny. The monkeys seemed quite tame! Slightly reassured, the gentleman agreed that they had had everything wrong. "From now on *you'll* be our god," he said, "and we'll do whatever you say!" He rubbed his hands together ingratiatingly.

The young man led him off to see the mayor, herding the monkeys along. His knock on the gate again got no answer.

"Open up!" the gentleman shouted. "I've got to speak to you! There'll be trouble otherwise!" This threat brought out the mayor, trembling with fear, to open up. At the sight of the sacrificial victim he threw himself prostrate on the ground. The young man led his monkeys into the house and spoke to them with fury in his eyes. "You've falsely called yourselves gods, and each year you've killed and eaten a human being. Now you're going to mend your ways!" He fitted an arrow to his bowstring and took aim. The monkeys screamed in abject fear, and the mayor was so alarmed that he asked the gentleman, "Is he going to kill us, too? Save us!"

"Keep calm," the gentleman answered. "Nothing will happen as long as I'm here."

"All right," the young man went on, "I won't have your lives. But if you ever show yourselves here again, and try any mischief against the people, I promise I'll shoot you."

He gave each monkey twenty blows of his staff, then sent the villagers to smash and burn what was left of the shrine. Next, he drove the monkeys out of the village. They ran off, limping, deep into the mountains and were never seen again.

Now the greatest man in the village, the young man stayed on with his wife. The villagers were at his beck and call. Perhaps he told this story when he came back to our land for a secret visit. Since the people beyond the waterfall had no cattle, horses, or dogs he brought them puppies (dogs are great enemies of monkeys) and foals for them to put to work, and these all multiplied. But although he sometimes visited our land, no one from here ever visited his.

1 8 9 .

CANNIBAL ISLAND

A man from Kyushu once set off by boat, with a good crew of men, to trade in parts unknown. On the return voyage the ship's first landfall was a large island far off the southwestern coast of Kyushu. It seemed inhabited, and the crew were all for putting in and taking on some provisions. When they landed, some wandered off to look over the island while others scattered to replenish their supply of chopsticks.

The soon heard a large group of people coming down from the heights of the island. For all they knew, the islanders could be demons. Rushing back to the ship, they quickly put some sea between themselves and the shore.

More than a hundred natives hove into view, dressed in white with tall, nodding caps on their heads. It was a familiar costume. Thank goodness they were humans after all! Apparently there was nothing to fear. Still, in so remote a spot these fellows could easily be murderous enough, and there certainly were a lot of them. The men kept rowing.

The islanders reached the edge of the water, saw that the boat was retreating, and came straight on into the sea. Being fighters, the crew were well armed. Every man had an arrow fitted to the string as they warned their pursuers off. The completely unarmed islanders glared at the ship a moment in silence, then turned round and disappeared again up onto the island.

What had the islanders had in mind? The crew did not really want to find out, and since the islanders could perfectly well try coming after them again, they followed the prompting of their fear and rowed away for good.

Back in Kyushu they told everyone they met about the incident. An old man who heard the story said they had been on Tora Island. As far as he knew, the islanders did indeed have human form, but were actually cannibals who would overpower any unwary visitor and kill and eat him. "You boys did well to get away from there," he declared. "If they'd gotten at you, you'd have all been dead, armed or not!" The men quaked afresh at this news and wondered at their narrow escape.

H A U N T S   I I

1 9 0 .

NO NONSENSE!

The splendid mansion of Tōru, the Minister of the Left, was called Kawara-no-in, or Riverside. Tōru was especially proud of its elaborate garden. When he died, his heirs offered the place to Retired Emperor Uda.

Late one night Uda heard someone open a storeroom in the west wing and come rustling toward him. Peering into the darkness he saw, kneeling now some six feet away, a gentleman in elegant everyday dress, carrying a courtier's baton and wearing a sword in the manner of a very great lord.

"Who are you?" Uda asked.

"The master of this house."

"You mean you're the Minister Tōru?"

"Yes, I am."

"What do you want?"

"Well, the house is mine, and if I may say so, your living here too makes the place a bit small for me. I wonder what you suggest."

"This is very odd," said Uda, his voice rising with anger. "When did I ever rob a man of his house? I live here because your heirs gave the place to *me*. Your being a ghost doesn't mean you talk sense. What's all this about?"

The ghost vanished instantly and was never seen again.

People were very impressed with His Majesty's handling of the incident. "No ordinary man," they said, "could possible have argued so forcefully with a ghost!"

1 9 1 .

QUITE A BIT OF NONSENSE

Once, Retired Emperor Uda took a carriage ride with one of his consorts to his Riverside Palace. The view from there was lovely, and that night the moon was very bright. Uda had the mats from his carriage spread out in one of the rooms, then he and the consort lay down. They were making love when a storeroom door opened and a voice spoke.

"Who's there?" Uda called.

"Tōru," said the voice. "I want your consort for *me.*"

"You were just a minister when you were alive," Uda retorted. "I'm an emperor. How dare you? Go away!"

The ghost clutched at Uda, who was half dead with fright. His servants were all too far away to hear him cry out. Only the little oxherd was nearby, tending the ox from the carriage while it grazed. Uda had him get the carriage brought round and helped his consort into it. She was ghastly pale and could not even stand.

As soon as Uda got home, he sent an exorcist to take care of the ghost. He was very lucky that the gods were still watching over him even though he had abdicated. There were sword cuts on the storeroom door, made by the gods as they slashed at Tōru's ghost and forced him back inside.

1 9 2 .

ONE MOUTHFUL

Long ago, Retired Emperor Yōzei lived in a haunted palace in northern Kyoto.

One night a guard was asleep in the Fishing Pavilion, a pavilion for parties and moon-viewing built out over the large garden pond. Suddenly he awoke to feel skinny fingers playing lightly over his face. Frightened by the eerie sensation, he drew his sword and seized the intruder. He had captured a miserable old man dressed all in pale blue.

"This is where *I* lived a long time ago," the old man said dolefully. "I'm Urashima's younger brother, you know, and I've been here for twelve hundred years. Please let me go! If only you'll build me a shrine and do me proper honor, I'll willingly protect the place!"

"But it isn't just up to *me*," the guard replied. "I'll have to consult His Majesty about it."

"Oh you will, will you?" snarled the old man. He kicked the guard high in the air three times. The last time the guard came down, as limp as a rag, he opened his mouth and swallowed him. At first he had loooked quite ordinary, but then he grew so huge that he made just one mouthful of that guard.

1 9 3 .

SUDDENLY, HORSE DUNG

One evening an imperial bath attendant (a woman) went off on a visit, taking her little son Akoboshi and some friends of his along with her. As twilight fell the boys began a wrestling game outside the house. Suddenly something like a huge curtain (they never did get a good look it) came down over them from the wall they were playing under, and Akoboshi disappeared. The other boys ran off, terrified. They were afraid to tell anyone what had happened.

The woman was very upset when she missed her son and hunted everywhere for him, but in vain. In the middle of the third night after his disappearance there was a knocking on her gate. Not daring to open it, she managed to cry out, "Who's there?"

"We want to give you back your son! Open up!"

She was too frightened to obey. Next, she heard voices on her roof and a roar of laughter. Something fell, or was thrown, to the ground. Fighting back her terror, she lit a torch and went for a look. It was Akoboshi, lying limp and still. The only sign of life in him was that he blinked.

She called a healer and his medium. When the medium went into her trance, Akoboshi was suddenly covered with some sort of brownish stuff. It turned out to be horse dung, three bucketfuls of it. Akoboshi never told what had happened to him, but he revived and was still alive ten years or so later.

This happened around 1215. I got this from someone who was there at the time.

1 9 4 ·

THE MONK IN WHITE ARMOR

Nakakane, the governor of Ōmi, was going every day to help his father, Lord Mitsutō, build the Hōjūji temple. He left the construction site one evening after sundown, and darkness fell while his carriage was rolling along in the vicinity of Tōji. There was no one behind him because all his attendants were running on ahead.

By the faint light of the stars Nakakane saw a monk in white armor walking behind his carriage. How very odd! Lifting the carriage's rear blind for a better look, he thought he recognized one Jirō, a monk whom his father had dismissed from his service and driven away. Perhaps Jirō was planning an attack. Still, it was all very strange.

Instead of warning his attendants, Nakakane gripped the sword that was kept in the carriage for emergencies, jumped down, and faced the monk.

"Is that you, Jirō?" he called threateningly. "What are you doing here? I don't like the look of you!" And he charged.

The monk grew huge, then seemed to vanish. Suddenly something knocked Nakakane's hat off from above and lifted him up by the hair. Slashing over his head with the sword, Nakakane struck something solid. Whatever it was let go, and he fell to the ground with blood all over his robe and his right arm.

Having no idea what had happened, Nakakane's servants went on to Lord Mitsutō's house as ordered. They only realized the carriage was empty when their master failed to get out of it. Back they went the way they had come, in great alarm, and discovered Nakakane in a field south of Tōji. He was dead, sword in hand. They carried him home and had a protective rite done over him for several days until he came back to life.

The Retired Emperor asked for the sword, and it ended up in the treasury of Sanjūsangendō.

DREAMS

1 9 5 .

LITTLE WHITE HAIRS

One day when the "Sage Minister" Sanesuke was still only a counselor, he dozed off in his carriage on the way out of the palace. Hovering between dream and waking, he noticed a little man all in white catching up with him fast. On reaching the carriage the little man lifted the rear blind. Sanesuke was indignant. "What do you want?" he growled. "I don't like you. Go away!"

"I'm from the king of hell," the little man answered. "My name is Little White Hairs." He jumped into the carriage, hopped onto Sanesuke's head, and disappeared.

Back at home Sanesuke looked in the mirror and saw his first white hair. He had never been much intererested in religion before, but after that he began to think about the life to come.

1 9 6 .

THE MAN WHO STOLE A DREAM

Hiki no Makibito, a county magistrate's son in Bitchū province, went to see a dream-reader about a puzzling dream he had had. Sitting chatting with the woman after she had given her reading, he heard a party of people approaching. It was the provincial governor's eldest son, a boy of sixteen or so, accompanied by half a dozen men.

The governor's son was very handsome. "It this the dream-reader woman's place?" he asked his men, and they told him it was. Makibito retired to an inner room and watched through a hole in the wall as the young man entered, told his dream, and asked what it meant. "That's a remarkable dream, sir," the woman replied. "It means you're sure to end up as a minister at court. Yes indeed, that's a wonderful dream! But be careful now, sir, don't tell anyone else about it." The young man looked very pleased. On leaving he gave her his cloak.

Makibito emerged from the back. "I hear it's possible to take over someone else's dream," he said. "Why not let me have that young gentleman's? The governor will be off to the Capital again once his four-year term is over, but I'm your neighbor and always will be. Besides, my father's the county magistrate and you might as well be nice to me."

The woman agreed and told him what to do. "Come in just as the young gentleman did," she said, "and tell me his dream exactly as he told it himself." Makibito cheerfully imitated the gentleman's entrance and narration in every detail, and the woman gave him precesely the interpretation she had just given. Makibito removed his cloak, gave it to her, and left.

After that he applied himself so studiously to his books that his scholarship came to the attention of the court. When tested, he did so well that he was sent to study in China, returning home after a long and fruitful stay to find favor with the emperor. In time he was promoted to minister.

So it pays to steal someone else's dream. The governor's son never got an official post at all. Had he kept his dream he would have been a minister. You should keep your dreams to yourself!

197 ·

THE BUDDHA-OX

During his tenure as governor of Echizen, Taira no Nakakata received from his province the gift of a black ox. After riding the animal for years, he at last gave it to a monk he knew at Kiyomizu in Kyoto, and the monk in turn passed it on to one Masanori who lived in Ōtsu at the southern end of Lake Biwa.

When the holy man of Sekidera began rebuilding this venerable temple from the ruins left by long neglect, he found that although he had a good wagon to haul building materials in, he had no ox to pull it. Masanori, not far away in Ōtsu, heard of the problem and gave him the black ox. The holy man put it straight to work.

The ox had finished its job when a great monk had a dream. Myōson, of Miidera near Ōtsu, dreamed that he went to Sekidera and found a black ox tethered before the main hall. He asked what it was doing there. "I am the Buddha Kashō," the ox itself replied. "I came to Sekidera in the form of an ox to help the temple and spread the holy Teaching." Then Myōson woke up.

He was so impressed that in the morning he sent a disciple to find out whether there really was a black ox at Sekidera, one used for hauling construction materials. The disciple reported that the temple did indeed have a big black ox with rather flattened horns. It was tethered in front of the holy man's lodging. According to the holy man, it hauled the materials for rebuilding the temple.

Amazed, Myōson set out on foot for Sekidera with a crowd of his most distinguished monks. The ox was nowhere to be seen, but the holy man explained that he had sent it up on the hillside to graze, and promised to have it fetched right away. Actually the ox came down the hillside behind the main hall even as the boy sent for it started up. Myōson wanted it caught, but this proved impossible. At last, filled with pious reverence, Myōson declared that he would not insist further. "I'll worship it from a distance, wherever it may roam," he said, and prostrated himself repeatedly toward the ox. All the monks with him did the same.

Having circled the hall three times clockwise, the ox lay down in front of it facing the altar. Myōson and his monks circumambulated the hall three times in turn. The more saintly-looking among them were all in tears.

After Myōson left, news of the ox spread till every single inhabitant of the Capital, all the great lords and nobles, and even the regent himself with his wife, came to Sekidera to worship it. Sanesuke, the Minister of the Right, was the only one not to come.

When Kin'sue, the chancellor, made the pilgrimage he met such a press of commoners at the temple that he thought it unsafe to get out of his carriage (as even so great a man as he would normally have done) before entering the temple grounds. Instead, he had his carriage drive straight in and up to the ox's stall. The ox seemed deeply offended by this sacrilege because it suddenly broke its tether and bolted for the hills. The chancellor got out at once and burst into tears at the thought that his conduct had displeased the ox and made it run away.

Perhaps moved by his heartfelt repentance, the ox soon came slowly back down the hillside and lay down again in its stall. The chancellor fed it grass he had gathered with his own hands; and when it ate the grass, although clearly not very hungry, he covered his face with his sleeve and sobbed. So did everyone looking on.

After the mass pilgrimage had continued for four or five days, the holy man dreamed that the ox spoke to him. "My work at this temple is done now," it said, "and in the evening of the day after tomorrow I'll be going home." The holy man wept when he woke up, and quickly reported the dream to Myōson. Myōson too was in tears. He told the holy man that someone at Miidera had had the same dream.

Word of this fresh development brought even greater throngs to Sekidera. On the day, all the monks of Miidera and Mount Hiei were there, and the surrounding hills rang with their chanting of the Amida Sutra. The scene recalled nothing so much as that other day so long ago when the Buddha Shakyamuni lay dying, surrounded by all the countless grieving beings who loved him.

As the day wore on and the ox still looked quite normal, certain perverse individuals in the crowd began joking that it seemed in no hurry to kick the bucket. But when evening came the recumbent ox got up, lumbered to the main hall, then twice ran a set of three circumambulations round it. Suddenly it seemed in pain and began abruptly lying down and getting up again; but it still managed to complete two or three more sets of circumambulations before it returned to its stall and lay down with its head, like the Buddha's on his deathbed, facing the north. Then it stretched out full length on its side, with its legs extended, and died. All the pilgrims gathered for the occasion — lords and ladies, common men and women of every degree, monks and laymen — burst into loud sobs and chanted the Amida Sutra with abandoned fervor.

After the crowd had left, they dragged the ox a little way up the hillside and buried it. The grave was topped with a proper marker and surrounded with a simple picket fence. Although it was summer and the carcass had been buried rather than cremated, the grave gave off no odor at all. Every seven days thereafter sutras were read at the grave until the forty-ninth day was past; and services continued to be performed in the same way, at the proper intervals, until the anniversary of the ox's passing.

The buddha of Sekidera is Miroku. It can be fairly said that every person who travels between the Capital and the eastern or northern provinces worships at Sekidera, and that a single act of heartfelt worship here has assured each pilgrim of the karma to be born again into Miroku's perfect world. It was to give us the chance to gain such merit that Kashō took the form of an ox and urged us to greater faith. How strange and wonderful a tale the story makes!

THE FALCONER'S DREAM

A falconer with many sons once lived in the western part of the Capital, near Saga Moor. Falconry was his whole life. He kept seven or eight hawks at home (just feeding them, especially in summer, meant killing so many creatures!) and twice that number of dogs. Nights he would sit till dawn with a hawk on his fist; and every day, whatever the season, he would be out in the fields hunting pheasants.

When he was old, he came down with a little illness and one night was unable to sleep. Toward dawn when he finally dozed off, he had this dream.

There was a hole in a mound on Saga Moor, and he lived in it with his wife and children. They had been awfully cold that winter, but now spring was here and the day was so warm they all went out to sun themselves and pick fresh greens. The nice weather made them wander off in all directions a long way from home.

Suddenly a babble of voices rose from the wood north of Uzumasa, mingled with the jingling of bells. The sound all but stopped his heart with terror. From the top of a rise he saw men approaching on swift horses, wearing brocade caps, spotted cloaks, bearskin chaps, and swords in boarhide scabbards. The fiendish hawks on their fists had tiny bells on and were straining to fly.

On they came, spread across Saga Moor, and others walked before them in rush hats, dark-blue cloaks, red leather sleeves, leather trousers, and boots of fur. These were beating the thickets with sticks; and huge, belled dogs, like lions, ran beside them, jingling like the hawks but in deeper tones.

His eyes went dim and his head swam. "I've got to warn my wife and children!" he thought. "I've got to hide them!" But they were widely scattered and could not possibly hear him. He dove in panic into a deep thicket while Tarō, his eldest and dearest son, hid in another nearby.

The dog-keepers and falconers were all over the moor. In horror he watched a dog-keeper head for Tarō's thicket, beating the tall, dense pampas grasses flat while the dog, its bell jingling, followed, intently sniffing the ground. It was all over for Tarō.

Sure enough, Tarō started up and the keeper gave a shout. The falconer, who had hung back a little, released his hawk. Tarō flew desperately, high in the air, with the hawk in fierce pursuit; then dropped again, exhausted. From below, the hawk seized his breast and head. The two fell. The dog-keeper rushed up, pulled off the hawk, picked up Tarō, and wrung his neck. Tarō let out a pitiful cry that pierced the poor father's heart like a sword.

And what about his second son, Jirō? He saw a dog, sniffing its way toward Jirō's thicket, suddenly charge and catch Jirō in its jaws. Though Jirō flapped his wings frantically, the keeper ran up and wrung his neck, too.

"And my third son, Saburō?" he wondered. Another dog was sniffing toward Saburō's thicket. When the trapped Saburō started up, the keeper knocked him down with a blow on the head from his stick.

With all his sons now dead, the father prayed in anguish that at least his wife might escape. He watched her fly up before the dogs reached her and make for the hills to the north. A falconer loosed his hawk and galloped in pursuit. She raced for cover in a thicket under a distant pine, but a dog right behind her caught her in its jaws. The falconer retrieved his hawk, which had perched on the tree.

The witness to this carnage had taken refuge deep in a clump of thick grasses and tangled brambles. Now he saw not one but half a dozen dogs, their bells jingling, sniffing their way toward him. It was too much for him and he too tried fleeing toward the hills. Hawk after hawk filled the sky in pursuit, some high, some low; and below on the ground a horde of dogs followed amid a dreadful din of bells. Behind them galloped the falconers, and the dog-keepers came after, beating the thickets with their sticks. He raced on and dove with a last effort into another deep thicket. The hawks perched on a tall tree nearby and jingled their bells to let the dogs know where he was. The dogs soon found his hideout. There was no escape. The dog-keepers' shouts were like thunder. Knowing he was finished, he did the last thing he could: he hid his head in the muddy floor of the thicket, leaving only his tail sticking up. The dogs were very close. "Now!" he thought—and woke up.

He was drenched in sweat. Realizing he had dreamed it all, he saw that what he had dreamed was the hunting he himself had enjoyed all his life. He had killed so many pheasants! Now at last he knew what he had done, and understood with horror that he had sinned past reckoning. Too impatient to wait for dawn, he immediately freed all his hawks and dogs, then gathered their gear together and burned it. Having told the dream, in tears, to his wife and children, he went straight to a mountain temple, shaved his head, and became a monk. For ten years he called Amida's Name day and night until he achieved a holy passing.

POVERTY

A miserably poor monk of Miidera decided that the temple had nothing to offer him, and that if he meant to claim the success he deserved he would have to try elsewhere. Not wanting to leave in broad daylight, especially looking as shabby as he did, he stole off in the darkness before dawn. Having a long, hard road ahead of him, he soon lay down for a nap.

He dreamed of a pale, sad, skinny youth, clearly a traveler like himself, whom he had not seen before. "Who are you?" he asked.

"Your servant these many years," the youth replied. "We've never been apart and I'm coming with you now."

"I don't know you. What's your name?"

"I'm not exactly a person so I don't have a normal name. But people who catch a glimpse of me call me Poverty."

The monk woke up and understood his real future. With that youth beside him he might as well stay put. Back he went to Miidera, lost in thought.

S C A R E S

A N D

N I G H T M A R E S

THE NIGHTMARE

It was during Emperor Konoe's reign that the great warrior Yorimasa performed the most famous of all his deeds.

Every night the emperor was oppressed by a mysterious agony which the holiest monks, working all their healing rites, seemed unable to relieve. In the small hours a black cloud would rise from a wood some way off and settle over the palace. Then His Majesty's ordeal would begin.

The court held a council and recalled that something like this had happened in the past. General Yoshiie had stood guard that time, twanged his bow when the moment came, and roared out his name and titles just as a warrior does before fighting a human enemy. His Majesty got better at once. So the court decided to post another warrior guard.

They chose Yorimasa, who was not then of very high rank. The command troubled him, and he protested that a warrior's job was to suppress rebellion or to impose the imperial will on the recalcitrant. "Who has ever been ordered to subdue an invisible monster?" he demanded to know. But since he could not very well refuse, he presented himself at the palace just the same, with a single lieutenant.

His lieutenant's arrows were feathered with eagle pinions, while Yorimasa had chosen for himself two barbed arrows feathered from a mountain pheasant's tail. With his black-lacquered bow in hand Yorimasa stood guard before the palace's south entrance. He held both arrows ready, reflecting that if he missed the monster with the first he could always use the second to shoot the clever fellow who had put him up for this duty.

The black cloud moved over the palace with a strange shape inside it. His whole career at stake, Yorimasa fitted an arrow to the string, called silently on his clan god Hachiman, and let fly.

There was no doubt about the hit. His bow arm felt it instantly and he yelled in triumph. The thing fell. His lieutenant moved in swiftly, pinned it to the ground, and ran it through nine times with his sword. When light arrived, they saw a beast with a monkey's head, a badger's body, a snake's tail, and a tiger's paws. Its moaning cry had sounded like a night thrush. It certainly looked frightening.

Overcome with relief and gratitude, the emperor gave Yorimasa an imperial sword named Lion King. After that Yorimasa's name was honored at court. The monster's body was stuffed into a hollow log and sent floating down the river. His Majesty was never bothered again.

THE DOUBLE

Lord Minamoto no Masamichi lived south of Fourth Avenue and west of Muromachi Street in Kyoto. His son, not yet two years old, was playing by himself outside when suddenly Masamichi heard him howl, and there were loud shouts from the nurse looking after him.

Masamichi picked up his sword and ran from the other side of the house to investigate. He found not one but two identical nurses struggling for possession of the boy. Each had hold of an arm and a leg. Clearly one of them must be a fox, though he had no idea which. As he charged, brandishing his sword, one of the nurses vanished.

The other nurse and the boy collapsed on the ground. Masamichi had his servants call in a healer of proven power, and after the healer had worked his rites awhile the nurse came to. At last Masamichi was able to question her.

"I was letting the young master play a little by himself, sir, when a woman I'd never seen before came out of the house and claimed the young master was hers. In fact she tried to take the young master away, and I held on to him to stop her. When you ran up with your sword, she let go and rushed back into the house."

Masamichi was seriously frightened. He never found out whether the double had actually been a fox or some sort of angry spirit. People commented, though, that you just shouldn't let little children play by themselves.

BEWITCHED

The Kamo Virgin, an imperial princess, was the high priestess of the Kamo Shrine in Kyoto.

An officer of the Bureau of Civil Affairs named Yorikiyo was serving as director of the Kamo Virgin's household when unfortunately the Virgin's displeasure forced him to retire to an estate he owned at Kohata, south of the Capital.

Omoto, one of his servants, had her own house in the city and so got leave to stay behind when he moved away. One day a messenger from him asked her to come immediately. Something had happened at Kohata, and Yorikiyo had left the day before for Yamashiro, the neighboring province to the north, where he was now renting a house. The messenger pleaded with Omoto to come quickly. She responded by picking up her four-year-old son and setting out.

When she arrived her master's wife greeted her with unusual warmth, fed her well, and put her to work dyeing cloth. After the two women had worked together for several days, the lady asked Omoto to take a secret message to a watchman she had left at the Kohata house. Omoto left her son with a fellow servant.

She naturally imagined that the Kohata house would be gloomy and deserted; she found there, on the contrary, everyone she had just left. One of the first people she met was her master's wife in person. She thought she must be dreaming and stood there in a daze while the others gathered around her. "Well, well," they were saying, "here's Omoto! What kept you so long? The Kamo Virgin has pardoned our master and we sent someone to let you know, but your neighbors said you'd left two or three days ago. Where were you?"

Trembling all over, the terrified Omoto told her tale. Almost everyone in the household was frightened, including her mistress, but a few laughed.

Convinced now that her son must be dead, Omoto begged to be allowed to lead a party back to the place she had just come from. On arrival she found no house at all, only a broad expanse of moor. After hunting desperately far and wide, she found her son wailing in a thick clump of pampas grasses and joyfully took him in her arms.

Back at Kohata she reported the outcome of the trip. Her mistress declared that she must have invented the whole thing, and her fellow servants looked at her very doubtfully.

But would she really have abandoned her little boy on a wild moor? It's far more likely that foxes tricked her. At any rate, people often came after that to talk with Omoto about her experience and to marvel that the boy was still alive.

THE FUNERAL

Once a professional courier, on his way up in haste from the western provinces to Kyoto, passed through Inamino in Harima province. Since it was nearly sundown he looked for somewhere to spend the night, but far out in the fields where he was he could see no promising house, only a miserable hut for the people who in season guarded the crops. The hut would have to do. He went in.

Though traveling light, he still wore a sword. In a lonely spot like this he felt safer not even undressing, and instead lay down as he was, watchful and silent. Late at night he heard a faint sound of bells to the west and a chorus of voices chanting the Buddha's Name. Oddly enough, the voices were coming his way. Peering outside, he saw a chanting crowd carrying torches and accompanied by priests ringing bells. Apparently it was a funeral. The closer they came the more worried he got, till he hardly knew what to do with himself.

The crowd stopped nearby, laid the coffin down, and began the ceremony. The courier kept more silent and still than ever, and reminded himself over and over that should he be discovered he would say quite plainly who he was and why he was there. But he also wondered about one very strange thing: whereas the spot for a burial is normally marked clearly beforehand, he had noticed nothing of the kind when he arrived even though it had been daylight at the time.

When the funeral was over, a large force of laborers armed with mattocks and spades built a mound on top of which they planted a gravemarker. Then they tidied up and put their tools away, and the crowd dispersed.

Being so close to a fresh grave horrified the courier more than the eerie funeral itself, and the hair rose on his head when he thought of it. He longed for the night to be over, but meanwhile kept an eye on the mound. All at once he thought he saw something on it move. Surely his eyes were deceiving him. But no, something on the mound *was* moving. Whatever it was, it was coming up little by little from the earth. At last a naked human form emerged and charged the hut, blowing and slapping at the flames that danced over its body. All the courier could see in the darkness was that the figure was ghastly and huge.

He knew that where a funeral has taken place there is bound to be a demon. Obviously the demon was now rushing to eat him and he was finished. Still, if he had to die he might as well get out of the hut before the demon reached it and try a direct attack. Drawing his sword he dashed out, charged the demon, and whacked off its head with one blow. The demon crashed over backwards.

The courier did not wait to see more. He raced on till he got to a village (it was a painfully long run), stole up to a house, and crouched by it in terror. The next morning he presented himself to the villagers and told them why he was there. Disturbed by his story, they decided to investigate.

He led the bravest young men of the village to the spot, but they found no mound or grave-marker, and no sign either of torches or fire. There was nothing there but a huge, headless boar. How horrible!

Apparently the boar had seen the traveler go into the hut and decided to give him a scare. "What a dumb way to get yourself killed!" murmured the villagers as they gazed at the corpse.

2 0 4 .

THE GRINNING FACE OF
AN OLD WOMAN

People often went hunting to an old pond in the Minase Hills which was frequented by flocks of water birds, but something in the pond would catch the hunters and many of them died.

Three brothers, personal guards at the retired emperor's palace on the Minase River, were just setting off hunting when someone warned them to stay away from the pond. One of the three, Nakatoshi, refused to believe the story, and feeling anyway that it would be unworthy of him not to brave the pond's dangers, he set off undaunted, with just one young attendant.

It was evening and too dark even to see the path, but Nakatoshi got through the hills, found the pond, and waited on the bank under the overhanging branches of a pine. Deep in the night the water trembled and waves rolled across the pond. The frightened Nakatoshi fitted an arrow to his bowstring. Next, a luminous mass rose out of the pond and flew over the pine. As soon as Nakatoshi drew his bow the thing flew back to the pond, returning only when he relaxed and removed the arrow from the string. This happened several times till Nakatoshi understood that his bow would be no use. He put it down and drew his sword instead. This time the luminous mass came so close that Nakatoshi saw in the light the grinning face of an old woman.

With the light so unexpectedly close and the form inside it so clear, he dropped his sword and attacked barehanded. When the thing tried to drag him into the pond, he braced himself against the roots of the pine and resisted until he could draw his dagger and stab it. The light went out.

A hairy beast lay dead at Nakatoshi's feet. It was a badger. Nakatoshi carried it back to his room at the Minase Palace and went to bed. The next morning his two brothers came to find out how his expedition had gone.

"Look at that!" cried Nakatoshi, and threw the badger out to them.

They were deeply impressed.

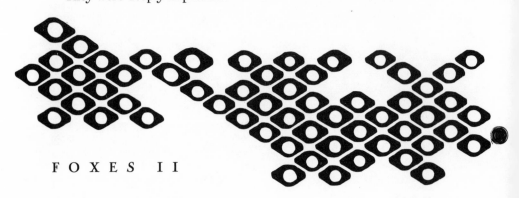

FOXES II

205.

FOX ARSON

A retainer who served the governor of Kai was heading home one sundown from the governor's mansion when he saw a fox, gave chase, and shot at it with the kind of noisemaker arrow used for scaring off dogs. He hit it in a back leg.

The fox yelped in pain, rolled over, and dove limping into the brush. As the retainer went to retrieve his arrow the fox reappeared in front of him, and he was about to shoot at it again when it vanished.

A quarter of a mile from home he saw the fox running ahead of him carrying a flaming brand in its mouth. What could it be up to? He spurred his horse on. On reaching the house, the fox changed into a human being and set the house on fire. The retainer was ready to shoot as soon as he got within range, but the human changed right back into a fox and got away. The house burned down.

Beings like that exact swift vengeance. It's better to leave them alone.

2 0 6 .

THE FOX'S BALL

A healer and his woman medium were once called to get rid of the spirit that was making someone ill. The spirit declared through the medium that it was a fox. "I didn't mean to put a curse on anyone," it said. "I only came because I thought you might have something good to eat. You didn't have to shut me up like this!"

The medium drew from the fold at the breast of her robe a little white ball (foxes often have one), and began tossing it in the air and catching it. The people present thought the ball pretty enough, but they were sure the medium had hidden it in her robe beforehand to trick them. One among them, a brave young man, waited for the medium to toss the ball into the air again, then quickly stuck out his hand, caught the ball, and popped it into the front of his own robe.

"Confound you!" snapped the fox. "Give me back my ball!" The man ignored its pleas till finally it said tearfully, "All right, you've got the ball, but you don't know how to keep it. It won't be any good to you. For me, it's a terrible loss. I tell you, if you don't give it back I'll be your enemy forever. If you *do* give it back, though, I'll stick to you like a protector god."

The young man decided the whole thing was a waste of time. "So you'll protect me?" he asked.

"Of course I will. Creatures like me never tell lies, and we always repay a debt of gratitude."

"Will the guardian spirit who caught you vouch for you now?"

"Listen, guardian spirit!" cried the fox. "I swear I'll protect him if he gives me back my ball!"

The man took the ball out and returned it to the woman, which made the fox very happy. Next, the healer dismissed the spirit and the fox left.

The people seized the medium immediately, before she could get up, and searched her. The ball was not on her. She really had been possessed.

Sometime later the man was on his way home after dark from a visit to the great temple at Uzumasa. When he reached the Ōten Gate he became afraid, for the neighborhood was well known to be dangerous at night. Visions of all the awful things that could happen to him ran through his head. Then he remembered that the fox had sworn to protect him. All alone in the darkness he called, "Fox! Fox!" A series of sharp barks rang out in answer, and in a moment the fox was before him.

"You *did* keep your word, fox!" he said. "I'm touched. You see, I'm afraid to go through this area and I want you to stay with me."

The fox seemed to understand. It went ahead, looking carefully all around and avoiding the usual path, while the man followed. Eventually it stopped, arched its back, and moved forward again only with the lightest steps, glancing about even more cautiously than before. The man tiptoed. He soon caught the sound of human voices and a glimpse of human shapes moving just beyond a fence. Through the gloom he spied a large group of armed men. They seemed to be talking something over, and shortly he gathered what it was: they were discussing where to commit their next robbery. The fox had led him this way—a way no ordinary person would know—just because the bandits would not be looking for a traveler to pass so close. The fox disappeared once he was safely by, and he reached home without further difficulty.

The fox stayed faithfully with him and often rescued him again. More and more touched by its fidelity, he was very glad indeed that he had had the good sense to return that ball.

2   0   7   .

SINGED FUR

Kōya Brook runs east of Ninnaji, just northwest of the Capital. One evening at dusk a pretty young woman stood on the bank. When a man rode by toward the city, she asked him to let her up behind and take her with him. With a brief word of assent he had her get on. After a quarter of a mile she jumped down and ran. She turned into a fox as he chased her and got clean away, barking.

This happened more than once and the word spread. One day the warriors of the Palace Guard were passing the time among themselves when the story came up in the conversation. A brave and clever young warrior swore he would catch the girl and mocked all those who had let her get away. The rest of the guards were sure he would fail, but he ignored them and promised he would do it that very evening.

He rode to Kōya Brook alone on a good horse. When he first crossed the stream there was no sign of the girl, but once he turned back toward Kyoto she was there on the bank. "Please take me up behind you, sir!" she called, smiling sweetly at him.

"All right!" he answered. "Where are you going?"

"To the city, sir. It's already sundown, you see, and I wonder if I mightn't ride with you."

She got on. Quick as a flash he tied her to the saddle with a rope he had ready. "Oh sir, what are you doing?" she cried.

"You're coming to bed with me, so I just want to make sure you don't get away."

Darkness fell. He rode east along First Avenue and had just passed West Omiya when he saw torches coming his way, accompanying a procession of carriages. Servants were going before the procession with loud and imperious shouts to clear the road. Obviously a person of quality was on his way somewhere. He cautiously turned south down Omiya, continuing east when he reached Second Avenue. Finally, after a long detour south around the palace compound, he reached the gate where he had told his fellow guards to meet him. They were all there.

Untying the girl, he roughly pulled her to the ground, seized her arms, and forced her in through the gate. Guards with torches lit his way to their headquarters where the rest of the men were waiting. "Here she is!" he announced. The girl, terrified by so many men, was crying and begging him in vain to let her go. The guards surrounded him and his captive.

Torches blazing, the guards urged him to let her go in the circle. He said no, she would get away if he did, but they insisted and a dozen drew their bows, shouting what fun it would be. "We'll shoot her miserable butt!" they cried. When he gave in and let her go, she instantly turned into a fox and darted off, barking.

The fire and the circle of men vanished. He was alone in the dark.

Completely confused, he called to his companions over and over but got no response. A glance at the surroundings told him that he was somewhere (he had no idea where) out in the wilds. Though his heart pounded and he was overcome with dread, he managed not to lose control of himself. From the look of the hills and the lie of the land he judged that he must be in the great burning ground at Toribeno. Naturally his horse was nowhere to be seen.

The trouble must have started when he turned down Omiya Avenue to avoid the procession of carriages. After that he had only believed he was heading for the Tsuchimikado Gate, but had actually been coming here. All those torches on First Avenue had been fox-fires. He started walking and reached home late in the night.

The next day he was almost dying. The guards who had missed him the night before were meanwhile having a good laugh at his expense and pressing him to join them. Late on the third day he finally went, still looking far from well, to face their questions and taunts. They demanded to know what he had done with the fox. He answered that he had suddenly become ill and had not been able to go after the fox after all. "But tonight," he promised, "I'll try again."

"Well then, bring us *two* foxes!" his companions cried. Taciturn as ever, he left without another word.

He did not really suppose that the fox would be foolish enough to appear again, but if it did he was prepared to hold on to it all night if necessary. If it did not, he would hide himself from the world forever.

This time he took the strongest of his own men with him. He thought as they rode how mad he was to risk his whole career on such nonsense, though of course his promise left him no other choice.

There was no sign of the girl when they crossed Kōya Brook. Then they turned back and there she was. At least, there *a* girl was, because the face was different from last time. As before she asked to ride behind him and he let her get up; and as before he tied her securely to the saddle and continued on toward town along First Avenue.

By now it was dark. He had some of his men ride ahead of him with torches and kept others right beside him. The band reached their gate without meeting a soul and dismounted. He seized the girl by the hair and forced her, despite her tears and cries, to the same spot as before.

His fellow guards were all there, clamoring for news. "Here she is!" he replied again. This time he had tied her up so tightly that she kept her human form for some time, but the men tormented her till she turned into a fox in the end, despite being a prisoner. They singed the fox's fur off with their torches and shot it over and over with stinging arrows, shouting at it all the while never to try its tricks again. In the end they let it go without killing it, and it managed somehow to run off, although it could hardly walk. Only then did the warrior confess how the fox had fooled him the first time and led him off all the way to Toribeno.

Ten days later he decided to visit Kōya Brook again. A very sick-looking girl, loitering on the bank, declined his invitation to get up behind him. "I'd like to," she said, "but you burned me so badly last time!" Then she disappeared.

2 0 8 .

NOT REALLY A TREE AT ALL

Chūdaifu lived in Nara since his uncle was the high priest of the Kasuga Shrine. Late one afternoon Chūdaifu's horse disappeared while out grazing. Chūdaifu and a servant set out eastward toward the mountains to look for it, armed with bows.

They had not gotten far when the sun set and night fell. There was only the dimmest light from a veiled moon. As they walked on, still hoping to find the stray animal, Chūdaifu glimpsed through the gathering shadows a colossal cryptomeria tree, twelve feet thick and a good two hundred feet tall. He stopped dead in his tracks. "Am I seeing things?" he exclaimed. "Has some spirit addled our brains? Do *you* see that cryptomeria too?" The servant answered that he did. "Then it's not my imagination," said Chūdaifu. "We must have met one of those gods who get you lost, and he's led us off goodness knows where. Where in the whole province of Yamato are you going to find a cryptomeria like that?"

"I've no idea, sir," the servant replied. "I've seen a few cryptomerias here and there, of course, but they've all been quite small."

"That's it, then. We've been bewitched and now we're lost. What are we going to do? I'm frightened, you know. I think we'd better get on back. I wonder how far we've come. This is terrible!"

"It's a strange business we've run into, sir, but it would be too bad just to go home again without trying anything ourselves. I suggest, sir, that you shoot an arrow into that tree, then come back tomorrow morning and check it."

Chūdaifu heartily approved and said they should both shoot the tree. When their arrows hit the tree it suddenly vanished. "Sure enough," said Chūdaifu, "we've met a spirit! Let's get away from here!" They practically ran home.

Early the next morning Chūdaifu and his servant returned to the scene. They found a bald old fox lying dead with a cryptomeria branch in his jaws and pierced through the belly by two arrows. "Aha!" they exclaimed. *"Here's* the fellow who had us so confused!"

Before leaving, they retrieved their arrows from the corpse.

THE WHITE FOX: FOUR DREAMS

*Shaped like a fat, falling drop, the Wishing Jewel
is an emblem of good fortune. The tails of magic foxes
sometimes end in a Wishing Jewel shape.*

Four nights ago someone brought me what he said was a picture of the Kasuga God, though I couldn't see what the god looked like.

The night before last I watched the evening star and a bright moon rise over Flower Mountain. Star and moon were the same size.

Last night in the fields I came to a big stone that looked like a Wishing Jewel, and I touched it. It was warm. North of the stone lay three foxes. I picked the white tuft off one's tail and saw it was a big white fox. "Wear red," the fox said, "when you bring me offerings."

At dawn I got twenty golden relics of the Buddha.

As I write down this marvelous sequence of dreams, I shiver again with joy and awe.

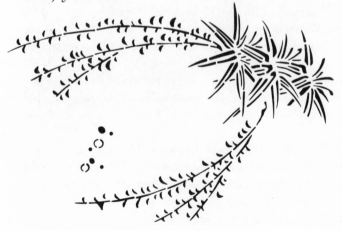

210.

THE TELLTALE FISH

Once upon a time a monk went visiting. His host served him wine and a special delicacy: some tiny, delicious fish which had just come into season. Of course monks are not supposed to eat fish at all, but the host may have suspected that this one would be broad-minded.

Having excused himself a moment, the host noticed on his return that there were now fewer fish in the dish than when he had left the room. Naturally he said nothing. But while the two chatted, a little fish suddenly popped out the monk's nose.

"Pardon me," said the host, "but how'd that fish get up your nose?"

"Oh, these little fish, you know, they're coming out eyes and noses everywhere lately!" replied the monk without missing a beat.

Both men roared with laughter.

211.

A TASTE FOR FISH

Rin'e, a monk from Nara, was on his way up to the Capital when he stopped at a house by the Kizu River and asked for fresh fish. The request shocked his host, who knew that monks are not supposed to eat the meat from any living creature.

The man's wife had been suffering from an abnormally swollen belly and to all appearances was dying. That night she dreamed that eight boys, announcing themselves as Rin'e's familiars, tapped her on the belly and expelled all the foulness from it. She awoke perfectly well and found the impure matter from inside her all over her sleeping mat.

When she told her husband, he realized that Rin'e was no average monk. First thing next morning he brought Rin'e more fish.

Accomplished holy men certainly do sometimes eat both fish and fowl. For example, they say that Ninkai ate small birds. Not that ordinary monks ought to imitate them!

2 1 2 .

THE PROMISE

*It is unclear whether or not this Ninkai really
is the same monk as in no. 211.*

Ninkai, a monk in Nara, was peerlessly talented as a scholar, but one day he decided to give up his temple and its conventionally studious atmosphere in order to devote himself more freely to true religious practice. Unfortunately, the abbot would not hear of his plan.

Ninkai resorted to courting a woman who lived across town, and soon people were gossiping about his affair. To make sure everyone knew, he would stand behind her at her gate with his arms around her. The passersby were properly shocked. Actually, though, he never slept with her. Instead he spent his nights, sleepless and weeping, before an altar.

This reached the ears of the abbot, who revered Ninkai all the more and began to want his company all the time. The desperate Ninkai ran off, married a local official's daughter some distance away, and even gave up carrying his rosary. But he only longed for enlightenment the more.

A county magistrate who noticed Ninkai became deeply attached to him. For some time he and his wife accompanied Ninkai everywhere and prepared his food, clothing, and bath. They did so, as they told Ninkai himself, out of pure reverence for his sanctity. "We have only one concern," they confessed. "How can we make sure to be with you when you pass away?" Ninkai reassured them. "Don't worry," he said, "I'll be with you." Then he went his way.

Years later, at nightfall on a snowy winter day, Ninkai came to their house. They greeted him gladly, excused their servants, and brought him food themselves. Then he took a bath and lay down.

The next morning the couple rose early. As they were preparing breakfast a marvelous fragrance from Ninkai's room filled the whole house. They decided he must be burning some rare incense. He had said he wanted to leave early, but it was light by now and he still was not up. When the morning gruel was ready they asked a disciple to let him know. The disciple refused. "My master has quite a temper," he said, "and if I bother him he'll only beat me. I'm sure he'll be up any moment."

By sunrise the couple were worried enough to call Ninkai through the door. There was no answer. When they entered they found him seated facing the west with his palms together in prayer. He was dead. Deeply stirred, they prostrated themselves with Ninkai's disciples before the husk of the saint. At dawn they had smelled the perfume of Amida's welcome to Ninkai's soul. Ninkai had known when he would die and had kept his promise to his friends.

2 1 3 .

THE JELLYFISH'S BONES

The renowned monk Zōga was born in Kyoto, but his parents soon moved to the East. They built for the journey a sort of palanquin which they mounted on a horse, and installed in it a wet nurse with their little son in her arms. Unfortunately, it was such a long way that the wet nurse fell asleep and dropped the baby. Little Zōga tumbled to the ground.

Nearly a mile further on, the wet nurse woke up and realized the baby must have fallen out, though goodness knows where. The news drove Zōga's parents wild. They ranted and raved about how all the passing horses, oxen, and people must have trampled him to death, but they turned back anyway since they still wanted his poor body. They found the baby on his back in the middle of the narrow trail, smiling happily. There was not a spot of mud or a wet patch on him.

It was a miracle. That night Zōga's parents had a dream. A sumptuous couch spread with a costly coverlet rode on an expanse of mud, and on it lay little Zōga. Four exquisite boys, one at each corner of the couch, chanted in the language of the scriptures:

This child is born from the Buddha's mouth,
wherefore we keep him from all harm.

Now Zōga's parents knew their son was unusual, and they raised him tenderly.

When he was five, little Zōga announced that he would soon be going to master the Lotus Sutra on Mount Hiei. His parents thought him much too young to be saying things like that and feared some spirit might be talking through him. But soon his mother dreamed that even as she nursed her boy he grew into a mature monk with a sutra scroll in his hand; and beside him stood another monk who explained that it was her son's destiny to enter religion. Zōga's parents stopped opposing their son's plan and were happy about it instead.

When he was eleven, Zōga found a distinguished master on Mount Hiei. After a few years everyone recognized his piety and learning. He caused quite a stir, though, when he came back starked naked from the Ise Shrine, having been inspired by a dream (a voice told him, "Forget the body!") to take off all his clothes and pass them out to the beggars. People thought he was mad, and though his master more or less understood, he felt obliged to remind Zōga that the wish to transcend worldly ambition did not necessarily exempt him from behaving normally. Another time, when his master had just been promoted to the highest ecclesiastical rank, Zōga joined the triumphal procession mounted on a bony old ox, with a dried salmon at his waist instead of a sword.

Respectability and success really meant nothing to Zōga, who wanted above all a quieter place to live. He chose Tōnomine in the hills south of Nara. When the abbot refused him leave to go, he quickly changed the abbot's mind. He stopped sending a servant to fetch his meals but instead came with a blackened and filthy sort of box to collect them himself. Then he would squat by the path with the workmen, pick up a couple of twigs for chopsticks, and share out his dinner as he ate. People decided he was crazy and the abbot was glad enough to let him go.

Zōga found the top of the mountain at Tōnomine too thick with the demons that hinder enlightenment and instead built a hut at an inconspicuous spot in the valley. Alas, he was so revered by now that the emperor insisted on naming him to his personal staff of healers, and naturally other great nobles demanded his services as well. Zōga generally ignored these calls, but when he did go he behaved like a madman and got out of the Capital as fast as he could.

There was, for example, the empress's ordination. Planning to retire into the religious life, the Sanjō Empress invited Zōga to preside at the ceremony. Her messenger thought this a fine idea, since so holy a man would no doubt make the empress into a properly worthy nun.

Zōga's disciples assumed their master would fly into a rage and perhaps even beat the messenger, but he did nothing of the kind. He accompanied the messenger back to the empress's palace without a murmur.

All sorts of great nobles and monks had gathered for the rite. There was even someone to represent the emperor. They all noted Zōga's fierce eyes and impressive bearing, but thought he seemed a little unwell.

Zōga went right up to the empress's curtains and started the ceremony. At the appropriate moment the empress put her long, beautiful hair out through the curtains and Zōga, in the gesture which above all divides the worldly from the religious life, cut it off. Within the curtains the empress's ladies wept as though their hearts would break.

Having done his bit Zōga tidied up, then addressed the empress in ringing tones. "What did you want me for, anyway?" he complained. "I don't get it. Did you hear I've got a big dick or something? Well yes, it's bigger than most, but it's as limp as silk floss right now."

All over the rooms eyes popped and jaws dropped. Who knows how the empress felt? It was unbelievable! The holy aura was gone and the speechless assembly broke out instead in a cold sweat.

Zōga's farewell followed. "I'm an old man, you know," he went on. "My insides don't work and I've got the trots so bad all the time that I shouldn't have come at all. The honor was just too tempting, I suppose. But now, you understand, I can't hold it in any more and, begging your pardon, I've just got to go."

He squatted on the veranda, tucked up his skirts, and let it squirt. The noise was revolting and the stench a horror. Both hit the empress full force. The younger courtiers went into convulsions of laughter, while the monks muttered to each other that Her Majesty was crazy herself to have called in such a lunatic. But nothing Zōga could do seemed to tarnish his unwanted fame.

He was past eighty, as sound as ever in body and spirit, when he understood he was to die in ten days. "At last I'll have what I've always prayed for!" he exclaimed. "Soon I'll leave this world behind and be reborn in paradise!" He had his disciples write verses on going to paradise, and cheerfully made one up himself from a classic paradox:

> *Eighty years of patience,*
> *with age slowly wrinkling me*
> *into an old man!*
> *What a joy at last to find*
> *the jellyfish's bones!*

Zōga announced the great day himself. When he called for a *go* board his disciples brought him one from next door, assuming he wanted to put the Buddha on it. But no, he demanded to be propped up and in a weak voice invited a close friend to play.

The friend was shocked and saddened that at a time like this, when Zōga should have been calling on Lord Amida and looking forward to his welcome, he was thinking of such foolishness instead. Why, he must be out of his mind! But Zōga was so eminent that the friend dared not disobey. He sat down at the board, and he and Zōga each placed their first ten stones. "All right," said Zōga, "no more," and swept the stones from the board.

"Why did you want to play *go*?" the friend asked timidly.

"I've watched people play ever since I was a boy, and as I was calling the Name just now I wanted to try it too."

Now Zōga demanded to be propped up again. "Get me a pair of stirrup guards," he commanded, meaning the leather guards that protect a rider's feet. When they came, he had them tied together and hung round his neck. Then he opened his arms wide, though it was clearly painful for him to do so, and announced he would dance. After doing a little dance he had them removed.

"When I was first on the mountain," he explained, "a bunch of young monks lived next door and they had a very good time. Once I saw one hang a pair of stirrup guards round his neck and dance to the tune of a clever song which I suppose he'd just made up. It really tickled me. I'd forgotten all about it, but the memory came back just now and I felt like doing it too. That's all, though. I've nothing more on my mind."

The Venerable Zōga then sent everyone away and retired to an inner room, where he sat in a crude chair facing the west and chanted the Lotus Sutra till he passed into Nirvana.

2 1 4 .

THE STINKING HUT

A monk once roamed the provinces, worshipping at each holy place, till in Kyushu one day he got lost in a deserted stretch of mountains. For days he saw no sign of another human being.

He was enormously relieved to find a hut at last, but the woman who came to the door warned him that this was no house for him to stay in. He protested that he was a pilgrim, exhausted and lost. "I don't care what your house is like," he said, "as long as I can rest for a while." In the end the woman gave in and agreed to let him spend the night.

She led him inside, spread a clean mat, and fed him a good meal which he ate gratefully. After dark a man came in with a big bundle on his shoulders and set it down. He was in a religious robe but his hair was cut short, not shaven, and he was too disgustingly filthy to go near.

"Who's this?" he asked on seeing the monk, and when the woman told him, muttered that he was a bit surprised since no one like that had been around for years. Next, he began eating some of the stuff he had brought in. It was all chunks of cattle and horse meat.

By this time the monk was wondering what sort of place he had come to. Obviously the man not only ate meat but lived by supplying the local hunters with meat to feed their dogs. To a pious soul the very thought was horrifying, but in the dark there was nowhere else to go. The monk was stuck, disgusted and miserable, in the little stinking hut.

Very late at night the man got up, washed in warm water, changed into a fresh robe, and went out behind the hut. The curious monk saw him enter a tiny chapel and light the altar lamps and incense. He went on to do the Lotus Confession rite, then chanted the Lotus Sutra through. Finally, after prostrating himself before the altar, he intoned the Name of the Buddha Amida. His voice was deeply holy.

When he left his chapel at dawn, he and the monk found themselves face to face. He said his name was Jōson and he quickly apologized for his ignorance and uncouthness. He acknowledged that despite having been born in a human body he was still committing terrible sins. "If only I could really follow the Buddha's Teaching!" he cried. "But I can't, and that's why I live off meat, which normal people won't touch. I'm so glad karma has brought you here, though, because years from now, on a date I'll tell you, I'm going to leave this world behind and be reborn into the Land of Bliss. Come again then, if you'd like to have the blessing of my passing!"

The monk saw that the man he had taken for an especially brutish sort of beggar was actually a saint, and he promised to return. Then he went his way.

He came back on the date named by Jōson, curious to see whether or not the prediction would come true. Jōson, now properly shaven and bathed and wearing a clean robe, greeted him joyfully. "I haven't touched meat for months," he said, "and tonight I'm going to be reborn in paradise!" His wife was now a nun.

The couple spent the night in their chapel, calling Amida's Name. As dawn broke, light burst through the chapel door. The monk heard the sweetest of music resound in the sky and move slowly away toward the west, while a delicious fragrance filled the air. At daylight he went into the chapel. Jōson and the nun were seated together facing the west with their palms pressed together in prayer. They had passed away.

The weeping monk prostrated himself in reverence and awe. He never left again, and everyone in the province who heard the story came to receive the blessing of the place.

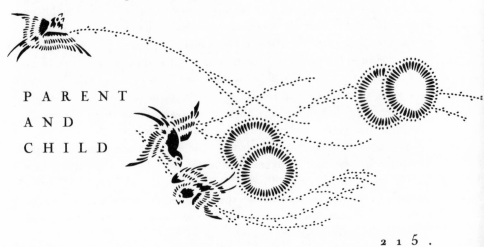

PARENT

AND

CHILD

2   1   5   .

BE GOOD TO YOUR MOTHER
AND FATHER!

Koma no Yukimitsu, a dancer attached to the Kasuga Shrine in Nara, had learned the dance *Katen* from his father when he was fifteen. Since then he had often danced it all by himself at the shrine, just for the god's pleasure.

Once he fell ill. Then his breathing stopped and he found himself at the palace of Emma, the king of hell. When a majestic gentleman arrived, Emma welcomed him with every sign of respect.

"This man has been loyal to me ever since he was fifteen," the gentleman declared. "I want him released."

King Emma obeyed, and the gentleman led Yukimitsu away.

"My lord," said the amazed Yukimitsu, "I thank you for having gotten me pardoned. But who are you?"

"I'm the God of Kasuga," the gentleman answered. "Would you care to see hell?"

"Yes, please," said Yukimitsu.

The god took him right off to show him hell. Yukimitsu saw so many kinds of horrible suffering that it would be impossible to describe them all, and afterwards he begged to be told how he could escape the same awful fate.

"Be good to your mother and father!" said the god. "That's the highest virtue. If you cultivate it, you won't fall into hell."

2 1 6 .

HELL IN BROAD DAY

Having contracted a painful illness, the wife of a provincial official in Etchū eventually died. Her husband and three sons looked after the funeral as well as they could and had the proper rites performed for seven whole days, but when the seven days were over the sons found that their grief was as fresh as ever.

They wanted at least to find out where their mother had been reborn, and they knew that to do this they would have to visit Tateyama, a steep and forbidding mountain in the same province, covered with hot hell-springs and other such horrors. In this unearthly landscape you could sometimes get news of the dead. So they persuaded a holy man to join them and set off without delay to see the hells of Tateyama burn, and to discover what had become of their mother.

They visited hell after hell on the mountain and felt as though they themselves were burning, because all around them water was boiling up amid curls of flame. Even from a distance the heat was terrible, and it was awful to imagine the torments of the unhappy spirits immersed in such fierce waters. They had the holy man shake his staff, tipped with jangling brass rings, in powerful rhythm as he chanted a litany for these spirits, and they had him preach the Lotus Sutra. When he did this, the flames of the hell they were in would plainly die down.

At last, in a hell that was even hotter and more hideous than the rest, they had the holy man shake his staff and proclaim the Teaching as before. The flames had just dimmed a little when they heard their dear mother's voice calling her eldest son's name from a cleft in the rocks: "Tarō, Tarō!" At first they refused to believe their ears and did not answer, but the cry came again and again till they were terrified. "Who's calling?" Tarō cried. The voice from the cleft answered, "How can you ask? Could a son not know his mother's voice? In life I was mean and committed many sins, and now I suffer endless and unspeakable agony!"

The sons had heard of the dead visiting the living in dreams, but never of the dead speaking to the living in broad daylight. Yet the voice was their mother's. "How can we help you?" they cried in reply.

The voice came again: "There's no easy way for you to lighten the suffering my sins have brought me. You're too poor to afford the good works that would help me. It wil be eons before I escape from this hell!"

"But what *would* it take to free you?" her sons insisted.

"The only way is to make a thousand copies of the Lotus Sutra and dedicate them all for me on the same day."

The sons knew how hard it was to do one copy a day. Not ten, not a hundred, but a thousand copies were clearly impossible, but now that they had seen their mother's agony with their own eyes they could not simply ignore her and leave. Each would far rather have taken her place in hell. The holy man had to remind them that although one might take another's place in *this* world, in the afterlife we all receive the impartial reward for our own actions so that no one can be punished for another's sins. "Go home," he urged them, "copy the Sutra as best you can! Even a single copy will help her a little!"

They went home stunned with grief and told their father what they had seen and heard. He acknowledged that a thousand Lotus Sutras was more than they could manage. Since they would just have to do what they could, they decided to start off with a goal of three hundred.

When the governor of the province heard what had happened, he called in the father and got the whole story from him. Pious and compassionate, he responded by vowing to join in the Sutra copying and encouraged everyone he knew in the neighboring provinces to do the same. A thousand copies were soon done and the dedication rite performed.

Knowing that their mother was now delivered from the torments of hell the sons rejoiced, and the eldest had a dream. His mother came to him, exquisitely beautiful, and told him that their care had lifted her up to rebirth in the Tōri Heaven. Then she flew off into the sky. Naturally he broadcast this dream far and wide, and it gladdened everyone who heard it.

Later on the sons returned to Tateyama and went round the hells again, but this time no voice came from the rocks.

The hells themselves, of course, are still there.

THE OLD WOMAN ON
THE MOUNTAIN

An old woman living with a younger couple at Sarashina in Shinano province looked after them for many years like a mother. But the wife, who in her heart detested her, hated especially the way the old woman was being deformed by age. She kept harping to her husband about how awful the old woman was. He tried to discourage her complaints, but he too ended up as often as not neglecting the old woman, whose body in the meantime had bent almost in two.

Finally the wife could take no more. Why, the hag did not even have the grace to die! Telling her husband she had had enough, she ordered him to take the old woman somewhere far into the mountains and abandon her. He did not like the idea a bit and at first did nothing, but she pestered him mercilessly till he was fed up and gave in.

It was the fifteenth night of the eighth moon, the great full-moon night of the year. Moonlight flooded the sky. "Come, dear," said the husband, "there's a very holy service at the temple. I'll take you there!"

The old woman was eager to go. He put her on his back and headed straight up the high mountain behind their village. When he was sure she could never get back by herself, he put her down and fled. She shouted after him in vain.

At home again he found he could not forget what his wife had made him do, and considering how kindly the old woman had once looked after them he wished he had not done it. All night long, with the moon bright over the mountain, he lay sleepless and his thoughts went out to her. As he lay there he murmured the poem:

> *This heart of mine*
> *refuses comfort,*
> *ah, Sarashina!*
> *as I watch the moon*
> *bright over Mount Obasute.*

Then he went back up the mountain, brought the old woman down, and cared for her as before.

So don't let your wife's unpleasant tongue turn your mind to unworthy thoughts. No doubt this sort of thing goes on even now, though.

As for the mountain, it's been called Obasuteyama ever since: "Mountain of the Deserted Crone." Until then people had always called it Kamuriyama, "The Cap," because it's shaped like the cap a gentleman wears.

MOTHER

Two brothers who hunted for a living went one day, as usual, into the mountains. Each had his lookout in the fork of a tall tree. The pair of trees were about fifty yards apart, and the brothers would wait for deer to drift in down below, between them.

It was a pitch-black night late in the ninth moon. Unable to see a thing, they waited patiently just to hear the deer. Hour after hour crept by. The deer did not come.

All of a sudden something reached down from higher up in the elder brother's tree, gripped his hair, and hauled him upward. He made a frantic grab at the top of his head and touched a wizened hand. A demon was dragging him off to eat him!

"If something had me by the hair and was pulling me up," he shouted to his younger brother across the way, "what would you do?"

"I'd take good aim and shoot it!"

"Well, do it! Because that's exactly what's happening!"

"All right, I'll aim by your voice!" The younger aimed at the spot just above where his brother's voice had come from and felt he had a hit. "Bet I got it!" he yelled.

The elder brother felt the top of his head again and his fingers closed on the hand, now severed at the wrist. "You cut its hand off!" he shouted. "Let's call it a night! I'll keep the hand!"

The pair climbed down from their trees and got home well past midnight.

Their mother, so old and tottery that she could hardly even stand, lived in a room between the two. They heard her groaning when they came in and called to ask what the matter was, but got no answer.

By the light of a lamp they examined the hand. It looked very like their mother's. In fact it *was* their mother's, beyond a doubt.

"Thanks a lot!" snarled their mother when they slid open her door.

She leapt to her feet and nearly hurled herself at them, but they just said, "Did you lose something, Mother?" then tossed the hand into the room and closed the door.

Soon she was dead. The poor thing had gotten so old and senile that she had turned into a demon and gone off to the mountains to eat her children.

2 1 9 .

PERILOUS GRATITUDE

A poor couple in Kyushu lived by the sea, and every day the wife would go out to comb the shore. One day she went gathering shellfish with a neighbor's wife. On the beach she took the baby off her back, put it down on a flat rock, and set a child to watch it. The spot was close to the hills.

While working, the two women noticed a monkey by the water, apparently trying to catch fish. This deserved a closer look. They assumed the monkey would flee when they got too close, and it certainly seemed frightened; but it stayed crouched where it was, chattering furiously. Something was wrong.

They soon saw what it was. In reaching for a huge clam it hoped to eat, the monkey had stuck its hand into the clam's open shell. The clam had snapped shut and trapped the monkey's hand. Now the tide was coming in and the clam was burrowing deeper and deeper into the sand. Soon the monkey would be overwhelmed by the sea.

The women took in the scene and laughed heartily. The neighbor's wife picked up a big stone to bash at the monkey with but her friend, the woman with the baby, reproved her sharply and snatched the stone away. "I only want to kill it so I can roast it for dinner," the neighbor's wife complained. But the baby's mother insisted, and with a bit of wood pried the clam open far enough for the monkey to get its hand out. Then she declared it would also be wrong to kill the clam, and so even though both women were actually there to collect shellfish she carefully removed the clam from their harvest and buried it again in the sand.

After running a little way off, the monkey turned back toward its savior with an ingratiating expression on its face. "Well, you're safe now," said the woman, "and I hope you appreciate all my trouble. I know you're only an animal, but still, you should be grateful."

The monkey seemed to listen, then scampered toward the hills. On the way it headed, of all places, for the rock where the baby lay, picked up the baby, and ran on. The child watching the baby took fright and burst into tears. The mother looked on in dismay as the monkey darted into the hills with her baby, and she raged at its ingratitude.

"Well," said her friend, "that'll teach you! A lot of appreciation you get from a fur-face like that! If I'd killed it, it would have made me a meal and *you* wouldn't have had your baby stolen. The nasty brute!"

The two women ran after the monkey and found it took care not to get more than about a hundred yards ahead of them. When they ran at top speed, the monkey matched them; when they slowed down, it slowed down too.

Finally the women stopped. "Ignorant beast!" the mother shouted after it. "Here I saved your life, you could at least show some gratitude! How dare you steal my baby! I suppose you'll eat him. Couldn't you give me his life for yours?" But the monkey ran on and carried the baby to the top of a tall tree.

The weeping mother gazed up from below while the monkey sat in a fork high aloft. Next, the monkey held a good-sized branch bent far back, at the same time jiggling the baby under its arm. The baby began to cry. When it stopped, the monkey jiggled it again and made it cry some more. The sound quickly attracted an eagle, which swooped in to seize the prey. Obviously the baby was going to be eaten one way or another, if not by the monkey then by the eagle. But the monkey bent the branch a little further, then released it with perfect timing. It caught the eagle in the head and the bird plummeted to the ground.

Again the monkey bent the branch and made the baby cry, and again an eagle came swooping in. It went the way of the first. The mother understood that the monkey had never meant actually to steal her child. It had just wanted to repay its debt by killing eagles for her.

"I understand, monkey, I understand!" she called through her tears. "But that's enough now! Please, please bring my baby back down!"

By now the monkey had killed five eagles. It descended from tree to tree, laid the baby gently near its mother, then leapt into the tree again and sat there, scratching.

Smiling through her tears, the mother nursed her child. When her husband dashed up, the monkey vanished into the forest. Under the tree lay five dead eagles.

The husband wondered at the story he got from his wife. He cut off the five eagles' wings and tails and took them home with his family. Bit by bit he sold the eagle feathers for basic necessities, so that in the end the monkey did repay its debt — but at the price of what agony for the mother before she understood!

2 2 0 .

THE UGLY SON

Long ago a gambler had a son whose eyes and nose looked as though they had been squashed together by main force. This made the young man outstandingly ugly. His parents were wondering how on earth they were to get him married when they heard that a rich man was seeking a handsome bridegroom for his beloved daughter. They let the father know that the "fairest youth in all the land" wanted to marry the girl. The rich man accepted the match and set the date for the betrothal.

On the couple's first night the brotherhood of gamblers gathered in borrowed finery and escorted the young man to his bride, doing their best to hide their faces under a brilliant moon. The groom looked quite presentable among them. This was how he began his nightly visits to the girl, in accordance with custom.

But all too soon came the dreaded night (the one that would seal the marriage forever) when the young man would have to lie with his betrothed right through dawn and into day. Undaunted, the gamblers thought up a plan.

One of them got up over the ceiling of the couple's room, trod the boards till they creaked and groaned, and bellowed in a terrible voice, "Fairest youth in all the land!"

The household quaked to hear him, for they recalled countless stories of supernatural visitations that had started exactly this way. The terrified groom called back, "I hear I'm the one people call fairest in the land. What do you want?" Three times the voice over the ceiling roared and three times the groom replied.

The family wanted to know why he answered at all. "I can't help myself!" he explained.

"The daughter of this house," the demon bellowed, "has been mine for three years, and I want to know what you think you're doing sleeping with her!"

"But, but," stammered the groom, "I had no idea! I didn't know! Please don't hurt me!"

"You nasty sneak!" the demon roared. "I'll ask you just one thing before I go. Which do you cherish most, your life or your looks?"

"How can I answer that?" protested the bridegroom.

His parents-in-law whispered frantically to him that he shouldn't mind his looks as long as he kept his life. "Tell him your looks!" they said.

He obeyed.

The demon replied with a horrid sort of sucking noise. The groom screamed, buried his face in his arms, and collapsed. The demon left.

What had happened to the groom's face? A lamp was brought in, and by its light they saw that his eyes and nose looked as though they had been jammed together. "Oh, if only I'd told him my life!" he sobbed. "How can I live among people with a face like this? And to think that you never once saw me as I used to be! What an awful mistake it was to get involved with a girl claimed by a horrible demon!"

Moved by this complaint, the girl's father promised him his fortune in compensation. In fact, to the young man's entire satisfaction, his father-in-law took excellent care of him and even built a separate house for him, on the pretext that the present one's possibly faulty location might have had something to do with the calamity. The young man lived a very pleasant life indeed.

SOURCES AND NOTES

When possible, I have given approximate dates for the events described in the tales, or the internal evidence which makes it possible to date them. (Not that these events are necessarily historically true!) Dates mentioned in the tales are noted again here.

1. *Konjaku* 31/37.
2. *Konjaku* 28/40.
3. *Uji shūi* 3/16.
4. *Konjaku* 31/33.
5. *Shasekishū* 7/17.
6. *Kokonchomonjū* 246.
7. *Konjaku* 28/25. Sanesuke lived 957–1046.
8. *Konjaku* 28/5. Tamemori was appointed governor of Echizen in 1029.
9. *Konjaku* 28/39.
10. *Konjaku* 28/41. Sons of the court nobility studied at the Academy.
11. *Konjaku* 27/9. 9th century.
12. *Konjaku* 27/7.
13. *Konjaku* 27/21. Third quarter of 11th century.
14. *Konjaku* 27/13.
15. *Uji shūi* 3/15.
16. *Konjaku* 27/1.
17. *Shasekishū* 8/11.
18. *Konjaku* 28/12.
19. *Uji shūi* 2/7.
20. *Kohon setsuwashū* 62.
21. *Konjaku* 28/11. Kaishū died in 1016.
22. *Konjaku* 11/29. Tenji reigned 661–668.
23. *Konjaku* 11/13. Second quarter of 8th century.
24. *Konjaku* 11/7. 736.
25. *Konjaku* 12/7. 752.
26. *Konjaku* 11/25, 11/9. Kōbō Daishi returned from China in 804 and died in 835.
27. *Kōfukuji ranshōki.* 1007–1013.
28. *Konjaku* 21/11. Ban no Yoshio was exiled in 866 and died in 868.
29. *Konjaku* 31/15.
30. *Konjaku* 19/32. Ca. 1000.
31. *Kasuga Gongen genki* 17, *Kasuga Daimyōjin gotakusenki.* 1202. In *Gotakusenki* the god (speaking through the medium) introduces himself as "this old man." The passage about the god having been higher than Myōe after all is from *Gotakusenki.*
32. *Shintōshū* 8. Ca. 460–70.
33. *Konjaku* 20/1. Ca. 880s.
34. *Konjaku* 20/2. Ca. 980.
35. *Konjaku* 20/11.
36. *Konjaku* 13/33. Perhaps 8th century.
37. *Uji shūi* 11/6.
38. *Senjūshō* 6/10. Shōkū lived 910–1007.
39. *Kokonchomonjū* 386. Kazan abdicated in 986 and died in 1008.
40. *Tsurezuregusa* 69. See note 38.
41. *Hosshinshū* 4/10.
42. *Hosshinshū* 6/12. Saigyō lived 1118–1190.
43. *Jikkinshō* 10/24. Early 1200s. Tennōji, one of the first temples founded in Japan, is now in Osaka, which did not exist then. Its relics were famous. In an important myth the Sun God-

dess, angered by her brother's outrageous conduct, hid herself in a cave and so plunged the world into darkness. She had to be lured out again by the other gods.

44. *Konjaku* 24/1. Makoto died in 868.

45. *Kasuga Gongen genki* 10. Rin'e lived 950–1025. He became abbot in 1017.

46. Jikkinshō 10/25.

47. *Kokonchomonjū* 265. 1107.

48. *Jikkinshō* 10/22. Noritaka lived 999–1076.

49. *Uji shūi* 3/4.

50. *Senjūshō* 5/15. Saigyō lived 1118–1190.

51. *Uji shūi* 14/11. Perhaps mid-11th century.

52. *Uji shūi* 9/1, *Konjaku* 20/10. Yōzei reigned 877–884.

53. *Konjaku* 27/19. Perhaps first quarter of 11th century. Sanesuke lived 957–1046.

54. *Uji shūi* 1/14. Minamoto no Sadafusa lived 1130–1188.

55. *Uji shūi* 9/7.

56. *Kohon setsuwashū* 19. Ca. 900.

57. *Konjaku* 30/1. Heichū died in 923.

58. *Uji shūi* 3/2. Tadaie, a poet, lived 1032–1091.

59. *Uji shūi* 2/8. Abe no Seimei lived 921–1005.

60. *Uji shūi* 11/3. See note 59.

61. *Konjaku* 24/19.

62. *Uji shūi* 11/3. See note 59.

63. *Uji shūi* 14/10. Michinaga (966–1027) built Hōjōji in 1020.

64. *Konjaku* 24/24. Murakami reigned 946–967. Hakuga no Sammi (918–980) is also known as Minamoto no Hiromasa.

65. *Konjaku* 29/18.

66. *Konjaku* 13/10.

67. *Konjaku* 25/11. Yorinobu (968–1048) became governor of Kōzuke in 999.

68. *Uji shūi* 13/6. Early 11th century.

69. *Jikkinshō* 10/27.

70. *Shasekishū* 7/24. 1278.

71. *Uji shūi* 15/6. Not Kanemichi but Mototsune founded Gokurakuji; he lived 836–891.

72. *Uji shūi* 8/3. Emperor Daigo reigned 897–930.

73. *Uji shūi* 15/8. Sōō lived 831–918. He founded Mudōji in 856. The Somedono Empress, daughter of Fujiwara no Yoshifusa, lived 829–900.

74. *Konjaku* 16/32.

75. *Uji shūi* 13/10. Ennin lived 794–864. He returned from China in 847.

76. *Konjaku* 16/20. Perhaps ca. 950.

77. *Uji shūi* 10/6.

78. *Konjaku* 29/28.

79. *Uji shūi* 7/4. Perhaps second quarter of 10th century.

80. *Kokonchomonjū* 606. Ca. 1180s.

81. *Kokonchomonjū* 681.

82. *Konjaku* 16/17. 896.

83. *Uji shūi* 1/18. Perhaps ca. 900.

84. *Konjaku* 27/31. Kiyoyuki lived 847–918.

85. *Uji shūi* 8/7. Jōkan lived 843–927.

86. *Konjaku* 13/2.

87. *Uji shūi* 13/13.

88. *Nara ehon* "En no Gyōja." En no Gyōja was exiled in 699 and disappeared in 701. I chose this version of his story because the *Konjaku* version is incomplete, and because it is fuller than the standard account in *Nihon ryōiki* (ca. 822).

89. *Jikkinshō* 7/1.

90. *Konjaku* 28/24. Montoku reigned 850–858.

91. *Konjaku* 31/17. Ca. 1025.

92. *Kokonchomonjū* 599. 1171.

93. *Konjaku* 28/28. "Our own time" must be the early 12th century.

94. *Konjaku* 28/18.

95. *Uji shūi* 3/6.

96. *Kokonchomonjū* 385. Uda abdicated in 897 and died in 931.

97. *Uji shūi* 11/10. Nichizō lived 905?–985?

98. *Konjaku* 14/43. Perhaps early 10th century.

99. *Konjaku* 31/13.

100. *Konjaku* 13/1. 941.

101. *Fusō Ryakki* 25. *Genkō shakusho* 9 supplied the ending about the "vajra-handled bell," etc.

102. *Uji shūi* 2/4.

103. *Kokonchomonjū* 45. 930 or 931. The original has 931, but I have changed the date to agree with no. 101. Other documents have 930 for the bolt of lightning hitting the palace. Where this version has the god as half salmon, another *(Shingonden)* has him as half frog.

104. *Konjaku* 17/26.

105. *Konjaku* 19/29. Yamakage lived 825–889.

106. *Tango Fudoki.* I used this version because the one in *Kojidan* is a little garbled, and lacks the closing passage. *Nihongi* supplied the date, 477.

107. *Kokonchomonjū* 682.

108. *Shasekishū* 7/18. Between 1264 and 1275.

109. *Konjaku* 29/40.

110. *Konjaku* 29/39.

111. *Konjaku* 14/3.

112. *Shasekishū* 7/2. 1270s.

113. *Konjaku* 15/20.

114. *Konjaku* 15/1. Ca. 770–780.

115. *Konjaku* 19/14.

116. *Uji shūi* 11/9.

117. *Konjaku* 15/23. Ca. 1040.

118. *Uji shūi* 13/9.

119. *Uji shūi* 2/14. Daigo reigned 897–930. According to *Konjaku*, the Minister of the Right was Minamoto no Hikaru, who died in 913.

120. *Jikkinshō* 1/7. Reizei reigned 967–969.

121. *Uji shūi* 8/6.

122. *Kokonchomonjū* 607.

123. *Shasekishū* 7/20.

124. *Uji shūi* 4/1.

125. *Konjaku* 20/7. The Somedono Empress, daughter of the Regent Yoshifusa, lived 829–900. Montoku, her son, reigned 850–858.

126. *Konjaku* 20/4. En'yū reigned 969–984. The original indicates that the characters for Kōzen are to be pronounced "Kaguyama," but the reading "Kōzen" is well attested elsewhere. I have adopted "Kōzen" to make the place recognizably the same as the place where the dragon lived in no. 183.

127. *Konjaku* 14/44.

128. *Uji shūi* 12/5. Kinsue lived 956–1029. This incident cannot be earlier than 981.

129. *Konjaku* 30/14.

130. *Konjaku* 31/9. Koretaka, the eldest son of Emperor Montoku, died in 897.

131. *Konjaku* 31/8. Kochūjō served Empress Shōshi (988–1074).

132. *Konjaku* 31/7. Mid-11th century.

133. *Konjaku* 27/24.

134. *Konjaku* 31/10.

135. *Jikkinshō* 10/26.

136. *Konjaku* 23/22.

137. *Uji shūi* 6/5.

138. *Uji shūi* 4/5.

139. *Konjaku* 13/43.

140. *Konjaku* 29/1.

141. *Konjaku* 29/36.

142. *Konjaku* 29/21. Ca. 1000.

143. *Konjaku* 29/17.

144. *Konjaku* 29/19. Ca. 1000.

145. *Uji shūi* 2/10. Fujiwara no Yasumasa, the husband of the poet Izumi Shikibu (no. 178), lived 958–1036.

146. *Konjaku* 17/42.

147. *Konjaku* 14/7.

148. *Konjaku* 12/28.

149. *Uji shūi* 8/4. Fujiwara no Toshiyuki died in 901 or 907.

150. *Uji shūi* 10/10.

151. *Konjaku* 13/41.

152. *Uji shūi* 1/12.

153. *Tsurezuregusa* 53.

154. *Uji shūi* 5/9. Zōyo lived 1032–1116.

155. *Konjaku* 17/44.

156. *Uji shūi* 1/13.

157. *Hosshinshū* 3/5.

158. *Konjaku* 12/31. Kōken reigned 749–758.

159. *Konjaku* 13/34.

160. *Konjaku* 15/41.
161. *Hosshinshū* 3/8. Probably 1176.
162. *Konjaku* 24/15. Perhaps ca. 1000. Tadayuki was the father of Jakushin (no. 179) as well as of little Yasunori.
163. *Uji shūi* 10/9. Mochisuke died 958.
164. *Konjaku* 28/29. Ki no Haseo lived 845–912.
165. *Konjaku* 29/5. Ca. 1000.
166. *Konjaku* 24/20.
167. *Jikkinshō* 10/20. Hakuga no Sammi lived 918–980.
168. *Konjaku* 14/42. First quarter of 10th century.
169. *Uji shūi* 1/3.
170. *Uji shūi* 12/24.
171. *Jikkinshō* 6/18. Genshō reigned 715–724.
172. *Konjaku* 17/47.
173. *Konjaku* 16/29.
174. *Uji shūi* 7/5.
175. *Konjaku* 26/11.
176. *Uji shūi* 6/2.
177. *Konjaku* 17/33.
178. *Uji shūi* 1/1. Dōmyō died in 1020. Izumi Shikibu's husband appears in no. 145.
179. *Konjaku* 19/3. Yoshishige no Yasutane became a monk in 986 and died in 1002. His father was Kamo no Tadayuki (nos. 162, 165).
180. *Konjaku* 17/17.
181. *Konjaku* 27/5.
182. *Senjūshō* 6/3, 7/4, 7/5. Chūsan lived 935–976.
183. *Kojidan* 5/24.
184. *Konjaku* 16/15.
185. *Shasekishū* 7/3. Ca. 1270.
186. *Uji shūi* 4/4.
187. *Konjaku* 26/9.
188. *Konjaku* 26/8.
189. *Konjaku* 31/12.
190. *Konjaku* 27/2. Uda abdicated in 897 and died in 931.
191. *Kojidan* 1/7. See note 190.
192. *Uji shūi* 12/22. Yōzei abdicated in 884 and died in 949.
193. *Kokonchomonjū* 605. Ca. 1215.
194. *Kokonchomonjū* 601. Ca. 1200.

195. *Hosshinshū* 7/6. Sanesuke lived 957–1046.
196. *Uji shūi* 13/5. Possibly early 8th century.
197. *Konjaku* 12/24. The regent, Fujiwara no Michinaga, recorded his pilgrimage to worship the Buddha-Ox in his diary. He went to Sekidera in the spring of 1025 (Manju 2.5.17).
198. *Konjaku* 19/8.
199. *Hosshinshū* 7/7.
200. *Heike monogatari* 4. Between 1151 and 1154. Although this source is unlike my others, I thought the composite monster motif made the story worth including.
201. *Konjaku* 27/29. Masamichi died in 1017.
202. *Konjaku* 27/32.
203. *Konjaku* 27/36.
204. *Kokonchomonjū* 603. The Minase Palace belonged to Emperor Go-Toba, who abdicated in 1198 and died in 1239.
205. *Uji shūi* 3/20.
206. *Konjaku* 27/40.
207. *Konjaku* 27/41.
208. *Konjaku* 27/37.
209. *Tamon'in nikki* 43. This series of dreams was recorded by a monk in his diary under the date 1578, 2nd moon, 15th day. He had dreamed them during the four previous nights. "Flower Mountain" is Hanayama in the Kasuga Hills.
210. *Uji shūi* 5/10.
211. *Jikkinshō* 7/11. Rin'e lived 950–1025.
212. *Uji shūi* 15/9.
213. *Konjaku* 12/33, *Uji shūi* 12/7, *Senjūshō* 1/1, *Hosshinshū* 1/5. Zōga lived 917–1003.
214. *Konjaku* 15/28.
215. *Kasuga Gongen genki* 6. Yukimitsu lived 1090–1152.
216. *Konjaku* 14/8.
217. *Konjaku* 30/9.
218. *Konjaku* 27/22.
219. *Konjaku* 29/35.
220. *Uji shūi* 9/8.

THE WORKS
THESE TALES
COME FROM

These capsule descriptions of the works the tales come from omit a few supplementary sources which gave me only a paragraph or two. Such supplementary sources are indicated in "Sources and Notes" and in the list "Tales Classified by Sources."

En no Gyōja (1 tale). A popular illustrated booklet of the *Nara ehon* ("Nara picture book") type, in simple Japanese. Perhaps 16th century. Anonymous.

Fusō ryakki, "A Summary History of Japan" (1 tale). A 12th-century history of Japan, written in Chinese by the monk Kōen.

Heike monogatari, "The Tale of the Heike" (1 tale). An epic on the wars of the late 12th century, and one of the masterpieces of Japanese literature. The work developed over time and has no single author. It was originally sung by wandering entertainers, to the accompaniment of the *biwa*.

Hosshinshū, "Those Who Awoke to Faith" (6 tales). Stories in fine, sober Japanese about Buddhist believers who achieved salvation, mingled with reflections on the lessons to be drawn from their examples. Early 13th century, by Kamo no Chōmei (1153?–1216), a minor courtier and poet from the priestly family of the Kamo Shrine, who became a monk late in life. Chōmei's brief *Hōjōki* ("An Account of My Hut") is one of the most famous works of classical Japanese literature.

Jikkinshō, "Ten Moral Teachings" (10 tales). Tales on many subjects, organized so as to provide examples of moral instruction. Chapters have such titles as "The Need to Avoid Pride" and "The Need to Choose One's Friends." Many tales are rather drily told. The work is dated 1252. Anonymous.

Kasuga Gongen genki, "The Miracles of the Kasuga God" (3 tales). A set of illustrated scrolls narrating the miraculous deeds of the Kasuga God, in Japanese. Completed in 1309. The text was put together by Kakuen (1277–1340), a Kōfukuji monk of extremely high birth; and copied out by a former regent and his three sons, one of whom was regent at the time.

Kōfukuji ranshōki, "The Beginnings of Kōfukuji" (1 tale). A compilation of lore on Kōfukuji, in Chinese. Of uncertain date. Anonymous.

Kohon setsuwashū, "Old Tale Collection" (2 tales). A collection of stories in pure Japanese, dating perhaps from the 12th century, but rediscovered only in the 20th. The original title is lost. Anonymous.

Kojidan, "Anecdotes of the Past" (2 tales). Anecdotes on various subjects, noted down in an inconsistent style ranging from Chinese to hybrid Sino-Japanese; historically valuable but generally poor reading. Compiled ca. 1212–1215 by Minamoto no Akikane (1160–1215), a courtier and official.

Kokonchomonjū, "Things Seen and Heard, Old and New" (13 tales). A large collection on a wide range of themes, organized under convenient topics like "Gods," "Poetry," "Music," "Gambling," "Frightening Prodigies." The text, in Japanese, is written in a pleasing, studiedly understated style. Dated 1254. By Tachibana no Narisue, a minor courtier and official whose dates are unknown.

Konjaku monogatarishū, "Tales of Times Now Past" (111 tales). This monument of Japanese literature includes over a thousand tales and probably dates from about 1100. Even though a few sections are missing, the standard modern edition is in five closely printed volumes of which the first is devoted to tales from India and the second to tales from China. The Japanese section covers many themes, religious or secular, serious or humorous. *Konjaku* is in a rather "preachy" sort of Japanese, written so as to look as much like Chinese as possible, but the stories are lovingly and often expertly developed. Each tale begins and ends with set formulas, as noted in the Introduction, but this only contributes to the collection's greatness. Having the same format, the stories fit well together in long sequences, linked to one another by a play of association. Reading *Konjaku* can be like gliding down a broad river past an ever-changing landscape.

Senjūshō, "A Choice of Tales" (3 tales). Tales of Buddhist piety, freely mingled with reflections on their significance. The ornamented Japanese style and the lyrical tone are both agreeable. Compiled perhaps in the mid-13th century. The author was long thought to be the monk Saigyō (1118–1190), one of Japan's finest poets (see nos. 42 and 50), but is now considered unknown.

Shasekishū, "A Book of Sand and Pebbles" (7 tales). Buddhist tales in unadorned Japanese, usually serious but sometimes amusing, gathered together by the monk Mujū Ichien (1226–1312) in 1287. Mujū was particularly interested in recent stories, noting at times that he had gotten the story straight from its source, or even that he had witnessed the event himself.

Shintōshū, "Tales of the Gods" (1 tale). Tales about important native gods, probably intended as notes for popular preaching. 14th century. Anonymous.

Tamon'in nikki, "The Tamon'in Diary" (1 tale). The massive diary of a series of monks at Kōfukuji, covering the years between 1478 and 1617.

Tango fudoki, "Account of the Province of Tango" (1 tale). In 713 each province was ordered by the court to prepare an account of its history and special features. Most of these accounts are lost, and for Tango, only this fragment has been preserved. The language is quasi-Chinese, read as archaic Japanese.

Tsurezuregusa, "Essays in Idleness" (2 tales). A book of musings and anecdotes, and one of the most distinguished works of classical Japanese literature. Written ca. 1330 by the poet, courtier, and man of letters Yoshida Kenkō (1283?–1350?).

Uji shūi monogatari, "A Collection of Uji Tales" (54 tales). A book of tales of all kinds, in no particular order, datable to the early 13th century. This is, in many ways, the finest of the medieval tale collections. Its pure Japanese is light to read, and its stories are told with wonderful wit and grace. The author's wry, knowing insight contrasts sharply with the overall seriousness of most collections.

T A L E S
C L A S S I F I E D   B Y
S O U R C E S

The number before each title indicates the tale's number or location in the original. The number in this book follows each title. Secondary sources are indicated in parentheses.

BIBLIOGRAPHY

1. Works in Western Languages

Blacker, Carmen. *The Catalpa Bow: A Study of Shamanistic Practices in Japan.* Totowa, N.J.: Rowman & Littlefield, 1975.

Dorson, Richard M. *Folk Legends of Japan.* Rutland, Vt.: Charles E. Tuttle, 1962.

Frank, Bernard. *Histoires qui sont maintenant du passé.* Paris: Gallimard, 1968.

Kelsey, W. Michael. *Konjaku Monogatari-shū.* Boston: Twayne Publishers, 1982.

Kobayashi, Hiroko. *The Human Comedy of Heian Japan: A Study of the Secular Stories in the Twelfth-Century Collection of Tales, Konjaku Monogatarishū.* Tokyo: The Centre for East Asian Cultural Studies, 1979.

McCullough, William H., and Helen Craig McCullough. *A Tale of Flowering Fortunes: Annals of Japanese Aristocratic Life in the Heian Period* (2 vols.). Stanford, Calif.: Stanford University Press, 1980.

Mayer, Fanny Hagin. *Ancient Tales in Modern Japan: An Anthology of Japanese Folk Tales.* Bloomington: Indiana University Press, 1984.

Mills, D. E. *A Collection of Tales from Uji: A Study and Translation of Uji Shūi Monogatari.* Cambridge and New York: Cambridge University Press, 1970.

Morris, Ivan. *The World of the Shining Prince: Court Life in Ancient Japan.* New York: Alfred A. Knopf, 1964.

Mujū, Ichien. *Collection de sable et de pierres: Shasekishū.* Translation, preface, and commentaries by Hartmut O. Rotermund. Paris: Gallimard, 1979.

Seki, Keigo, ed. *Folktales of Japan.* Translated by Robert J. Adams. Chicago: University of Chicago Press, 1963.

Ury, Marian. *Tales of Times Now Past.* Berkeley, Los Angeles, and London: University of California Press, 1979.

Yanagita, Kunio. *The Legends of Tōno.* Translated by Ronald A. Morse. Tokyo: The Japan Foundation, 1975.

2. Japanese Sources

En no Gyōja in *Muromachi jidai monogatari taisei,* vol. 3, edited by Yokoyama Shigeru and Matsumoto Takanobu. Tokyo: Kadokawa, 1975.

Fusō ryakki (by Kōen). In *Kaitei shiseki shūran,* edited by Kondō Heijō. Tokyo: Kondō Kappansho, 1900.

Genkō shakusho (by Kokan Shiren). In *Shintei zōho kokushi taikei,* vol. 31, edited by Kokushi Taikei Henshū Kai. Tokyo: Yoshikawa Kōbunkan, 1965.

Heike monogatari. Edited by Takagi Ichinosuke, Ozawa Masao, et al. (Nihon koten bungaku taikei, vols. 32, 33.) Tokyo: Iwanami, 1959–60.

Hoṣṣhinṣhū (by Kamo no Chōmei). In *Hōjōki, Hoṣṣhinṣhū,* edited by Miki Sumito (Shinchō Nihon koten shūsei). Tokyo: Shinchōsha, 1976.

Jikkinṣhō. Edited by Nagazumi Yasuaki. (Iwanami bunko, vol. 30–120–1.) Tokyo: Iwanami, 1942.

Kaṣuga Gongen genki and *Kaṣuga Daimyōjin gotakuṣenki.* In *Gunṣho ruijū,* vol. 2, edited by Hanawa Hokiichi. Tokyo: Zoku Gunsho Ruijū Kansei Kai, 1972.

Kōfukuji ranṣhōki. In *Dainihon bukkyō zenṣho,* edited by Bussho Kankō Kai, vol. 119. Tokyo: Bussho Kankō Kai, 1915.

Kohon ṣetṣuwaṣhū. In *Kohon ṣetṣuwaṣhū zenchūkai,* edited by Takahashi Mitsugu. Tokyo: Yūseidō Shuppan, 1985.

Kojiðan (by Minamoto Akikane). Edited by Kobayashi Yasuharu. (Koten bunko, vols. 60, 62.) Tokyo: Gendai Shichōsha, 1981.

Kokonchomonjū (by Tachibana Narisue). Edited by Nagazumi Yasuaki and Shimada Isao. (Nihon koten bungaku taikei, vol. 84.) Toyko: Iwanami, 1966.

Konjaku monogatariṣhū, books 19–31. Edited by Yamada Yoshio, Yamada Tadao, et al. (Nihon koten bungaku taikei, vols. 24–26.) Tokyo: Iwanami, 1961–63.

Nihon ṣhoki. Edited by Sakamoto Tarō, Ienaga Saburō, et al. (Nihon koten bungaku taikei, vols. 67, 68.) Tokyo: Iwanami, 1967.

Senjūṣhō. Edited by Nishio Kōichi. (Iwanami bunko, vol. 30–024–1.) Tokyo: Iwanami, 1970.

Shaṣekiṣhū (by Mujū Ichien). Edited by Watanabe Tsunaya. (Nihon koten bungaku taikei, vol. 85.) Tokyo: Iwanami, 1966.

Shigematsu, Akihisa. *Uraṣhima-ṣhi ðen* (Koten bunko, vol. 55). Tokyo: Gendai Shichōsha, 1981.

Shintōṣhū. Edited by Kondō Kihaku. Tokyo: Kadokawa, 1967.

Tamon'in nikki. Edited by Tsuji Zennosuke. In *Mugenki* (a collection of the diarist's dreams), vol. 3. Tokyo: Kadokawa, 1965.

Tṣurezureguṣa (by Yoshida Kenkō). Edited by Nishio Minoru. (Nihon koten bungaku taikei, vol. 30.) Tokyo: Iwanami, 1957.

Uji ṣhūi monogatari. Edited by Kobayashi Chishō. (Nihon koten bungaku zenshū, vol. 28.) Toyko: Shōgakkan, 1973.

INDEX

The numbers after the entries are tale numbers, not pages. People are listed under their personal names.

ABOUT THE AUTHOR

Born in England in 1936, Royall Tyler has lived in the United States,
Canada, France, and Japan. After receiving his B.A. in Japanese
from Harvard and his Ph.D. in Japanese Literature from Columbia
University, he taught Japanese language and literature at the
University of Toronto, the Ohio State University, and the University
of Wisconsin at Madison. Since 1984 he has been teaching at the
University of Oslo. He has previously translated the writings
of a seventeenth-century Zen master and two volumes
of Noh and *kyōgen* plays.

THE PANTHEON FAIRY TALE AND FOLKLORE LIBRARY

African Folktales: Traditional Stories of the Black World,
selected and retold by Roger D. Abrahams

Afro-American Folktales: Stories from Black Traditions in the New World,
selected and edited by Roger D. Abrahams

*America in Legend: Folklore from the Colonial
Period to the Present*, by Richard M. Dorson

American Indian Myths and Legends,
selected and edited by Richard Erdoes and Alfonso Ortiz

Arab Folktales, translated and edited by Inea Bushnaq

British Folktales, by Katharine Briggs

Chinese Fairy Tales and Fantasies, translated and
edited by Moss Roberts

The Complete Grimm's Fairy Tales, introduced by Padraic Colum

Eighty Fairy Tales, by Hans Christian Andersen

*An Encyclopedia of Fairies: Hobgoblins, Brownies, Bogies,
and Other Supernatural Creatures*, by Katharine Briggs

Favorite Folktales from Around the World, edited by Jane Yolen

Gods and Heroes: Myths and Epics of Ancient Greece, by Gustav Schwab

Irish Folktales, edited by Henry Glassie

Italian Folktales, selected and retold by Italo Calvino

Japanese Tales, selected, edited, and translated by Royall Tyler

The Norse Myths, introduced and retold by Kevin Crossley-Holland

Norweigian Folk Tales, collected by Peter Christen Asbjørnsen
and Jørgen Moe

Russian Fairy Tales, collected by Aleksandr Afanas'ev